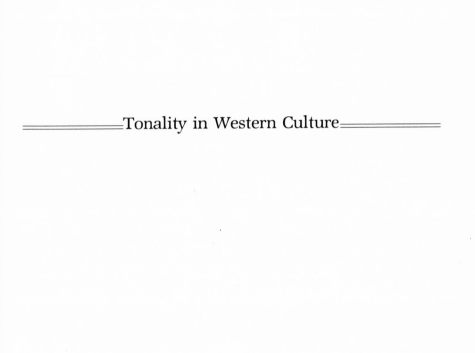

Tonality in Western Culture

*The assertion that because a certain combination
of musical sounds seems to satisfy the human ear,
it must therefore be founded on natural law,
is easily disproved by simply changing the audience.*

—Arthur J. Mundy, *"The Philosophy of Music"*
Famous Composers and Their Works, *1910*

Tonality in Western Culture

A Critical and Historical Perspective

Richard Norton

The Pennsylvania State University Press
University Park and London

Library of Congress Cataloging in Publication Data
Norton, Richard, 1938–
Tonality in western culture.
Includes bibliography and index.
1. Tonality.   2. Music—Philosophy and aesthetics.
I. Title.
ML3811.N67   1984   781'.22   83-43030
ISBN 0-271-00359-6

To Donald Lock

Contents

Preface

If a linguist were to develop an analytical system to study the nature of the English language as spoken and written from 1600 to 1900 and then have the presumption to call that system the totality of an understanding of "English," men of intelligence everywhere would call him mad. If our myopic scholar failed to understand how Greek, Latin, Celtic, Norse, Low German, Anglo-Saxon, and French resonate in the works of Elizabethan playwrights; or if he chose to remain ignorant of the fields of anthropology, sociology, psychology, philosophy, semiotics, human aural anatomy, and psychoacoustics and still claimed that he had established the principles of English, we would declare him madder still. And should someone have the temerity to inform him that there was English spoken before 1600, and our scholar replied, "Well, of course, there was English spoken before 1600, but people didn't really hear it that way," we would doubtless remove ourselves from his presence lest we become mad as well.

When we turn to the study of tonality, however, we discover that similar untenable assumptions are unfortunate points of fact. These assumptions are held generally by musicians everywhere and by music theorists and musicologists in particular, who seldom question the materials of sonic nature from which their art is created or the rationalizations they bring to bear upon explanatory systems that have historically assumed the character of ideologies. These systems come into and pass out of fashion only to be replaced by other ones with no greater dialectic or precision than those which they replace.

It is not the intent of this book to advance still another system of tonality other than to place key-centered music (so-called tonality and "*the* tonal system") within its proper historical context, that of the whole of Western tonal consciousness. The following chapters define the map of this tonal odyssey, one which I never envisioned at the beginning that I would or could make. It is a journey that began with a sabbatical year when I generously gave myself an opportunity to study Greek music philosophy and music theory in depth, without the slightest notion where that study would end. It has terminated here, in a book that contains only one chapter from my research of that year; yet during that time I began vaguely to intuit that tonality was something quite other than what I had been taught to believe. Perhaps only a fool would assume that he could outline a history of Western tonal consciousness in a single volume, but it was my stubbornness regarding the validity of sweeping generalities that are customarily made about tonality (particularly the overtone series and harmonic vitalism) that tempted me to make and to test even greater ones of my own. Pragmatically speaking, it was when I attempted to teach to nonmusicians any notion of tonality whatsoever that I realized their cognitive abilities and disabilities formed the very critique of a lost subjectivity within tonal speculation which I now believe is the only dialectic that will restore the musical object to its creator. As defined in this book, tonality is a decision made against the chaos of audible nature, a bewildering abundance of sonic potential that perhaps only the contemporary composer at his electronic synthesizer can fully appreciate. If this definition is true, then all music is tonal or none of it is. That the definition is not only adequate for my intentions but also absolutely necessary for a genuine dialectic of tonal speculation is I hope proved in the chapters to follow.

This book contains very few musical examples, but the major portion of its readers will be quite familiar with the music I discuss or will have ready access to it. I was once criticized for analyzing music from such an "unreliable" source as the *Historical Anthology of Music*, Vol. I, where sensitivity to the most recent editorial practices regarding medieval and Renaissance music is, of course, not found. But I now believe that when as students we sang and performed those pieces ourselves in graduate school because "*HAM I*" had not yet been recorded; when we puzzled over the various ways that *musica ficta* enhanced or detracted from the printed score; and when we evaluated those performances against the tonality already ingrained in our ears, we were carrying out some of those same judgments—reflective or otherwise—that made this music the specific historical phenomenon that it was. Tonality became again a decision against the delightful chaos of medieval and Renaissance sonic potential.

I wish to thank those who encouraged and helped me in this long project.

Since what they do has been more important to this book than where they are, I list here their fields of expertise: John Bokina (Political Theory), Nancy Rockmore Cirillo (Comparative Literature), Paul Norton (Physics), Howard Schechter (Acoustics), Agnes Crawford Schuldt (Contemporary Music). I am profoundly grateful to the staff of The Pennsylvania State University Press and to its readers, Jurgen Thym, Herbert Brün, and Mark Behm, who encouraged me and argued this book into its present form. And, finally, to the unknown reader for a different press who years ago read my initial manuscript and wrote one of the most negative reviews I have read in modern times, I publicly offer my sincere thanks. Only when I had absorbed and understood the nature of that criticism did I realize that the path I was about to take was—for me, at least—the only one available.

Introduction

T his book describes and evaluates the concept of tonality in Western
music from Antiquity to the present. To date, the general concept of
human tonal consciousness, however understood, has been thoroughly uncritical and uniquely lacking in substance. While it is admitted that such a
comprehensive notion of tonality must mean "loyalty to a tonic, in the
broadest sense of the word,"[1] the critique of how such loyalty is carried
forth in the human tonal project, or even if it is carried forth, has remained
until now an unwritten chapter in the history of Western musical consciousness. In fact, any customary association of "tonal" with "tonic" in
such definitions, while forcibly attempting to encompass the broadest dimensions of human sonic interests, nevertheless excludes through its assumed generosity so much of Western music that one must judge it to be
presumptuous, abandon it, and begin the investigation of tonality with new
and critical insights.

From a terminological standpoint, of course, the problem has been historically generated and fostered. It has been the successful project of mainstream Western scholarship since Jean-Phillipe Rameau to reserve "tonality"
for itself, a project which has been rigorously examined, measured, and
argued within the confines of theoretical treatises, academic seminars, music theory courses, books of diverse sorts, and the learned journals. A good
portion of current music theorists and musicologists are so committed to
the special tonal functions of the "common-practice" period—from about
1600 to 1900—that Norman Cazden could state in 1954,

There seems no good purpose in stretching the term tonality to cover any and all methods of organizing tones in music, in hope of proving it a universal and eternal principle of the art. For if the definition of tonality be made so abstract and inclusive, it ceases to be a useful term, and some other name would still be needed for *the* tonal system.[2]

But a quick survey of recent musicological and theoretical literature reveals that what is "tonal" about "tonality" is not as easily confined to the common-practice period as some would assert. Since Professor Cazden made his statement in the mid-fifties, a generalization about the notion of tonality has taken place in an effort to embrace musics that were composed before and after the common-practice era when all composers participated in the articulation of a single prevailing and encompassing tonal idiom. On the one hand, one need only read two major contributions to the study of medieval music—*Music in the Middle Ages* (1940), by Gustave Reese, and *Medieval Music* (1978), by Richard Hoppin—to realize that the adjective *tonal* is understood quite differently by these scholars. Forty years ago, Reese simply ignored the term: medieval music was modal. It was to be understood as based on a system of ecclesiastical modes whose hegemony over tonal consciousness was historically annulled through the gradual infiltration and eventual subjugation by the major-minor scale system. Hoppin, however, writing in a time when affinities of modality and tonality for one another seemed more apparent, even acceptable, frequently used the term *tonal* when describing certain aspects of monophonic music. On the other hand, there is George Perle's *Twelve-Tone Tonality* (1978), which seeks to outline a carefully structured network of pitch-class and formal relations that can compositionally serve as points of reference for a system of tonal development. To the vast army of advocates of common-practice tonality, however, these activities can only appear as curious excursions to a land of tonal Oz for a principle of sonic consciousness that does not, and apparently cannot, exist. What normative musicology does offer as an analytical model for monophonic and polyphonic tonality, on the one hand, and "post-tonal" music, on the other, continues to be one that runs the gamut roughly from Rameau to Heinrich Schenker, with whatever epithets one cares to apply from the tortured jargon of the most recent scholarship. What normative music theory offers is the admission of an uncritical pluralism that both confuses and discourages those who seriously approach the problem. This situation reflects an aspect of musicology and music theory even greater and thus more problematic than the concept of tonality itself.

Tonal methodology—to the extent that it is a cohesive methodology at all—is an ill-fitting aggregate of philosophical concepts drawn from the eighteenth to twentieth centuries. Generally housed in the realm of logical positivism and scientific empiricism, tonal methodology has, in addition, consistently flirted with idealism and vitalism whenever it felt the need to do so, though quite unconsciously. I can only suggest here, in highly selective statements, the historical path that these wandering generalities have taken over the course of the last hundred years, but the historical moment of its public appearance in American musicology is instructive.

The espousal of Neo-Positivism was publicly made by Arthur Mendel in 1961 at the New York meeting of the International Musicological Society, when he encouraged the application of Carl Hempel's "covering-law model" for descriptive analysis to the discipline of musicology. That is, "the occurrence of an event is explained when a statement describing that event is deduced from general laws and statements of antecedent conditions; a general law is explained when it is deduced from more comprehensive laws."[3] What Mendel recommended was a positivist approach to musical objects and the historical data surrounding them. Musical analysis and writing about music should reject all explanatory procedures that did not depend totally upon sense data; propositions should assert only that which had an empirical referent and could be demonstrated by logical analysis. It was a significant recommendation, and it coincided with a unique phenomenon in modern musicological research and music publishing. The virtual explosion of the "Collected Edition" of composers' complete works—which had begun in earnest after World War II—provided scholars everywhere a direct and fresh encounter with the musical object as the composer himself had created it.

Historically, it was a felicitous period, during which the frequently romantic approach to the historical past began to fade from view. This transition, of course, was much more complex than any one example can suggest, but perhaps the gradual disenchantment with Albert Schweitzer's monumental study on the music of J. S. Bach, which sought to objectify the "essence" of Bach's music, will serve. Ironically, Schweitzer himself had argued for the "authentic" reproduction of historical instruments for the realization of the composer's original intent, but he also thought that a chorus of a hundred and fifty singers was appropriate for performing Bach's large choral works. In the case of Bach (and the Bach family), Karl Geiringer provided a new model for musicological writing that demonstrated precision, historical insight, and scholarly rigor. And this transition was also subtle and rarely evaluated other than to reaffirm its positive results. I do not recall ever hearing much about the essence of music in my formative years in graduate school. The sheer data of the score overwhelmed that very humanistic inspiration which had given it birth.

Attendant on the gradual crystalization of the positivist method in musicology and music theory, and specifically with regard to tonal speculation, these disciplines continued almost unnoticed to carry as baggage at least two other—to me, crippling—philosophic components: idealism and vitalism. Nowhere in the study of music are these notions more entrenched than in our conceptions of tonality. The nineteenth-century concept of historical continuity, derived from the theory of evolution and the metaphysics of Hegelian idealism upon tonality, is critical. Unlike the other arts in that it produces its own material which is totally assimilated by its form, music was easily absorbed by idealism, particularly through Walter Pater's revision of Hegelian aesthetics. Vitalism as a metaphysical doctrine concerning the nature of living organisms was generalized primarily through Henri Bergson into a comprehensive metaphysics applicable to all phenomena. Although I have not seen it stated in these terms, tonal vitalism understands that a passage of music somehow exhibits the presence of a substantial entity that animates and moves the tonal activity experienced there and that this entity imparts powers to the tonal system which are not possessed by the materials of which it is created, that is, musical tones. (Schenker even wanted the tones themselves to possess this power.) The unwitting conflation of vitalism with the interests of theorists who sought to explain harmonic motion appears prophetically in Rameau and is confirmed by Schenker with disastrous results. These problems are taken up in chapters 1 and 2.

If tonality is not just the durable tonic-dominant model that chiefly characterizes the period from 1600 to 1900, with a "pre-tonal" stage before it and a "post-tonal" stage after it, what then is it? Can we neatly scoop up all the residue that does not fit into customary definitions of the above-mentioned specific tonality and thrust it upon a larger, general theory of tonality and call it "loyalty to a tonic, in the broadest sense of the word?" What is the broadest sense of the word? What is loyalty? What is a tonic? And, finally, is music that is devoid of tonics and loyalties to them without tonality?

What is tonality? The thesis of this book is that tonality is a decision made against the chaos of pitch. This seemingly vacuous definition immediately restores the subject to its created object, without which the musical object has no meaning, for tonality is a product of the human mind and ear in collaboration with the given of nature. This dialectic has been ignored from Pythagoras to Rameau to Schenker. In fact, the basic problem with all current views of tonality, in addition to their attempts to be recognized as absolute tonal truth, is that the subjective ego has been removed from the sphere of thought itself. Tonality has become an object that is viewed only in the physical presence of the musical score. The ear, the mind, the intricate processes of aural cognition, the behavioral methods by which as children we learn to distinguish music from language (and these from noise), the very societal framework in which humans become tonal—all these are ignored, shunted to one side as the tonal project is carried forth by the music theorist and the musicologist who uncritically speak of "harmonic motion" or "local linear expansion of the V chord." But the truth is that harmony does not "move" any more than motion pictures "move." One hears single tones in time and relates them through habit, not because one tone "wants" to disappear from existence as it fulfills some metaphysical annulment in the sonic actuality of some other tone. The same is true of intervals and chord complexes. The tonal motion we hear may be the aesthetic imperative of the gesture we call music, but it is a planned illusion. If we were to generate electronically a major seventh continuously for the next hundred years it would not ever attempt to resolve itself to the octave or to the sixth, any more than the nouns in this book will someday change into verbs when we are not watching. Tonality cannot be explained as a product of vitalism, Henri Bergson and Schenker notwithstanding.

This is no idle criticism. Throughout his theoretical system, Schenker frequently wrote of "our ear," an ear that both expected and wanted harmony to resolve by certain means, specifically and eventually, to the tonic, a tonic that was artistically to be delayed if the music in question was to be longer than the few seconds actually necessary to reach it. What did Schenker mean? "Our ear" was of course the Schenkerian ear and not an ear at that, but a mind oriented to the tonal tradition of the nineteenth century that was not overly generous about what it found to be exemplary there. Schenker built his system of tonal analysis from the music of hardly more than a dozen composers who were natives almost exclusively of Germany and Austria. In this respect at least, orthodox Schenkerians have been properly cautious about any application of Schenker's methodology to the music beyond the geographical and historical consciousness of Schenker's own musical interests. This is not to say that Schenker's project is without merit when analyzing the very music he cherished, but it is to say that Schenker's own consciousness must be taken into consideration when evaluating what he sought to explain and why he sought to do it.

By way of introduction, I think it is instructive to state what this book is not. It does not present an analytical method, a theory of tonal consciousness for all the music of Western culture, from ancient Jewish psalmody to the tantalizing sounds of Steve Reich's Six Pianos, although both of these expressions and everything between them give evidence that specific aspects of chapter 3 are germane to human tonal consciousness and form the bedrock of tonal communication.

Because of its special commitment to the general modeling of tonal consciousness, my critique has had to assume the form of essays juxtaposed upon the vast tonal project of Western history. The first two chapters are a critique of the scope and methodology of current tonal theory. They seek to examine the systems of Rameau, who formed the basis of what I call "bourgeois scholarship" regarding Western tonal speculation, and of Schenker, who has subdued all but a few scholars into a complacent—and at the same time apparently tireless—examination of the most specific features of harmonic consciousness, with its attendant and periodic rehearsal of "natural" causes for human tonal activity and its facile (because unexamined) capitulation to a deterministic view of the course of musical creativity.

The underlying theme of this book is that mainstream Western musical thought is what social scientists and social historians describe as "culture-bound" and is a product of the culture best described as "bourgeois." The term is infrequently used in these chapters to identify the historical growth and development of European capitalism that gradually absorbed a nexus of musical activities—composition, performance, audience consumption, and finally the study of music itself—which formerly had been largely the concern, and therefore under the control, of the Roman church and the nobility. A positive characteristic of this new, cultural movement was that version of societal expression called individualism, which had decisive and lasting consequences for the arts, philosophy, and science. To be sure, individualism had been tolerated, even encouraged, by popes and kings alike, but only to the degree that it was subjected to and glorified their own interests. The emergent individualism of bourgeois society, however, had a liberating aspect. According to Raymond Williams, bourgeois consciousness contained within it "an idea of a society as a neutral area within which each individual is free to pursue his own development and his own advantage as a natural right."[4] Within the context of this individualism, musical expressivity was personalized in a fashion hitherto unknown, even unsuspected. That is, the expressive content of music was no longer obligated only to objectify the greater glory of God or to soothe the frazzled nerves of monarchs: its responsibility now also lay within the very subjectivity of its creator. The composer, particularly in the nineteenth century, became a vehicle of expression for men and women like himself who expected him to objectify feelings that ran the gamut from their most private yearnings to espousals of public virtue. At the same time, the advantage this individualism provided the composer to pursue his own development as a "natural right" also forced him to produce commodities with exchange value, that is, salable works of art, if he was to maintain his existence. Thus, as he sought to maximize the exchange value of his works, he was also forced to present that music in a universally accepted language or idiom. Nowhere is this more evident than in the realm of tonality, as I hope to demonstrate later in this book. This is to say that bourgeois carries here none of the condemnation frequently associated with that term. My point is not to deprecate bourgeois individualism, but simply to define the culture in which Western music and musical thought have been shaped.

Chapter 3 suggests a point of departure for a phenomenology of tonal consciousness. To be sure, I do not call myself a philosopher of music, but, rather, a musicologist who has reluctantly decided that his profession has failed to achieve its goal, that is, if within the purview of its interests there lies any serious commitment to the very nature of those historical appearances of music which have given that profession its reason for existence. If tonality is a form of human consciousness, then, clearly, we know little about it. An incessant rehearsal of three hundred years of its activity through the ostensible objectivity of the musical score will only continue to produce the same cadence at the end of all analytic endeavors and polite applause from an academic quarter that has benumbed itself through scholarly convention. Let me state quite plainly here that chapter 3 does not present a methodology for tonal analysis. It is, rather, a series of observations about the activity of creating and making music when one purposely turns away from the notated score of whatever era is under investigation and asks why there are musical scores and how they came about. In fact, four of the components of tonal phenomena that characterize Western music seem to have emerged without the assistance of notation. To be sure, the invention of Western harmony necessitated notation (although Pygmy culture—however consciously or unconsciously—seems to create harmonized music quite nicely without it), but tonality was not forged in the crucible of harmony: harmony was forged in the crucible of tonality. In short, chapter 3 is an assertion that the origins of tonality are so deeply embedded within consciousness that the whole begins to quiver and vibrate when thought itself turns with sincerity and openness toward its sonic object.

Chapters 4 through 11 are examinations of critical aspects of the tonal project in Western music history that remain problematic both in current theoretical and musicological literature. I cannot say that I have solved these problems once and for all, but I have attempted to set them in a perspective which I found lacking in the literature that dealt with them—either superficially or in detail. It is a not so curious feature of current musicology that we either tend to ignore altogether or attempt to trivialize into benignancy those very features of our tonal consciousness that are the most crucial to our understanding of how we hear and how we think we hear. For instance, chapter 6, "Medieval and Renaissance Hearing," is a particular case in point. While I believe that a proper resolution to its most fundamental questions lies within the field of cognition itself, this problem is far from solved and needs much thought, research, and observation.

Specifically, in the frequent scholarly debate over the vertical versus the horizontal aspect of Renaissance polyphony, musicologists do not ask the right kinds of questions. The problem is not to rummage through the theoretical literature for the most respected evidence to support one's position, but to ask instead why a given medieval or Renaissance theorist took the position he did in the first place. Knowledge and human interests are all of a piece.

In the interests of comprehensibility it is also instructive to offer a few comments about my terminology, which may not immediately signify to the reader what it has come to mean to me over the course of several years of thought. There is no particular merit in rendering the fundamental musical tone and its attendant envelope of harmonics as *Klang* other than the fact that no proper English word corresponds with it. What is important to its conceptualization is the fact that no natural tone is a single tone, that within its envelope of partials are critical components which cognition must and unwittingly does attend to in its comprehension and shaping of the tonal image. Certain phenomena within the *Klang* are indeed responsible for the historical development of the notion of consonance and dissonance and timbre, although probably not as responsible as some have wished and others have assumed. The world of musical tone is a durable one, but I do not believe that Western music has followed an inevitable historical development up through the overtone series: if it had, the course of that development would be other than what currently characterizes modern tonality in the form of equal temperament. We can no more lay the blame for tonality ultimately upon the overtone series than we can blame the color brown upon the rainbow or light refracted through a prism.

Melos has a specific meaning in this book, close to the Greek one, "that which is composed of words, melody, and rhythm." As with the Greeks, it is always distinguished here from *organikon melos*, or—to them—the less important instrumental melos. Each time it is used it means the collective vocal tradition of a specific or general community of singers. It also means an oral tradition or an oral tradition that gradually became crystallized through notation. I readily admit that I have paid scant attention to the rhythmic aspect of the collective melos, which certainly merits a study of its own, but tonality was first conceived in the minds of people who sang more than they played (and their playing was attendant upon their singing), and the interrelation between the three elements—words, melody, and rhythm—is implied even though I have left rhythm in a sort of temporal limbo. I do not feel, however, that a study of rhythm and its relation to tonality will vitiate my work, but, rather, will serve further to confirm it.

Ratio, as it is used here, is probably only my understanding of that term, and I apologize to those who may be disturbed by its perhaps indiscriminate use. To me, it means that operation of the mind upon the objective given of nature, how it rationalizes and explains that existence to itself, how it appropriates that object for its own use. In terms of tonality, this has historically defined itself within the context of mathematics, which enjoyed an unassailable position with music in the Greek quadrivium, and within the later activity of the Cartesian *cogito* and the empirical (but also frequently speculative) activities of the Enlightment and the beginnings of modern science. Within a given historical context, the collective *ratio* assumes the nature of an ideology. Certainly this is true of our current notions of tonality, due chiefly to the reverence that we tacitly offer to the thought of Rameau and openly to Schenker. When this sense of *ratio* is intended, it is italicized; otherwise, ratio (as found in chapter 4 and elsewhere) means numerical proportion.

Harmonia is a term of such profound implications in Greek music philosophy and theory that I have not even attempted to give it an English equivalent. Its content is briefly developed in chapter 4, where it is pertinent, but I can only suggest that it be viewed with respect and in light of two critical sources that define the early and late contexts of its meaning: the fragments of Philolaus and the writings of Aristotle, particularly the *Poetics*.

In order to restore a forgotten subjectivity with regard to the tonal object, throughout these essays I have relied heavily on two English terms, *cognitive* and *sonic*, which designate specific tonal operations and properties. The mental operation of cognition is not as finite for me as it is in psychologist J. P. Guilford's resourceful "structure of intellect" model of the sixties, but the operations—cognition, memory, divergent thinking, convergent thinking, and evaluation—that Guilford describes through that model reflect the kind of tonal thinking I attempt to identify in this book. *Tonal cognition* is as active a process of the mind and body as tying one's shoe. It is therefore just as difficult to scrutinize. Only when we do it wrong do the operations of memory and evaluation (higher orders in Guilford's model) correct and alter the situation at hand. That is, missing a shoe eyelet and playing a B natural in the fifth note of the opening theme of Mozart's K. 333 Piano Sonata are of the same order. At that point, psychology and neuropsychology—not to mention one's mother—simply take over; judgments are pronounced and the activity is altered to bring it into conformity with expected and accepted patterns of human behavior. The very simplicity of this operation is the truth of its coherence and order. With every mention of *cognitive* and *cognition* I imply an active process of human mentality, however uncritical or nonreflective that process is judged to be in the activity so identified. Like language, tonality continually makes itself, even when we are not listening.

As for *sonic*, its abundant use in these pages simply ignores a now popular and fairly recent application of that term, which has to do with airplanes and breaking the sound barrier. Here its meaning is that vast beauty of a vibrating world at our ears, irrevocably to be subjected to manipulation and judgment by thoroughly human interests. Sonic means the heard materials of nature from which tonality is physically wrested and made aesthetically (and therefore rationally) true. To be sure, sonic is frequently used here as a substitute for tonal, but only to thrust it back in the a priori sphere of its yet unchallenged freedom. From the ancient "First Delphic Hymn" to John Cage and beyond, every tonal creation acknowledges this freedom at the same time that it willingly restricts itself to the totality of the musical object at hand in order to express a quite human love for audible truth. From my meager understanding of physics, I believe that only the octave is universally pure: all other intervals that man creates from a vibrating cosmos necessarily and critically reflect a relationship between his consciousness and heard phenomena, with a continuity of reason that inevitably reveals the abilities and disabilities of his perception and the capacities of his understanding. Man is capable of differentiating well over thirteen hundred pitches within the audible spectrum of sound. Why he has historically selected only eighty-eight tones (and very infrequently all of those) from that vast reservoir of sonic material with which to compose his motets and concertos is the most puzzling and most important question that this book attempts to answer.

It is to be regretted that modern technology has so precisely defined sonic, restricting the meaning of this wonderful old Latin term. I ask the reader to consider what generosity those Italian composers exhibited: when they composed a new and remarkable form of instrumental music in the seventeenth century, a form not restricted to the exigencies of textual demands; when they literally created a term that had its roots in the same Latin source, that similarly revealed its rhapsodic freedom; when they called that new and resonating freedom *sonata*, something merely *per sonare* and thereby liberating and full of human potential and unique utterance.

And finally, there is the term *tonality* itself, which I render interchangeably as "tonal consciousness."[5] There is a specific reason for this. To turn tonality into an adjective with relation to consciousness is an attempt to restore the subjective ego to its proper relationship with the object it both creates and cognizes. The chief fault of mainstream scholarship has been to ignore (even to fail to recognize) this relationship. There can be no ontology of tonality as a human endeavor until this relationship is brought into proper perspective—through physics and neurophysics, through psychology and sociology, through acoustics and psychoacoustics, and through politics and economics. Until this project is actively taken up by the musicological community there can be no progress toward the historical definition of our tonal consciousness.

Within the pages of this book I cannot define and evaluate the whole human tonal project, nor was it ever my intent to do so. I have necessarily restricted myself to certain dimensions of the tradition which I have inherited, into which I was born and think. But within that tradition, the great tradition of Machaut, Bach, Mahler, and Ives, I have become comfortable with a small group of concepts which tell me that I have intimate connections with the man who first catalogued the tuning systems of ancient Ugarit, the musician who played at peasant dances in tenth-century Spain, and the rock star in the seventies, who wore a live snake around his body and smashed his guitar as coda to his performance because his own tonal consciousness no longer served him with the necessary components of integrity, forcefulness, and expression that his inherited sonic legacy once guaranteed. It is all of a piece and I am part of it.

Because the history of tonal speculation has been largely characterized by an ever-increasing and frequently deadening objectivity, we have reduced tonality down to the tone, the triad, the cadence, and the chord progression. With its basic sonic components thus shattered under our scrutiny, it is not surprising that the most popular analytical method for tonal speculation today seeks harmonically "to prolong" these objects in order to afford the subject a continuing reason to exist. Happily, tonality will survive. Because it is the remarkable product of sonic knowledge and human interests, it is an object capable of truth, expressivity, even self-correction. Had I not believed this, the chapters that follow would not have been written.

1 The Activity of Tonal Speculation

T o comprehend tonality itself, not just to fit and register it in its system of reference, is nothing but to perceive the individual moment in its immanent connection with other moments.[1] This paraphrase of a statement by Theodor Adorno critically exposes the failure of the musicological establishment to take cognizance of the historical nature of Western tonality, that is, its attendant ignorance of the assumptions upon which its tonal theories are constructed, which has proved to be its largest single embarrassment. True, there has been erected a clearly defined system for a single historical era, the "common-practice" period, as it is frequently called, which was in effect in Western music from roughly 1600 to 1900. This tonal era, which parallels the ascendance of capitalism and the development of the modern nation-states in Western Europe and North America, produced a great body of musical literature and acquired a cultural hegemony now dominant in the industrialized nations of the world. This era of "classic tonality" contains the major portion of that music which an active public of millions of listeners considers both "popular" and "serious." It is sustained by world media to the point of universality. There is something utterly amazing in the fact that a large music festival, for instance, may draw peoples from dozens of nations, who sit down together and—without speaking with one another because they cannot—listen to a Mozart piano concerto which addresses each person through a common sonic language. The tonal saturation of the global village via electronic communication need only be mentioned. Tonality is a critical part of this aesthetic communication and achieves it in a fashion that utterly escapes linguistic behavior.[2]

The importance of this wealth of tonal utterance, however, has also tended to discourage proper reflection upon its own historical position within the development of human culture as sonic communication. What is taken as "the tonal era," as stated above, is assumed to be the whole rather than Adorno's individual moment in its immanent connection with all other tonal moments. More critically, "the tonal era," as many refer to it, is merely but very importantly an era in Western tonal consciousness that is correctly identified as creating and producing "key-centered music." Therefore, to erect a conceptual model of this music as the historical fulfillment of tonal truth takes, to borrow the words of Adorno again, "as fetishistic a view of the concept as the concept does in interpreting itself naively in its own domain."[3] For purposes of explicit clarification, however, let us continue to use tonality in this restricted classical sense for the remainder of this chapter in order to pursue its implications to their necessary conclusion.

Chief among the weaknesses of this naive interpretation has been the assumption that tonality reached—through a series of minute refinements of its rules—an idealized historical state within real historical appearance. Thus tonality is thought to be something that had to emerge; it had to develop; there was frequently a problem as it "evolved" into mature expressions of its assumed essence. In the same fashion that liberals conceive the history of political theory, which is thought "naturally" to culminate in the American Constitution and attendant documents and practices, everything else is musically pre-, proto-, post-, or wrong. From cocktail chatter to graduate seminars presided over by the most prestigious academic elite, how many battles are waged from this very platform?

Our faith in this developmental point of view has what appear to be logical tenets. As Leo Treitler points out, its extreme statement appears in a form that Karl Popper has called "essentialism" that is based on the assumption that there must be something in tonality that is recognizably the same even while it changes constantly with respect to its "outer" form.[4] Treitler warns us that, armed with a faith in the developmental point of view, we assume three general characteristics about the tonal object: 1) Tonality is regarded as the embodiment of an essence; 2) tonality is understood in terms of its antecedents and its consequences; and 3) tonality is seen in the context of a process that culminates in fulfillment and perfection. The Mozart Piano Sonata in B-flat Major (K. 333), for example, would allow the construction of as classic a case as could be made.[5] Mozart, for one, is judged to be a culmination of this process, and over him and other tonal composers, well-trained, professional minds hasten to take sides and wage harmonic war until the work of music is broken asunder. We have not been remiss in our academic duty to this classically conceived tonal concept since its early concretization by the now famous *Traité de l'harmonie* of Jean-Phillipe Rameau in 1722. Through a series of books, monographs, and dissertations we have carried forth Rameau's initial project of tonal modeling in works of music thought either to possess it outright or to allude in some way to it. These scholarly activities are easily identified by the incipit "Tonality in . . . ," followed by "the Early Operas of Verdi," "the Middle Quartets of Beethoven," "the Large Orchestral Works of Richard Strauss," or what have you. Within the narrow parameters of the common-practice era it matters little who of several dozen composers are chosen for this analytical exercise. Schubert will suffice as well as Mozart, Chopin as well as Beethoven. From a harmonic arsenal of chromatic chords, "far reaching" modulations, the abusive caveat of "tonal ambiguity," and so forth, one respectfully chooses those sonic weapons that are appropriate to his task. For instance, to Ernst Křenek in 1939, Beethoven represented the apex of tonality. Tonality became "overripe" with Schubert, who somehow "remained wholeheartedly true to the basic harmonic principle of tonality," by which token "he was exceedingly progressive." A "triumphant return of chromaticism" was effected by Richard Wagner, which, along with "*ersatz* tonalities" such as are found "frequently" in Debussy, brought the whole of music to "the threshold of atonality."[6]

But such attempts as these to define the limits of tonality have also led us to believe that perhaps the vast body of music composed *before* the common-practice period is also in some fashion tonal. From the birth of Christian chant in Syria and its neighbor countries in the Eastern Mediterranean crescent to the late Masses of Palestrina in Rome at the end of the sixteenth century there lies a vast tonal consciousness that is thought to have yearned for the coming of an ideal sonic appearance. So with renewed vigor but considerably less armor we sally forth first into the Renaissance, then into the Middle Ages, in a concerted effort to ferret out this hidden dimension which we then subdue with what remains of a shabby and battle-scarred methodology.

Our victory is Pyrrhic. Modal music, so-called, fails to measure up to the tonal expectations we have for it. The final triad is not a triad at all but an "empty" fifth; the leading-tone triad (a surrogate dominant) declines to resist us, tottering through its cadential progression, in inverted position, standing tonality on its head! But our rigor proves consequential, for our analytical view—which is seldom questioned—has proved the developmental thesis once again. In its elemental (read, modal) stages, each new composition in the Middle Ages and the Renaissance is assumed to be yearning toward a supposed *tonal* "thing-in-itself." The generality of tonal modeling becomes the normative aspect of the system and the individuality of the work (here as elsewhere) is dismissed as an aberrant appearance.

Carlo Gesualdo, for example, becomes a neurotic harmonist who threatens tonal suicide and thus can be analyzed only on psychological (that is, what is believed to constitute extramusical) grounds. Composers who do not fall within the precision of the method are judged totally insane. *Musica ficta*, a persistent Hegelian contradiction of the promulgated thesis of Renaissance music theory, is treated as an interesting anomaly of performance practice: its true historical dimensionality as the clay of tonal praxis from which theoretical models were molded into ever new models is shunted aside in favor of modal clarity and analytical neatness. Since tonality has been falsely objectified into a paradigm stage, any extension of it works under the greatest frustration in what is felt to be its pre-paradigm existence. But since it must achieve its goal there springs up still another batch of monographs, books, and dissertations which testifies to the generally held notion that if nothing else in world reality ever achieved the fitful process from becoming to being, tonality at least can be exhibited as a phenomenon of which metaphysics can be justifiably proud, e.g., "The Emergence of Tonality"; *Tonality and Atonality in Sixteenth-Century Music;* "Tonality in Early Polyphony: Towards a History of Tonality"; "The Evolution of the Leading Tone in Western European Music to *circa* 1600 A.D." Characteristic of this group of studies are the "emergent" and "evolutionary" natures of tonality, thus reifying the developmental aspects of an inadequate methodology. The normative aspects of classic tonal modeling are tediously searched out in an effort that projects the sonic creation of the medieval composer—with prophetic vision—into a tonal future to which he had no commitment, in which he had no logical participation. The Italian lutanist Joan Ambrosio Dalza is not permitted merely to compose a collection of dances for the rising bourgeois citizenry of early sixteenth-century Venice: his pavanes are wrested from him and treated as harbingers of the tonal perfection for which his fatigued modal spirit yearned instead.

At the other end of this transhistorical reductionism, tonality is simply left to fend for itself. Having run a course of tonal perfection during classicism, tonality's uncanny tendency toward disintegration is first privately felt (in the works of Beethoven) and then publicly acknowledged (in the works of Wolf, Mahler, Strauss, and early Schoenberg). Tonality has run the course of its usefulness and must be abandoned. There is, of course, a reason for this, which I shall call the "shredder syndrome," and it is the inevitable product of the developmental theory. Leo Treitler notes that analysis done under the aegis of the developmental theory assumes that "musical materials have to be used up, shredding the material down to its constituent fibers,"[7] so that nothing is left but to engage in a search for more audible substance upon which to perform the same sonic operation. While entire eras are subjected to this type of analysis, such as the last half of the nineteenth century, single composers are sometimes brought forth as specimen shredders of individual merit. How many papers and lectures have we heard on "Beethoven's Harmonic Development" that accomplish this process in the ubiquitous early, middle, and late stages so dear to musicologists?

Obviously, tonality as essence, while apparently universal, was a fragile creation and could be exhausted. Under the operation of the shredder syndrome tonality was simply chewed up. The late nineteenth century unfolds as the silver years of this process of tonal attenuation and disintegration. Fully pensioned now, the musics of Wolf, Mahler, Strauss, and Scriabin become the wasted residue of what was once young and strong. "Excessive chromaticism" and "tonal disintegration" are the epithets of *Salome* and Mahler's Seventh Symphony. It is customary at this point to make significant pronouncements about the death of tonality. The specter of sonic chaos hovers in the background. The death knell sounds not one tone but all twelve pitches of the chromatic scale, at first in what seems only random order but then with a bewitching, serialized stubbornness: It had to happen. In an age of tonal anxiety for composer and public alike it is every man for himself. The curtain falls here for the developmental theorist. The negation has come.

It is here, in the twentieth century, that we should be most embarrassed at our failure to recognize the ahistorical reductionism that exemplifies our common notions of tonal consciousness. This failure, however, was predetermined and lay at the very heart of modern tonal speculation. After all, what *was* the meaning of twentieth-century music if not the negation of tonality? If "atonality" alone appeared to theorists as the most rational (and threatening) consequence of the developmental theory, it was only because tonality in its prosperity was deemed also to be rational, a mirror of the mentality that produced it. From the standpoint of Webernian speculation atonality *could* be the logical consequence of something that was thought to be organic and aesthetically true.[8]

Thus it was thought (and feared) by some theorists that atonality would one day reign supreme in the sonic affections of Western musical consciousness. But atonality did not achieve this. There was no dreaded triumph of atonality. It did not become *der Tonkunst der Zukunft*. It could not, for tonality from Pittsburgh to Peking became an extended marketable consciousness. Now as before, its here and now are legislated as audible commodities: at home by the public's demand for tonal reification, which does of course find Schoenberg "interesting" but mentally and emotionally inaccessible; and abroad by party congresses, which apparently find him too emotionally accessible and therefore unacceptable. Somehow, the developmental theory and the shredder syndrome of tonality fail to account for the persistence of tonality in a modern world. Although pronounced dead by the avant-garde a half century ago, tonality remains not as "the downright new quality leaping forth from the definite negation; it is the return of what was negated. Dialectical progress is always a recourse as well, to that which fell victim to the progressing concept; the concept's progressive concretion is its self-correction."[9] Atonality was but a species of moment in a general negation, felt at the turn of the century, that manifested itself among a plurality of less radical tonal appearances: bitonality, polytonality, pantonality, neomodality, neoprimitivism, neoclassicism, futurism, and neoromanticism. Each of these possessed its own harmonic mode of disintegration; each flashed before sonic cognition as a hammer with which to smash the generalizing and leveling tendency of tonal consciousness. Historically, the collision and cross-fertilization of these tonal pluralities have produced and are producing a reified tonality, the return of what was negated, that has reinstated itself in the musical consciousness of man for purely nonmusical reasons. It is beyond the comprehension of theorists and musicologists that classic tonality appeared as and how it did through economic, social, political, philosophical, cognitive, and aesthetic as well as "natural" means. Therefore, it will not be an easy task to convince them that it became its own negation through the same processes.

How accurate is the picture sketched in the paragraphs above? As the editors of prestigious musicological presses have been quick to advise me, "nobody believes the developmental thesis any more," and I am "whipping a dead horse." Music styles do not wax better and better any more, they just change; and the progressive attitude of musical change has been discreetly retired to the back of the closet. To be sure, there seems to be a reversal of attitude among some musicologists and theorists who currently write about music. There is, however, only so much tinkering that can be done with the empirical methodology that characterizes current musicology. It is impossible here to offer a thorough critique of all aspects of this consciousness, its complexity, and its internal contradictions. So complete an exploration will have to wait for some future time, but in light of the subject of these essays, a critical point must be made.

If tonality does not progress to a perfect state at which its fundamental components can be fixed, then the most popular analytical system for examining tonal modeling must be abandoned. The latest craze in academic music theory orbits around the thought of Heinrich Schenker, whose technique of layer analysis has filtered all the way down to the undergraduate level. (Readers will recall how little of Schenker was known among American academic circles even twenty years ago.) But the Schenkerian model is an ideal one: The *Ursatz* is an "externalization" of the idea of tonal nature (the *Klang*); and, as Eugene Narmour points out, the idealism of Schenker's philosophy "is accompanied by the usual embarrassing metaphysics."[10] The essence of the Schenkerian system is "tonality as chord prolongation," which has inspired strange analytic excursions into early polyphony, where the triad begins mischieviously to appear and take its place in the hierarchy of the *Klang*. These Neo-Schenkerians have decisively separated themselves from their "traditional tonalist" origins. The traditional tonalist believes that triads and progressions of triads in medieval music are not to be thought as having the kind of harmonic motion found in later music, for the medieval composer did not hear his harmonies as we do. In its present state, tonal speculation has no other means of survival but revisionism: one idealism is replaced by another.

But if nobody believes the developmental thesis any more, as I am told theorists no longer do, if tonality does not progress toward an assumed perfection, what then does it do? The implication here is that there is a vague historical dialectic at work, for demonstrable reasons. But these reasons, precisely because they lie in the subjective activity of man as tonal producer, are either ignored or attacked. In the meantime, Schenkerian idealism is both pruned and embellished: it is reified in each new study of tonality that appears. Theorists disavow association with Schenker at the same time that they labor to extend his principles via their own private metalanguages for tonal consciousness.

Perhaps the most extensive of these attempts is Wallace Berry's *Structural Functions in Music*, published in 1976. In one of the longest chapters on tonality to date, Berry seeks to describe "the practice of hierarchic systems of tonal order, by which the concept of tonality is engendered."[11] Tonality is thus broadly conceived as

> a formal system in which pitch content is perceived as functionally related to a specific pitch-class or pitch-class-complex of resolution, often preestablished and preconditioned, as a basis for structure at some understood level of perception. The foregoing definition of tonality is applicable not just to the "tonal period" in which the most familiar conventions of tonal function are practiced (roughly the eighteenth and nineteenth centuries), but through early modality and more recent free tonal applications as well.[12]

To be sure, Berry is able to extend his analytical model (which I will not evaluate here) to encompass music from Josquin to Berio, with an occasional excursion even into monophonic chant. But his bias toward his model and what it explains is weakened every time he is forced to use the term "quasi-tonal" for what it does not explain. (Note, for instance, on page 172 the conjectural set of *fifteen* classifications for levels of significance of tonal function, including "Absolute" atonality and "Irrelevant" tonality!) After all the analysis there is still a tonal residue left over which cannot be decreed away. The most serious flaw to be found in Berry's system of structural functions in tonality is one which he curiously passes off as a virtue rather than permitting its contradiction of his system to spoil his version of the dialectic: "Questions of the establishment of tonal reference by harmonic-melodic succession, and of the nature of tonal fluctuation, like that of conjectured tonal allusion in *antitonal* styles, are necessarily somewhat subjective. . . ."[13]

But herein lies the fault in all present systems of tonal analysis: they are not subjective enough. The subject, in fact, has been removed; his cognitive abilities and disabilities have been completely ignored; and his ear ("our ear," as Schenker was fond of calling it) has been disembodied to serve the ends of analytical validity. This problem is briefly addressed by Bennett Reimer but dismissed by his pointing out that everybody is born into tonality and internalizes it without much effort:

> The listener need not know the functional technicalities, for they are so much a part of our lives, like the language we learn as babies, that they can be regarded as given, as one of the basic ways our minds operate. Tonal music makes sense to us because we have internalized the system. Particular pieces of tonal music may be more or less understandable, as particular books in English are more or less understandable, depending on their complexity and the experience of the reader. But the basis for understanding is present, in tonal music or in a book of English; neither requires that a new language be learned.[14]

But as long as the internalization of tonality remains unknown, we have no platform from which to launch a discussion of the sonic phenomenon, a phenomenon which is a reciprocal relationship between subject and object, composer and score, listener and performer. As Reimer clearly states, we are not born tonal. We are made tonal by society. Moreover, in the history of music we see clear indication of the development of those cognitive abilities which have rendered the image as historically tonal. These developments are in fact reflected anew each time we teach the young how to become tonally conscious. The societal repository of scales, the process of centonization, the growth of polyphony, the competition of tuning systems in the Renaissance and baroque eras, the establishment of equal temperament, the fixation of concert pitch, and the "invention" of perfect pitch—all these are operations of the subject in its activity of rationalizing its object. But the subjective nature of tonality is ignored, while the theorists offer ever more sophisticated models of how the composer's mind is assumed to work in the process of creation and how the listener must respond in order to understand it. At the moment, Schenkerian analysis is one of the most speculative systems of musical cognition ever designed. What evidence has been offered to establish the empirical reality of the prolongation of the triad, layered hearing, and the complex relationships between background and foreground elements in the actual process of hearing during which tonal understanding is required to take place? In short, the reductive activities of the theorists have been offered as true forms of tonal consciousness. But they are, unfortunately, only their notions of the concept; they are not the forms of consciousness of tonal cognition between subject and object. When will evidence appear that listener A understood sixty percent of the tonal work on level 2, listener B made it all the way to the background, while listener C never made it past the foreground? Future writers of dissertations will be either alarmed or pleased to learn that these statistics must be forthcoming for the Schenkerian legacy to be valid. Once this problem is solved, however, we may gleefully apply the method to the most fundamental levels of appreciation and begin to grade students on their abilities to hear the "tonicizing" factors of a work of music; symphony audiences will read a different kind of program note on how to layer their hearing in order to hear "the interior manifestations of the IV chord"; and both the actual and virtual temporality of the surface of the work will disappear in a reductive internalization of time that I fail to understand.

Since Schenker will be examined in the next chapter, I will omit further discussion of his system here. But it should be noted in passing that what the modern theorist is doing can only be understood as an act of self-preservation. We have stopped vilifying Schenker; we completely ignore his outrageous historical bias against any system but his own; and we are manipulating the major aspects of his system in order to legitimize further the discipline of music theory. We must be objective, we keep telling ourselves; layer analysis is good analysis. But the necessary relation of this analysis to the heard work of music is shunted aside and the listener is expected to comprehend meaning within the context of a reductive temporality in which the work itself does not and cannot reside.

Music is like language in so many ways that it has been called one. The nature of this tonal language is one of the most profound communicative activities of human mentality. It is now possible to hear a Hurrian cult song from ancient Ugarit, first sung perhaps sometime about 1400 B.C. There is no spoken language which has enjoyed an active history of thirty-four hundred years. In fact, the words of this ancient song, which may be addressed to the goddess Nikkal, wife of the moon god, are largely undecipherable. And yet its four-note melody haunts the ear with tonal gestures of sonic comprehension, expression, and beauty. What is this tonal link with our cultural past? What primitive cognitive abilities and disabilities are reflected in every piece of music we hear? What is *Homo tonifex?* These questions have yet to be answered.

If the reader has sensed that classic tonality per se is under attack he has not sensed rightly. Many hundreds of composers have used and are using even today—especially today—the tonality that Rameau was so delighted to establish through scientific precepts. But Rameau did not establish tonality; rather, he established a concept of it, a set of rules, authoritative in nature, in order that music might be (and remain, Schenker hoped) tonal. The notion of classic tonality as conceived by Rameau and extended by Schenker is but a historical gesture of human tonal consciousness. It is as historically related to polyphonic tonality of the Middle Ages and the Renaissance as to its apparent negation in the works of Schoenberg, which we shall discover are not "atonal" at all but are, rather, both an annulment and a preservation of tonality in its historical dimension. To be sure, this may initially trouble the contemporary musicologist or theorist who has reserved "tonality" for a given historical species of general tonality, and he might indeed hope for an adequate definition of general tonality to bail him out of confusion, even if only momentarily. But the dialectic of tonality will not permit a definition of it other than one that restores the *subject* to its proper place in the tonal act: tonality is a decision made against the chaos of pitch. There is no single truth of tonality except the willingness of this historical *subject* to seek a genuine understanding of its own thought about tonal appearance. The necessity for piercing this subject's persistent reification of assumed tonal truth has not yet been understood; instead, tonality is hypostatized through the activities of a thoroughly entrenched ideology.

2 The Hypostatization of Classic Tonality

I t is one of the anomalies of our cultural history that "classical music" does not refer to the music of ancient Greece. While classical architecture, sculpture, drama, poetry, philosophy, and law tend to indicate finite Greek and Roman legacies, the music from the ancient past is necessarily meager and largely undecipherable. Instead, classic music and what theorists refer to as "classic tonality" isolates a definable segment of Western music history, roughly from 1600 to 1900, with the customary internal stylistic divisions of Baroque, Classic, and Romantic. This arbitrary but popular designation for a music to be treated as good, true, and beautiful is of our own invention. It reflects no particular esteem for the music of ancient Greece, which, because of the predominantly oral tradition in which it thrived, remains a curiosity for the musicologist and is usually summarily dismissed as being irrelevant, primitive, and "not very tonal."

The purpose of this essay is to examine this arbitrary classic tonality of modern Europe on its own merits, to establish its historical parameters as judged by mainstream scholarship, and to assess its validity in determining the true nature of tonal consciousness. Since World War II there has been abundant research in theories of tonality. It must be granted at the outset, however, that the question of tonality remains one that is more or less neatly framed within the theoretical activities of Jean-Phillipe Rameau (1683–1764) and Heinrich Schenker (1868–1935).[1] To judge from current writing on music, to see any other aspect of tonal consciousness as anything but a frustrating series of footnotes to this historical framework is willfully to ignore the bias under which theorists currently operate. The very words *modal*, *atonal*, and *post-tonal* indicate that the modern music historian does not quite grasp the true nature of his own tonal consciousness, his historical past, or his culpability in perpetrating his prejudices under the guise of scientific objectivism and scholarly rigor. This is not to denigrate out of hand the careful work and insight of those who have constructed the platform of tonal speculation upon which academic music has built its theoretical edifice. Rather, what I seek to accomplish here is to put those efforts in their proper historical perspective. There is a tendency in current musicology to ignore the historical consciousness of the scholars who have molded our discipline, particularly their historical biases, at the same time that we extract from their writings and thought those features that are attractive and that lend themselves to subsequent revision. But revision produces revisionism, and I find it instructive to disentangle from the texture of tonal history those threads that have become the warp, the very backbone of current consciousness about human tonal acts.

Today we fix the *terminus ad quem* for classic tonality by the appearance of atonality, twelve-tone technique, Schoenberg, and expressionism. The search for its origin is more difficult. To Manfred Bukofzer and others, tonality was in its infancy in the first part of the seventeenth century. Not surprisingly, it thrived on Descartes, as we shall see. In 1690 it was a fledgling composer from Verona, then playing tenor viol in the orchestra at the great basilica in Bologna. But it is unfair to single out Bologna and young Giuseppe Torelli. There was, Bukofzer reminds us, also Naples and its thriving opera houses, which were frequented and appreciated by nobility and the new urban bourgeoisie alike.

By the early eighteenth century this tonality had become so harmonically stable as a vehicle of sonic motion that Rameau could characterize it in a single volume. Its basic tenets can be summarized in a few pages. This is not to say that Rameau was consistent throughout his long life as a composer and theorist. Taken as a whole, his theoretical *oeuvre* exhibits a maturation of thought about harmony. Rameau argued with and corrected himself. He was progressive, and he spent the latter part of his life trying to fit together all the pieces into his tonal puzzle. Some of them never did fit.

The popular notion of classic tonality with which an entire generation of post-war American students grew up was published in 1947, in a book now read by thousands, Bukofzer's *Music in the Baroque Era*. To be sure, Bukofzer did not invent the concept or the term, although he is among the first to delineate so carefully for English readers two distinct early stages of tonal modeling which preceded the rage for Neapolitan opera that brought about the infiltration of eighteenth-century Italian tonality in the great capitals of Western Europe.[2] It is instructive to examine the Bukofzer model in its entirety.

> Tonality was not "invented" by a single composer or a single school. It emerged at approximately the same time in the Neapolitan opera and in the instrumental music of the Bologna school and was codified by Rameau more than a generation after its first appearance in music. Tonality established a gradated system of chordal relations between a tonal center (the tonic triad in major or minor) and the other triads (or seventh chords) of the diatonic scale. None of these chords was in itself new, but they now served a new function, namely that of circumscribing the key. While in middle baroque harmony this function had been performed chiefly by the two dominants, it was now extended to all chords. Significantly, this inclusive system of chordal functions is known as functional harmony.[3]

Note that fully "emerged" tonality embraced a hierarchical system of relations between the tonic triad and the remaining six triads of the diatonic scale. Middle baroque harmony sees this hierarchy sustained "chiefly" by the two dominants. There remains only the establishment of the defining limits of early baroque harmony, and this Bukofzer supplied in the preface of the same book.

> The harmony of the early baroque was already clearly conceived in terms of chords and therefore "modern," but it was as yet free from the directive force of tonality, and this preserved a vestige of the renaissance tradition.[4]

It was Bukofzer's understanding that the "melodic laws of part-writing" of Renaissance music and the regulation of intervallic combinations precluded the necessity or even the possibility of a tonality whose "directive force" came from chordal harmony.

> In renaissance music, harmony was restricted to the regulation of intervallic combinations. The progression from any one combination to any other, or what in modern terminology would be called the chord progressions, were dictated not by a tonal or harmonic principle, but by the melodic laws of part-writing. Since the individual parts were in turn guided by the rules of the melodic modes, the intervallic harmony was indirectly governed by modality. The intervallic harmony of renaissance music was directed by modality, the chordal harmony of the late baroque by tonality.[5]

Thus, the identity of homophonic tonality gained credence by stating what was assumed to be its nonidentity: modal and tonal became falsely separated in an effort to locate the architecture of the latter. Nor was this concept invented by Bukofzer, who merely brought forth a nineteenth-century idea in modern dress. Bryan Simms notes that the term tonality

> had a clear and handy meaning when first used, referring to the scale-type basis of music of some era, that is, whether the music was based on the church modes or major and minor keys. Renaissance counterpoint, for example, was written in "tonalité ancienne," or as we would say, in the modes; later music was written in "tonalité moderne," or major and minor keys.[6]

The term *tonalité* as used in this sense began to appear in French theoretical literature in the early part of the nineteenth century. It was not invented by François-Joseph Fétis, as has often been stated: it seems to have been first used around 1810 by Alexandre Etienne Choron to point out the above distinction.[7] But this separation of modal and key-centered tonal modeling from the beginning already exhibited an embedded tonal vitalism that theorists were incapable of understanding even when they were aware of it. For Fétis, for example, the principle of modern tonality clearly involved a specific type of scale—major or minor. But there was more to tonality than just notes of a given scale. There were, notes Simms, " 'mysterious' relationships between the scale degrees which served to generate the scale in the first place, and then act *through* the scale as the ultimate source of chord structure, classification and succession."[8] This notion that certain scale degrees, intervals, and chords were imbued with the sensation of repose while others lacked it would puzzle Rameau (but not Schenker) and eventually serve to deter consciousness itself from questions about the role of human will that—however dimly—sought any clarification of its own activity within the tonal act. We will take up the notion of tonal vitalism later in the chapter. What directly concerns us here is the fact that the romantic distinction of old and new tonalities gradually but firmly became one of nonidentity rather than a critical understanding of the principles of identity and difference within a general and historical sphere of advancing tonal consciousness. This romantic distinction lingers on. Here is a quote from one of the most popular music appreciation texts of the mid-fifties of this century:

> The word *modality* refers to the old modes and their use in a contrapuntal-melodic system. *Tonality* is mainly concerned with the major and minor and with a complete system of keys related by harmonies. Tonality, in the modern sense, began to evolve in the seventeenth century. Prior to that time the system of modality was in force.[9]

Occasionally, in modern texts, the false tonal dichotomy of modal versus tonal is tacitly admitted by the contemporary scholar but then quickly forgotten. Note the use of quotes in the following sentence to indicate that the author may himself suspect he is subscribing to a convention in lieu of examining the equally important tonal features of both systems: "All these conditions resulted in an outcome decisive for the whole history of music: namely the rise of modern 'tonality' out of the old 'modality.' "[10] Once one has discreetly slipped the terminology into the discussion, however, he is absolved from any further commitment to acknowledge that it is false. Later in the same paragraph we read:

> In the late Baroque era, however, about from Lully and Corelli on, modality is transformed into tonality, which is to say that the basic succession of chords becomes on principle a grouping around fixed centers: tonic, dominant, and subdominant (this being the order of their importance in Baroque music) become the focal points of these groups, and these centers stand to each other in the functional relationship of modern major-minor tonality.[11]

These remarks are typical of the manner in which good tonality is reserved for a specific order of historical tonal modeling. Furthermore, the aesthetic value of all tonal consciousness is weighted in favor of the music of the bourgeois age. As late as the 1970s it is still possible to read in a new music text, "The old ecclesiastical modes have a less definite, less clear-cut sound than the major/minor system of tonality."[12] I am uncertain what this statement means, but its implied historical bias is remarkable indeed.

One of the most frustrating results of the modal/tonal dichotomy is the sheer sonic chaos of the tonal consciousnesses thought to characterize the musics of late Renaissance and early baroque composers who of course never knew that they were afflicted by the march of tonal progress. Between Renaissance modal harmony and baroque tonal harmony an audible wasteland has arisen in current literature, a combat zone which is claimed by thoroughly partisan interests. The length of this era of transition from medieval mode to classic tonal scale and the assumed tonal ambiguity historically caused by their simultaneous use depends on the bias of the scholar who determined it. For Edward E. Lowinsky, who was surprised to discover pieces in Joan Ambrosio Dalza's *Intabolatura de lauto libro quatro* (1508) that were "written in crystal clear C Major,"[13] this conflict lasted about a century. For Robert W. Wienpahl, the emergence of tonality lasted from 1500 to 1700, with modal and tonal modeling so fused at one point that he coined the curious term *monality* for the process of infiltration and interdependent structuring.[14]

But these analyses are not attempts to break free from the limits of the common-practice model of tonality. Collectively, they testify to the notion, mentioned earlier, that pre-paradigm tonality yearned for a tonality that was a thing-in-itself, a goal which was not fully realized until the late seventeenth century in Naples and Bologna. It is of the utmost importance to focus this notion properly; three decades ago it was generally held among the scholarly community, and it has thwarted nearly all attempts to understand tonality in medieval and Renaissance music, not to mention in antiquity and the "post-tonal" works of contemporary music.

Let us narrow our discussion for a moment to a certain phrase of Bukofzer's definition: "a gradated system of chordal relations between a tonal center (the tonic triad in major or minor) and the other triads (or seventh chords) of the diatonic scale." Clearly, what Bukofzer sought to establish was not tonality but rather the nature and content of functional harmony, to which he applied the term "tonality" by force of tradition. There were three general aspects of this process: an assumed dichotomy between chordal and melodic structuring in harmonic entities, a topic which is still being debated in the theoretical journals; the obvious reduction of the rich repository of medieval modes into two characteristic but highly plastic modes—major and minor; and the stability and hierarchy of tonal place as defined by a tonic or key center. Bukofzer thought tonality to be a whole, audible gestalt defined by a qualitative polarity between a center (in which dwells the tonic) and other triads, including the dominant, built on the remaining diatonic scale steps. It was assumed that this qualitative polarity was intended by the composer when he constructed his sonic canvas and that it was discernible by the listener. At the level of aesthetic perception, the understanding of the tonal composition was chiefly anchored in the pivotal relationship between the tonic of a given key and its dominant, the bare bones of tonal cognition in an abstract sense as well as the particularization of its essence in terms of cadential appearance in the temporal gestalt. Without this assumption classic tonality falls apart. Of fundamental importance to classic theorists is the idea that this modeling is chordal and thereby vertical. Historically, there is a reason that this conceptualization should appear as truth. The era in which it evolved as a theory was a chordal era in which even polyphony was thought to be only an infiltration of chordal, tonal structuring. Hence our problems with previous historical eras, which I shall take up in later chapters.

It would be quite unfair to malign Bukofzer for his own insight into specific tonal modeling in baroque music, nor is this my intent. But it must be readily admitted that for an entire generation of American scholars Bukofzer's statements were authority enough: functional harmony, common-practice period, and tonality gradually became virtually synonymous terms for the great age of bourgeois music.

How much have we changed our attitudes in the last thirty years? The degree to which our consciousness has been expanded can be tellingly demonstrated by the use of the word *tonal* in the previously mentioned books on medieval music, *Music in the Middle Ages* (1940), by Gustave Reese, and

Medieval Music (1978), by Richard Hoppin. The term is largely absent in Reese's early study. It is frequently used in Hoppin's book to indicate features of sonic modeling which the author senses in medieval music. Does the abundant use of the adjective "tonal" in a new book on medieval music indicate that at last we have seen the light and that our problems are over? No, for there is no consistency in this usage nor any general agreement among scholars as to what is meant by the use of the term *tonality*. On the one hand, Charles Rosen states that "tonality is a hierarchical arrangement of the triads based on the natural harmonics or overtones of a note."[15] On the other, Hoppin writes that "the Marian antiphon, *Alma Redemptoris Mater*, already cited for its constant use of B-flat in Mode 5, provides a particularly striking example of this new type of tonal organization."[16] Obviously, there are no chords to prolong in *Alma Redemptoris Mater*, so it must be tonal in some other sense than that indicated by Rosen.

I think the camp is hopelessly divided. Those who choose not to think about tonality at all before the common-practice era will continue to use the modal/tonal dichotomy because they feel comfortable with the terminology and do not wish to question it. Those who have sensed that tonal consciousness is somehow all of a piece and wish to subscribe to this notion, however uncritically, have begun to search for a more generalized terminology that will disguise their inadequate methodology, which they also do not wish to question. Thus while we begin to witness a general drift in current writing toward a broader definition of tonality, there is no agreement among members of the musical community as to what this definition should be. We can document this transition to a more generalized conceptualization of tonality with several citations. These citations are characterized by a gradual capitulation to the general sense of tonality as broadly stated in music dictionaries, music appreciation texts (where the deception is the most pernicious because it is least suspected), and the modern music theory text. Tonality is "loyalty to a tonic, in the broadest sense of the word."[17] It is thought that by simply abandoning a conceptualization of tonality within the limits of triadic harmony, as stated before by Rosen, we have corrected our myopia and are looking at the historical past and present with the proper perspective. The following statements are representative:

> The tonic (1) of a key, the center of the tonal universe, determines a complete hierarchy of notes in which each note functions as an individual or as part of a chord; the tonic is home base, the static point, the point of rest.[18]

While *harmony* still remains a possibility in this definition, the following one has become so bland that tonal harmonic interpretation per se is left up to the reader:

We have already learned that tonality is that quality in music according to which one tone, the tonic, is heard as a focal pitch toward which the other pitches of a particular piece or section all point. . . . That is, in a specific tonality the pitches will have certain interval relations to each other, and some pitches will be heard as more important than others.[19]

And finally, through the jargon of theoretical authenticity, tonality becomes broadly conceived as

a formal system in which pitch content is perceived as functionally related to a specific pitch-class or pitch-class-complex of resolution, often preestablished and preconditioned, as a basis for structure at some understood level of perception.[20]

Here the monophonic tonic (pitch-class) and harmonic tonic (pitch-class-complex) are safely disguised, and the definition seems now capable of sitting up and taking solid food—even atonal music—although the fault of this definition and the principles it implies are frequently seen in Berry's use of such terms as "quasi-tonal" for those musical appearances which fall beyond the parameters of his definition.

The current problem regarding definitions of our tonal consciousness is fairly clear. Music becomes tonal only to the degree that a specific definition of tonality will permit it to do so. A given definition, Fétis's or Reimer's or Berry's, creates pre-paradigm, paradigm, and post-paradigm stages for tonality in terms of it. This is to say that as long as the definition is in vogue, one era, one composer, one piece of music is more tonal than another. But composers never viewed themselves in this fashion. They did not struggle to become tonal: they already were tonal. Tonality must be something quite other than we conceive it to be. It is the thesis of these essays that this is the case; that while the general definition of tonality, "loyalty to a tonic," serves to open the field of sonic investigation, it cannot ultimately encompass and restore the thinking subject to its proper place within the tonal act. The reason is clear: loyalty to a tonic does not permit the subject to make its own decision against the chaos of pitch and become tonal in any sense but that governed by the activity of being loyal. It excludes twelve-tone music from the ranks of tonal consciousness, something that Schoenberg himself insisted was not the case. Just as all language is linguistic, so all music is tonal or none of it is. And what we have been describing from the first extant Greek music theory treatises to the latest issue of the Journal of Music Theory is our historical consciousness of acceptable (and not so acceptable) orders of sonic change. But in the meantime the ontology of tonal consciousness remains hidden.

I have attempted to sketch above as briefly and clearly as possible the trend in tonal thinking since World War II because it is the concept under which my generation of teachers have taught, students have learned, and musicians have interpreted and played their music. It would be pleasant to report that the proper questions are now being posed about what tonality is, but they are not. To a marked degree the major portion of the academic community follows a quasi-homophonic model of tonality which it attempts—with questionable results—to push back into the Middle Ages and drags—with no little frustration—through a maze of contemporary music that frequently runs far ahead of acceptable tonal expectations. Karlheinz Stockhausen's *Stimmung* (1968) and Dieter Schnebel's *Atemzüge* (1970–71) are unique instances of this problem. How tonal are these works by any of the definitions cited above? But since the homophonic model of tonality is so popular, so apparently durable, and so intellectually seductive, I would like now to examine the principles upon which it was built. The most significant thinking about homophonic tonality has been carried out by Rameau and Schenker.

It is customary in current writing to demonstrate how Rameau and Schenker differ from one another in their speculation about tonal music, and the latter is usually awarded high praise for the sophistication of his thought. There are differences, of course, and the Schenkerian model displays a number of features that far exceed Rameau's program. But their similarities will also concern us here, since they testify to the mutual consistency of their respective ideologies. In the end, we shall discover that, despite the historical perspective of his era or perhaps because of it, Rameau was more scientific than Schenker and less willing to surrender to metaphysics those features of tonality that he could not explain. Both are indebted to Pythagorean music philosophy (see chapter 4) in the same fashion that all philosophical idealism after antiquity is indebted to Plato.

The awareness of the tonic as an embodiment of unique sonic features is similar in Rameau and Schenker and is defined in the harmonic generation of the triad. The definition of triadic generation as sensation is thus already, in itself, what the system would like to set forth as conscious formation. Let us take up its mathematical suppositions first.

In 1722 the young Rameau, then an organist at the cathedral at Clermont-Ferrand, published his *Traité de l'harmonie reduite à ses principes naturels*, divided into four books. The first book of this treatise treats chords, ratios, and proportions, and the relations that exist between them. Enlightened by the *Discours de la méthode* (1637) and the *Compendium musicae* (ca. 1628), of René Descartes, Rameau understood the relationships expressed between the pitch of a vibrating string and the different pitches realized by numerical division of that string to be ontologically pure because they were dictated by nature and established by mathematics. To be sure, there is compelling truth in this concept which traces its lineage at least back to Pythagorean thought.

Rameau's concretion of a highly objectified tonality unfolds briefly as follows. When a string length is divided according to the first six integers, the intervals that arise (if C is taken to represent the sound of the entire string) correspond to the notes, C, c, g, c', e', and g'. Intervallically, we find octave, fifth, fourth, major and minor thirds. Now Rameau called the repetition at the octave *replica*. Any replica, or octave repetition, is thus merged in its own principle and represents it. Rameau then eliminates octave repetition through this principle of identity, which thereby eliminates the intervals of the fourth and the minor third. There then remains only C, g, and e'. Within the structure of the overtone series this represents fundamental, twelfth, and seventeenth, but at the time Rameau was quite unaware of it. Rameau then collapsed his three pitches into their closest possible formation, the major triad in root position. The basis of classic tonality thus begins with the major triad, a vertical sonority, a natural unfolding of the mathematical proportions within the *Klang*. Schenker's view is the same.

But this perfect chord of nature, Gioseffo Zarlino's *harmonia perfetta*, while awarding the tonic major virtually metaphysical status, does not explain the other triads in the diatonic major scale (let alone the minor). This caused Rameau to abandon the "natural principle" in chapter 3 of book I of the *Traité* because the perfect chord can also be established from another point of view that freed it early on from the necessary deduction of a tonality composed of nothing but major triads. This was the principle that when the E splits the perfect fifth of C–G, two thirds of unequal size result. A fifth can then be viewed as two superimposed thirds. If this is the case, then there are actually four types of triad, determined by the position of the major and the minor thirds, which resulted when E severed the previously derived fifth into unequal halves. This additive construction of all possible combinations of major and minor thirds yielded major, minor, diminished, and augmented triads, all those to be found in the major and minor scales.[21]

One of the most exciting moments in Rameau's life must have occurred between the publication of his *Traité de l'harmonie* and his *Nouveau système de théorique*, which appeared four years later, for it was during this time that he become acquainted with the acoustical research of Marin Mersenne (1588–1648) and the French acoustician and mathematician Joseph Sauveur (1653–1716).

Sauveur was among the first to investigate the nature of partial tones, or harmonics. Inspired by Descartes's attempt to build a philosophy with "the help of mathematics" and "by reason alone," Rameau became a Cartesian and sought to establish the natural principles of tonal harmony. But their physical confirmation, Sauveur discovered, had resided in the vibrating string all along! With the *Nouveau système*, Rameau happily announced that the sounds arising from the first six mathematical divisions of a string, which had furnished him with his fundamental principle of harmony, were present in the string *during* its vibration. This meant that

> the string or other sonorous body not only vibrates in its totality, that is, throughout its whole length, but in vibrating *naturally* divides itself into sections (segments) which vibrate independently; these sections corresponding exactly with those resulting from the harmonic division (1, ½, ⅓, ¼, ⅕, ⅙, etc.) of the sonorous body.[22]

Schenker, of course, could assume this, but Rameau, at the beginning, had not, and the bulk of the *Nouveau système* is taken up by Rameau's "citing every acoustical phenomenon which he imagines can in any way serve to demonstrate the correctness of his theories."[23]

The wedding of mathematical theories of harmony by Zarlino, Descartes, and the early Rameau with the acoustical theories initiated by men like Sauveur was a critical moment in music history. Rameau ended his life satisfied that he had discovered the *natural*, and furthermore *rational*, basis of harmony. Despite the criticism of the French Encyclopaedists (from Rousseau, d'Alembert, and others), the spell of the laboratory captured not only Rameau but generations of theorists who followed him, even Helmholtz, who appeared at times to mistrust it.[24]

A short summary here will prove helpful. All theories which treat in any fashion the nature of the overtone series, beats, and combination tones, partake in the "natural" theory of tonality, which is thought to be scientifically established through physics and physiology, and epistemologically sustained through the psychological motions of cognition and memory. In addition, all theories of mathematical origin—the simplicity of intervallic ratios, et al.—are annexed to the physical structure of the *Klang*, whether they are carried out by the disciples of Pythagoras, of Rameau, or of Schenker. All features of this methodology cannot be discussed at once, but, shored up with mathematical calculation and empirical verification, a vast body of theoretical literature has arisen, extending from the psychological testing of musical talent to the completely respectable theories of the physical basis of intervallic quality in modern acoustics. In short, academia has done its homework well.

Having generated the major triad from the primal *Klang* of nature, we have now to concern ourselves with the notion of how one triad, the tonic, constructed on the the first degree of the diatonic scale, assumes for itself the centric focusing implied in the statement by Bukofzer. In defining tonality as a motion in consciousness that results from "chordal relations between a tonal center (the tonic triad in major or minor) and the other triads (or seventh chords) of the diatonic scale," harmonic progression is implied as both self-evident and self-sustaining. How did this thinking come about for the classic tonal theorists? On what suppositions is it based? We shall find that these suppositions form the backbone of any qualitative identity of tonal modeling and its attendant phenomenon of harmonic progression. And we shall discover that, regardless of the care with which he constructs his sonic edifice, the tonal theorist comes ultimately to a metaphysical aspect of tonal identity that vitiates the system so evolved. This aspect is already apparent in Rameau; it is championed by Schenker.

It is assumed that in the generation of chords lie also the laws which govern their succession. The similarity between Rameau and Schenker here is remarkable. The perfect progression for Rameau is that one in which the *fundamental bass* descends a fifth, as in the perfect cadence, V–I. The perfection of this progression is secured by the perfection of the consonance of the fifth; it is the first interval (exterior to the replica) generated mathematically and acoustically in the *Klang*. This explains for Rameau the superiority of a falling fifth progression (either in genuine root movement or implied through his rules for the fundamental bass and the inversion of chords).[25] The perfection of this progression by fifths, as in the perfect cadence, is allegedly due to the "directness" and "closeness" of the relationship existing between the two tones that constitute the fifth. Rameau clearly understands this from the statement in book II, chapter 18 of the *Traité*, where he states that "in the perfect cadence the fifth returns, as it were, to its source." Schenker is similarly inclined. In the *Harmonielehre* of 1906, he asks:

> Which two tones are most naturally related? Nature has already given her answer. If G has revealed itself as the most potent overtone emanating from the root tone C, the potency and privilege of this close relationship is preserved also in those cases where, in the life of a composition, C meets G as an independent root tone: the ascendant, so to speak, recognizes the descendent.[26]

It is difficult to understand how the modern Schenkerian can treat a statement like this one without some amusement. The proposition that the tones C and G have wills of their own, that they "meet" and "recognize" each other in the life of a composition is something that belongs in an animated movie cartoon, not as the foundation of a theory of tonality. Nevertheless, this *hypostatization* of the form of the fifth is achieved when Schenker calls "this primary and most natural relationship between two tones the fifth-relationship."[27] Thus a relationship comes to govern where only pitch instances within the *Klang* stood before. Both Rameau and Schenker are guilty of substantively qualifying the tones of the *Klang* in order to explain tonal motion, why one tone appears to gravitate to another. This is precisely what is meant by the title of this chapter. A relationship is erected through a linguistic wizardry that nobody ever questions.

The "natural" superiority of the intervallic fifth, secured by the overtone series for both Rameau and Schenker, obviates any critical examination of the scale as a theoretically stated tonal substance. The major scale is simply taken to be the expression of the system's root tones which have obeyed the laws of fifth evolution. But not quite, for we find it necessary to derive an involution as well. In an upward cycle of fifths we derive, as Schenker remarks, the following "stately retinue of tones" from C: C, G, D, A, E, B. The cycle cannot be extended any further because F-sharp is the next perfect fifth; and the raised fourth is not found in the major scale. Here Schenker performed the same operation as did Rameau. If the interval of the fifth is of the highest value, then F-natural can be derived by inverting the fifth downward from C: Presto, the major scale waxes complete! The subdominant appears, then, as another kind of dominant, a dominant below the tonic instead of above it. This is the meaning of the prefix "sub-," not its appearance in the scale as the lower neighbor of the fifth tone in the scale. Schenker assures us that "what is usually called a 'fourth' is thus, in reality, and considered as a root tone, a fifth in descending order."[28]

Despite the mathematical sleight of hand by which Rameau secured through inversion the fourth tone of the scale, he still sought for decades for a natural explanation of its appearance. In the *Génération harmonique*, which appeared in 1737, Rameau derived the fourth tone from a misobservation of a scientific experiment. Joan Ferris states that from it he concluded that "a given string may cause to vibrate other strings, which are its multiples in length, at their respective fundamentals."[29] The creation of these "undertones" means, however, that the fundamental of the *Klang* is not actually as fundamental as one might wish, thus destroying the integrity of the overtone system itself. Thirteen years later, Rameau corrected his error in his *Démonstration du principe de l'harmonie*. Ferris summarizes this passage:

> The long string is caused to vibrate by an agitating string of whose length its length is a multiple, but this longer string vibrates only in segments corresponding to the unison of the agitating string. This, unfortunately, leaves the subdominant without any basis in fact. Rameau concludes that nature gives the indication that there is a relationship between one string and another several times as long; in other words, the subdominant is a product of art.[30]

Rameau is certain of one thing, however, that the dominant is superior to the subdominant. But in 1752 he tried again to explain the basis of the subdominant. The *Nouvelles réflexions* is a work of both speculative and empirical dimensions. The subdominant can be found, he says now, if the overtone series is extended beyond the sixteenth partial, but this assumedly natural subdominant tone is woefully out of tune. In the second part of the *Code de musique pratique* of 1760, Rameau attempted to summarize his theories. He rejected the statements he had made years earlier about the erroneous undertones, but clung stubbornly to the notion that music comes from a single natural principle, thus divesting the artist of any right or need to create his own sonic material. Because of this he was forced to consider tones as far removed as the 45th partial.

Although Schenker dismissed Rameau's work as trivial, the similarity of their systems up to this point is fundamental. It is the generation of the fourth degree of the scale that critically separates them, for Schenker capitulates to human invention (art) when nature fails to provide the necessary sonic material for musical creation.

Rameau did not initially feel that there was anything irrational or unnatural in inverting the fifth. He was in search of a complete set of triads on the degrees of the major scale. When the subdominant failed to appear in the cycle of fifths in the overtone series, he went elsewhere. It is probable that his misobservation of 1737 arose from his being overwhelmed with faulty empirical data. When he discovered that he had made an error he criticized himself fitfully for years, but he was unable to shake the view that the material components of the art he called music had any but natural bases.

For Schenker, however, the fourth tone was admitted outright to be the contribution of the artist to the incomplete ladder of the major scale. He even said why the artist felt compelled to do this: the act was mimetic. To be sure, Schenker is to be praised for ascribing any credit to the artist in the evolution of his own sonic material; but the remarks in subheadings 16 and 17 of chapter 1 of *Harmonielehre* form a cogent internal critique of his own system.

In order to achieve "good artistic effect," he says, the "inversion from the tonic to the subdominant fifth in particular became well-established. There thus arose the need of assigning to this tone a place in the tonal system."[31] Schenker certainly never claimed that artificial and natural components did not both dwell in tonal music. Throughout the pages of *Harmonielehre* we find the artist. (Actually, a more accurate reading of the text is given if we call him "Schenker's artist," since not everybody who makes music becomes automatically a creator in the Schenkerian musical world, as he frequently and gleefully told his readership—particularly in *Der freie Satz:* only those who had intuited or understood his method were true artists.) But the important fact here is that the recourse to ungrounded naturalness reveals an incomplete system that encouraged the artist to construe the fifth-relationship in an inverse direction, thus creating an artistic counterpart of nature's proposition. Schenker thoroughly believed this, and he could soften the blow made to consciousness by this artificial involution only when he resorted to an oblique Platonic twist. A purely artificial process, a phenomenon extraneous to nature, became comprehensible when the artist created a mirror-reflection of the a priori given by nature, the rising fifth. By so doing, "he discovered the subdominant fifth F, which represents, metaphorically speaking, a piece of the past history of the tonic C."[32] It is this kind of garbled logic, with which the Schenkerian system is fraught, that ultimately renders it as the private musings of a romantic idealist; and it is upon this platform that the modern music theorist has curiously chosen to ground his methodology. Even metaphorically speaking, what is a piece of the past history of the tonic C? Let us examine the extension of this particular feature of Schenker's system more carefully.

Once the artificiality and originality of the artist have been established, Schenker can erect artifice in all places where nature has left a void. The whole of the minor mode system is an artificial one claimed by the artist. Schenker summarily declares this in a single sentence that constitutes subheading 24, "The Artificial System as the Claim of the Artist": "In this sense, the minor mode springs from the originality of the artist, whereas the sources, at least, of the major mode flow, so to speak, spontaneously from Nature."[33]

With this statement, however, Schenker opened a Pandora's box, and the supposed facts crowd him uncomfortably into a tight corner. Thus, he immediately has to rescind the freedom of artistic creativity and finds himself battling what he erroneously takes to be the primal repository of scale phenomena. This is seen in subheading 25, "The Occurrence of the Minor Mode among Primitive Peoples Does Not Disprove Its Artificial Character." From the standpoint of ethnomusicological observation, we can ignore Schenker's "well-known fact that many primitive peoples seem to take to the minor much more easily than the major mode." But because he himself could not, he felt compelled to clarify the irrationality created by his natural/artificial dichotomy to which page after page of *Harmonielehre* gives testimony. His explanations are marred by the same indefiniteness which he found in the first groping steps from chaotic and primal music expression toward the "real art" of tonal music. The following is typical:

> It is one of the mystifying features of our art that its truth is not penetrated any more esaily for having its roots in Nature! Today we know that the major mode has been, so to speak, designed and recommended by Nature; and yet

we needed hecatombs of artists, a universe of generations and artistic experiments, to penetrate the secrets of Nature and attain her approval. . . . If art is
considered as a final and correct understanding of Nature and if music is
seen moving in a direction of art so defined, I would consider the minor
mode as a stepping stone, perhaps the ultimate one or nearly so, leading up
to the real and most solemn truth of Nature, i.e., the major mode.[34]

It is difficult to take these remarks with any degree of seriousness. The
"hecatombs of artists" summons forth an image of the Nibelungen, clang-
ing away on their anvils, hammering out sonic substance for the gods.

A second fundamental difference between Rameau and Schenker is the
nature of consonance and dissonance as it relates harmonically to tonal
modeling. Recognizing the *plurivalent* quality of the major triad in the
major scale (I, IV, and V are major), Rameau was at a loss to explain why—
besides the previously established superiority of the fifth as a root tone—
certain chord progressions sounded more conclusive than others. By his
own reasoning he discovered that in a V–I succession (the term *progression*
is intentionally avoided here), in which both triads constitute perfect harmonies of nature, "one is unable to judge which of these chords is the true
chord of repose."[35] The problem is acute: one cannot hear the acoustically
and mathematically determined superiority of the fifth as a root tone. For
Rameau, dissonance became necessary for the proper determination of harmonic motion, of key, of tonality.

It is necessary to break off here and write a short paragraph about a
concept that forms one of the structural pillars in the aesthetics of
music—the nature of consonance and dissonance. Consonance and dissonance form a melodic and harmonic polarity that is thought by many to
be mandatory in any adequate explanation of why one tone should
"move" to another. Its substantive nature has been sought in music all the
way back to the early medieval period (Mackey's "The Evolution of the
Leading Tone in Western European Music to *circa* 1600 A.D.")[36] Consonance and dissonance currently constitute a significant part of the ontology of the expression theory of music. Together they form the structure of
what may be called for purposes of clarity "the resolution syndrome." The
answers that are given to the question of what causes harmonic resolution
in music are most frequently theories of nature. How the ear responds,
how the mind interprets the response, what meaning is given to the
response—all these would seem to originate in a physical manifestation
of *tuned* nature. And yet the initial act of tuning nature is forgotten in the
bustle of the activity of the *ratio.* It must come from without. This is to
say that the isolation of harmonic motion in eighteenth-century music
alone will produce the very state of affairs which Rameau discovered, a set

of possible mathematical and physical explanations as to why the mind perceives the activity of one harmonic entity moving to another. There can be no explanation of harmonic motion, however, exterior to an examination of the sociology, psychology, and physiology of music, but Rameau did not know this. Thus his explanations, however satisfactory they seemed to be, were one-dimensional. But to that end he simply annexed the seventh chord, particularly the dominant seventh, to provide—through the tension felt to inhere in it—harmonic motion. Zarlino furnished him with the rule for the proper resolution of the four tones in the chord, although this "proper resolution" was simply shelved in favor of the new demands made upon it by the principles of figured bass. What is important to realize is that harmonic motion was *already* a part of historical consciousness. Let us return to Rameau's problem.

It defies logic to assume that the chord succession V_7–I is more tonal than V–I, but Rameau apparently felt that the harmonic motion immanent within the nature of tonality could be secured only by the juxtaposition of consonant and dissonant elements discretely arranged. If there appears a perfect cadence in which the seventh is not actually present, Rameau states that it must be understood. Without tension there is no harmonic motion, and without motion there is no tonal consciousness.[37] His middle and late works reveal the persistent difficulties with his treatment of dissonance, but amid them all Rameau held to his initial concept of the seventh chord and its necessary resolution as a fundamental law of tonal motion.

Now Schenker conceived the nature of consonance and dissonance quite differently than did Rameau. It does violence to the totality of his system to treat dissonance as an isolated phenomenon, since it is thereby extracted from the comprehensive features of the *scale-step* and *tonicization*; but some facts can be fairly well established here in order to compare them with Rameau.

For Schenker, there are initially only eighteen consonances and dissonances, to which he later added two more. In all, we have the following: Consonances are the intervals of prime, octave, fifth, fourth (as inversion of the fifth), third, and sixth (as inversion of the third). These are consonant because either in root position or inverted they can be reduced to the simple proportions of 1, 2, 3, and 5 in the series of overtones.[38] Dissonances are the intervals of second, seventh, and all augmented and diminished intervals. Later, Schenker added—through chromatic alteration—the diminished third and the augmented sixth.

It cannot be said, as Rameau assumed, that dissonance must be held accountable for harmonic motion. Music moves when there is none. For Schenker, dissonance simply is not harmony at all and is regulated to passing or neighbor functions that appear to act as appropriate spices enhance *haute cuisine*. Schenker was fond of saying "the dissonance never constitutes harmonies" and even wrote an article to that point.[39] He sought to qualify harmonic motion by other means than by direct dependence on dissonance and his reversal was sincere. What evolved could have been established by psychological means, and Schenker occasionally drew upon his intuitions about the cognitive process, but his intuitions faltered in the absence of hard data and he frequently capitulated to metaphysics, sometimes willingly.

This is how Schenker explained harmonic motion. Take, for instance, a passage from an allemande by Bach in which the dominant may assume the dimensions of a fundamental harmonic entity for a beat or several beats. Alone, the dominant triad is consonant. In the running line of the top or other voice, however, the seventh or some other nontriadic tone (ninth) or any chromatic tone appears. This note is dissonant but it does not constitute the "harmony" of the passage. It is perhaps even unnecessary. It appears, Schenker would say, due to the voice-leading of the free composition *and* to the genius and will of the composer. To repeat: dissonance and dissonant entities, for Schenker, never constitute harmonies. This requires that the backbone of harmonic motion consist of major and minor triads, and such is the assumption of *middle ground* and *background* structuring by Schenker in the later development of *der freie Satz*, the free composition. How then does this harmonic modeling, scrubbed bare of any dissonant contaminants, actually appear to move? What constitutes harmonic motion? Let us turn to those features which make concrete organic harmonic life for Schenker.

First, there is the concept of the *scale-step*. It "is a higher and more abstract unit" than had been hitherto objectified in tonal cognition. This conceptualization enables the "ear" to assume the structuring power of a single root tone in the diatonic system, "to gather, so to speak, a large sequence of contrapuntal parts into a unity." Not every chord is to be analyzed as a discrete harmonic entity. Chords have different harmonic intensities. The tonic is king of scale-steps and reigns over the others as a sovereign over subjects. Rather than a complicated series of individually named harmonies (some chromatically at variance with their neighbors in the phrase or period), Schenker proposes the scale-step as the *ratio* for guiding tonal consciousness through the maze of immediate harmonic temporality.

Next in importance and strength is the scale-step of the dominant, although other root tones may also become the basis for marshaling and planning both small and large portions of musical material. With carefully chosen examples from the Bach, Chopin, and Wagner literature, Schenker illustrates for us how genius conceived of this higher level of harmonic unity.[40] As we work through any customary analysis of a tonal composition, it becomes apparent that the identity of each particular and successive triad and chord is a gratuitous exercise: the result is a string of chords from nearly or distantly related tonal areas which seem to possess such individual characters of their own that the composition manifests a roadmap of quickly suggested key centers. All that is proved by this analytical operation is that there seem to be numerous ways to avoid the principal and ultimate key location. But, by setting down "the principle that not every vertical coincidence of tones as such must be considered an interval," or a structurally formal triad, we come to the realization that the abstraction of the scale-step reorganizes temporal consciousness into a field-theory notion of tonal ordering. The scale-step becomes "a superior factor in composition, a factor dominating the individual harmonic phenomena."[41]

Curiously, the scale-step is a plea—first formalized by Adele T. Katz in 1945—for *less* of a certain kind of analysis that was the norm in theory and analysis courses in the fifties and sixties. Despite the fact that the extended harmonic progression is momentarily and occasionally shot through with particular notes, intervals, triads, and chords that have constituted the grist for many a harmony debate as to exact identity and function, these appearances never vitiate the a priori temporal strength of the tonic—even though it may be the dominant that appears within the harmonic space.[42] True, these aberrant harmonies may be placed on the weak parts of beats, but it is not merely position within the measure that weakens their identity: the strength of the tonic (or other root tone) in motion "prevents us from hearing them as independent scale-steps."

When scale-step progression does occur, the most natural is a root movement by fifths, up and down. There is also step progression by thirds and seconds. It is the unfolding of these scale-steps, through the interpreter of the musical motif, that constitutes the organic content of the harmony. Schenker concludes, therefore, that "each harmony is not merely asserted but is also unfolded and demonstrated in this unfolding; as content and harmony join each other, the feeling for the scale-step awakens in us."[43]

This part of Schenker's discussion in *Harmonielehre* is thin, although one can see in it the early conceptualization of the middle ground of the free composition.[44] But while he states clearly that "harmonic concepts must be unfolded," the theory of the abstract, high-level scale-step *cannot* manifest itself, nor even incorporate tonal consciousness for itself. The necessary motion is not provided by the superiority of the fifth in the overtone series; that is merely the direction that the fifth as scale-step progression will assume when it does move. For the ontology of harmonic motion, Schenker must turn to the psychology of the step progression, and here he radically differs from Rameau. From this point on, however, his system assumes such subjective proportions that it becomes clear that he is writing of *his* expectations as a music theorist and not of any intrinsic properties in triads that compel them to move. A harmony's identity becomes a source of confusion to itself and "calls for a further clarification, which, in turn, creates in us the need and expectation of a continuation—in us, and, naturally, in the composer as well."[45] The scale-step forsakes its potential for unfolding and seeks a "certain satisfaction" that will be harmonic as well as conceptual: it seeks a sufficiently "clear demarcation" of its content by initiating a progression to the dominant. This passage to the dominant is the tailoring of the middle ground of Schenker's later analytical system, but here in the *Harmonielehre* of 1906 he simply opens a new chapter and begins to describe his clear demarcations by a discussion of different kinds of psychological conclusions—cadences, formalized by the expectations of the listener.

When the "valuation theory" of the scale-step is presented in section two of Schenker's "practical application" of his harmonic system, it is clear that the scale-step is the composer's will, breathing life into the harmony. Note this lively will.

> Each scale-step manifests an irresistible urge to attain the value of the tonic for itself as that of the strongest scale-step. If the composer yields to this urge of the scale-step within the diatonic system of which this scale-step forms part, I call this process *tonicalization* and the phenomenon itself *chromatic*.[46]

This process is effected when "the scale-step in question, without any ceremony, usurps quite directly the rank of the tonic, without bothering about the diatonic system of which it still forms a part." In the area of tonicization, a given triad—with relation to the triads surrounding it—becomes its own tonic and satisfies its yearning for the value of a tonic quite alone.[47] Tonicization is attained chiefly by descending fifths and thirds, but also by the upward progression by a second.

Not only can tonicization effect the scale-step, as a comprehensive unit of a higher order, it can arise through an individual tone of only secondary importance. Schenker calls this the microtonicization of individual tones.[48]

In the process of tonicization, chromaticism is seen not as a threat to the principal key, but as the tonal space in which freely breathes each tone, interval, or triad as it manifests itself through the normal means of unfolding; indeed, "Chromatic change is an element which does not destroy the diatonic system but which rather emphasizes and confirms it."[49]

It would seem from this motion in thought that modulation as such would disappear almost completely from the Schenkerian model and in fact it nearly does. Modulation, to him, must not be construed as "those changes to chromatically simulated keys which are changes only apparently, while in reality they are fuller elaborations of a strictly diatonic scale-step, whereby the diatonic system must be assumed to continue." Modulation, true modulation, means a complete change from one key to another, which happens in three ways: 1) modulation by changing the meaning of a harmony; 2) modulation by chromatic change; and 3) modulation by enharmonic change.[50]

To illustrate only one of these ways, modulation is attained by changing the meaning of a harmony. This is possible due to the plurivalent quality of triads within the system. We are all familiar with it—the common chord between two key systems; and "we recognize it only by its consequences, i.e., by the fact that the new key, initiated by the change of meaning of certain scale-steps, asserts itself in the subsequent harmonies." A cadence in the new key proves the most suitable means to fortify the new tonality and makes the modulation real and complete. It is to be readily admitted that on this principle tonal composers built the large sonic edifices of sonata, rondo, and operatic scene. Now the unfolding of a scale-step can occur only on a consonance, such as the dominant triad. As the dominant extends itself as a scale-step, tonicization may take place: the nontonic becomes its own tonic. The successful execution of the process constitutes a modulation—such as happens immediately prior to the second theme in a Mozart sonata exposition. The phenomenon is chromatic. The new theme unfolds in the dominant key, accruing tonal capital for itself. There may not be another genuine modulation until immediately before the recapitulation and the unfolding of the principal theme in the tonic once again.

This long description of the basic points of *Harmonielehre* does not in the end explain why harmony moves, other than to state that Schenker wanted it to move—as I shall demonstrate shortly. There is no hint in his section on the full close that indicates any dissatisfaction with the previous "natural" principles of tone, interval, or triad generation—the haphazard role of the artist notwithstanding. The extension of these principles into the sphere of organic tonal motion is assumed to be naturally developed. The seventh chord is not mentioned. While both dominant and tonic triads are major (with perfect fifths), which perplexed Rameau, they may in Schenker be held accountable for the complete and absolute satisfaction which—as harmonic progression—they create for the definition and particularization of tonality. Schenker offers two reasons for the perfection of the full close, one formal, the other harmonic. Formally, it becomes complete through the processes of repetition demanded by our psychological need for association. Unfortunately, this is as close as Schenker ever came to understanding the cognitive abilities and disabilities that constitute the consciousness of the tonal act. But he does not see the actual content of his statement and furthermore houses it poorly within a vague formal component. Form of what? Harmonically, it is absolute because of the dominant's proximity to the tonic as root tones in the overtone series. Rameau, of course, did state the latter, although he found it difficult to sustain credibility in his own statement, without the tension felt in the dissonance guaranteed by the seventh chord.

In contrast to Rameau, Schenker felt no compelling need for dissonance to reside in a polarity with consonance in order to prove that harmony possessed an intrinsic motion of its own. For Schenker, his random philosophical babblings to the contrary notwithstanding, tonality was not something that wrested itself from the chaos of tones. Tonality could exist in frozen and crystalline form, as the later dogma of the *Ursatz* gave ample testimony. Dissonance became the right of the composer (in the sense of true artificer) to express himself within the model he had inherited. It could be as proper and engaging as Bach or as diffuse as Wagner; as long as it resided within certain historical boundaries determined by Schenker, he could readily explain it.

Schenker's cogent conceptualizations of the scale-step, of tonicization, and harmonizability are no mean achievements in the structural analysis of classical tonal music. They are not altogether new, but they are more carefully and clearly worked out as a systematic activity in harmonic speculation than any theorist prior to *Harmonielehre* had been able to establish. Several variations of these features in other harmonic speculations which we could have discussed do not impair a cogent—if closed—system from this highly ambiguous and thoroughly egotistical personality.[51] Hugo Riemann's earlier "functional harmony," to which Bukofzer refers, is the most notable foreshadowing of the structural elements of tonality provided by a study of *Harmonielehre*.[52] But there are two aspects of Schenker's system which impair its attempts to explain tonal consciousness. One is a historical caution that Schenker himself exercised upon his own thought; the other is an academic hubris that hypostatizes itself in the form of pseudointellectual ratiocination.

As the volumes of *The Musical Forum* testify, the Schenkerian system has been historically extended on both sides of the common-practice era. True Schenkerians disavow this. There is nothing to be gained, they state, by subjecting the madrigals of Francesco Landini or the symphonies of Hans Werner Henze to principles of Schenkerian analysis.

The other aspect is more damning because it is more subtle and comes from Schenker's own attitude about the truth of tonality. I mean by this the creation of the Schenkerian "ear," a construct that testifies to the narrowness of his vision for music as history. In an assumedly real and continuous conflict within the tonal context of the composition, a conflict between the artificial and artistic system of the composer and the "revengefulness of Nature" (Schenker's own phrase) which triumphs over tonal creations, the ear is intellectualized into a thinking entity of no mean dimensions. I will excuse Schenker for his choice of anatomy. I assume his "ear" means his educated tonal understanding, that fusion of body and mind within which the sonic world is mediated as real; but this is precisely the point to be stressed as its inherent weakness. In page after page, there surfaces in Schenker the demand for a disembodied "ear" (or mind) which perceives and understands the subleties that his system asserts. It is true that he did not try to escape from the demands of his own thinking; indeed, he found it quite adequate to the task. "Our ear" becomes the reification of the "demands of nature" which proclaim "a solemn truth." "Our ear," a kind of collective Schenkerian mentality, objectified only in true artist and dedicated audience, listens attentively in the void of sonic nature, yearning for the tonic. Apparently, this is an activity consciously manipulated by the composer and unconsciously applauded by the audience. As the tonal object becomes an object of cognition, and as each scale-step seeks the attainment of the value of the tonic for itself, the physical nature of the composition is spiritualized by a translation into epistemology.[53] These subtle borderline transitions, unsubtly evaluated from biological points of view, ultimately refute the supposed solidity of tonal facts. One thing is certain: "our ear" can never be accused of naive realism.

In part II of *Harmonielehre*, "our ear" surrenders to the animated spirit of the scale-step. The scale-step "manifests an irresistible urge to attain the value of the tonic"; the composer "yields to this urge." The scale-step "usurps" sonic territory; it does not "bother" with the diatonic system of which it still forms a part. It accrues interest for itself through unfolding its potential. These phrases from Schenker betray that it is actually the will of the composer that creates tonality for itself, regardless of the disguise of an animated scale-step which only appears to have a life of its own. Thinly concealed under the sponsorship of "practical application," Schenker announces a sonic vitalism for triads. What is actually being described is the bias of an early twentieth-century mind that unwittingly sympathized with and supported Hans Adolf Eduard Driesch's "entelechy" and Henri Bergson's *élan vital*. It is to be regretted that Schenker could not have become aware of this contradiction in his system.

If it is actually the will of the composer that creates tonality, and I believe that it is, we then place ourself on a firm Hegelian platform of creation within the sonic act: Man makes tonality through his own self-production. Unmediated sonic substance becomes mediated tonal material at the very moment that man listens in the void for tones—tones which he himself creates to fill that void. He was tonal long before he became conscious that he was tonal, and it is only by retracing the abandoned stages of reflection—to the extent that this is possible—that we can discover our true tonal consciousness. This will be the subject of subsequent chapters. All that can be said of Schenker is that, like Rameau, his system is but a moment in the history of tonal consciousness, and not a very critical one at that. If the subjective creativity of the composer and his audience is actually responsible for tonal consciousness, then this need for cognition, assurance, and evaluation cannot be created post hoc—after the priority of nature has been set up for "treatment." The dialectic which Schenker was able to maintain in certain instances is shipwrecked on this premise of a much higher order. Tonal thinking is obliged to transcend its unreflected subjectivity through more rigorous means than by merely rationalizing its activity in terms of an a priori conceptualization of nature and its "demands."[54] Such is the fate of all systems of tonal consciousness whose actualization initially and primarily depends upon the allegedly fundamental principle of primal sonic appearance—nature and her *Klang*. Hence Aristotle was extended a prolonged invitation to dwell in the house of the Platonic philosophical system. Everyone thought it would work.

What of Schenker today? Only a few years ago Schenkerian analysis of some sort or other was carried out by only a limited number of professors and their students, who were wont to regard—once they understood it— all competing theories of analysis with contempt. It was a difficult system to comprehend; one had to understand German to read it, and there were no short cuts or handy aids to comprehension. All that has changed and the Shenkerian comet is at the moment at its very brightest. By way of conclusion, therefore, it is instructive to see his theory and the transformation of it at work in the modern seminar and classroom, for it is there that our most recent, our freshest opinions concerning tonality are being forged. It ought to be stated outright that some who are the most indebted to Schenker are also eager to disavow any "genuine" inspiration to the thought of this remarkable theorist who was also an egotist of the first water.

The first attempt to bring Schenker before an English readership apparently was Michael Mann's article in *Music Review* in 1949, "Schenker's Contribution to Music Theory."[55] Somewhat prematurely, and with high praise, Mann sketched Schenker's position in history.

> Eternal supremacy of the major-minor system; immutability of the laws of counterpoint; alleged distinction between harmonic (structural) and melodic (prolonging and filling) functions and—closely allied with this—recognition of the triad as the sole directly intelligible harmony. . . .

These elements were the important features of Schenkerian thought, and Mann "could think of no other elements by which they would be supplemented in the *Ursatz* doctrine."[56]

But there was much more to Schenker than this. By 1952 Schenker could be studied through his pupil Felix Salzer, whose *Structural Hearing* (which included a volume of examples demonstrating structural hearing at work) brought Schenker to the public platform of academic theory.

In 1959 Allen Forte, in a masterful article of introduction, sought to describe Schenker in general terms and likened his work "to a particular kind of high-level achievement in science: the discovery or development of a fundamental principle which then opens the way for the disclosure of further new relations, new meanings."[57] Forte even compared Schenker to his Austrian contemporary Sigmund Freud: the diverse patterns of overt musical behavior were actually controlled by certain underlying patterns of fundamentally internal organization. Schenker's general conceptualization and his specialized terminology were discreetly housed under the concept of structural levels. There is no doubt that modern theorists are profoundly indebted to Schenker—whatever their immediate aims—for the particular analytical systems now in vogue in American universities, however distant they seem from him and despite their ready disavowal of his influence.

I have treated the early formulation of Schenker's thought in *Harmonielehre* in order to demonstrate its similarity to and divergence from that of Rameau. The culmination of Schenker's system appeared in *Der freie Satz* (1935), whose major points bear directly on a large body of current tonal analysis. It developed the notion that a total musical structure was to be regarded as an interacting composite of three main levels of composition, none of them meant to be audible, although they appear on musical staves and seem to be oddly pianistic. A musical composition's tonal cohesion can be reduced to a number of linear spans proportionate to the actual length of the composition; or they are not proportionally governed and merely represent collapsed visual views of the work's surface audibility.

The major "surface elements" of the piece are designated in the level called the *foreground*. Anything not found in this level will be found in the actual heard piece itself. On the level of the foreground actual durational values are rapidly sacrificed or mutilated in favor of emphasis on "structural weight." Behind the foreground is the *middle ground*. Here the tonal stuff of the composition is further reduced so that there appear fundamental chords with relation to one tonic (the key of the piece) and a group of subordinate chords of neighbor, embellishing, or passing functions. This reduction represents a series of scale-steps that are the sonic skeleton of the music's audibly living body. Finally, there is the *background* in which appears the synthetic and distilled essence of the work's tonality, a projection of the work's tonic triad or its fundamental progression, depending on one's interpretation of Schenker. Despite its existence in an incredibly reduced state, the background "progression" is still somewhat plastic. The configurations appearing in the deepest background level Schenker called the *Ursatz*, the "overall structure," or the "fundamental shape." *Ursatz* figures underlie compositions or movements. Gerald Warfield explains:

> In that the *Ursatz* spans an entire piece it should be pointed out that major portions of the compositions may be represented by single notes of this configuration. For instance, the initial *Ursatz* bass note may represent more than half of the total time of the piece. The structural dominant may represent an entire section of the piece in the key of the dominant. In a minor key the following bass line is common in the background. The second note of this con-

> figuration may represent an entire section in the key of the relative major.[58]

From its reduced state the structural framework of an assumed "ur-tonality" can be expanded back to the totality of its audible substance through the progress of *prolongation*. In fact, it is implied by some that this process is what composers somehow accomplish when they compose music. Harmonic motion resides in the prolongation of single chords or of the expansion of a progression from one chord to another. The purpose of the famous graphs developed by Schenker was to show tonal coherence in gradual stages, which Salzer and others thought necessary "if we are to explain in a systematic way what we hear."

The reader may perhaps personally recall his early encounters with this system. About twenty years ago, a debate arose concerning the Schenkerian principles and percolated merrily around the country. Schenker attracted friends and made enemies. One of the system's chief problems was its applicability, whether or not the system could be expanded backward and forward in history, to musics written before and after the common-practice period. If the *Ursatz* had to be a I–V–I progression, if tonal rectitude was the triad, then of course it could not be so projected. But a coterie of contributors to the yearbook *The Musical Forum* felt that the *Ursatz* could be projected and took analytical steps in that direction.

But it was then that the system made a leap over its own historical limitations quite unwittingly. Gradually to be realized was the notion that the real issue of this type of analysis was not the concretized features of *Ursatz* and *Urlinie* but rather the notion of layer analysis as such, and on any level with any component or group of components—melody, harmony, rhythm, tone color, and what have you. It is this expanded and transformed notion of sonic design that decisively marks many of the current studies about the nature of musical structure. In general, there occurred a convergence between the basically antithetic ideas of Rameau's *Traité de l'harmonie* and J. J. Fux's *Gradus ad Parnassum*, although these treatises were now regarded as historical precedents of one-sided views about sonic design. In the last few years there has been a trend away from the "linear" conceptualization of music, which analytically characterizes the historical consciousness from 1600 to 1900, toward a more comprehensive and spatial sonic entity, a kind of continuum that is more or less tightly partitioned or packed with musical components—meters, volumes, motives, harmonies, and tone colors.[59]

Tonally, the expanded system brought into focus a picture of "the ideas of primacy and hierarchy among pitch-classes and pitch-class-complexes," which would be able to illuminate both *generic* and *particular* tonal systems. Wallace Berry explains this in a passage I quote at length:

> In the projection of a primary factor with the PC (pitch-class) content of a musical work (or style) much of the weight of historical practice suggests the chief importance of its relation to the pitch a semitone below (and, in some styles, above) and the pitch a 4th below or 5th above. The "leading" or "leaning" force of the proximate pitch in semitonal relation, and the strong "natural" relation of the 5th and its inversion, emerge throughout tonal practice of all kinds as preeminent affiliations by which the central factor in the hierarchic order is approached and understood. The primacy of the tonic is a function too of its role as the ultimate point of cadential arrival.
>
> The hierarchic *tonal system* can be referred to as one of generic applicability—i.e., the tonal system of a style might be conceived as that embracing, for example, a diatonic set together with vertical PCC derivatives of common usage and expanded by subsidiary collections of chromatic affiliates usual in such a given style. Thus, the "tonal system of a style" would represent *the normal range and ordering of PC material* reasonably to be expected. In the same way, the tonal system of any class of works might be theoretically conceived.
>
> Of more immediate concern is the concept of tonal system as it applies to a particular musical instance, a particular work and the experience of that work, as opposed to the theoretical system generic to the class of which the work is a member. The generic system might be, for example, the phrygian scale together with predictable secondary leading-tones attending (and inflating, or tonicizing) certain of its degrees, or the diatonic scale of C comparably expanded. The tonal system specific to a composition represents the total resource of PC content basic to that work, and the hierarchic ordering of the content *as expressed in the formulations of that particular work*.[60]

In other words: tonality is a decision on the part of composers against the total chaos of available pitch data. But note that the people (actually, no human mentality seems to be at work in the above) who make these decisions are still obeying "natural" orders and demands. I seriously doubt the validity of isolating the semitone as a "leading" or "leaning" force in that tonal era of longest duration, antiquity. And the "natural" relation of the fifth and its inversion again surrenders to Pythagoras, Rameau, and Schenker all the ground otherwise covered by some expert thinking. In no way may it be stated that the fifth and its inversion emerged as preeminent throughout the music of Jewish cantillation and early Christian chant. The third is just as important. Ergo, we are left again with a large portion, the largest one, of our tonal history that is compelled to be less tonal than another by virtue of the definition. This means that the definition is wrong. Once again the thing-in-itself muddles the theorist's thought. The generic applicability of the hierarchic tonal system is merely erected as an analytic retreat from the actual historical problem of accepting *all* historical moments of tonal modeling as particularized and authentic formulations of general and societal tonal communication. This fault cannot be corrected until the listener, the tangible music maker, *Homo tonifex*, is restored to his proper place in the creation of tonal consciousness; and Schenkerians and structural functionalists censure any close relation to music's audience. To begin with, the composer would have to be considered immediately, and there is no way to determine if the composer conceives his music as a series of layers that radiate from the throne of a reigning triad or progression.

The weakest internal feature of Schenkerian tonal analysis and the systems of structural levels it has inspired is its gross neglect of music's actual temporality and its immanent relation to tonal consciousness. The collapse, reduction, and mutilation of what is heard as tonal in actual music is apparently thought inconsequential in light of gains that are achieved by conceiving sonic phenomena in terms of their tonal structural weight or structural coherence. This is all very fine for an analyst, but the immediacy of tonality cannot be suspended while the listener interconnects one level with the other, taking random shots at this or that progression in order to capture its tonal essence—not to mention what cognitive process would be necessary to prolong the structural weight of a dominant triad "horizontalized" for seventy-five measures through constantly moving chromatic harmony. Only the cognitive operation of perfect pitch or a musical score will tell the listener that the Mahler Ninth Symphony begins in D minor and ends in D-flat major, but even the untutored listener hears that work as remarkably and particularly tonal in an immediate sense that eludes the attempts of the hierarchical system to grasp it. Only a phenomenology of tonality will correct this weakness within current tonal modeling, and to perform one here would require an extensive platform I am incapable of supplying.

Still to be determined, however, is how prolongation of a progression cognitively accounts for the actual tonal awareness of all who listen. In what sense does the knowing subject understand, in the various moments of hearing, that this triad or that progression is structurally related to music he has not yet heard? How is he aware of the fact that a neighbor or embellishing harmony is only that until he hears its function completed? Does he know even then? Tonal consciousness for Schenker requires both analytic reflection and prophetic vision, which are curious mental states to demand of two thousand years of listeners who apparently operated quite successfully without them. Schenker and his followers were eager to point out that their analytic system, although they recommended it to students and performers as an aid for assessing the true schema of a piece of music, was not a recipe for the manner in which composers *thought* when they composed their music, Schenker was wise, of course, in not stating that composers actually followed any such necessary schema in the process of composition, but by this decision he also tacitly admitted that perhaps nobody's cognitive activity of tonal consciousness was being described but his own.

There are the facts of hearing tonal music, and they remain functional to what tonality is when it is heard rather than viewed. To be sure, the least detail of the most extended piece of music may be in a "proper relation to the meaning of the whole," but the listener does not immediately hear it that way, simply because he cannot hear the whole at once and because, paradoxically, any given moment of hearing is the whole of what there is to hear. Only to a certain extent is a given passage of music judged against the whole, that is, against the reduced tonal structure that Schenker demands as indicative of true harmonic excellence. While hearing the secondary theme in a sonata, the average listener is not also judging its tonal structural weight against the development section, where the theme will be repeated, fractured, combined, and presented in a variety of key areas; nor is he cognizant that it will return in the recapitulation in the home key and perhaps be used in the coda at the end of the movement. But he *is* in an immediate constellation of sonic facts, with certain expectations related to the psychological activity of expectation and fulfillment. These are provided by both short- and long-term repetitions, by imitations, continuations, variations, digressions, and returns. Both immediately and ultimately, the work is and remains tonal for him because, as he hears, he is not given too many different bits of tonal information. Within the given context of the historical composition, he totally understands because the pitch data are systematically and immediately arranged in a fashion that his mind can comprehend. The pitch data may appear to be infinite, but they cannot operate at great variance with the accepted comprehensibility of the system in which it exists at the moment.

We seem to have drifted away from Schenker but actually we are examining him from several points of view. Tonality is a societal expression; it is heard and judged as an immediate historical moment. Schenkerian and other layer analyses fail to comprehend this fact. By virtue of the logic which his system claimed one would assume that, with the score of *Tristan und Isolde* and a batch of his graphs tucked under his arm, Schenker could have marched back to Leipzig and convinced J. S. Bach that because their *fundamental structuring* was the same Bach would have eagerly awarded a judgment of tonality to Richard Wagner. Any argument through "fundamental structure" or "overall shape" would have availed nothing, for the very societal reservoir of pitch data in Bach's opinion would have been violated. Bach could no more have accepted the freedom of Wagner's chromaticism than he could have accepted his morality. To Bach both would have appeared as promiscuous. But were not the same twelve pitches at work in both Bach and Wagner? Indeed, they were, and here a vital principle of tonal modeling is brought to the surface. The same pitches of the chromatic scale were active in both Bach and Wagner, but the societal view towards the utilization of that pool of pitch data was very differently conceived. Like language, tonality is historically characterized by its unfreedom. All the words of a given language may be available but they are accepted or rejected according to a given society's mores and laws. One cannot say in public what he can say in private. Certain words are guarded and controlled. It is the same with tonality. There is not, in a given historical moment, a total possibility for tonal expression; there is only what that society accepts as tonal expression, and that expression is complete. There is no yearning for the fulfillment of an assumed tonal thing-in-itself. The seemingly empty definition of tonality given in this book begins to acquire its proper significance: tonality is a judgment made against the societal reservoir of pitches. Tonal consciousness is not free any more than linguistic or moral consciousness is free. True, it is freer in some societies than others, but that is not the issue here. The issue is what actually constitutes tonal consciousness between the composer and his audience. Internally, this issue may be determined on the basis of internal structural integrity, as the theorists avow; but externally, it is also historically determined by quite different but critical factors: religious ideology (the Church legislated tonality for over a millennium); or bourgeois respectability (Chopin in the salons of Paris); or market economy (tonality is what will make a profit). It is a pity that the theorist—of whom Salzer is as good an example as any—will acknowledge that a "complete explanation" of the development and interpretation of music "will never neglect" the vital activity of comprehending music in "aesthetic, cultural, historical, philosophical, psychological and physiological terms," and then in the next sentence will offer his ignorance as a virtue as he turns his own efforts toward a "musical understanding of music."[61]

As long as the theorist insists on a "musical understanding" of tonal consciousness he is doomed to play internal structural games: musical understanding is not enough. He and his fellow theorists may do this with a disarming ingenuity, but they will be unable to offer any ultimate explanation about why a work is tonal. No amount of analytic dismantling in order to comprehend structural weight will tell you that a door is an entry into a building. You must also know that people enter buildings through doors rather than through windows. Nor will analysis from the inside alone reveal that a chord progression or a melodic phrase is a vehicle by which a listener enters into a relationship of tonal significance in a piece of music. You must also know that people have certain (but highly flexible) mental behavior patterns by which they both structure and evaluate their cognitive perceptions.

I believe that the current inadequacy of modern music theory to comprehend the nature of its tonal object is directly related to its method, now well-entrenched in the American academic system. We will make no further progress by embellishing the principles of Schenkerian idealism. Thus, the ultimate critique of current analytic techniques concerning tonal modeling comes not from within but from without—in the unconscious positivistic connections that are made between theoretical work and social life-processes. This may be a curious turn of affairs for many readers, but I ask them to consider with me the following close paraphrase and quotations from critical theorist Max Horkheimer.

Doubtless the positivist music theorist considers the prevision and usefulness of his results to be a scientific task, but, in fact, this does not guarantee that the theory of tonality which he develops will be of value to anyone but himself. In reality, notes Horkheimer,

> this sense of practical purpose, this belief in the social value of his calling is a purely private conviction of the scholar. He may just as well believe in an independent, "suprasocial," detached knowledge as in the social importance of his expertise: such opposed interpretations do not influence his real activity in the slightest. The scholar and his science are incorporated in the apparatus of society; his achievements are a factor in the conservation and continuous renewal of the existing state of affairs, no matter what fine names he gives to what he does. His knowledge and results, it is expected, will correspond to their proper "concept." . . .[62]

This is to say that the contemporary music theorist shields himself from his actual social function and from the actual cognitive operation of the object he contemplates, in this case, tonal consciousness. He speaks not of what theory means in the human creation of music, but only of what it means in the isolated sphere in which for purely historical reasons his thought has come into existence.[63] At the moment, the particular traits of tonal modeling described above are being elevated to the rank of universal categories, much to the depreciation of tonality as it temporally exists in the consciousness of men and women. The ideal to be presently sought for is a unitary system of tonal science that will be all-powerful. Everything about the object is reduced to conceptual determinations, and the end result of the theorist's work is based on a platform that must constantly reveal its unifying function as elemental. The theorist's production is the production of a unity, and this production is itself the product.[64]

I see no steps being taken to heal the breach between the facts of tonal music and the activity of the theorists who ostensibly know the most about them. The world that is given to the listening individual who hears music daily, the sonic world that he must accept and take into account, is, in its present and continuing form, a product of the tonal activity of society as a whole.

> The objects we perceive in our surroundings—cities, villages, fields, and woods—bear the mark of having been worked on by man. It is not only in clothing and appearance, in outward form and emotional make-up that men are the product of history. Even the way they see and *hear* is inseparable from the social life-process as it has evolved over the millennia.[65]

Not only does the theorist ignore the separation that critically divides his theory from actual practice, he cannot even conceive of the necessity to reconcile them. From the viewpoint of the theory of knowledge this is merely the product of the Cartesian dualism of thought and being. Thought is the theorist's self-aggrandizement through the construction of self-acclaimed "universal" tonal models placed here and there in history upon the works of composers who live a special and transhistorical life in the mind of the tonal theorist, confirming him in his belief that his models are a picture of what actually happened. This musing of the theorist exonerates him from any concern with the being of tonal consciousness as it lives out its daily activity immediately before him. In short, any tonal theory which the theorist will erect will be partisan. He is as ignorant of the tonal consciousness of the average (but active) listener outside a sheltered academy as he is about what that listener ate for dinner. When the listener cares to raise *his* level of consciousness, he must submit to the espoused superior-

ity of the savant. Then and only then will the listener be told what tonal truth is: he is assumed to possess none of his own. To quote Horkheimer again, the dualism that exists between thought and being

> is congenial both to nature and to bourgeois society in so far as the latter resembles a natural mechanism. The idea of a theory which becomes a genuine force, consisting in the self-awareness of the subjects of a great historical revolution, is beyond the grasp of a mentality typified by such a dualism. If scholars do not merely think about such a dualism but really take it seriously, they cannot act independently. In keeping with their own way of thinking, they can put into practice only what the closed causal system of reality determines them to do, or they count only as individual units in a statistic for which the individual unit really has no significance. As rational beings they are helpless and isolated. The realization that such a state of affairs exists is indeed a step towards changing it, but unfortunately the situation enters bourgeois awareness only in a metaphysical, ahistorical shape. In the form of a faith in the unchangeableness of the social structure it dominates the present. Reflecting on themselves men see themselves only as onlookers, passive participants in a mighty process which may be forseen but not modified.[66]

Critical tonal thinking is not the function of the isolated individual; nor is it the sum total of the academic community as displayed in its periodicals, books, conventions, seminars, and colloquia. Its subject is rather a definite individual who stands in a real relation to the music of other individuals and groups; his consciousness is the resultant web of relationships with the social totality of class interests and with nature. Among the professions of music, the music theorist considers himself to be the most autonomous representative, a special privilege he grants himself because of an illusion about the subject, which he approaches with a Cartesian idealism that has become an ideology in the strict sense. Within this ideology's limited freedom he puts on an illusory form of perfect freedom and autonomy. In the meantime the work of music and its real tonal significance vanish beneath his scrutiny.[67]

What is needed is a radical reconsideration of music, not only by the music theorist, the musicologist, the ethnomusicologist, and the music educator, but by the knowing tonal individual as such. The conditions of the hearer's tonal consciousness, of the music maker's, of the composer's must also become the objects of their perceptions. The distinctions within this complex totality between what belongs to unconscious tonal receptivity residual in the nature of hearing and what belongs to the action of the listener, the performer, and the composer cannot be drawn in concrete detail.[68] Because they cannot, theorists have decided not to attempt to draw them at all. The genesis of their particular tonal facts, the practical application of the conceptual systems by which they treat their facts, and the rule of such systems in action, are all taken to be external to theoretical thinking itself. There is an estrangement that is unheeded as long as the theorist can make himself and his constituency believe that his work is not opposed either in its aim or in its other ambitions to the usual activities that go on within classificatory tonal science. Unfortunately, not only is this alienation largely unheeded by the vast portion of all who in any fashion theoretically concern themselves with tonal speculation of sonic phenomena: in all but the most exceptional instances it is not even recognized.

3 The Nature of Tonal Phenomena

I t is occasionally admitted by some scholars that there is no totally satisfactory definition of tonality. Those specific theories which have been evolved in order to describe the tonal modeling of Western music from about 1600 to 1900 become impoverished when applied to what are erroneously judged to be pre- and post-tonal systems of music. While a general definition of tonality is admitted, this is supplied more in the interests of encyclopedic thoroughness than in a genuine attempt to understand the nature of all tonal phenomena: the notion "loyalty to a tonic" has been so carelessly conceived that to utilize it in any analytical activity with given works would once again render general tonal consciousness as historically progressing to fulfillment and perfection in specific tonal creations from Monteverdi to Mahler. For over a century, theorists have been hard at work searching for the perfect analytic model to explain how so-called common-practice tonality operates in the creation of sonic acts. Tonality is thought to be the unfolding of a chord, or creative obedience to natural orders within the *Klang* (that demand specific treatment related to their acoustical properties), or to the presence of key centers, or the conflict of interest between active and inactive sonic events within musical structure (which are frequently evaluated in terms of predetermined commitments to consonance and dissonance). More recent definitions have lapsed into the generality of a tonal Weltanschauung that, when the last sharp and flat have been analyzed, still leaves a residue of "irrelevant tonality" or "tonality of ambivalent conventions." While these theories seek to and can accomplish much classificatory and analytical work within the fixed historical appearance of the classical tradition, they are incapable of distinguishing what elements of tonal phenomena, if any, are common to all music in Western culture, from the psalmody of ancient Israel to yesterday's popular song.

It is unnecessary here to rehearse further the weaknesses of our present notions of tonal modeling in music. But in the face of this admitted deficiency of thought to comprehend the nature of its object, we can do more than continue to criticize the theoretical status quo, which is fraught with schools, quarrels, and even lampoons (Schenker) against those who are not fortunate enough to subscribe to a given analytical system. What is sought is illumination of those properties of musical appearance which render tonal consciousness valid for vast groups of people. How are these properties cognitively attained? What is their historical dimensionality? How does the same tonal music express the sonic intelligence and emotional lives of whole nations whose economic, political, and social systems differ so widely? Could tonality be the "universal" part of the often quoted maxim "Music is a universal language"? Of course, no particular music is a universal language, but it is apparent that the manipulation of the societal repository of pitches in Western culture has had a durable and effective life for centuries and among many peoples. How did this phenomenon come about?

These questions cannot all be given definitive answers. It will be seen from the remarks that follow, however, that a thoughtful consideration of tonal appearance reveals general components or elements of tonal consciousness which bear directly upon all historical eras of Western music; that this great repertory of music is tonally all of a piece; and that we can no longer thrust traditional tonal theory upon music history as an absolute or even near-perfect model to describe the whole of music as a cultural artifact. I shall thus ignore here the historical emergence of tonal consciousness as conceived by such theorists as Rameau, Hauptman, Riemann, von Oettigen, Durth, Schenker, Hindemith, plus a growing academy of neo-Schenkerians in America. What is proffered here, instead, is a prolegomenon to tonal modeling that can operate as a basis for investigation into all Western music. These diverse musics share common properties which, if properly approached, reveal fundamental limitations and potentialities in the creation of sonic works of art. These properties are characterized by their temporality, their very sonic historicality, yet at the same time are contradicted by it; they are both annulled and preserved in each higher stage of sonic reflection. Thus, while it seems that to state these generalizing components with a view toward their historical truth would render them so analytically vacuous that they would tend to be and remain meaningless, we shall discover instead a fundamental ontology of tonal consciousness: to isolate them as tendencies is to appreciate the wealth of human invention and creativity that characterizes the music of Western culture in its most concrete objective expressivity. It is instructive to break tonality down into a series of *interconnected* principles, none of which operates alone, although each exhibits particular features that distinguish it from the others. These elements secure validity for tonal expression: 1) pitch selectivity; 2) melodic gesture; 3) linguistic performation; 4) durational preeminence; and 5) vertical motion.

PITCH SELECTIVITY

Tonality is a decision made against the chaos of pitch. This statement, although negatively cast, immediately restores tonality to its proper relationship to both knowledge and human interests, separated from which it has no meaning. As a characteristic of tonal art, pitch selectivity is so obvious a component that we tend to leave its content unexamined. It signifies that group of pitches from which specific musics are created, but in so doing it reveals the cognitive abilities and disabilities as well as the expectations and interests of the already tonal hearer. I shall not attempt to formalize this subjective component, although the very presentation of the data substantiates its importance.

The world of pitch is virtually infinite and—with the exception of the octave—irrational. Let us consider it. When we run our fingers over the keys of a finely tuned piano we bring into play one of the most finite systems of pitch data every created. Here are eighty-eight tones, each equidistant from its neighbor on either side, with the entire series precisely tuned to an international standard of frequency measure that is currently more accepted and widespread than the metric system.

Opposed to this finely tuned pitch system of eighty-eight tones, the sum total of which is very infrequently used in the creation of music, human hearing affords a staggering potential for virtually infinite pitch discrimination. Experimental data have shown that, depending on the frequency region of the tones, their intensity, the capacities of the observer, and individual "tonal fatigue," the human ear can detect well over thirteen hundred "just noticeable differences" between tones within the sonic reservoir of pitches. But take note here of all musical artifacts—past and present. There has not been and probably never will be a system of tonality that makes even a modest attempt to exploit this human capacity for pitch identification and differentiation. Humans tend, rather, to be terribly conservative in their approach to pitch. From the Babylonians to the Beatles, or roughly three and a half millennia of music making, there seems to be a reluctance to structure a tonal system in which the actual number of different pitches is many rather than few (usually less than eighty). The oldest extant tuning texts, from the Assyrian and Babylonian cultures of ancient Mesopotamia, suggest heptatonic scales, with seven strings or pitches to the octave.[1] To be sure, the interior of the octave has been historically manipulated in diverse ways. We know that the ancient Greeks divided some tetrachords so as to permit quarter-tones. But we must ask how important was the quarter-tone in Greek music. The "profound influence" that the Greeks are frequently assumed to have had upon Western music did not ever inspire the early Christians to create and sing quarter-tone music. This failure in itself encourages conservative evaluation of any marked presence of quarter-tone activity in Greek music and, I think more critically, of the historical influence that Greek music is allegedly said to have had upon the *early* development of Western music. In modern times the most rigorous attempt to create such music in the twentieth century (Alois Hába) remains absolutely unprofitable on the economic market of world music which—like it or not—presently controls the destiny of tonality. Moreover, while we have evolved a working system of twelve equally spaced half-steps (no mean historical feat), that is, the tempered chromatic scale, we must still admit that the 7 + 5 relationship that began to evolve with the first chromatic pitch B-flat in medieval theory is a fact of tonal life which Schoenberg could alter only at the risk of removing himself from the sphere of public tonality. What are the causes for such limited tonal vision regarding the chaos of pitch when the act of hearing liberally demonstrates such remarkable flexibility and potential? We shall return to this question shortly.

Pitch is also irrational. Despite the initial simplicity of the overtone series, one can hold it accountable as a *natural* reason why a particular group of pitches is culturally adopted for use *only* if he also acknowledges that arbitrary decisions are made for and against the series at the whim of theorists and composers. Since French acoustician Joseph Sauveur discovered overtones in the early eighteenth century and Rameau so very much delighted in them, there has been a false tonal teleology afoot which both publicly and privately assumes that modern tonality (and by implication, all Western tonality) evolved as it did in response to the truth of the overtone series. This teleology, for example, forms the bedrock of the Schenkerian system (see chapter 2). But it is a false teleology and was so from the start. When Rameau discovered that the true 7th, 11th, 13th, and 14th partials of the overtone series were in fact out of tune with the way in which eighteenth-century theorists had *already* tempered their system of pitches, he did not hesitate to discard them. They were absent from the artificial tonal system that had already been created for musical expression, and upon discovery they were ignored—natural or not. In short, if the overtone series had truly dictated the development of tonality, then tonality would be something quite other than what it is today.

The first catalyst in the ratiocination of tonality, however, was not the overtone series, which was not discovered until the eighteenth century, but was rather mathematics, which was brought to bear upon tonal appearance as early as the Babylonians. But the simplicity of prime integer numbers—aesthetically cherished since Pythagoras—from which the assumed rationality was said to be derived, was also shunted aside in historical theory (even Greek theory) whenever it conflicted with the reduction of finite tonal space from the natural chaos of pitch. The true Pythagorean fifth with its precise numerical ratio of 2:3 left an irrational residue of pitch space, a small comma of sound that was variously absorbed within the scale until the early nineteenth century and the general adoption of equal temperament.[2] Similarly, all other intervals but the octave and the unison have been so adjusted. While we can look to mathematics for the historical rationalization of what theorists have thought pitch formation should be, the primary, that is, *societal*, creation of pitch lies *before* mathematical consciousness. This is to say that initially theorists inherited societal pitch data which had been created through basically nontheoretical means. This repository of pitches was determined a priori by both cognitive and pragmatic factors that operated simultaneously.

In terms of practical music-making where tonality is forged, the assimilation of the total pitch area that is cognizable by human hearers has been a slow process. While it is possible to perceive as many as 1378 just-noticeable differences between the frequencies of 20 and 20,000 cps, no such discrimination has been historically demanded of any tonal hearer outside the acoustics laboratory. Historically, the tonal hearer began to work in a gross sonic field, establishing high and low pitches within a spectrum of sounds that more or less reflected his own vocal range. The masculine adjective is intended. While it would seem from the evidence of the Greek's Greater Perfect System that some consideration was given to female singers, medieval notation that begins to reveal more or less accurate registers was fixed over the gamut of the male voice first and developed chiefly upward. This is to be expected when the singers were predominately men and adolescent boys. By the time of Ockeghem (in the fifteenth century!) the bass range had been extended downward to the comfortable limits of the average male voice, around E. By the end of the Renaissance, secular vocal music had expanded upward to the limits of comfortable pitches for female singers. Instruments were constructed largely to duplicate the ambitus of these singers. Even the remarkable advance of technology in the seventeenth century contributed only gradually to the expansion of the functional ambitus up and down through the tonal system. The baroque composer, who should have been the most interested in greater ambitus potential, was in practice slow to exploit it. Although the craft of violin making was to reach unparalleled execellence in the seventeenth century, string writing in the higher registers was rare. While the sopranino recorder existed during the Baroque era, Handel treated it as a novelty, the high-pitched sounds suggesting something humorous ("O Ruddier than the Cherry"). The reluctance to consider all parts of the pitch spectrum as tonally equal and interesting may reflect built-in human limitations or mere aural laziness. Even today, extreme ambituses that cannot be duplicated by humans are pretty much ignored, and the list of piccolo, contrabassoon, tuba, and even bassoon concertos is a relatively short one.

When we accept the prior status of melodic construction before the theory that seeks to rationalize it, we are thrust upon the immediate functionality of pitch selectivity within human tonal production. Thus, pitch often depends on how the sonic vocabulary is used. In a non-notational society it means simplicity and memorability within functional musical activity. There are several teleological procedures by which tones were canonized into the sonic corpus of acceptable societal expression. Certainly an important early one was their use in magic that served cultic and medical needs. Tones were thereby "subject to stereotyping to which any magically important action or object is inevitably exposed," notes Max Weber. Deviation from the acceptable pitch series (in the form of magic formulae) that had proved effective in cultic function would have destroyed its potency; therefore, "the exact memorization of the tone formulae was a vital matter."[3]

There is no reason forthcoming why the whole-step so successfully accommodates the great portion of the early monophonic melos. While quarter-tones and other microtonal inflections are evident in the musics of the world, they hardly predominate in the tonal systems in which they operate. Nor is there a tonal system in which the half-step is the common denominator for *melodic* consciousness, although of course it is crucial to the development of Western harmony. At present one can only explain this in curious and arbitrary ways. On the one hand, there are the fundamental laws of the Neo-Pythagorean philosopher Gurdjieff who, like Schenker, went looking for "a piece of the past history of C."[4] On the other, there is the psychoacoustics of the ear, which, if determined to be inviolate within certain parameters, may indeed prove to be the final court of appeal in explaining why we hear pitches and their incumbent overtones in the fashion that we do. In addition, there is a puzzling feature of our pitch consciousness that has critically surfaced with the advent of electronic music: why do we prefer discrete pitches, each separated from the next by at least a half-step, and not a kind of sweep-tone effect that is easily available on the electronic synthesizer? This effect existed early on with the invention of the slide mechanism of the medieval sackbut and the later trombone, but was never exploited as a pitch phenomenon. Perhaps this is related to another of the principles to be discussed later, which is linguistic preformation.

MELODIC GESTURE

Except for the accurate production of tones which concerns musicians generally, pitch systems are primarily the concern of the music theorist, who inherits them, evaluates them, and tells how the composer manipulates them. But as has just been stated, pitch also became historically important through its function; this function, for one, is housed necessarily within the concept of melodic gesture. By this is meant that melodic construction is never random—except sometimes in the twentieth century when the explicit intent is to make it so—and because melodic construction is never random, pitch selectivity is both stabilized and rationalized by it. Nor is melodic construction the gratuitous exercise of the harmonic externalization of the *Klang*, a kind of sonic lagniappe for having properly unfolded the triad. As a further critique of the poverty of Schenkerian tonal methodology, it must be said that Schenker simply pulverizes melody under the wheels of harmonic prolongation. The highest status that melody can acquire in Schenkerian analysis is one which realizes, externalizes, and prolongs harmony "through the interpreter of the motif." This notion is utterly frivolous and renders the monophonic era (the longest in world history) as several millennia of nonsense syllables in search of a triad. (Even a capitalist critique of this notion will not tolerate it. To my knowledge, one can copyright a melody; he seldom—if ever—attempts to copyright "a harmony.")

A melody is normally thought of as a horizontal arrangement of tones, articulated by phrases that are its basic structural units. (The utmost importance of the *phrase* to the melodic act will be considered in the next section.) While there are "melodies" in which a single tone is rhythmically repeated, or melodies built of two tones only, even the primitive ancient Veda and Jewish psalmodic cantillations customarily exhibit more tones in the construction of melodies. A melody is built up through many repetitions of the pitch data-pool. This expectancy of tone frequency in melody reveals a necessary component for human tonal consciousness: a melody must be *for someone*. (The reason why we do not utilize the more than thirteen hundred pitches that are cognitively available to melodic consciousness is the same reason we have not been able to construct a meaningful tonal language with the some 379,000,600 possible twelve-tone successions available in the chromatic scale. We cannot remember them and because we cannot remember them they cannot become significant as tonal expression.) This is a semiotic phenomenon that resides in the very nature of music as tonal gesture. To be sure, there is a difference between the oldest melody any musicologist has been able to transcribe, an ancient, four-note Hurrian cultsong from Ugarit (ca. 1400 B.C.), and the opening theme of Henze's Second Piano Concerto (see p. 253), but it is a difference of only eight tones, not the more than thirteen hundred that are cognitively available to consciousness. The difference between human cognitive abilities and human responsiveness to the semiotic systems created by humans is enormous and sets up an opposition between the greatest amount of information to be gleaned and the least amount of mental effort required to keep any given system expressive. Between these extremes lies all of Western music. To be sure, melody in its externalization historically became complex: the melodies (and consequently the tonality) of Bach are more complex than Landini; Wagner than Bach; and Schoenberg than Wagner. But this does not defeat the argument; it only confirms it. For, from the abundance of his own creativity the composer externalizes his own consciousness through self-production; he produces a tonal object that he thinks will—or ought to—speak for his listeners; and he desires that they appropriate his consciousness in the object by understanding and appreciating it. Not surprisingly, this process did not begin clearly to manifest itself in music until the Church lost its hegemony over the creativity of the melos, beginning about the time of the Reformation.

The basis for the notion that a melody and its tonal content must be a melody for *someone* has both social and economic components. The economic component may be distasteful to the positivist theorist, but it cannot be disposed of by even the most rigorous of analyses. A melody is a product of the subjective creativity of the composer. Production, writes Marx,

> is thus at the same time consumption, and consumption is at the same time production. Each is directly its own counterpart. But at the same time an intermediary movement goes on between the two. Production furthers consumption *by creating material for the latter which otherwise would lack its object.* But consumption in its turn furthers production, by providing for the products the individual for whom they are products. . . . Consumption furnishes the impulse for production as well as its object, which plays in production the part of its guiding aim. It is clear that while production furnishes the material object of consumption, consumption provides the ideal object of production, as its image, its want, its impulse and its purpose. It furnishes the object of production in its subjective form.[5]

This relationship cannot be disavowed, and it is no more apparent than in the late stages of musical capitalism. The absolute glut of popular melody is a precise barometer of the "ideal object of production" as provided by consumption. Each new melody, painstakingly diatonic and at variance with its competition in only the slightest sonic detail, vies for a small corner of the tonal market, its tenuous place on weekly popularity charts, and its ephemeral existence in the mind of the consumer, who must be able to identify the past production of the composer with any new image he provides *at the same time* that the consumer is seduced into believing that he is hearing something quite different.

But Marx's statement has also its purely societal component, which is ably demonstrated in the passage above. The composer, as the producer of melodies, is the agent by which the substance of sonic nature is materially created for the listener, who without the composer's activity would have no tonal object of his own. Since a melody is *for* someone, it must be comprehensible *to* him. This necessity is historically determined. The tonal act is successful because it is conceived as a statement from the societal repository of melodic gestures—those the listener has acquired for himself through the habitual process of melodic identification. It is also progressive, not in the sense of achieving greater states of perfection, but in the sense of expanding the listener's consciousness in terms of the potential for melodic configurations.[6] Thus melody as form is constantly in the process of annulling its present tonal content. This process is the positive appearance of new tonal material which preserves the form of older melodic types at the same time that it guides the listener into ever higher stages of consciousness with regard to the subjective creativity of the composer. Thus, Bach could understand the melodic configurations of the *stile antico* as found in the works of, say, Palestrina—and did so in a remarkable fashion in his own motets—while Palestrina would have rejected Bach's motets because, historically, had he ever been able magically to hear them, they would have violated the Palestrinian rules of counterpoint and the control of dissonance.

This is the great office of the artist as self-conscious creator for those less musical than himself. To quote Lukács in analogical melodic terms, the emergence of the new melodic act as the tonal act "is not simply or immediately identical with its everyday activity." The composer's own creativity

> demands from him a generalizing on himself, a movement upward from his particular singularity to aesthetic uniqueness. . . . The real content of this generalization, which (objectively as well as subjectively) deepens and enriches—but never departs from—the individuality, is the social character of human personality. . . . The subject in the audience imitates in his aesthetic pleasure every movement which receives form in the creation of the individuality of work: a "reality" which, with respect to differentiation, is more intense than the experienced quality of the objective reality itself, and which in this intensity immediately reveals the essential features concealed in reality.[7]

This means that tonal content, generalized through the social character of human personality, succeeds, deepens, and enriches because the listener believes he is being addressed through the individual melodic act of the composer. It is not primarily the harmony that a listener carries home with him in his head: it is the melody.[8]

LINGUISTIC PREFORMATION

There is nothing remarkable in the fact that no Western tonal system ever evolved via instrumental music alone, that is, without the influence of the linguistic forms with which it simultaneously appeared. The basic gesture of sonic structure is the musical phrase, *directly* analogous to the statement of speech as well as intrinscially committed to it. *The domination of the linguistic act upon tonal utterance is prior to its rationalization through various reflective acts.* Purely instrumental forms of music adopt but also exploit the structural potential of verbal gestures when they operate alone. (This usage will be demonstrated in chapter 8 with regard to the doctrine of the affections.) It is quite easy, then, to explain the Schenkerian deficiency to grasp the deep and many-layered meanings of the relationship between word and tone. Schenker built his system in the great age of bourgeois music, in which instrumental music had found a permanent place in the hearts of music lovers. That he should reduce melodic content "through the interpreter of the motif" to a mere unfolding of nature's *Klang* is not commensurate with the economic interests of opera, oratorio, and art song of the era; but it becomes so when it is realized that these vocal forms actively competed for the public's attention *along with* concertos, symphonies, and chamber music of all sorts and in such abundance that the dominance of the latter quite overpowered Schenker's theoretical frame of reference.

It is not feasible to speculate at length on the primitive song of mankind, but the prior assumptions that modern ethnomusicologists have frequently formulated must be mentioned in passing. The notion that music begins simply and waxes complex culturally is not at stake here. Certainly, the history of Western music bears this out. But we cannot, therefore, assume that all early melodic traditions grew from one-note recitations to few-note cantillations to many-note melodies, thereby establishing a melodic ontology of primitive aesthetic creation. The reason is that we do not know when and how song separated itself from spoken language. This is to say that the early vocal communication of primitive man may have been quite fused in character: the distinguishing features of melody—vowel elongation, greater ambitus, and text repetition—may also have characterized early speech in a curious fashion that we would casually label today as "sing-song."[9] But this probable fusion is the point. Until primitive man became conscious of the functional aspects of his encompassing vocal communication, there could be no specific elements that could belong to two separate spheres of sonic delivery. Speculatively to be sure, this is to say that rapidity of thought as spoken in time of danger, excitement, or didactic communication had to develop in consciousness, as it became necessary to project specific information quickly and efficiently. The rapid pattern of dialogue had to extract itself from the subjective human spirit that was objectively given in a proto-language of emotional crooning, more or less tonal babbling, verbal signs, and the repetitive configurations of magic and/or religious sonic charms. For music to become tonal it had to identify something that could be specifically regarded as *tones*, sonic events that could stand alone and in opposition to spoken vocal sounds. (How many thousands of years did this process take?) But among the pitifully meager and largely uninformative records of man's earliest languages there lies the fact that—when we do find them—song and speech are already somehow separated from one another by their functions.

Some light was shed upon this dichotomy, in 1911, by Max Weber, who noted that primitive tonality had much to do with magical and sacred factors in the determination of their early constitutive substance, factors which it never shed in the ratiocination that two thousand years of Western culture imposed upon it. For instance, primitive music seems to be tied early on to the realm of practical requirements.

> It was addressed to magical ends, particularly apotropaic (cult) and exorcistic (medicinal) needs. Therewith it was subjected to the stereotyping to which any magically important action or object is inevitably exposed. . . . Since any deviation from a magical formula once proved to be effective destroys its potency, in fact, since such deviation can attract the wrath of metaphysical powers, the exact memorization of the tone formulae was a vital mater. The wrong rendition of a tone formula was an offense which often could be atoned for only through the instantaneous murder of the offender. Once canonized for any reason, stereotyped tone intervals were of extraordinary influence.[10]

Disregarding the somewhat movie-script scenario of punishment for inattentive singers who altered magic formulae, there is here, nevertheless, an important notion concerning the sanctity of the primitive melos. While it is unlikely that even the most careful reflection will ever enable us to leap over the speculative nature of these remarks, they do characterize a type of consciousness about melodies that still exists today in nonliterate societies. Beyond this we may not go, but our problem does begin to assume more tangible shape at various points of entry in the music of the ancients— particularly where we know that it bears directly upon the development of the Western melos, ancient Jewish psalmody. By way of example of the fundamental importance of the linguistic, performative aspects of tonal consciousness, let us take up the topic of cantillation.

There are at least two distinct stylistic levels of musical consciousness discernible in the music of ancient Asiatic rituals. Each of these reflects a particular facet of speech and song, the *logos* and *melos* of our communication. One level would seem to be exorcistic and magic. Oral communication in its address to the god or spirit becomes itself spirit-like and not human. The voice (is it even singing?) confers upon itself an audible mask. It may adopt what it thinks is the god's voice; it may imitate the sounds of nature around it; it may mimic the cries of animals and the songs of birds. Only by becoming what it vocally is not can the human "speak" to, gain the attention of the god. But there is another level, states Edith Gerson-Kiwi in her remarks on these primitive types of melody, that

> makes use not of naive imitation, but of conscious stylization of the spoken word in the speech-melody of chant. The structure of chant closely follows that of the text, and the bulk of the text is recited on a single axial note, while the beginning and end of the sentences, and in general the main points of punctuation, are marked by high notes or brief melodic flourishes.[11]

This description isolates a general method and practice of "intoning" sacred texts. It is called *cantillation* and it is the cradle of Western tonality. Cantillation is witnessed audibly throughout ancient Asia—in Tibet, in Persia, in Japan, and in India—but these musics are all aspects of the same appearance: a solemn form of speech-melody is adopted for the reciting of sacred texts. Here is a typical example.[12]

v'- a - mar   sol-lu, sol-lu, pan-nu do-rekh

ha - ri - mu mikh - shol mid-de-rekh' am-mi. ___

Hebrew Bible Cantillation: Isaiah 57, v. 14 (from Baghdad)
(Collection of E. Gerson-Kiwi)

How did such chant come about? Two features of the chant's utilization afford insight into the societal nature of the question. First, such chant is created for a specific function: the elevated delivery of religious texts of high moral quality. To the primitive worshipers, it represents the instruction of divine intelligence. It directs behavior in that it encourages the faithful to acceptable collective action. It is not just any tribal communication: it is the word of the god, to be protected and carefully preserved. It is other than we are but it is for us. To that end, special modes of presentation are reserved for it so that confusion will not result.

A second feature supports the "otherness" of primitive chant. It is the fact that, while the secular regional musics of the above-mentioned societies went through profound historical changes, and while each of these musics may be structurally quite different from those of neighboring cultures, the musical structure of all types of cantillation is remarkably similar in style, being roughly approximate to the description and example given above. Cantillation bridges national boundaries, even—to some extent—those of race and religion. "Thus Shintoist, Buddhist, Brahman, Moslem and Hebrew sacred chant reveal a strikingly similarity to one another, while they differ greatly from the secular musics of their respective countries."[13]

But bridging their national boundaries was certainly not uppermost in the consciousness and thought of these nations, widely separated as they were by geographic reality. Can a general phenomenon then account for stylistic similarity at all? Perhaps. Hypothetically, there is the grammatical form of cantillation itself. It is a form of elevated speech. As such it clarifies and focuses the "natural" delivery of the linguistic sentence in which the pitch level and intensity are more or less unconscious and assumed. In a spoken sentence, the linguistic flow of words emerges from silence, on a pitch that is comfortable and naturally placed by the speaker. It rises slightly to a point at which the main body of the sentence is delivered. When the sentence is nearly finished, however, the pitch level tends to fall back to or near the pitch at which the sentence commenced. There are exceptions of course. Questions tend to end in the upper register: questions incidentally were specifically treated in musical terms in both Jewish and Christian chant. The point to be stressed is that the melodic transformation of such a sentence parallels and does not oppose the general conformation of everyday speech. To be sure, this is not meant to restrict all the utterances of everyday communication into a rigid form of verbal articulation. There are many types of expression and numerous geographic patterns of vocalization. But there is a leveling tendency particular to the act of reading aloud that constitutes a general speech model. If natural means are being sought for tonal consciousness, then surely this positive fact must be considered: cantillation is a tonally conceived form of elevated speech.

Among the chain of cantillation styles from the Near to the Far East, we find this style of chanting in the Hebrew recitation of the Bible. At the point where we can begin to document it, it actually represents a late and elaborate system of primitive cantillation, but it illuminates for us a proper and necessary entry into the focusing of Western tonal consciousness. By this is meant, of course, the Psalter, the *tehillim*, a large collection of collections of

sacred Hebrew poetry for use in the post-exilic worship of the Temple and
the Synagogue. The importance of these "praise-songs" for both Jewish and
Christian faiths can hardly be overstressed. The petitions, laments, impre-
cations, and meditations of the psalms have formed the backbone of public
worship and private devotion for over two millennia. But psalmody as a
term means more than a collection of poetry. Psalmody also means, states
Eric Werner,

> a type of musical setting which is governed by a coordination of syntactic and
> melodic accents. Not only do texts of the Psalter belong to this category but
> also any scriptural or liturgical passages, chanted in a manner whereby the
> structure of the sentence determines the length, the flow, and the phrasing of
> the syllabic melody.[14]

To what extent can we say that the structure of the psalm sentence
follows—as it does in pan-Asiatic chant—that of the text? Let us look at
the general shape of a typical psalm formula.[15]

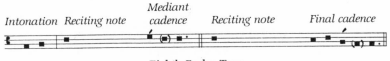

| Intonation | Reciting note | Mediant cadence | Reciting note | Final cadence |

Eighth Psalm Tone

This formulaic melody concurs with the general description of cantillation
by Gerson-Kiwi. The bulk of the text is recited on a single axial note, while
the beginning and end of the sentence, and in general the main points of
punctuation, are marked by high notes or brief melodic flourishes.

Now there is a critical relationship between the note and the word in
psalmody, and it is a negative one. The individual note is of little importance; nor is the individual word of great importance either. Only the whole
thought or sentence, with its caesura and cadence, makes a musical unit.
Hence the musical line is rendered serviceable to the idea to be expressed.
We find melodic movement only at significant places of the sentence. There
is the beginning, the pause ('atnah), and the final cadence. With Werner we
conclude, "The rest of the sentence is recited upon the tenor without any
melos."[16]

But this relationship is only superficially to be judged as negative, since it
also positively establishes a fundamental quality that places tonal consciousness within the context of actual sonic utility. One cannot speak of
scale tones and of their inherent and essential activity; instead there are
selected tones that are articulated by their function within predetermined
linguistic structural limits. Once established, these places of sonic focus

may be repeated, embellished, retarded, ignored, thwarted, or abused, but this does not invalidate their dominant position over the whole of the temporal unit. Here can be seen and heard the quivering life of a tonal system—a nexus of sonic events in which structure is grammatically judged and built.[17] Given the grammatical nature of this music and the pragmatic nature of its activity, it is quite unlikely that the Jewish and the early Christian singer reflected in any tonally theoretical sense on the tones that he used as the *Urstoff* of music. But he did hear tones as portions of a tonal whole, each needing to be complemented and each pointing in some fashion beyond itself. In this sense the whole was known before the parts. Through grammatical structure, the melos was conceived as a whole framework that housed (but musically) another whole framework, i.e., the sentence itself. Once established, this fusion of text and tonal unit—the musical phrase and period—could be manipulated at will. Within the requirements of rhythm and sentence length other words could be utilized in the *same* musical space. This process is the historical key to the later autonomous musical phrase, one that will stand alone without the option or necessity of subscribing to the demands of a given text. A musical meaning comes to stand in place of a textual-meaning-with-musical-support. This notion, which is embedded in the structure of our early tonal consciousness, is suggested by recent research in the studies of congeneric musical meaning and in the semiotics of music. There is more truth in the oft-quoted statement "Music is a tonal language" than can possibly be articulated here in passing. The remarkable dominance of vocal over instrumental music in its historical development should have led us to this notion long before it did.

The principle of linguistic preformation appeared historically before the great ages of instrumental music and has continued to effect its development right up to the present. The classical form of the eight-measure period, articulated by a half cadence after four measures and a whole cadence at the end, became the formal model for both instrumental and vocal melody in the latter eighteenth century but was not at variance with the structure of *parallelismus membrorum*. It merely brought into critical focus the contrasting aspects of tonic and nontonic (specifically, the dominant) modeling. As might be expected, freed from the demands of delivering a phrase of text, instrumental melody internalized its content. A Mozart theme, while falling neatly within the parameter of the classical structural period, is frequently a facile group of shorter melodic and rhythmic units that begin to assume a life of their own when they move from simple presentation to tonal development. This process housed its own contradiction. Beethoven's middle and late works in particular tend to demonstrate the developmental potential of themes from the very beginning of their appearance in the musical form: melodic presentation became thematic activity in and of itself.

In the meantime, vocal melody continued its course in art song, recitative, and aria. The melodic phrase, which usually sets only a part of a sentence of text, has remained one of the most durable elements of man's musical creations. Considering only Western music (and its Near Eastern infancy and childhood), we find it all the way from Paul McCartney back to the ancient hymn from Ugarit. If the structure of language had been different than it is, so would have been the tonal cohesion of music. A hundred million melodic phrases (most of them about seven seconds in length) establish the substantive relationship between the *logos* and the *melos*.

DURATIONAL PREEMINENCE

The utilization of pitch data is characteristically flexible but also carefully coordinated within heard sonic structure in terms of temporality itself. In terms of the *successive temporality* of a given work, one pitch (and its functioning substitutes) dominate durational substance through extension and repetition. This coordination and preeminence serves to render the work tonally valid with regard to what is frequently called a tone center in monophonic music and a key center in harmonized music.

This component of tonal consciousness has been thoroughly misunderstood, and the reason why is clear: its true content lies in the realm of the phenomenology of hearing and *not* intrinsically within the created tonal object which is only its externalized reflection. After studying it intermittently for a number of years, I must admit that I have no particular expertise in phenomenology. The remarks that follow, therefore, will be of a humbler cognitive sort. They are not meant to depreciate the value of studies in the phenomenology of music currently being carried out by a few scholars, although some of these studies are quite woolly. What I wish to describe here is the activity of tones in time and how cognition is affected by the temporal phenomenon of durational preeminence, at least how music theorists intend that cognition should be affected. These remarks are carried out with the assumption that, tonally speaking, what extends over longer periods of time in music is cognitively more memorable, can acquire greater importance, and is intentionally conceived to be more melodically or harmonically significant than what happens over shorter periods of time within the same musical context. It does not matter whether we examine this principle in monophonic or harmonized music. Let us therefore select a specific example from the latter, the familiar aria-theme of Bach's *Goldberg Variations*.

Without repetitions there are ninety-six beats in this symmetrical binary theme, and the harmonic changes are moderate, usually one to a measure. The piece is now as before experienced within the context of historical tonality. We could attempt phenomenologically to reduce this attitude to insignificance, but the work as created was not so reduced: Bach was a tonal hearer. Thus we bring to the experiencing of it our anticipation that it will normatively begin in its key, G major, and indeed it does. Tonic harmony in the first half of the theme amounts to 12% of the piece's total duration.[18] Bach spends much more time (20%) establishing the dominant, the tonal area in which the first half of the dance will end. But in the second half of the piece the tables are turned. The new key area (D major) has been established and its tonal weight must now be vitiated. The dominant here accounts for less than 10% of the total duration of the theme, and the tonic, which must reestablish its dominance, occurs 25% of the time. I am, of course, dealing only with tonic and dominant triads and ignore substitutes for them. But even on this level, especially on this level, I submit that durational preeminence has nothing to do with Schenker's "revengefulness of nature," or any other metaphysical notions of harmonic motion. It is, however, intrinsically related to the cognitive processes of *short-* and *long*-term memory. In their briefest definitions, short-term memory is that memory process that permits one to call the operator for a telephone number and retain it in mind long enough to dial it without writing it down. Ten or fifteen minutes later he will have forgotten the sequence of numbers, forgotten one or several of them, and tomorrow he will have to ask for the number again because he cannot remember it at all. It was not transferred to a long-term memory bank where important data remain in our brains for days, months, years, and decades. This mental operation is of course highly flexible and immensely complex.

This same process happens in terms of tonal consciousness. Through repetition, a phenomenological category of continuance builds up in cognition.[19] Since the listener is already to some degree a social tonal listener, the tonic in the first half of the theme need not be overstressed. He assumes a certain context of stability from the start, and this stability is quickly established by the tonic. But the dominant must acquire the greater portion of heard time or it will not be able to assert its own tonal strength, which is the same kind of harmony as the tonic, both major and perfect. This is not to say that the dominant itself "acquires" strength, but, rather, that the composer "makes" the dominant acquire strength and import by repeating it more often than he does the tonic. It must become its own tonic, which it does through duration via repetition or temporal extension.

At this point it must be admitted that we are actually talking about a fairly sophisticated tonal consciousness that concerns largely the musician and the critically tonal listener. For the nonmusician, however, the process of establishing the dominant as superior could happily stop at the end of the first half of the dance. My own classroom experiments with this process demonstrate that the unreflective tonal hearer feels no compulsion to return to the tonic, must be told that there is more music to follow, and that his musical experience is incomplete unless he hears the music return to its "natural" close. Nature, of course, has nothing to do with any "need" to return to the tonic. It is merely human will that wishes to bring the nonmusician within the sphere of a sociological value that the pedagogue thinks is worth sharing. But, while nature has nothing to do with it, self-production does. The ideology of current music theory on a pedagogical level has unfortunately taken it as its basic supposition that short-term memory processes are to be quickly transferred to longer memory spans and then used as indicators within the infrastructure of the work in order to fulfill the aesthetic demands of unity and variety. Actually, there is nothing wrong in this, since it was exactly what composers did as they historically objectified their own tonal consciousness in order to manifest this cognitive apparatus. We know that it requires about two years (longer for some) for students to establish in cognition the basic and customary harmonic components and patterns (intervals, cadences, progressions, modulations, et al.) that characterize the music of the "common-practice" era. We even tell students that the dominant "demands" resolution, that it "must resolve" to the tonic, etc., in order to hurry this allegedly "natural" phenomenon along. We punish the undergraduate who fails to understand and reproduce this phenomenon in his own consciousness by giving him poor marks when he falters. If he quite fails to perceive this phenomenon of harmonic motion, we fail him and label him "not a musician." He can love music all he wishes, but he is hopelessly consigned to the rank of an amateur and is not permitted to join the ranks of the professional elite. *This is an ideology in purely tonal terms.* It is not the truth of the dominant "wanting" to progress to the tonic, as Rameau fully understood. It is, rather, the expression of the ideology of a class that wishes common-practice tonality to remain the model for tonal consciousness. The network of tensions that this notion has created between the individual and the society in which his tonal interests are both limited and dictated cannot be discussed here. Let us return to the second half of the saraband.

In the second half of the theme the harmonic process is reversed. The acquired tonal strength of the dominant harmony must now be gradually attenuated, which is accomplished in both a general and a particular way. As the tonic assumes more and more of the work's temporality through repetition and extension, the dominant is now reevaluated. It is made to commit itself ultimately to its former function, as the servant of the tonic. General harmonic motion, the gradual process of going from V to I *as tonal essence* is also and finally particularized as objective reality in the final cadence. Curiously, it is attempted immediately over the double bar at midpoint in the piece: measures 17 and 18 contain the same harmonic progression, a foreshadowing of the real close, but not meant here actually to terminate the piece—for both harmonic and formal reasons. Harmonically, the cadence in these measures is not a cadence in fact, since it does not occur as a cadentially formal part of the musical phrase which it articulates: not every V–I progression is a cadence, only those which are expected to achieve that function and are critically positioned so that they do. In addition, the tonic is intentionally weakened in measure 18 by being placed in inverted form. And the formal reason is, in this case, the composer's previously determined intent for symmetry: each half contains the same number of beats.

There is something terribly Humean about the reason behind this kind of tonal motion, but it cannot be disavowed. It is largely habit that makes a person tonal, just as it is habit that makes him speak and understand Portuguese rather than English. Through countless repetitions, to be sure, this places the burden of tonal responsibility upon the composer (at least since the age of anonymous collective monophony), but this is precisely where it belongs. The composer is given the freedom to objectify his tonal consciousness, which he does by externalizing his subjective will upon the sonic substance of pitch; but since he is also a creator in a society, he is also bound by necessity to speak *to* society as well as *for it*.

But by what means is the principle of durational preeminence carried forth in twelve-tone music, where the expressed intent is to annul tonics and dominants and their incumbent loyalties? I think the answer lies in something that Schoenberg did not build into his system of "twelve tones that are related only to each other." While Schoenberg did equalize the appearance of pitch data, he did not equalize their durations, that is, demand that each tone, interval, or chord complex be as long as all others. Moreover, the exception to repeating a given note of the series was an *immediate* repetition of that note (before progressing with the remainder of the row), which in temporal terms means extension through repetition for a particular sonic event. In no sense did the fact that some sound events are longer than others create tonics for Schoenberg, since any sound event could be extended, but the fact that some tonal events are longer than others underscores a fact that serialists have not yet acknowledged: through the activity of duration, holding place in a stream of sonic events localizes temporality in consciousness and gives weight to certain sounds at the same time it minimizes others. If this were not part of the rationale of twelve-tone composition, any note, interval, or harmonic complex in Schoenberg's music could be temporally altered to any other duration with no loss of meaning. To test the validity of this premise one need only play any of Schoenberg's Opus 23 Piano Pieces and hold all notes, intervals, or chord complexes for the same duration, say, a quarter note at eighty beats per minute. If the experiment seems bizarre, how much more fundamental is the notion that tonal meaning depends not only upon what we hear but also how long we hear it?

VERTICAL SONORITY

The four preceding components of tonal consciousness—pitch selectivity, melodic gesture, linguistic preformation, and durational preeminence—operated together in Western music until the appearance of polyphony about the mid-ninth century. They were not annulled by the gradual emergence of harmonic consciousness, but instead were preserved within it at a higher level of sonic objectification. Because all but one of the remaining chapters of this book address certain aspects of harmonic tonality in specific historical contexts, I shall not duplicate those observations here. However, a few general comments are in order. What is the relation between knowledge, human interests, and vertical sonority in tonal consciousness? In its most fundamental physical component vertical sonority can be stated in the following. If the ear hears three pitches whose frequencies are quite close, say 440, 442, and 444 cps, it will resolve these three discrete sonic data into one pitch. This resolution is apparently due to a physical mechanism within the cognitive activity of the brain as it processes data gathered by the hearing organ, which seeks to be as efficient as possible. But if the ear hears two tones sufficiently separated in frequency it resolves two pitches (rather than fusing them together) and regards them as different and perhaps related tones. At this point, consciousness must make a decision whether or not it wishes the two tones to exist simultaneously and, if so, under what conditions.

"If so" and "under what conditions" house the whole history of Western harmonic consciousness with respect to tonality, indeed, of harmonic consciousness anywhere. Let us examine a couple of instances of this phenomenon in practice, realizing that the degree of conscious reflection in any given instance is of great importance.

The variative polyphony of the African pygmies, which includes such techniques as hocket, ostinato, canonic imitation, and parallel part movement largely in fourths and fifths, is judged by some to be a reflection of the "essentially democratic, non-hierarchical structure of pygmy social units."[20] The system of shared meanings and values that unite pygmy society are thus tonally embodied in a given performance that can be experienced by all members of the community. To what degree is the pygmy conscious of this harmonic praxis? To point out that pygmies possess no music theory books that explain it is not helpful: neither do they possess any written theory about their political system, which is relatively stable, understood by all members of its culture, and communicated when necessary by pygmies with subtlety that no doubt escapes the most careful of observations by outsiders. To the pygmy, "singing" means to carry out those harmonic techniques just mentioned rather than to subscribe exclusively to a collective monophonic melos.

But with the advent of the *Musica Enchiriadis* in mid-ninth-century Western Europe, whatever polyphonic activity preceded it, we historically encounter a decisive operation of *conscious* human interests upon vertical sonority. Yes, another voice may "ornament" an already established monophonic melos, but it may do so only under certain tonal conditions. There, harmonic organization admits the intervals of fourth and fifth (as with pygmy harmony); this harmonic ornamentation must organize itself beneath the monophonic melos; and these preferred intervals are not always welcome, specifically at the beginning and ending of the melodic phrase.

As will be stated several times elsewhere, here begins the concept of harmonic motion. Fritz Reckow notes that the early activity of the *vox organalis* may be in truth no more than an "ornament," but it is a great deal more than a mere "doubling" of the chant. "It creates sonorous tension by 'singing apart,' heightens this tension by changing the vertical intervals, and dissolves the tension at each of the caesuras as it establishes *a point of rest in the sonority.*"[21] I would only add to this excellent hypothesis that creating, heightening, and dissolving sonorous tension was *already* a part of the structure of the texted monophonic phrase itself and intrinsically related to the phrase's nexus of statement, expectation, and fulfillment. The semiotic referent of harmonic gesture initially paralleled and did not oppose the authenticity of the melos.

Gradually, the cadence critically determined its own substantive content as well as that of harmonic activity in general. Its particular component is closely related to the manner in which, historically, it came to support specific, melodic cadential patterns for the delivery of text. That is, it preserved the functions of partial and complete closure as seen first in the dichotomy of cantillation, of structural *parallelismus membrorum*, and later in the *ouvert* and *clos* endings of both monophonic and polyphonic secular song and dance. The general component of this harmonic cognition was the subjective extension of such objective particularity into the temporal vortices of vertical cognition itself. While the cadence was a specific motion, toward momentary and conditional repose or complete sonorous cessation, its essence could also operate on extended levels through sonic temporality itself: simultaneously with the notion of vertical sonority there evolves the concept of *harmonic motion* which in actual practice was very much like the cadence itself, only prolonged.

This cadential movement had, however, two aspects, a progression to a point of tonal stability and expectation and another away from it. This motion away from a note, interval, or chord center was no less important than motion toward it and early on offered composers the potential of modulation, a shift of tone center, the notion of being harmonically the same, governed by the same types of vertical complexes, but with shared or entirely different pitches. Whether or not this change of tone center truly takes place within a given composition is a game that theorists—particularly Schenkerians—love to play, with the rules laid down in advance and the outcome predictable in terms of wins and losses. For Schenker, there ultimately was only one key center, summarily stated in a prolonged I–( )–V–I progression or its minor variant. Tone centers other than that expressed by the overriding given tonic may be neighbors or passing tone centers that one may visit but must not take up residence in, even though cadential (and therefore structural) integrity guarantees tonal orientation and cohesiveness. Thus, both Johannes Ockeghem's popular virelai "Ma Maitresse" and Gustav Mahler's Ninth Symphony must be regarded as unwanted tonal aliens because both begin with clear loyalties to one tonic but disavow this allegiance and take up residence elsewhere. Regarding vertical sonorities and relationships within them, Schenker did not ever acknowledge that a complete relocation of tonal citizenship was feasible: since all good music subscribed to his formula of I–( )–V–I, or its minor variant, Mahler's Ninth Symphony was a mistake or did not exist. Who ever heard of an entire symphony whose tonal consciousness simply sank to its leading-tone key and forgot or refused to return home?

It must be clearly noted that the concept of harmonic motion as stated above is based upon the notion of the chord or triad as a unit, primary and indivisible, which accounts for an important era in Western harmony (1600 to 1900), but that harmonic motion is by no means absent when triads are absent or not perceived as triads when present. The inability of the contemporary theorist to understand or admit this truth provides its own critique. For example, Carl Dahlhaus notes that in the sixteenth century "the simultaneous sounding of D–F–B constituted neither a chord nor an incomplete inversion of a dominant 7th."[22] But neither did it constitute nothing at all. To be sure, Dahlhaus's caution against interpreting vertical complexes in medieval and Renaissance music as prophetic announcements of future harmonic realities is quite defensible. But fact that we do find D–F–B in abundance in early polyphony before C–G–C as a form of harmonic closure and do not find, say, an E-flat minor triad before the same final sonority should tell us that composers had very precise notions about vertical orders of successive tone complexes, however they conceived this activity melodically. The treatises of the theorists, particularly those that treat musica ficta, testify to the interplay between both linear and vertical components of a consciousness critical of its own interests, aware of possibilities, and willing to jettison stated rules of melodic and harmonic control over a two-dimensional polyphonic content when those rules inhibit aesthetic necessity in the form of subjective tonal invention. Not infrequently, a reason given for the transcendence of an inhibiting theoretical maxim was the perfectibility of imperfect intervals (major and minor thirds and sixths) "for the sake of sweeter harmony." To hold as many do that harmony before the baroque era was merely the gratuitous outcome of part writing does not award the polyphonic composer a high degree of harmonic intelligence.

At the other end of the spectrum, in the twentieth century, the composer acquires virtually limitless ways in which to build vertical structures and to juxtapose these structures in expressive forms of sonic comprehensibility. Frequently, this is carried out within the parameters of the chromatic scale. It is interesting to note that, despite experiments with microtonal systems, by far the largest portion of twentieth-century music has been composed with tones that lie a half-step apart and that the established pitch data of Western music, which are far from being indivisible (particularly on electronic instruments), apparently serves thousands of composers who have yet to exhaust its riches.

But "apparently" only illuminates the cultural contradictions of musical capitalism, and it is necessary by way of conclusion to realize that, harmonically speaking, the music of the spheres is currently orbiting around the dollar and not according to any expression of Pythagorean *harmonia*. Let us look at popular music first.

The "good" song, the harmonically marketable song, is one that contains fewer different chords than a fourteenth-century *ballata* by Francesco Landini; and the popular composer who intentionally removes himself from a restrictive sphere of public harmony does so not only at the risk of tonal misunderstanding but planned poverty as well. Harmonically speaking, the "liberal" society is the V–I society. It is both curious and amusing that the weekly "Words 'n Chords" tune that is copyrighted and cycled through the nation's Sunday newspapers, the latest tonal vision from the latest tonal prophet, pretends that the sequence of harmonies given there is actually privately owned. It is no more private property than were the ground basses of the seventeenth century. The song must be harmonized, but its "see-through" chords are merely the container in which the composer takes his melos to market, a melos conspicuous by its absence although suggested by the lyrics. If this one-dimensional, comic book harmony were unique, if it were personally expressive—as harmony once was—it would also be inac-

THE NATURE OF TONAL PHENOMENA 79

cessible to the limited tonal abilities of the potential consumer. As one of America's most popular and wealthiest band leaders once cautioned the staff arrangers who created the harmonies for his "easy listening" music, "Keep it simple, fellas, not too many diminished sevenths."

In the world of the so-called serious composer, the harmonic tables are completely turned. His vertical idiom must appear to be unique: for him to indulge in the Sunday supplement harmony of his more popular counterpart would mean committing aesthetic suicide before his peers. Nor may his harmony sound like Bartok or Debussy or anybody but himself. He must continue to mine the wasted residue of tertian consciousness for sonorities that have been overlooked by his contemporaries. Ultimately, they must survive academic analysis in the crucible of the doctoral dissertation in music theory and emerge free of the dross of any other composer's harmonic consciousness. The greater the difficulty in understanding his own harmonic thought, the more its aesthetic intent is legitimized.

In either case alienation and lack of freedom characterize harmonic thought. The popular composer may not deviate from an expected harmonic norm lest he compose himself out of the sphere of tonal productivity; the serious composer must not trespass on the harmonic fields of his neighbor lest he be accused of tonal plagiarism. Since he is not trying to or cannot make a living on his creations, they continue to foster the illusion that greatness always waits.

4 Retuning the Music of the Spheres

A lthough it cannot be assumed to be of exclusively classical origin, the notion that the cosmos is so well tuned that it sings is one of the great legacies of Western philosophy. When the ancient psalmist said "the morning stars sang together," he unwittingly uttered a prophetic theme that was to be created again by later Greek philosophers who knew nothing of him. We may attribute the psalmist's remark to a burst of poetic inspiration or privy counsel to divine intelligence. The Greek notion of a harmonic cosmology, however, does not bear the marks of inspiration or revelation; rather, it reflects philosophic speculation about a physical universe. While it is widely assumed that the pre-Socratic, Ionian Greek philosopher Pythagoras is somehow responsible for the harmony of the spheres, few are aware how this doctrine came about. Fewer still are aware that it has both musical and nonmusical components; that these components may have existed separately in their earliest historical stages; and that when they were joined together by the followers of Pythagoras, they crystallized into a belief that Pythagoras probably had not thought of himself. We might happily discard the notion of a cosmic music had it been not a persistent and widely held belief up through the seventeenth century. It is instructive, therefore, to examine as carefully as possible the historical origins of this harmonic cosmology. We shall find both fact and fiction, and the latter is no less important than the former if what we are seeking is an adequate account of the concept from which the essays in this book draw substance. It is only by retracing the abandoned stages of reflection of past ages that we will be able to understand historically what *harmonia* was like to its earliest known observers and what it meant to those who discovered it. Our discussion begins with the ancient philosophers of Ionian Greece.

The peculiar function of music in Ionian philosophy is no better attested to than by the activities of Xenophanes and Pythagoras. For Xenophanes, music was merely a pragmatic condition for communication; as a rhapsodist he made his living by singing his own verse, a lively testimony that poetry, as W. K. C. Guthrie says, "is no bar to philosophy." For Pythagoras, however, the contemplation of *harmonia* was the consciousness of cosmological proportion and unity. By force of a magnetic personality he developed this consciousness in a religious order of disciples who venerated him to heroic stature in his own lifetime; after his death he became the source of legends which followers and admirers repeated and embellished for half a millennium; and he inspired philosophers from the Academy to the medieval scholastics to consider music as a discipline worthy of the same intellectual rigor accorded geometry, astronomy, and arithmetic.

In order to assess the character of Pythagoras's philosophy it is necessary to determine as accurately as possible what testimony can be taken as fact and what is the product of ardent hero worship, and, in addition, to determine to which parts of Pythagoreanism later philosophers were attracted and why. This is no easy task. Pythagoras was both a mystic and a scientist, a man of unique mental powers, characterized by Bertrand Russell as a combination of Mary Baker Eddy and Albert Einstein. Many thinkers who genuinely respect Pythagoras's mathematical genius ignore or even malign his mysticism, so that Pythagorean philosophy has become a mirror in which philosophers consciously or unconsciously reflect their own temperaments and biases. This condition is as prominent in the twentieth century as it was in the time of the Academy; it surfaces early on in the meager testimonia that lie closest in time to the life of Pythagoras and the activity of his school.

Since the late nineteenth century it has been admitted that any reconstruction of pre-Socratic philosophy must depend on the original words of the men who made it. But in the case of Pythagoras we are faced with the vexing problem that he taught his philosophy to some three hundred men and women who were forbidden to write down what he said. After Pythagoras's death, however, this injunction was disregarded, particularly in mainland Greece where the society migrated to avoid persecution; and from the third century on, various books appeared about Pythagoras or allegedly even by him. The first name connected with this body of literature is Philolaus.

Little is known of Philolaus. He was perhaps a native of Tarentum. His teacher was Lysis, one of the two Pythagoreans who escaped to Tarentum after the massacre of the Pythagoreans at Croton in 454. Lysis later went to Thebes and became the tutor of Epaminondas. When Lysis died, Philolaus also migrated to Thebes, probably at the invitation of the large Pythagorean order there. He became the teacher of Cebes and Simmias, who were later pupils of Socrates and present with him at his death in 399. From Thebes, Philolaus apparently returned to Tarentum and became the teacher of the "last generation" of Pythagoreans, the generation including the mathematician Archytas.

According to both Diogenes Laertius and Iamblichus, Plato, sometime in the early fourth century, commissioned Dion in a letter to buy for him "from Philolaus" three "Pythagorean books" for the sum of a hundred minas. Walter Burkert feels that it is unlikely that Philolaus authored the three books. Rather, he brought forth or published writings previously unknown, perhaps even secret, but in any case already in existence for some time.[1] As might be expected, it was quickly assumed that Pythagoras himself had written the three books, and a trilogy circulated in Greece for several centuries as genuine works by the philosopher from Samos. Whatever their origin, we must subscribe to the evidence that Plato did have access to them by the middle of the fourth century, probably at the time of the writing of the *Timaeus*.

The Philolaic writings are extant only in scattered fragments attributed to his name, and not all of them are genuine. Of the twenty-three fragments, Nos. 1–7, 13, and 17 are believed to be authentic. The remaining fragments betray Platonic or Aristotelian philosophical terminology to such a degree that, along with the evidence from the doxographical tradition, they are judged to be spurious and cannot be included among the earliest written accounts of the philosophy of Pythagoras. We are forced to admit, then, that the only unassailable evidence for early Pythagorean philosophy is dependent on two sources. One is the authentic fragments of Philolaus; the other is the discussion of Pythagorean philosophy in Aristotle's *Metaphysics*, *Physics*, and *De Caelo*.[2] These are the only direct sources for determining the nature of Pythagorean philosophy before Plato, and it is upon them that we must depend for the early formulation of music philosophy with regard to a harmonic cosmology.

There is a simple experiment that will serve to place us neatly within the context of Pythagorean music philosophy. With a tape measure divide the G string on a violoncello in half. When the string is pressed against the fingerboard at midpoint, g at the octave above will sound when the string is plucked. The ratio of the vibrating length of string to its total length is 1:2. Now divide the string so that the ratio of string length is 2 to 3: d will sound when the string is plucked. Next, divide the string so that the ratio of string length is 3 to 4: c will sound when the string is plucked.

Now there is a feature of this experiment which needs immediately to be considered because it reveals how readily Pythagorean philosophy is complicated by assumption and subjective whim. In ancient Greece there was no musical instrument that had a fingerboard on which to stop the strings as suggested above. Since it was assumed that Pythagoras must have had an instrument which could be stopped at various intervals along its string length, antiquity created one for him and then claimed that he had invented it: the monochord or *kanon*. This scientific instrument consisted of a single string stretched over a resonating box; it was equipped with a movable bridge which traveled under the string along its entire length to permit division at any point. Calibrations enabled the experimentor to measure ratios accurately.

While the kanon is said to date from the fifth century, there is no circumstantial evidence for attributing its invention to Pythagoras. Aristides Quintilianus (third and fourth century A.D.), in his treatise *On Music*, and Diogenes Laertius (probably the first half of the third century A.D.), in the *Lives and Opinions of Famous Philosophers*, are the first to support the invention of the kanon by Pythagoras, apparently reporting from no longer extant writings of Xenocrates; from there the legend passed down into the Middle Ages and became firmly entrenched in all textbooks on music theory. The medieval monochord was constructed along elaborate designs, with several strings, and for centuries remained the most popular instrument for demonstrating the physical properties of sound.

The discovery of the musical ratios is first ascribed to Pythagoras by Xenocrates, a pupil of Plato and the successor of Speusippus as head of the Academy about 339. Xenocrates accompanied Plato on his third Sicilian journey, and, like Plato, was keenly interested in Pythagorean philosophy. The term "number theory," *arithmon theoria*, appears to be his invention, from the title of one of his books devoted to the general theory of numbers. (His writings are lost, except for fragments.) If Xenocrates had known *how* Pythagoras had discovered the musical ratios, it is unlikely that he would have omitted an explanation of so important an event in his books.

The fact that Pythagoras must have discovered the musical ratios through the observation of natural phenomena, prior to experimentation with the kanon, inspired an often-repeated legend of a physically impossible experiment. According to tradition, while passing a blacksmith's shop one day, Pythagoras noticed the sounds of the hammers ringing as the blacksmith worked at his forge. Upon examination, and with no little amazement, Pythagoras noticed that the sounds which four different hammers made when struck were related to their weights and that the ratios were 1:2, 2:3, and 3:4. The oldest testimony for this tradition is from Nicomachus and Adrastus. This tale also passed into medieval music theory unquestioned.

Typical of its popularity are the woodcuts in Franchino Gaforio's *Theorica Musicae* of 1492. In one panel Pythagoras is depicted in the background, striking six different bells numbered with their weights: 16, 12, 9, 8, 6, and 4, while in the foreground his follower Philolaus strikes six glasses filled with liquid to different levels, similarly numbered. The law presupposed here is one that states that the vibration and sound of a metallic body are directly proportional to its volume and weight. Unfortunately, it is not a law at all, but only a hypothesis. The vibration and sound of a metallic body, such as a bell, are not directly proportional to its volume and weight. Nevertheless, the legend was apparently not seriously challenged and the experiment not actually performed until the seventeenth century, when the French theorist Marin Mersenne demonstrated its physical impossibility in his *Questions Harmoniques* in 1634.

Before we take up the nonmusical—but equally important—aspect of Pythagorean *harmonia* a point must be stressed. It is indefensible to attribute all insight into the nature of musical ratios and the Greek scales solely to Pythagorean tradition. The pitch data of Greek musical culture in the sixth century was doubtless studied by other, non-Pythagorean theorists— e.g., Lasus of Hermione. Burkert suggests that "what distinguished the Pythagoreans was apparently not a special knowledge, inaccessible to others. Rather, something which may well have lost its interest for professional musicians came to be prized among them as fundamental insight into the nature of reality."[3] The achievement of Pythagoras is the fundamental notion that music was not tied to the world of man by mythic decree or aesthetic postulate but was rather realized from that world by virtue of its very physical essence, its constitutive substance. Music, says Burkert, was "captured in the net of number," like geometry, astronomy, and arithmetic. It offered confirmation that "number holds sway throughout the universe," and this consciousness awed Pythagoras and the Greeks no less than it did Whitehead and Russell.

It is generally agreed among scholars of pre-Socratic philosophy that the notion of a universe of disparate appearances "fitted together" (*harmochthe*) in an orderly fashion is of Pythagorean origin. This concept of *harmonia* appears in the fragments of Philolaus as a principle of musical proportion and cosmological design revealed through the nature of number. If it is permissible to paraphrase the ontological question, Why is there something rather than nothing? to, Why is there music rather than silence? we discover in the earliest metalanguage of music itself a term which is neither thoroughly musical nor philosophic in meaning but which illuminates the Pythagorean cosmology as a unified system of thought: *harmonia*.

Besides being the name of a mythological personage—Harmonia was the daughter of Aphrodite and Ares—*harmonia* encompassed several different meanings in Greek literature. As a nonmusical term in early Grecian dialects, it meant the joining or fitting together of physical things, such as we find in Homer:

> Kalypso, the shining goddess, at that time came back bringing him an auger, and he bored through them all and pinned them together with dowels, and then with cords he lashed [*harmoniesin*] his raft together.[4]

In the sense of fitting or joining together, *harmonia* proved a useful term in shipbuilding (Herodotus 2.96), masonry (Diodorus 2.8), and anatomy (Galen 2.555). In addition, it signified an agreement or a covenant, although not necessarily arbitration (Iliad 22.255). The sense of "fitting together" is present in Philolaus' fragments 1 and 2; in fragment 6 it is combined with the musical senses of *harmonia* as well.

> The *physis* [i.e., 'nature'] in the cosmos has been put together harmoniously [*harmochthe*] from unlimited and limiting (constituents), both the whole cosmos and all the things in it (B1).
> Existing things must be, all of them, either limiting, or unlimited, or both limiting and unlimited; but they would not be unlimited only ⟨or limiting only (?)⟩. Since, however, they are clearly neither made of limiting (constitutents) only nor of unlimited only, it is therefore obvious that from both limiting and unlimited (constituents) the cosmos and the things in it were harmoniously put together [*sunarmochthe*]. This is proved also by actual existing things; for those of them which are made of limiting (constituents) impose limit, whereas those made of both limiting and unlimited (constituents) both do and do not impose limit, and those made of unlimited (constituents) will appear unlimited (B2).[5]

The cosmology being discussed here can be explained briefly as follows. Pre-Socratic philosophers attempted to explain the generation of the world as a sequence in time. The Pythagoreans did this also by positing a universe of sensible objects from nonsensible first principles (*archai*). The term "first principles" needs to be understood in the only way in which Philolaus, as a Pythagorean, could have meant it. In pre-Socratic philosophy *arche* meant beginning; it did not mean cause. The word which meant cause was *aitia*, and this does not appear at all in Philolaus. Thus, the beginning of the physical universe was activated through a bonded pair of opposite qualities. (What happened before that, Philolaus says in fragment 6, "requires divine and not human intelligence.") These primary nonsensible and opposite qualities were the Limited and the Unlimited (B1). The formation of the cosmos transpired through the imposition of the Limited upon the Unlimited, as Aristotle explains Pythagorean philosophy in the *Physics* (213b), "the universe being supposed to breathe in the actual void, which keeps the different kinds of things apart; for they [the Pythagoreans] define void as that which separates and divides their nature." There is a picture here of the universe condensing in an unqualified and unquantified void which is nevertheless spatial and temporal. As physical matter, the Unlimited

> was that on which the nascent cosmos fed and by which it grew, as space, or extension, it was that which could submit to the imposition of mathematical form; but it had also a temporal aspect, as anything *apeiron* (unlimited) had.[6]

When Aristotle states that "this happens first in numbers; the void divides their nature," he is alluding to the spatial conceptualization of number revealed by the tetractys of the decad, a symbol attributed in numerous sources to Pythagoras himself. This symbol, initially no doubt a pebble

game, represented the number ten, and for Pythagoreans ten was considered "to be complete and to include every nature in numbers" (*Metaphysics* 986a). But also, in a more abstract way, the tetractys demonstrates how Pythagoreans conceptualized the opposite, nonsensible qualities of Limited and Unlimited as capable of bringing a thing forth into existence. The dots in the symbol represent the principle of Limit; they are fixed points in space. But the space between them represents the unlimited void from which the points or dots are "drawn in and limited." There was no sphere of existence where this duality was not manifest. The generation of geometric forms was accomplished by the structuring of space through the imposition of the first four integers expressed in the decad. From a single point (1) a line can be drawn to a second point (2); a third point (3) can be

placed to form a triangle; and a fourth point (4) generates the first three-dimensional figure, the tetrahedron. With each step the points draw in and limit unquantified space, so that position, length, area, and volume arise from the void. The opposite principles of Unlimited and Limited are physically manifested and "fitted together" through number.

The duality of the Philolaic system is, of course, readily apparent; but it is a polarity of opposites which could not have been united into an entity, be it universe, man, or bird, without the addition of *harmonia*, a fitting together of the separate qualities.

> This is the situation about *physis* ['nature'] and [*harmonias*]: the being (*esto*) of things, which is eternal, and *physis* itself admit of divine but not of human knowledge, except that it was impossible for any of the things that exist and are recognized by us to come to be if there were not the being (*esto*) of the things of which the cosmos was composed, both the limiting and the unlimited. And since these beginnings (*archai*) were not alike or of the same kind, it would have been impossible for them to be put together harmoniously if [*harmonia*] had not supervened [*ei me harmonia epegeneto*] — however it was that it came to be. It is not things that are alike and of the same kind that need [*harmonias*], but things unlike and different and of unequal speed; such things must be bonded together by [*harmonia*], if they are to be held together in a cosmos. . . . (B6; first half)[7]

Without the action of *harmonia*, there would be no material universe. *Harmonia*, commented one of the pseudo-Philolaus writers in fragment 10, "is a unity of many mixed elements, and an agreement between disagreeing elements." It is a necessary condition for nature; thus, says Burkert, it heals the breach which opens in the cosmos between the Unlimited and the Limited when "things" come into being. It is important to stress here that the Unlimited and the Limited are not quite the abstract entities that later philosophic definition is wont to make of them. The Unlimited and the Limited are *archai* (principles), beyond discovery by specific and direct experience, and yet, as *perainonta*, are "things" that have been generated by the active power of such a universal duality.

The discovery of this cosmic *harmonia*, the physical fitting together of things into a world, was achieved through the contemplation of number, and by way of number Pythagoreans united the musical meanings of *harmonia* with the nonmusical and perhaps earlier senses we have just discussed. Let us now turn to the musical aspects of the same term.

Musically, *harmonia* carried several different meanings in Greek literature: octave, tuning, scale, and mode. It is not always possible to determine which is signified in a given text, and occasionally multiple meanings can be implied simultaneously from the syntax. I shall argue that there are at least two senses of *harmonia* in the last half of B6. One is obvious: *harmonia* means octave. But I believe that Philolaus is careful to establish that there is more at stake than naming the most consonant interval: the major portion of the fragment is devoted to the "content" of the *harmonia*, and in this sense *harmonia* is a tuning, in fact, an ontologically pure tuning system, because it is grounded in the small integer numbers that are tonally represented in intervals which both fit within and constitute the whole. It has been argued that the two halves of B6 do not belong together. To be sure, the first half breaks off and the second section is about musical harmony, not nature and harmony. Exactly what came between the two sections we do not know. However, I shall argue that they are related to one another, although the reader is encouraged to form his own conclusions.

> The content of the *harmonia* (octave) is the *syllaba* (fourth) and *di' oxeian* (fifth); and the fifth is greater than the fourth by a whole-step; for from the highest string to the middle [string] is a fourth, and from the middle to the lowest string (highest note) is a fifth. From the lowest to the third string is a fourth; from the third to the highest string is a fifth. Between the middle and third strings is a whole-step. The fourth has the ratio 3:4; the fifth 2:3; and the octave 1:2. Thus the *harmonia* consists of five whole-steps and two half-steps; *di' oxeian* consists of three whole-steps and a half-step; and the *syllaba* consists of two whole-steps and a half-step (B6; second half).[8]

On the surface, this passage appears to be sheer gibberish. But we can clarify its meaning if we do so in stages, starting with its terminology. The translation of "octave," "fifth," and "fourth" for *harmonia, di' oxeian*, and *syllaba* is the product of Greek music theorists after Philolaus. The terms which he uses here are quite different in meaning and perhaps represent the earliest Greek attempt at naming musical intervals. *Harmonia* is that sound which is realized when the ratio of a vibrating string is expressed in the proportion of 1:2, a tuning, "the concord of the first and last strings" [*he dia pason chordon symphonia*—Damoxenus]. It cannot be without significance that *harmonia* was assigned by Pythagoreans to the simplest of the mathematical ratios, or that the octave expresses the most harmonious of all consonances. However, *harmonia* was dropped in the fourth century in favor of *dia pason*, "of the whole," and hence, *diapason*. In early Greek literature, *syllaba* meant "that which is held *together*," especially several letters taken together so as to form one sound, such as a syllable. Was Philolaus thinking of the tetrachord (literally, four strings) as a unit, or simply the fact that two tones are to be conceived as an entity in order to realize the audible space between them? *Syllaba* became a completely different word as well, *dia tessaron*, or the fourth. And *di' oxeian* originally meant "shrill" and "piercing." (See the numerous instances in the *Iliad*: 15.313; 17.89; 18.71, etc.) With specific reference to musical tones it meant high-pitched, as opposed to low-pitched. Again, Philolaus's term for the

interval of the fifth is something other than the concept of "fiveness"; *di'*
oxeian apparently was located in the higher register of the lyre. Thus it was
"shrill." In later Greek writings this term was dropped in favor of *dia pente*,
that is, the fifth.

When combined with the first half of fragment 6, this second section
comprises the longest authentic excerpt by Philolaus and contains the earliest
statement of the relationship between music and the cosmos. Since it is of
paramount importance to an understanding of the Pythagorean doctrine of
the "harmony of the spheres," we must examine it closely. Our next step is to
reconstruct the lyre upon which Philolaus could have made his observations.

The names of the strings indicate that Philolaus is speaking of a 7-string
lyre, with the outer strings tuned to an octave. There could be no "middle"
string on an 8-string lyre. For purposes of explanation we will use a scale
from e to e'.

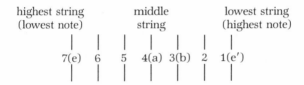

highest string	middle	lowest string
(lowest note)	string	(highest note)

7(e)   6   5   4(a) 3(b)   2   1(e')

From the highest string (physically, it was the string closest to the
player's body but the lowest sounding note on the lyre) to the middle string
is a perfect fourth (e–a); from the middle string to the lowest string (highest note) is a perfect fifth (a–e'). Next, Philolaus reverses the operation
because he has not yet separated the octave into two disjunct tetrachords;
from the lowest string (highest note) to the third string is a fourth (e'–b);
from the third to the highest string (lowest note) is a fifth (b–e). Last,
between the middle (a) and the third (b) strings is a whole-step. At the end
of the fragment Philolaus gives the size for each consonant interval in
whole- and half-steps; octave, fifth, and fourth. When the fourth ($2\frac{1}{2}$ steps)
is placed above the fifth ($3\frac{1}{2}$ steps) the result is a Dorian scale with diatonic
genus; but since Philolaus's lyre has no fingerboard, this complete scale
cannot be expressed on the seven strings.

e'	d'	c'	b	a	g	f	e
1	1	$\frac{1}{2}$	1	1	1	$\frac{1}{2}$	

It is clear that Philolaus is more interested in the derivation of the consonances from the expression of ratios between the first four integers than in
the construction of a particular scale; for the former, as we shall see, forms
the harmonic basis for his unique cosmology. This is further confirmed in
that the 8-string lyre was known from the early fifth century on, and
Philolaus could have used it had he been interested in the number eight as

a symbol of cosmic *harmonia,* but a point of clarification is in order. I do not mean to impose upon Philolaus thoughts which he may never have had, but we can supply some points of information about what he said within its own historical context. Philolaus is careful to position the two tetra-chords within the *harmonia;* he demonstrates the disjunct method of joining them, that is, with a whole-step between the two fourths. The way in which he states the sizes of the perfect intervals in the last sentence creates a problem. He seems merely to be "adding up" whole- and half-steps to determine the gross dimensions of the intervals in question. There was no Greek mode which was constructed of five whole-steps followed by two half-steps, and the statement about the octave appears to be one of simple addition. But there was a fourth and a fifth with the "additive" step sizes mentioned in the fragment—the ones in the Dorian mode as given above. Should we make a special note of the fact that Philolaus's scale reveals the *diatonic* genus of tetrachords instead of *enharmonic* or *chromatic* genera? And even these three genera of tetrachords represent only some of the many "shades" of interior scale formation mentioned later by Aristoxenus.

We assume from his and other writings that the ancient Greeks, like many European peoples, exhibited a rich repository of characteristic *meloi* with microtonal inflections of geographic and societal distribution. Philo-laus affords us no information as to the content of this modal consciousness other than what is implied in the passage about the Dorian mode. If he had, he would have been brought face to face with the conflict between the rationality of his system as secured through number and the expressive consciousness of men and women who were *already* tonal by nature of their interest and delight in sonic communication. This point must be kept in mind whether Philolaus addressed himself to it or not. In fact, the tedious state of affairs in which classical Greek music theory found itself by the time of Aristoxenus is precisely the conflict between a plethora of modal consciousnesses and an attempt to incorporate them within the discrete sphere of the numerical ratio. Human tonal production as a form of histori-cal consciousness that united many individuals was in fact an internal and subjective generality. It had to be externalized as a "configuration of con-sciousness" that was given both abstract and ethical authority through the power of number. Because the Greeks did develop and participate in this motion of spirit, they produced the first great age of music theory. Let us return to the cosmology of Philolaus.

Philolaus is concerned with the content of the *octave* as system. *Harmo-nia* here means more than just the octave ratio; it means as well the expression of the ratios 2:3 and 3:4 which fit within the octave as compo-nent lengths. The ratio of 1:2 defines the external limits of the octave, but the content of such *harmonia* is also the correct tuning of fourth and fifth located within it. "Fitted together" in a nonmusical sense of *harmonia*, these intervals constitute the whole operation as a musical tuning (also called a *harmonia*), symbolically contained in the prime vehicle of Pythagorean number consciousness, the tetractys of the decad. Not only does the sum of the first four integers 1, 2, 3, and 4 add up to ten, but the tetractys also expresses the musical ratios for the octave (1:2), the fifth (2:3), and the fourth (3:4). (See the second half of fragment 6.) The tetractys affords an audible spatialization of the number concept which the symbol visually represents; "the void divides their nature." Through the expression of the octave-system, the lyricist placed audible limits on the unlimited silence of the void; fixed between the actual pitches themselves was the prior unlimited and inaudible void from which articulate sounds were drawn forth into existence. Number is then *harmonia*, notes Burkert, "not only in a general way, as that which transcends the opposition of Limit and Unlimited, but even more so on the basis of the recognition that all musical intervals are determined by numerical ratios."[9] It is in this light that the tetractys became for Pythagoreans a symbol of the actual generation of the cosmos, and its power to reveal such proportion in universal design so awed them that they took their most solemn oaths by it.

It has been argued that the two parts of fragment 6 do not belong together; but the notion of *harmonia* is for Pythagoreans the basis of being (*esto*), and its significance is of no less importance even if the fragments represent isolated statements in Philolaus's "book" in the Pythagorean tradition. The meaning he wishes to express in the first instance is that meaning which he defines in the second, through a discussion of the tuning of musical pitches: the *harmonia* known to exist in the proportional tuning of music's very sonic material is a model of the principle of how the physical universe fits together as a whole, generated from the primal conditions of the Unlimited and the Limited.

We have laid the groundwork for the celebrated doctrine of the "harmony of the spheres." This Pythagorean belief states that "the whole heaven is a harmony and a number" (Aristotle, *Metaphysics* 986a), which follows from Philolaus; but virtually all descriptions of it in subsequent music theory have unwittingly assumed the accretions of post-Aristotelian commentaries as part of sixth-century Pythagorean philosophy. The doctrine is nowhere named "the harmony of spheres" by Philolaus; and, in fact, Burkert has pointed out that the poetic phrase is not justified by any of the other early sources. Before Eudoxus of Cnidus in the fourth century, when speaking of the cosmos, one spoke of bodies, wheels, rings, and circles in the heavens, but not, strictly speaking, of spheres.

The Myth of Er, related and embellished in the concluding chapter of the *Republic*, briefly suggests a cosmic harmony that testifies to Pythagorean influence on the late writings of Plato. "Perched above upon each of the circles is a Siren carried around along with it, singing one sound, one note, so that from all eight there was one accord."[10] That the note for each circle is provided by the singing Siren and not by the actual motion and velocity of the astral body itself is believed to be Plato's personal interpretation of the myth. In *De Caelo* (290b), Aristotle offers a more critical account of the Pythagorean celestial harmony. Because the planets are large and because they all move

> at a tremendous speed, it is incredible that they should fail to produce a noise of surpassing loudness. Taking this as their hypothesis, and also that the speeds of the stars, judged by their distances, are in the ratios of the musical consonances, they affirm that the sound of the stars as they revolve is concordant.

Aristotle is annoyed with the Pythagoreans for making assumptions which cannot be proved by direct observation, but he states fairly their position and the major objection to it. In response to the obvious question why the *harmonia* cannot be heard, the Pythagoreans, says Aristotle, accounted for it

> by saying that the sound is with us right from birth and has thus no contrast-ing silence to show it up; for voice and silence are perceived by contrast with each other, and so all mankind is undergoing an experience like that of a coppersmith, who becomes by long habit indifferent to the din around him.

Perhaps on this evidence Aristotle's pupil Eudemus credited the Pythago-reans as being the *first* astronomers to study the relative positions of the planets to each other within the cosmic system. The ratios of their relative distances were said to correspond not only to the musical consonances but to the notes of the complete octave scale as well, so that a perfect diatonic Greek mode sounded eternally throughout galactic space. This explanation was subsequently fixed into the historical tradition as fact and continued to elicit credence down through the Greco-Roman era. Not even the most severe of the ancient critics ever commented on the cacophony of a com-plete scale sounding simultaneously. Perhaps they did not think about it or were grateful that, according to tradition, only Pythagoras could hear it.

The fascination with seven or eight or ten celestial bodies strongly sug-gests to Burkert that "the idea of cosmic music is not bound to any particu-lar system. This concept has nothing to do with mathematical or musical theory, but comes from a deeper root; and this is why it was able to outlive even the Ptolemaic cosmology."[11] However, this does not vitiate the at-tempts of the astronomers to affix specific Greek music theory to observable and not so observable celestial phenomena. One such system was that of Philolaus, which was doomed to fail because he chose the number ten—as we might expect—to represent cosmic *harmonia*.

According to Aristotle and the doxographers, Philolaus believed that the cosmos contained at its center a central fire, which he called "the hearth of the universe" (B7). Closest to this center was the "counter-earth," followed by the earth itself, the moon, the sun, the five planets (Venus, Mercury, Mars, Jupiter, Saturn), and, last, the realm of the fixed stars. This unique system was neither geocentric nor heliocentric; the earth was merely one of the planetary bodies revolving around a fiery, invisible center. The counter-earth was so named because it lay exactly opposite the earth and was therefore never seen; the central fire was invisible for the same reason. Not without coincidence the number of celestial bodies totaled ten, which was also the sum of the tetractys. But the counter-earth was invented, complains Aristotle (*Metaphysics*, 986a), for that very reason, to bring the number up to ten. Thus, the Philolaic system is connected to the *harmonia* of the octave-system in that both are expressed by the sum of the first four integers.

There is no unassailable evidence to prove that the counter-earth theory was the invention of Pythagoras. It appears in the fifth century after various geocentric systems—albeit modest and simpler—had already been proposed. Pythagoras was undoubtedly aware of some of them. Detailed knowledge of the planets was introduced to Greece and Italy from Babylon sometime between Anaxagoras and Philolaus, but perhaps Pythagoras had acquired such knowledge in Egypt long before. A single reference in *Meteorologica* (342b) suggests that Aristotle knew of other "Pythagorean" systems which existed alongside the cosmology of Philolaus. Which of these was Pythagoras's own, if any, and exactly what it consisted of, is impossible to determine to anyone's satisfaction.

At any rate, the Philolaic system just described was short-lived. Plato, Aristotle, and Eudoxus placed the earth back in the center of the cosmos, and other Pythagorean philosophers supported geocentric theories (Ecphantus, for one; see Hippolytus, *Refutatio* I, 15); and the Philolaic cosmology aroused little interest among astronomers until Copernicus. Some Pythagoreans seemed to have had a penchant for cosmological systems which exhibit a kind of proto-science fiction. One Petron, a desert prophet from the Persian Gulf, who was not a Greek but apparently a Pythagorean, said there were 183 worlds arranged in a triangle;[12] and Hicetas of Syracuse maintained that everything in the universe stood still except the earth, "which by turning upon itself and rotating about its axis at high speed, produced the same effects as if the earth were stationary and the heavens in motion."[13]

There is good reason that other Pythagorean philosophers rejected the Philolaic cosmology and with it its own particular "Pythagorean" harmony of the spheres. Along with Aristotle, they refused to accept the counter-earth because it could not be seen; clearly it was invented to fill out a numerical scheme of ten celestial bodies. By the same token, the central fire around which the universe revolved was judged to be impracticable. A cosmological harmony based on this system, the equation of ten spheres with the consonances within the octave realized through the ratios expressed in the tetractys of the decad, was no longer useful. It became necessary to seek elsewhere for confirmation of the harmony of the spheres.

Post-Aristotelian Pythagoreans apparently preferred to connect their cosmological harmony of seven planets to the 7-string lyre, known from the time of the lyric poet Terpander in the seventh century. In bypassing Philolaus (and Plato) they reached back to a musical model which was as ancient as Pythagoras himself, an instrument which they felt was the one that Pythagoras might have used to explain the harmony of the spheres. Not even the advent of the later 8-string lyre, known at least by the early fifth century and which permitted a complete diatonic scale, tempted very many of them. Plato adopted it in the Myth of Er, but he had nothing at stake. Later Pythagoreans might have been uncertain that Pythagoras himself had equated the archaic Greek scale to the planets, but they correctly assumed that he had not used an 8-string lyre to do it.

Thus, subsequent Pythagorean explanations of the harmony of the spheres saved appearances by adjusting their number symbolism to more readily observable and acceptable cosmic schemes. They were aesthetically attractive, but when the chronology from Plato to the Greco-Roman philosophers is brought to bear upon them, the number symbolism expressed therein is Pythagorean only in that it seeks to reveal a cohesive Greek music theory that was consonant with accepted cosmologies. The assumption that the archaic Greek scale (with seven *or* eight tones) was a physical symbol of celestial order must be struck from the original Pythagorean tradition, for the evidence cannot be satisfactorily traced back to the school of Croton. When Plato states in his account of the Myth of Er that eight musical tones correspond to the eight planets, he is no doubt giving voice to popular notions about Pythagorean cosmology prevalent in fourth-century Athens. He also makes the statement within the context of myth, where he thinks number symbolism rightly belongs. What remains is the testimony of Aristotle and the Philolaic fragments.

Aristotle maintains as Pythagorean doctrine "that the speeds of the stars, judged by their distances, are in the ratios of the musical consonances," and the earliest ratios which can be attested as Pythagorean are those given by Philolaus in fragment 6, in which the mathematical properties of a vibrating string—the octave and the perfect intervals within it—are models of cosmological proportion. In this sense, the whole cosmos "is a harmony and number." Aristotle finds the system invalid because Pythagoreans (specifically Philolaus) collect only those facts which are consistent with the attributes of their system, and when there is a gap somewhere, "they readily made additions in order to make their whole system connected." He rejects the counterearth for two reasons: he cannot see it, and it was invented to preserve the numerology—as a symbolic relationship—which he finds useless in metaphysics. He has little to say about other "Pythagorean" cosmologies.

The doctrine of the harmony of the spheres handed down to the Middle Ages was essentially a loose aggregate of assumptions from the late Academy, subsumed into neo-Pythagoreanism of the first century A.D. The chief authority before Carolingian music theory was Boethius, who established new Latin terminology for the proportions and regarded *musica mundana*, the music of the spheres, as that perfection which the true musician should seek to reflect in his own music, as part of a vast celestial order. In the Renaissance, the music of the spheres drew forth its first critics—Johannes Tinctoris, Martin Agricola, and Vincenzo Galilei, the father of Galileo. But the doctrine was strongly supported by other theorists who upheld the Pythagorean notions of harmony and proportion; among them were Franchino Gaforio, mentioned earlier, Francisco Salinas, and Marin Mersenne, who nevertheless physically demonstrated the falsity of the "hammer discovery" whch had persisted for so many centuries. Perhaps Johannes Kepler is the last staunch supporter for the music of the spheres. Kepler's *De Harmonice Mundi*, published in 1619, which sets forth his famous third law of planetary motion, upholds the doctrine of the music of the spheres, which Kepler thought was heard only by the Being that animated the sun. While the idea of *harmonia* is a profound insight into the nature of number and the physical properties of audible phenomena, developed by the school of Croton and known to exist at least in the fifth century, through Philolaus, the particular notions of cosmic harmony which we hold dear as "Pythagorean" are as contestable as the fact that Pythagoras had a golden thigh or appeared in two places at the same time.

We might regard all of the above as an interesting piece of ancient music philosophy and consign it to Marx's dustbin of history were it not for the profound influence that Pythagorean philosophy played in the development of the tonal consciousness of the Latin theorists of the Middle Ages and the Renaissance, which was done through both veneration and misunderstanding of Boethius. In the remainder of this essay we shall turn our attention to this problem and concentrate on the transmission of Greek music theory in its most general aspects, its subsequent manipulation by the medieval theorists, and the particular manner in which this was accomplished through the authority of the Latin philosopher Boethius.

The position of Boethius in the shaping of medieval thought undergoes periodic evaluation. Some scholars feel that his importance has been "unduly stressed"; others judge Boethius as the father of modern music speculation, second not even to Augustine who preceded him.[14] Boethius did write two of the most important books of the Middle Ages, one of them while in his twenties, the other while awaiting execution at the hands of Theodoric the Ostrogoth whom he served; they testify to the remarkable intellect and catholic interests of a man who has often been called "the last of the Romans." His *De Institutione Musica*, an incomplete treatise in five books, was still a textbook at Oxford in the late eighteenth century. It is largely unread today; a complete English translation has been made only in the last few years.[15] The other book, *De Consolatione Philosophiae*, "was one of the two or three books of universal appeal throughout the Middle Ages."[16] While Boethius's treatises on logic and his commentaries were widely read by medieval monks and theologians, it was *The Consolation of Philosophy* that spoke directly of a kind of melancholy comfort and registered a resignation to divine providence that appealed to the men and women who suffered daily the risks and disasters of medieval life in Western Europe.[17] Alfred the Great (c. 890) translated this work into Anglo-Saxon; Notker Labeo (not the composer of sequences) made a translation into German at the turn of the millennium; both Chaucer and Elizabeth I translated it. Sixty-two Latin editions of it were printed before 1501.

Anicius Manlius Torquatus Severinus Boethius was born ca. 480 into a distinguished Italian family. His father was consul of Rome in 487 and twice prefect of the city. Orphaned at an early age, Boethius was raised by Symmachus, a leader of the Senate, whose daughter, Rusticiana, Boethius married. Perhaps he was educated in Athens. It is reported that as a young scholar he set for himself "the task of translating into Latin and commenting on all the works of Plato and Aristotle, with a view to a final harmonization of their teachings."[18] David Knowles believes that Boethius produced the following translations: the *Categories* (known as the *Isagoge*); the *Prior Analytics* and *Posterior Analytics*, the *Sophistic Arguments* and the *Topics* of Aristotle. But it is questionable, Knowles notes, "whether the Boethian translations are still extant among the various primitive translations that were supplanted by versions of Gerald of Cremona and others."[19] Boethius was carefully educated in the liberal arts. During his twenties he undertook a study of the disciplines of the quadrivium, and between 500 and 510 he wrote treatises on arithmetic, music, geometry, and perhaps astronomy.[20]

The substance of the medieval quadrivium was actually formulated by mathematicians during the age of Plato, and it was never doubted that arithmetic, geometry, music, and astronomy were proper disciplines for the education of the young in the Greek and Roman worlds. These subjects formed the *artes liberales*, the schooling of free Greek men who did not

have to earn their living by *techne banausike,* or craft. In the first century
B.C., Marcus Terentius Varro formulated the Roman view of the liberal arts
in his *Disciplinae* of nine books: they were grammar, dialectic, rhetoric,
geometry, arithmetic, astronomy, and music (the subsequent trivium and
quadrivium), in addition to medicine and architecture. Medicine and architecture were later dropped from the list of the liberal arts, and Varro's
classification become the model Roman preparation for each of the special
branches of learning—philosophy, medicine, or law.[21] Varro's *Disciplinae*
has been lost but its later influence on the medieval scholastics is certain.[22]

Boethius' own books on the quadrivium, however, are much more than
the popular "recipe" books by Latin authors on the various disciplines of the
artes liberales, which were quite common in the Roman world. His thrust is
markedly Platonic. Thus *De Institutione Musica* is not merely an *isagoge,*
that is, a general introduction for the student into the study of music, such
as we find in Isidore of Seville's compendious *Etymologie* of twenty books. It
is, rather, an "exhortation," a *protreptikos* to philosophy, "exhorting the
student to study music so that he can master that type of essence which
consists of harmoniously related quantity or multitude, contemplated and
judged by the reason alone."[23] The Platonic influence here is profound,
particularly the seventh chapter of the *Republic.* For Plato, the quadrivium
was not only an academic activity for free citizens. Its subjects were "hand-
maids and helpers" which, if properly contemplated, would release the soul
from the chains of perception, in an upward passage from an underground
of ignorance to the light of reason. They possessed a power for "stirring up
and bringing out the best in the soul to survey the best in things which
really are."[24] Or, in Boethius's words, the quadrivium was the *four-way*
path "by which one should come to those places where the more excellent
mind, having been delivered from our senses, is led to the certainty of
intelligence."[25]

Now the *exhortative* quality of *The Principles of Music* may or may not
have impressed the later medieval and Renaissance theorists, but through
Boethius's *De Institutione Musica* the transmission of Pythagorean *music
speculation* became the foundation of musical science and philosophy in
Western civilization for over a millennium. It was through this transmission
that the distinct mathematical conceptualization of music received an authoritative stamp that even today is only grudgingly relinquished. In short,
it was the authority of Boethius that sanctified the heritage of early Christian tonality that had for centuries ignored or had been largely unaware of
the relationship between the so-called fundamental properties of the *Klang*
and of number.

It is instructive here to mention the exact position of music within the
four disciplines of the quadrivium and the authority given to it through the

power of number. Magnitude *qua* number and considered in itself constitutes the subject matter of arithmetic. Magnitude *qua* number can also be applied to other things, that is, through the mental operation that sees relations *between* numbers, and this constitutes—among other things—the study of music. Magnitude spatially conceived without movement constitutes the study of geometry. And magnitude spatially conceived with movement constitutes the study of astronomy. Thus, music was one of the elect disciplines from which vantage point the true reality of its ontology, epistemology, and aesthetics was thought to unfold.

We cannot develop here or even trace all the ramifications of this marriage between sound and number, first developed by the Pythagoreans, later sanctioned by Greek philosophers in general, and rediscovered by the medieval theorists. (For example, there is the historical importance of numerical proportion in the aesthetics of medieval and Renaissance music.) But we do understand that through Boethius's *De Institutione Musica* there arose a tendency in medieval music that may accurately be called "the scientific method." When defining the general characteristics of Western music, perhaps this notion becomes our most distinctive attribute, as Walter Wiora has remarked:

> Western musical art was impregnated as no other by scholarly and, in the broad sense, scientific theory. In mensural rhythm, in the rules governing tonality, in harmony it was rationalized through and through. The seemingly irrational world of tone was laid down *imperio rationis*—under the command of reason, as was said following Boethius—in concepts and written signs. There took shape systems of relationship and forms of presentation, like the coordinating system of the score, metrical schemes using bar-line and time signature, and the well-tempered keyboard. More than anywhere else music was objective spirit and *scientia musica*.[26]

As is stated throughout these essays, no particular quarrel is to be sought with objective spirit and *scientia musica* other than to show their historical contradictions and limitations. In a historical sense, these limitations are not concerned with the ability of such a method to construct a sonic universe of reason and beauty. It did this perfectly well to nearly everybody's satisfaction. Its limitations lie rather in its inability to explain the causes behind tonal modeling in the first place. More particularly, *scientia musica* must be seen for what it actually did tonally, which was to give impetus to purely musical theories, those of intonation, of consonance and dissonance, of notation, and of modes and scales, around which the components of Western tonal art have orbited for many centuries. But the causes for tonality lie within the collective mentality of groups (both large and small) of people who, by already being tonal in specific senses, cognitively orient themselves within sonic potentiality. If this is so, and I believe that it is, then any claims for the "natural" foundations of tonality, à la Rameau and Schenker, et al., are destined to critique themselves (when they do) only upon their historical entry into tonal modeling already in progress and never at the threshold of tonal consciousness which these theorists have assumed as commensurate with their methods.

It is on this important point that the major portion of the musicological community founders, so perhaps it would be helpful to state it in still other terms. We may state that a given tonal system is secured by mathematical means. We may say that the whole of Western tonality has been historically guided by the mathematical concepts which we have brought to bear upon it. But we cannot also say that tonality is *natural* because it merely obeys or regards as authentic certain relationships and "laws" within the *Klang*, the sound as "given" in nature. This is a musical version of the philosophical concept called *physical determinism*. We should not be surprised to see physical determinism appear musically in the historical figure of Rameau (although of course it had antecedents). Until that time the whole approach to the study of nature had been largely philosophical and speculative, and was heavily influenced by Aristotle. In the seventeenth and eighteenth centuries, however, this tendency gradually gave way to deeper processes of observation and experiment and the methodical search for "natural laws." (These same developments are exactly paralleled in the history of political theory.) The best early example of physical determinism in a modern sense is the system of the English philosopher Thomas Hobbes (1588–1679). Musically, Rameau was a physical determinist; so was Heinrich Schenker. And regardless of what other methods of thought they use for their research and observation, when it comes to tonality, so are most current musicologists and music theorists. Since this book is an argument against the physical determinist view of tonality, it is unnecessary to discuss it further here except to point up a few consequences of its persistent application. It means that music, while known to be an artifice, a willful creation of man, had no choice but to become what it did. It means that tonality was destined in the physical order of sounds. And it also means that all the nations of the earth will become tonal in more or less the same fashion. Ignoring the influence of imperialism and the facts of a shrinking globe, it means that the Yamis of Orchid Island in the Western Pacific Ocean will eventually and inevitably produce their Ockeghem and their Mozart. Let us return to our examination of Boethius.

Despite the confusing testimony that Boethius's treatise is a translation of Pythagoras (who never wrote anything), the major sources for *De Institutione Musica* are the *Harmonics* of Ptolemy (the Alexandrine astronomer of the second century A.D.) and the *Manual of Harmonics* by Nicomachus of

Gerasa.[27] Nicomachus lived at the turn of the first century A.D. and was probably from the city east of the Jordan River in Syria.[28] Boethius supplemented these Hellenistic works by other theorists to whom credit is frequently given—Cicero, Albinus, Aristoxenus, Philolaus, Archytas, Eubulides, and Hippasus. The two main sources, Ptolemy and Nicomachus, reflect the curious state of affairs regarding the respective Pythagorean and Aristoxenian music theories of the Hellenistic age. Ptolemy had sensed their differences and attempted to reconcile them. Nicomachus conflated them, probably unwittingly. It is proper at least to suggest what the differences were, although we cannot pursue their long histories here.

Stated summarily, Pythagoreans were concerned with *harmonia* as an index of the properties of physical tone, from which devolved true music; Aristoxenians were concerned with *harmonia* as a compositional phenomenon, that is, with the erection of a system which would establish rules for what Greek composers actually did when they wrote music rather than with arguing for rules which those composers ought to be following because of their a priori truth, beauty, and simplicity. For Pythagoreans, the power of number to explain physical tone was translated into the power of number to dictate value in the musical image itself. This was the very notion that Aristoxenus sought to excise from the theory of music in the fourth century B.C.

What Pythagoras (or more properly, Pythagoreans) and Aristoxenus each sought to establish as true was indeed true. As Norman Cazden points out,

> Pythagoras correctly generalizes that standards for identifying harmonious agreement among musical tones are susceptible of numerical formulation. Aristoxenus correctly observes that this primitive level of the recognition of tones and their distances does not constitute the art of music, for music begins only when there is a musical system for the collocation of tones, and such a system is not given by external measurements but only by the ear of the musician nurtured in that system.[29]

But the different points of view of these two music theorists were conflated and promulgated by the earliest writers of the Christian era and from thence they disseminated into Renaissance Europe. To quote Cazden: "The natural law of consonance was taken not only to illuminate the secrets of the cosmos but also to control inexorably the particular procedures of musical art."[30] The need for metaphysical justification of music gradually fashioned common practice in such a way that, subtly and quite unconsciously, the Pythagorean tenet of the music of the spheres was actually orchestrated only on earth.

The literary fate of Aristoxenus's *Harmonics* is a many-faceted story with chapters still to be written, but it parallels the confusion with which subsequent theorists interpreted his central thesis. While his other philosophical and musical works were lost during the Hellenistic era, the *Harmonics* found its way to Egypt, to Rome, eventually to medieval Europe and the Near East. We can only trace a few of these complex threads. As Isobel Henderson suggests, ancient writers of manuals on technical subjects tended "whether for piety or fraud," to lend credibility to their subject matter by assuming the pseudonym of an appropriate authority. To such practice we owe spurious treatises by the physician Galen, and surely Aristoxenus did not actually write all 453 books ascribed to his name. Hack theorists disseminated a mixture of Aristoxenian theory, casually mixed with their own speculations, until Aristoxenus was ultimately made to support the very idea he sought to defeat—the principles of pitch measurement according to atomic microtones and the authoritative basis of Pythagorean number proportions. In this light it is difficult to ascertain what direction a given theorist of the early medieval period might have taken then, had he had before him an uncontaminated copy of the *Harmonics*. We have no idea what copy of the *Harmonics* Boethius used.

We must mention a few facts about Ptolemy. The most gifted theorist between Aristoxenus and Boethius was the astronomer and geographer Ptolemy in Alexandria in the second century A.D. History has not been overly kind to him, perhaps because he crystallized a cosmological error of the geocentric system under which Europe incorrectly assumed its position in the universe for over a millenium. Ptolemy's *Harmonics* has been totally ignored by all but a mere handful of scholars. J. F. Mountford read it carefully enough to declare it "the most scientific and best arranged treatise on the theory of musical scales that we possess in Greek." But after seventeen centuries it still exists only in Greek, Latin, and German. While he was critical of Aristoxenus's system of thirteen keys, Ptolemy's sensitivity to the Aristoxenian thesis of theory-as-system led him to state in book II of his own *Harmonics* that the sounds in the two-octave Greater Perfect System "are sometimes named after their position (*thetic*), i.e. in respect to their higher or lower situation. But sometimes we name them according to their relative significance or function (*dynamic*)."[31] But the Latin theorists, including the first of them, Boethius, did not see any marked opposition between the systems of Aristoxenian and Pythagorean philosophy; or, to those who did see it, Ptolemy appeared to reconcile them so effectively that no further worry about their differences was deemed necessary.

All this is to say that the later medieval theorists after Boethius looked beyond him into the past and saw there a long chain of Greek thinkers whose authority they both respected and revered. The transmission of Greek music theory through Boethius proved to be a mistake for the historical conceptualization of tonal consciousness, but the Latin theorists did not understand it as such. Moreover, Boethius himself is not to be blamed for what they inferred from his *De Institutione Musica*. I am of course referring to the long-held belief that the Latin modes were the progeny of the ancient Greek modes.

The discussion of the Greek modes, upon which subsequent Latin theory would become shipwrecked, is found beginning in chapter 15 of book IV of Boethius's treatise.

> Therefore the elements of music called "modes" are made from these species of the diapason consonance; but they are also called "tropes" or "tones." Moreover the systems of the tropes are in the total series of notes, and they are different according to their lowness and highness. . . . But if someone should move these total systems up or down in pitch according to the species of the diapason consonance discussed above, then he would make the seven modes. The names of these modes are as follows: hypodorian, hypophrygian, hypolydian, dorian, phrygian, lydian, mixolydian.[32]

The terms *tropus, modus,* and *tonus* are of such great importance to the tonal consciousness of the medieval theorists that I am forced to set them aside here for some future discussion of what they meant to the evolution of tonality. All that can be said for the moment is that for a long time the Latin theorists used them interchangeably. It cannot be said of this passage, however, that the term *mode* refers in any way to the ecclesiastical modes of medieval chant. Calvin Bower explains that

> Boethius is literally translating the Greek word *tropus* into the Latin word *modus*. The words *tropus* and *tonus*, which modes "are also called," are merely Latin transliterations of the Greek words *tropus* and *tonus*. Boethius is *not* confusing the diapason or octave species, the medieval and modern "modes," with the Greek tropes. He does not say that the modes "are" the species of the diapason, but rather they "are made from" or more literally "exist from" the species of the diapason consonance (*Ex diapason consonantiae specibus existunt qui appelantur modi*). This idea is taken from Ptolemy. . . .[33]

But if Boethius had even sought to make one, the distinction was too subtle. To the later medieval theorists the quoted passage looked like a clear reference to the existence of the church modes in ancient Greek music. Boethius unwittingly secured this connection further by adding an eighth mode to the previously mentioned seven. He did this purely for reasons of completeness. Here is the passage:

The reason for the addition of an eighth mode—the hypermixolydian—becomes evident in the following. Assume the following bisdiapason consonance:

A B C D E F G H I K L M N O P

A:H contains a diapason consonance, for it consists of eight notes. Thus we said that this is the first species of the diapason. The second is B:I; the third, C:K; the fourth, D:L; the fifth, E:M; the sixth, F:N; the seventh, G:O. Therefore there still remains H:P, and since it completes the total series, it is added to the others. This then is the eighth mode, which Ptolemy added to the top.[34]

Now Ptolemy *had* stated the possibility of an eighth mode, hypermixolydian by name, which could be added to the top, and he even discussed it in terms of letter notation. But he rejected this mode because it was "harmonically identical" with the first mode.[35]

From the standpoint of Boethius's text, however, an assumed scheme of eight scales attributed to the Greeks was ready for incorporation into the Latin theoretical canon of eight modes. It does not greatly matter exactly when this happened. It may be said to be implied in Aurelian of Rome's *Musica Disciplina* of the ninth century; it is directly stated in the *Alia Musica*, begun by an anonymous theorist soon thereafter. One of its several authors misinterprets Boethius and names his own modes by the old Greek names. The order in which he names them *is reversed* from that of the Greek octave-species. but even if this reversal had been corrected it would not have solved the larger problem of erroneously equating Greek octave-species with the church modes. Gustave Reese notes that another author of this treatise, "in commenting upon the passage ostensibly on the modi attributed to Ptolemy, merges the formulas and the scales and thus, for the first time, ascribes modal functions to degrees with octave-species. This is the beginning, in the medieval tracts, of the theory of the church modes as we ordinarily think of it today."[36]

This misinterpretation of Greek theory marks an important moment in the historical evolution of modern music theory. It initiates in the West the critical merger of mode and scale. That is, the societal repository of geographical mode types, derived from the characteristic features of a given melos as habitual melodic patterns, were brought under the leveling tendency of mathematical precision, thereby objectifying their substance. This had happened of course in ancient Greek theory during the time of Socrates, Plato, and Aristotle, perhaps even before. But to Christianity it was a new operation of the *ratio*, and this objectification of tonal substance marks the beginning of the tendency in medieval music theory (*medieval* meaning from Alcuin in the eighth century on) toward the aforementioned "scientific method." This rationalization of the sonic matter of music was as important to the tonality of Western culture as it was one-dimensional.

In summary, it cannot be said that Boethius had any particular vision in mind for the music of his own era, pre-Gregorian Latin chant. There is no hard evidence that he saw its practice as ultimately secured by an interpretation and evaluation of Greek theoretical concepts, and he differs in this from the later theorists. Like Plato, he felt the study of music to be a means only to higher and more important truths. But as an early Latin Christian he stood in a position of authority for theorists from the ninth century onward, not many of whom would have been able to read Greek even had the sources been available to them. Without Boethius medieval and Renaissance music theory would have been considerably different. We find him quoted in the Ars Antiqua by such writers as Jerome of Moravia and Walter Odington. Franco of Cologne compared Boethius's authority on music theory analogous to Gregory's authority on chant practice. Jacob of Liège drew heavily upon him for his *Speculum Musicae*. In the fifteenth century his musical mathematics was applied to the problems of musical rhythm by such theorists as Prosodocimus de Beldemandis, Guilelmus Monachus, Johannes Tinctoris, and Franchino Gaforio. The Boethian heritage was even continued in the Late Renaissance, when theorists (Pietro Aron, Heinrich Glareanus, Nicola Vincentio, Gioseffo Zarlino, and Francisco Salinas) were no longer dependent upon Latin translations of Greek theory. And in the seventeenth and eighteenth centuries music theory proceeded from basic inductions of sense perception using mathematical axioms to arrive at the numerical essences of each successive proof.[37] Promulgated by Rameau, tonality "as it really is" is the direct consequence of the faith in Pythagorean musical order brought to the modern world under the aegis of the "last of the Romans," who in all probability had hoped for something else.

Perhaps Boethius would even have considered any such practical applications as these historical ones as a contamination of his intent, which was to achieve "the more excellent mind," delivered from the senses and led to the certainty of divine intelligence. Recall that music in Rome of the sixth century formed a part of the liberal arts, the curriculum of free citizens, who did not study music in order to become professional musicians. A knowledge of music theory was considered a part of one's education in much the same way that biology or mathematics or social studies is part of the intellectual baggage that characterizes the education of the graduate of the modern university system. When Boethius does refer to music as a form of present experience, it is within the framework of a philosophical gesture. But if he sought no particular pragmatic application of what he understood, those who later read him certainly did.

5 The Origins of
Polyphony Reconsidered

T he practice of making music with two or more simultaneous sounds is
perhaps one of the great testimonies to the human struggle against
boredom. It renders music tonal in such a characteristic fashion that harmony is viewed as one of the most striking features of Western music. But if
we may trust Carl Stumpf's long-established observations regarding fusion
theory that 75% of the time nonmusicians do not know that they are
singing in octaves and that 50% of the time they also mistake the musical
interval of the fifth for a unison, then it is also proper to say by way of
introduction that polyphony is as much the result of a cognitive deficiency
as it is the result of any theoretical speculation upon its possibility. While
polyphony is commonly thought of as music "that combines several simultaneous voice-parts of individual design, in contrast to monophonic music,
which consists of a single melody, or homophonic music, which combines
several voice-parts of similar, rhythmically identical design,"[1] we soon discover that this definition itself is complex and ambiguous. For instance, if
homophony can be characterized by music which combines several voice-
parts of similar, rhythmically identical design, then the strict organum
described and notated in the ninth-century *Musica Enchiriadis*—which is
the earliest theoretical treatise that clearly demonstrates the principles of
polyphony—should be called *homophonic*, a term that is not very helpful
when discussing the music under scrutiny. Clearly, there are differences
other than rhythm that must be held accountable for the distinct nature of
polyphonic and homophonic music practices.

In fact, to use the term *combine* for the phenomenon we are about to examine exhibits a highly rational and post factum attitude that fails historically to illuminate the actual appearance of simultaneous sound in music. One "combines" elements that are seen as different but which are brought together to form some kind of unity. It is unlikely that any such judgment accompanied the sonic appearance of early polyphonic singing in Western practice or that any such underlies the polyphony of many contemporary nonliterate societies.

It is not necessary to determine exactly when polyphony entered Western music, although it is useful here to state the current notion held by academic musicology. The major portion of the English-speaking community, remarks Ross Ellison, seems "to assume that early Christian polyphony first developed within the context of the Church itself,"[2] starting sometime in the ninth century. The current evidence of folk polyphony in nonliterate societies is quietly shunted over to the department of ethnomusicology, whose members are supposed to exhibit the proper scientific attitudes toward it. However, there are a few scholars who have searched for an alternative to the much-honored ninth-century appearance theory. They have gathered a small group of data that is generally regarded as reliable because of the evidence from reports and field recordings of nonliterate societies. Icelandic "twin-song," Welsh canonic rounds, two-part singing in northern England, Georgian folk polyphony, and canons sung by "primitive" tribes—these phenomena so greatly weaken the ninth-century invention theory of polyphony that we are forced to regard it not as a beginning of polyphony at all but as a "first culmination" of a development whose origin is permitted to exist anywhere (for example, Oriental or primitive music) as long as it does not get in the way of the historical musicologist.

In short, the general agreement among the major portion of musicologists that "there is no scientific evidence proving polyphonic practice before the ninth century"[3] is due to their positivistic inability or refusal to think about music when there is no score in front of them. In addition, what they offer as theories of origin for polyphonic consciousness has not advanced beyond even the most obvious of speculations. Furthermore, nobody is willing to place very much faith in these theories because even taken as a whole they are tentative and inconclusive. Let us quickly review them here.

Traditionally, the origin of polyphonic music has been explained as the outgrowth of the theoretical speculation on its possibility. We may call this the *boredom theory*. Medieval singers simply became weary of their monophonic melodies and to their delight found that they could sing them simultaneously at different intervals, hence the parallel organum of the ninth century. Second, there is the natural division of tessituras among human voices. We may call this the *placement theory*, which is usually shored up with some unavoidable facts concerning the physiology of the human vocal apparatus and the additional feature of cognitive disability. When men and women sing together they must do so in octaves, which has a venerable tradition, called magadizing, dating back to the ancient Greeks. There is the possibility that the early Christian church continued this practice in its singing schools in Rome and elsewhere when boys and men together sang ostensibly monophonic Latin chant. For some scholars it seems a small step to assume a development from the singing of a melody in octaves to singing it at the interval of the fifth and hence at any other interval within reason. The fifth and the fourth do gain some credibility as possible intervals in the placement theory, since tenors and baritones, for instance, have normal tessituras that lie approximately this distance apart from one another. And finally there is the problem of inattention to pitch or a tone-deaf singer. We may call this the *accident theory*, which is assumed to have been formalized through constant repetition and perhaps a personal stubborn delight in deviating from the monophonic regimen of the melos. This accidental harmony, or *heterophony* as it frequently is called, gains credence as a kind of peripheral consciousness of those who did not take their music seriously.

These three theories are, of course, interrelated and need not, indeed should not, be isolated as single causes for polyphonic consciousness. But it seems to me that we have failed through lack of imagination and observation to gain a better insight into the origin of our polyphonic consciousness. The fact is that the "birth" of polyphony is daily available for audible examination, but we do not hear it.

As I shall demonstrate shortly, I think that the answer to the problem of the origin of polyphony *does* lie in its heterophonic appearance, if we attribute to that concept the cognitive processes which it actually does imply. Plato first used the term *heterophony* in the *Laws* (812d) to describe a musical practice that was not quite or not yet monophonic. Among modern musicologists, heterophony was first used by Stumpf "to describe an improvisational type of polyphony, namely, the simultaneous use of slightly or elaborately modified versions of the same melody by two (or more) performers, e.g., a singer and an instrumentalist adding a few extra tones or ornaments to the singer's melody."[4] This definition, however, is weighted in favor of a type of heterophony which may or may not occur much in actual practice.

Clearly, we must first decide if heterophony is an accidental or an intended act. The fact that we describe it as "an improvisation," as a "simultaneous use," as "slightly or elaborately modified," and as "adding a few extra tones or ornaments" is clear indication that opinion is weighted on the side of some kind of mental and self-conscious operation. One does not improve, use, modify, and add through total ignorance. These terms simply do not add up to an accident. I think that we are guilty here of oversight on a fundamental point. Heterophony is poorly defined as "accidental harmony," because the phrase is so simplistic that it tends to discourage thought before it ever gets started. The point is that heterophony is so vacuous a term that it can easily be shaped to mean anything one wishes. Thus we must view its use by Stumpf, Guido Adler, and Curt Sachs as historical rather than ontic, for whom heterophony came "to mean the unison ornamented by a second voice, and thus a melodic variation of the main voice by the second. Sachs has glossed the term with the phrase 'that kind of simultaneous tone production that occurs on the basis of tradition and improvisation.' "[5] This latter is an interesting remark, but when carefully considered it opens a series of questions about polyphony for which there are no immediate answers. What is the nature of tradition, polyphonically speaking? To what extent is it consciously articulated? Similarly, to what extent does improvisation account for polyphonic appearance, and when does improvisation become so fixed as a societal norm that it cannot be omitted in any adequate account for a given musical expression? And finally, does ethnomusicology hold the key to our own polyphonic consciousness, or is there some other phenomenon that will reveal it to us?

We may begin our investigation by realizing that heterophony can be reduced neither to an accident nor to an occasional or frequent improvisation. The reason lies in the nature of accident itself. Heterophony is not an accident any more than the pre-speech of infants is an accident. Both are *events* of the utmost cognitive importance, which critically reveal how linguistic and monophonic consciousnesses are respectively taught and enforced as societal values. Consequently, as a sonic phenomenon, heterophony might better be posited *before* monophony rather than *between* monophony and polyphony, where we have customarily posited it both tacitly and openly, that is, as a kind of halfway house between two historical stages in Western music. Although it will have to be proved, I recommend this positioning of heterophonic musical expression simply because that is where it falls in the consciousness of the singing human being.

I would like now to put the origin of polyphony in its proper evolutionary *and* cognitive context. Just as the pre-speech of infants and small children precedes their membership in the community of language users, so polyphony is grounded in an early childhood activity of pre-monophonic consciousness which is gradually but decisively repressed in favor of singing melodies in unison. Anyone who has ever listened to children sing knows this to be true. When young children sing or attempt to sing a unison melody, they fail for the same reasons that their speech is not exactly like that of their parents. They have not yet learned to discriminate all the acceptable sounds of adult linguistic behavior. The imitate and they approximate; through practice, observation, encouragement, and correction they learn gradually to produce the phonetic material of their family, tribe, clan, state, and nation. So they do with music. Monophonic consciousness is *developed* in children; it does not just appear like their first molar teeth at about six years of age. Perhaps the relating of a personal experience is in order here, although the phenomenon to be described can be experienced wherever young children sing.

Several years ago I attended some professional meetings in Toronto. In the bustle of a Saturday morning while packing and leaving my hotel, I turned on the television set. For some minutes I watched a Canadian version of "Sesame Street." On this particular day some children were learning a new song. Apparently some of them had begun to learn the song the day or several days before. They formed the core of young singers who "knew" the song, or so the program's host said. But musical abilities being what they are in the very young, some "knew" it better than others who remembered only scraps of melodic phrases and words. That is, the establishment of the song's intended melodic line was still very much in jeopardy. One little girl vigorously sang along in what occasionally could be called an augmented fourth, but even this interval faded in and out of what amounted to an organum of a random species of parallel intervals most of which have yet to be recognized in Western music theory books. Children also sang who had not heard the song before. Their performance was even more erratic in terms of an ostensibly desired unison performance. Some wavered around certain notes, swooping up and down through the melos as they heard—always too late—the contour of the song unfold in their presence. And others simply produced a sing-song pattern of repeated pitches modulating up and down in a narrow compass of notes: whatever they were doing fit their own private and untutored notions of singing and not speaking. In addition, there was no general agreement as to the precise length of phrases. Some children simply sang through the phrase endings, breathing when they ran out of breath, and rushing the next group of words in order to catch up.

This tuneful disaster merits our serious consideration, for in it lie the natural origins of our polyphonic tradition. Children are not born with a monophonic consciousness. It is a societal value that is taught, just as speaking French and toilet training are taught—with a system of rewards and punishments. They are gradually educated out of their uncritical ur-polyphony as they are taught to sing. The random-fourth singer is told that she "is not doing it right"; she is told "to listen." If ultimately she cannot be trained to match pitches, she is judged tone-deaf and is sent off to art class where, it is to be hoped, she will not insist on drawing feathers on all her pictures of dogs and cats.

What I have described here is, of course, Stumpf's fusion theory in poly-phonic dress, that is, the tendency for judging two pitches as one. Societies have not been successful in evicting this phenomenon from the consciousness of their singers; nor have they tried. In fact, there is reason to assume that the pre-monophonic singing of children, their unreflected ur-polyphony, is the developmental model for the manner in which societies around the world gradually became predominately—but certainly not exclusively—mono-phonically conscious. Except for the music of children, we cannot observe this ur-polyphony in its embryonic state, but it nevertheless merits considera-tion as a process of sonic consciousness which ought to be viewed as a cognitive stage *before* monophony and not *after* it, as we have been led to believe. That historical notion is wrong which assumes that monophony came first, and was then followed by some accidental heterophonic stirrings that were ultimately rigidified and crystallized in the early polyphony of the ninth century in France. It was not a short step from this ur-polyphony to consciously tuned polyphony: it was a very long evolutionary one that enjoyed particular developments in particular societies, each of which created and re-created its own expressive elements that bear some resemblance to one another, owing perhaps to the placement theory mentioned above. It seems logical to assume that primitive man exercised little or no discrimination in the pitches he used when singing or that it very much mattered that he sang in unison with his fellows. But as the collective consciousness of the tribe shaped his individual expression linguistically, so also did it determine the monophonic *and* the polyphonic consciousness of his music. It is not neces-sary, therefore, to posit this ur-polyphony as a thing that had always to be extracted and removed from the societal expression of all primitive culture. There are numerous societies that have developed the ur-polyphonic ele-ments of their musical communication into successful polyphonic expression in addition to and in conjunction with the development of a monophonic expression. This is not a mandate for all cultures, but unless we allow it as a possibility from some, we are forced to accept the rather curious notion that all societies of the world which have polyphony received their impetus for that expression from a central appearance of polyphony that they imported directly or indirectly from medieval France sometime after the ninth century.

Certainly it is time that we espoused a multiple appearance of polyphony in world musics, one which is in accordance with the abundant evidence of ethnomusicological research.[6] Moreover, we can focus our investigation more clearly on its true nature by using a different term than did Plato, who was hostile rather than sympathetic to its presence in his society. Like heterophony, ur-polyphony also tends to affirm an inferior status for a phenomenon that can no longer be treated as primitive, untutored, or yearning for culmination in some future perfected state. A far superior term for the whole of this polyphonic consciousness is *variative polyphony*, a term and a concept developed by the Hungarian musicologist János Maróthy.[7] Variative polyphony does not mean the same thing as hetero-phony, which, as we have seen, has been historically mutilated to serve particular needs. Variative polyphony reflects the constant reworking of musical material that ethnomusicologists have discovered is characteristic of much of the communal re-creation of music in primitive societies, not all of which is conscious and very little of which is ever articulated in terms of public compositional norms, although it may be tacitly assumed as an expressive, social value. Maróthy sees variative polyphony as an ever-vital process in collective creativity and posits polyphony in the form of hetero-phonic thinking as simply (but very importantly) a part of collective-varia-tive performance within primitive communities, which landed sometime near the ninth century on the European soil of serf-peasant and proto-bour-geois development towards songlike thinking.

The significance of variative polyphony is that it restores and preserves the consciousness of polyphony, which may be practiced unknowingly by societies around the world. On the other hand, while unarticulated, varia-tive polyphony may be conscious to the degree that it is regarded as an authentic method of making music even though it exhibits no theoretical canons—scientific or otherwise—to support its activity. The important thing is that variative polyphony is grounded in actual cognitive life: that is, a society could have begun such a practice in ignorance (which is not an accident); later, through gradually deepened awareness and long stages of development, it could have formalized what it discovered itself to be doing via "tradition and improvisation."

With this cognitive orientation and variative polyphony we are thus able cogently to explain the various states of polyphonic consciousness that we find in different societies around the world—including in retrospect the polyphony of medieval Europe in the first ten centuries of the modern era, whose sounds have long since vanished. The assumedly tone-deaf little girl from Canada demonstrates more truth about our polyphonic evolution than we might expect. If the random fourth singer were never corrected, if there existed no societal value that imposed conformity to a norm, or if that value was itself a consciousness that took centuries to develop, what direction might her singing take? In a society of predominately unison singers she eventually might hear the difference between her performance and theirs and adjust to the norm. But if no value were placed on unison singing, if it were as random as intervallic singing, the cognitive operation necessary to distinguish intervals would tend to lie dormant and unnoticed. This is to say that a unison melos as a societal value is accompanied by a concomi-tant demand for the operation of a cognitive ability to secure it. If fusion theory has any validity at all, it would seem that the development of a consciousness of monophony and polyphony was gradual, regional, and societal, and that it was accompanied by appropriate values that encouraged the operation of cognitive abilities to secure these quite different forms of musical activity. Thus ethnomusicologists have discovered polyphony arrested in various degrees or stages of development in particular societies. In some musics variative polyphony is an integral part of the sonic expression of the tribe; in others it is randomly present and little or no thought is given to it. There is no absolute goal in the development of this polyphony; it will not necessarily culminate in the early polyphony of the ninth century any more than a nonliterate language in the middle of Africa will of necessity ultimately transform itself into Ukrainian.

We are now in a position to examine early polyphony in Western music in a more critical fashion than we have in the recent past. What the ninth-century Latin theorists wrote about in their treatises was not a phenomenon that they created *ex nihilo* because of boredom, although they certainly are to be credited with the first rational attempts to articulate its particular musical features. I would like to suggest some of the errors and wrong attitudes that have prevented an adequate assessment of the actual state of affairs in the ninth century in France, which we have customarily designated as "the birth of polyphony."

The musicologist is not accustomed to think about his discipline in broad, encompassing terms, that is, by millennia, and his knowledge of the cognitive operations by which music is sustained as an ongoing mental activity is virtually nonexistent. Considering the academic training that he receives, this is not surprising, but his myopia too often prevents him from seeing the proper cognitive and societal solutions to his problems. His first error is to attempt to treat the development of monophonic consciousness as totally separate from polyphonic consciousness. Indeed, the development of Christian music for nearly a thousand years seems to be a great flowering of monophonic consciousness; but we cannot argue from this knowledge that there was no polyphony during the same long centuries. Suppose ethnomusicologists took the same stance today. They too can say that the primitive musics of Africa and elsewhere seem to indicate a great flowering of monophonic consciousness. Should they then ignore all polyphonic expression because it is much less abundant? But because we do take this attitude about the monophonic era in Western Europe, we are quite confused by those few reports that we have of polyphonic activity during the centuries of Boethius, Augustine, Isidore, and Scotus Erigena—so much so that we usually interpret their remarks as "they aren't really talking about what they seem to be talking about." In this fashion we keep the monophonic era scrubbed clean of contamination from any polyphonic leaven.

This attitude is even reversed, so as to question the "purity" of primitive cultures which do have polyphony but which are not to be trusted because of alleged acculturation. Lincoln Spiess suggested some twenty years ago that "it does seem that during the one thousand years that polyphony has definitely known to have been in existence (exclusive of the heterophony of classical antiquity) some influence, however indirect, may have reached . . . aboriginal nations and tribes."[8] This impurity would thus vitiate the attempt to set up primitive polyphonies as models for any sort of comparative evolutionary consciousness. But the amount of evidence from current ethnomusicology indicates that the problem at hand is much more complex. Spiess's reservation seems ultimately to stem not from any genuine critique of the purity of primitive polyphony but from a last-ditch effort to safeguard a purity for the great monophonic era of Latin chant which it may never have possessed historically and certainly never claimed. We may assume that, despite the distinctly monophonic melos that Christianity developed via Judaism, it is no longer necessary to require a total monophonic consciousness in Christian music—neither in its early centuries in the Near East nor in the subsequent advancement of its interests in medieval Europe.

An example of this divide and conquer technique can be found in Karl H. Worner's history of music, in which there is a brief treatment of non-European polyphony.

> We may distinguish several types of non-European polyphony, for there are many different ways in which tones may sound together: in heterophony, in parallelism, in imitation of each other, with one voice serving as a drone or ostinato, and with all voices combining in accordance with primary forms of sonority.[9]

This paragraph has all the appearance of scholarly care, but its author has been seduced by his rage for categories. Not only is monophony cleanly separated from polyphony, there are now five categories for the latter, so that their connections with monophonic consciousness are even further separated from any important relationship to it. Worner's intent becomes clear as he describes his data. For instance, he notes that "still another type of non-European polyphony occurs when voices imitate each other in the course of antiphonal singing. The result may be an overlapping between two choruses or between the leader and the chorus, which produced *true* polyphony."[10] Once again, to be simultaneously polyphonic and anything but European is regarded as some sort of sonic misfortune that can be cured only by becoming properly clothed, educated, and bourgeois.

The musicologist's second error is closely linked to his first one: by separating monophonic from polyphonic consciousness he facilitates the process of an embedded positivistic development demanded by his a priori belief in historical progress in music. In polyphonic terms, perhaps the most curious of these chains is that propounded by Marius Schneider in his *Geschichte der Mehrstimmigkeit* some years ago. The thrust of Schneider's thesis is a kind of comparative musicology with a good deal of slippage due to his own a priori prejudices. He divided primitive music into four spheres of cultures, "according to the music idiosyncrasies of the various races and the complexity of their polyphony, ranging from the most primitive sphere comprising music of southern Asiatic and South American tribes to the comparatively highly developed sphere represented by the music of certain African tribes."[11] This is not to say that primitive music as such influenced medieval polyphony, but rather that there are evolutionary stages through which polyphonic consciousness must somehow pass. Spiess tells us: "According to Schneider, the organum of the ninth century is the culmination of a development in which aboriginal polyphony (such as, for instance, still exists today in certain parts of Africa) is the earliest stage, and in which Greek heterophony was an intermediate development."[12] Here the musicologist's most seductive tempter wins again: all musical change must be demonstrable in terms of early, middle, and late stages. Schneider's particular evolutionary path is hopeless. As models, he first sets up "primitive" polyphony, which may or may not be conscious behavior and which is accompanied by few, if any, theoretical canons or articulated aesthetic attitudes, although it is carried out in practice much to the satisfaction of all. This is followed by a heterophony characterized in ancient Greece—if we can believe Plato—as something that rational people (professional musicians) wanted to do but were told they should not because it was bad for them and their society. I might also add that we know virtually nothing about this "model" nor the cognitive operations that produced it. And the "culmination" in the ninth century is a type of polyphony that could be used only if it was willing to bear the burden of a historical melos of great age (Latin chant), although probably no polyphony that had ever existed before it had been required to perform such a heavy task. The point is that we may not erect discrete and tidy categories of polyphonic consciousness—which we then wrench into evolutionary chains of development—at the expense of the cognitive abilities and disabilities or the societal norms and values that brought them into existence.

The problem with our approach to early polyphony and its origins is ultimately betrayed by the invidious vocabulary we use to describe it. A "first culmination" of polyphony leads automatically forward and lends even greater respectability to the second culmination (I assume it would be the sixteenth century) and to any subsequent era we might decide to offer to the unwary as indicative of the progressive march of polyphonic consciousness. Because of their complexity, I cannot set forth here what steps are necessary to escape from this trap, but if the reader assumes that they are anything less than radical, he has been misguided. Instead, I conclude with a brief examination of two attitudes (totally unreflective in substance and widely separated in time) that more than anything I have stated above demonstrate quite adequately the reason that we have yet to realize the true nature of our polyphonic consciousness—in any era.

It is not difficult to interpret negatively the reports of polyphony by early medieval theorists and philosophers: their own attitudes were negative. Beginning with Plato, educated opinion held polyphony in the form of heterophony as something to be extracted from a monophonic melos. Plato thought that the laws of a just city ought to do something to secure monophony against the deliberate and not so deliberate intrusion of heterophonic elements upon the music of its citizens. And much later, while the Church was eventually to develop the art of polyphony in remarkable fashion, its initial reaction to the practice was not entirely positive. As Gustave Reese and others have noticed, "the author of the *Musica Enchiriadis*, in fact, seems to apologize slightly for its presence there, when, at the end of his treatise, he says he has just discussed 'a kind of surface (*superficies*) of musical science intended for the decoration of the ecclesiastical chants.' "[13] Considering the Church's gradually intensified authoritative control over its melos, this is only logical. If polyphony existed already in the musics of medieval Europe, as I believe that it did, then the Church's initial attitude toward it could only have been one of decoration upon a melos that had developed quite nicely without it. Polyphony could not have been regarded as something vitally important to—but lacking in—divinely inspired chant. As with the ecclesiastical modes themselves, the first clear mention of polyphony in liturgical practice is not to be construed as the invention of polyphony; it is rather an early (and surely not the earliest) attempt to comprehend a practice already present in the melos of a secular consciousness that the Church was in the process of evangelizing. This practice was accompanied by few or no theoretical canons, aesthetic attitudes, or performance norms. We have a tendency as music theorists and musicologists to assume that because we carefully quantify a musical phenomenon, it is thereby readily understood as a cognitive process in the ears of all who hear and that it can be accurately reproduced upon demand. This is not so. As anyone who has examined the results of his efforts to teach music appreciation courses to large groups of nonmusical students will be forced to admit, the major portion of the people, at least in this nation, live out their entire lives without being able to distinguish major from minor. This simple musical ability is an unimportant cognitive operation and only a societal value (in the form of a liberal education) brings it to the foreground of consciousness. Unless we can posit a curious kind of guardian-ship over the musics of medieval Europe, one which would require an extensive educational program of music instruction quite at variance with the facts we now possess, we are forced to admit that the polyphony that the Church first began discussing in the ninth century had unsystematically evolved here and there with little conscious operation on the part of its singers in the various regional expressions. In this light, the rationalization that the Church brought to this cultural phenomenon is a remarkable internalization of a practice for which it initially deserves no more credit than it does for any other cultural force in medieval pagan society. Its early negative attitude is quite understandable.

If this historical moment tends to be somewhat irretrievable because of a lack of abundant evidence, the second moment is close to home and criti-cally exposes a similar attitude. If you read even a modest portion of the research that has been conducted in the last forty years on the musical abilities of small children, you will soon discover that as educators we have quite missed the significance of the phenomenon of polyphonic conscious-ness. There is no evidence in this vast literature to indicate that *what* children do when they sing is a *natural* activity; there is rather a concerted effort to suggest how to get them to do what they ought to do, which is to sing monophonically. Contemporary music educators readily concur that chief among the accomplishments for young singers is the "ability to carry a melody." Those who cannot are classified as "minimally," "moderately," or "acutely" monotone singers, and ingenious programs are evolved to bring these musical misfits into the community of unison singers. The ability to sing in unison with one's peers is not stated as a value: it is merely implied at the outset. The successful singer is the monophonic singer—at least in his early years of musical activity. The irony of this is that we teach children to be monophonic so that we may later then teach them to be polyphonic and to sing in parts—at a period in their educational life when music educators have decided that their polyphonic consciousness is at last cap-able of development.

The diagnosis of this situation is clear. Pragmatically speaking, the situa-tion is remarkably similar to that of the ninth century. Our society values a monophonic melos, and we take pedagogic steps to secure that value. The same may be said for other societies in world culture. But surely we might reflect on why we value a monophonic melos in the fashion that we do. It is not because collective monophony as a type of consciousness is part of the ontology of being human. We have only made it so.

6 Medieval and Renaissance Hearing

O ne occasionally reads statements in the scholarly and pedagogical literature on medieval and Renaissance music to the effect that the cognitive operation by which it was composed and heard was quite different from the manner in which we hear (and write as classroom exercises) such music today. The elements of this problem are not well defined, but there are so many remarks now in circulation that it is instructive to gather representative samples from several sources for a closer and more methodical examination than has been so far attempted. Since this topic ought to have an unambiguous title, we may call it the nature of polyphonic cognition. It was clearly stated some years ago by Richard L. Crocker, who does not happen to believe it:

> This view holds that medieval polyphony is "linear," and that these sonorities are fortuitous. If the medieval composer did pay attention to vertical sonority, it was only to ensure the use of perfect consonances, that is, unison, fourth, fifth, and octave.[1]

That was 1962. Fifteen years later we find that we have advanced this theory into the Renaissance as well as proved it with a clinching argument from historical evidence. In his *Istitutioni Harmoniche* of 1558, the theorist Gioseffo Zarlino tells us that "we should always take care to make the cadence principally in the tenor, this part being the principal guide for each mode, over which the song is composed; and from this the composer should take the invention of the other parts."[2] This led Joel Lester to state recently that "any systematic treatment of harmony according to the intervals over the bass would be alien to Zarlino's theories."[3] The problem has settled down more or less neatly over the entire medieval and Renaissance eras. While there are differences between Crocker's identification of the medieval aspect of the belief and Zarlino's statement that it obtained for the Renaissance composer as well, we may ignore them for the moment. Summarily, they speak to the same issue: medieval and Renaissance polyphony was so conceived that melodic linearity dictated harmonic content; because not everything was harmonically possible under the operation of this principle, there resulted a certain accidental quality in the harmony so governed. Particularly in the Middle Ages, both composer and listener were aware of the accidental features of the resultant harmony, but they were not overly concerned about it.

I would like to examine and challenge this notion in the pages that follow, but first a few other comments will be helpful, for Zarlino's recommendation only identifies a single moral imperative and not the ontology of polyphonic consciousness. There is also a prevailing pedagogical assumption expressed in the way we teach students how properly to hear and write music within the parameters of an assumedly authentic polyphonic style. For instance, the linear theory is advanced in Donald J. Grout's popular *History of Western Music* (example III-16), in a discussion of medieval harmony.[4] He supports the assumption by quoting a passage from a Montpellier motet, which indeed sounds like a rejected sketch from Bartok's *Mikrokosmos*. No sensitive medieval composer could have listened very carefully to the vertical aspect of his work and produced such a piece of music.[5] There are still doubts, however, about the later aspects of this harmonic modeling, which are revealed in Lloyd Ultan's *Music Theory: Problems and Practices in the Middle Ages and Renaissance* (1977), a book that seeks to teach the modern music student how to analyze and write Renaissance music. When writing in the style of Dufay, for instance, one is to proceed in the following fashion, after laying out the tenor in the next to bottom voice.

> Several possible choices exist for the next step, and students should proceed in the manner which they find most comfortable. Stylistically it is more appropriate to compose each line as a complete entity, adding each subsequent line to the completed ones. This may more successfully contribute a sense of linear motion which, of course, is the nature of so much of this music. It is also possible to compose all lines simultaneously measure-by-measure, if one is continuously alert to the danger of homophonic rather than polyphonic factors playing a principal role in decision making. Both

forces are evident and vertical considerations are of great importance in achieving a successful representation of the style. *But foremost this music must be linear in conception and effect.*[6]

This is a recent statement that accurately reflects our notions of the polyphonic/harmonic dichotomy. I shall refrain from any judgment about the philosophical and pedagogical value of teaching students how to compose fifteenth-century polyphony. Perhaps it is as important as instructing literature majors in our universities how to write *terza rima* in the Tuscan dialect of Dante and Petrarch. At any rate, it identifies a particular value in the current teaching of music history and theory. More important, there is a decided preference on the part of the author for what he believes to constitute the Renaissance sound ideal in music. "So much of this music" *does* exhibit a characteristic style that is "linear in conception and effect" that it requires one to avoid the danger of homophonic factors playing a principal role in decision making. To be sure, Ultan does devote two of his eighteen chapters to the more homophonic forms of secular music, but he sees their evolution in terms of "a lessening dependence on contrapuntal practices and an increasing interest in harmonic possibilities."[7] According to Ultan, this interest in harmonic possibilities apparently appeared late in Renaissance consciousness and was not a fundamental principle in effect in all the music of the Middle Ages and the Renaissance. Since this passage quite clearly reinforces common academic opinions that are held about the dichotomy of polyphonic and harmonic consciousness in our historical past, I shall return to it later in this chapter. For the moment, however, we may leave open the possibility that the Renaissance composer wrote in both of the methods suggested; perhaps Zarlino's statement will even support it. But we are not much closer to solving our problem as to how early music was heard.

Hearing music, of course, while it is our business to teach people how to do it, is not an entirely objective activity; and it is hearing and thinking about hearing that have produced the present state of affairs. Because there is a definite subjective element in the hearing of music, Crocker sought to explain why that subjectivity manifested itself in our current notions of how medieval and Renaissance composers both created and heard their music. Our notion of how this music actually sounded, he suggests,

> seems to have arisen when modern ears were first confronted with medieval sounds; accustomed to "traditional harmony," the ear found the sound of medieval music meaningless or intolerable. But when viewed as the result of simultaneous melodies, the crudity of the progressions became acceptable, even interesting. In this way medieval music was made accessible to the

modern mind, which was willing to attribute philosophic brilliance but not common sense perception to the musical contemporaries of St. Thomas Aquinas.[8]

I would like to suggest that Crocker's remark testifies to a common deficiency with the musicologist's perceptions and conceptualizations of heard music: we do not know a great deal about the phenomenon of our own hearing, let alone that of past ages. If we did, we might understand more accurately how medieval and Renaissance composers wrote their music. Since we do not, we have evolved a loose aggregate of inconclusive and curious assumptions based on formal, rather than necessary cognitive, features of the sonic experience. To be sure, the current notion concerning the medieval musical mind makes its assumptions from what appears to be the unique nature of polyphony itself. It is assumed that since polyphony is intrinsically a linear phenomenon, the cognition of its harmony was therefore linearly conceived. Certainly, the historical evidence of *successive composition* fundamentally supports this position. One recalls the role of Perotin, who re-composed the music of his predecessor Leonin by adding more voices to the organa dupla; the early history of the motet frequently demonstrates that its polyphony was enriched by melodic addition to two-voice pieces; and the theorists themselves tell us how to compose music in this fashion.[9] But this procedure produces genuine havoc with the fundamental building block of Western harmony, the triad, whose historical integrity is usually ignored by a myopic reduction of the facts. There are triads, a good number of them, already in the music of the Ars Nova, but since they signify "tonality" to the modern theorist and since he is not ready historically for its appearance, he can merely reason that "of course, the composer did not think that way." It is "a commendable reservation," notes Crocker, but it raises the urgent and obvious question: how *did* he think of his harmony?

Crocker's article on discant, counterpoint, and harmony speaks for itself. I hope that the reader will take it down from his shelves and read it again. Here, I would like to expand and develop the medieval and Renaissance hearing problem by examining some ideas about hearing itself and about current notions of harmony and counterpoint. Since these thoughts are two aspects of the same problem, polyphonic consciousness, I shall treat them together, letting each provide a critique of the other when appropriate. A proper entry into the phenomenon of polyphonic consciousness can logically begin by retracing our steps back to the Church's early awareness and treatment of polyphonic consciousness.

The rules for early organum as described in the ninth-century *Musica Enchiriadis*, its companion *Scholia*, and *De Organo* are well known to this readership, but I will summarize them here as to types: 1) organum at the fifth, with the chant melos, or *vox principalis*, in the top voice, usually called "strict simple organum"; 2) the same, with the vox principalis doubled at the octave below, and the lower voice, the *vox organalis*, doubled at the octave above, usually called "strict composite organum"; 3) the same simple and composite forms with the vox organalis at the fourth below; and 4) a kind of free organum at the fourth in which the organal voice occasionally remains stationary for the lowest notes for reasons of gamut and intervallic integrity.

We note that the vox principalis was initially placed in the top voice, at least when the organum was not composite. Approximately two hundred years later, we also note that the author of *Ad Organum Faciendum* made a decisive and systematic change by placing the vox principalis on the bottom of the musical complex. This change was no doubt regionally carried out and over a considerable period of time; but until the appearance of the *contratenor bassus* some years later, the chant melos lay at the foundation of the harmonic order, organizing sound from below instead of above—as was initially the case. Why was this change made?

It is the opinion of many, myself included, that the ecclesiastical chant was originally placed in the top voice or organum for purely theological reasons. It was a common medieval belief that the chants had been divinely inspired; therefore, if polyphony was to exist, it could do so only by assuming a subsidiary role of enhancement and ornament, as the author of the *Musica Enchiriadis* stated.[10] The political-philosophical correlate is so strikingly similar that it must be mentioned here. The feudal theory of law extended from heaven to earth. God reigned from above, down through the king, who was his vicar on earth; the king granted his lands to his barons in return for certain specified services; and they in turn had series of tenants under them; at the very bottom were the serfs, upon whose labor the successful operation of the entire system depended. Early ecclesiastical polyphony sonically reflected this hierarchy. Considering the alleged origin of the chant, the Church had no choice but to assume a role of superior melodic importance in the absorption of polyphonic consciousness, which it did physically by placing its melos above any additional elements that were permitted to coexist with it. But this process was rather schizophrenic if, indeed, an assumed melodic superiority was at stake. Consider, for example, composite organum *a* 4 in which the vox principalis was embedded within the texture, the vox organalis being doubled at the octave above and thus on top of the vox principalis.

Or consider more specifically what particular cognitive operations might be activated when three singers sang organum *a* 3. First, there is the singer of the chant itself, which is the vox principalis. Second, there is the singer of the vox organalis, which we shall hypothetically assume was taken at the interval of the fourth. Did he think his intervals a fourth *down* from the vox principalis? One would think so. We have no written evidence that the early medieval singer of organum cognized his harmony and structured his intervals from a bass tone up to a tone above it; the hierarchical position of the vox principalis would tend to indicate that he did not. But third, there is the singer who doubles the organal voice at the octave above. Did this third singer actually think his part an octave above the organal voice, that is, *up* from the bottom line? or did he think it a fifth up from the chant instead? If the new harmony was something to be thought of as being organized from a melody *down* to its virtual duplication at some interval below it, which is what the second singer was apparently doing, the third singer nevertheless had *two* options: he could understand that he was singing *up* from the bass or *up* from the chant; or he could think of himself in the same fashion as did the second singer and organize his line by thinking *down* to the chant which lay a fifth below his own part or to the organal voice an octave below him, which he was ostensibly duplicating as a third part of the texture. All this sounds very complex, and perhaps the singers did not "think" about it very much at all. This is to say that the force lines of up and down were perhaps not as important to these singers as they have become historically important to us. But we do know that there *were* some force lines in early polyphony because the rules for the *occursus*, the cadence, clearly indicate this. And we also know that whatever cognitive operations early medieval singers did evolve for organizing the harmonic relationships of intervals to the chant line underwent remarkable change— however unconscious these operations may appear to be on the surface.

   The first change occurred around 1100, when the vox principalis (or tenor, as it was soon to be called) was moved to the lowest voice in the texture: this clearly organized the harmonic structure from the bottom up—a practice that seems quite natural to us. This harmonic consciousness existed for about three centuries, although by the time of Dufay we realize that four-voice polyphony had established a secure beachhead. With the advent of four-part writing, the tenor made a permanent move to the second lowest position in the polyphonic complex and the contratenor bassus was placed beneath it. It was a dramatic step, although it was only gradually taken and not everywhere in Europe at the same time. The variations and exceptions that occurred in this development are ably demonstrated by the research of the last few decades.[11] From this second lowest position, the tenor apparently, according to Zarlino, governed harmony now above and below it. Thus, during the space of half a millennium the tenor assumed all possible positions within polyphonic texture: top (early organum), bottom (from about 1100 to well into the fifteenth century), and middle (with the establishment of four-part writing, about the time of Dufay). It would seem that whatever control the tenor claimed over the harmonic complex, several centuries passed before musicians determined from which place in the texture that control was to be executed. Harmonically, our story ends in the sixteenth century, when we sense but cannot yet prove that vertical sonorities were organized from the bass, although Lester wants to deny us this intuition, citing Zarlino to prove that we are only chasing a harmonic ghost.

To be sure, although we have realized that the tenor—which controlled harmonic consciousness—went through stages of migration, we have not yet said anything to defeat or even clarify the linear harmonic thesis which is commonly assumed to be "the way the medieval and Renaissance composer thought." And there are questions still lurking in the background, which I would like now to bring forward. Why was bass-oriented (although called tenor) harmonic consciousness given up (historically, the Ars Antiqua, the Ars Nova, and a portion of the music of the early Renaissance) when the tenor moved upstairs in the polyphonic complex? Was it given up? Let us return to the migration of the early vox principalis, since proper consideration of its activity will also shed some light on the larger problem just raised. Whatever the cognitive operations were that initially secured the intervallic perceptions for early medieval singers, as mentioned, by 1100 and the time of *Ad Organum Faciendum* and the *Winchester Troper*, we find the vox principalis below the vox organalis. This seems like a natural development to us. A gradual shift in consciousness divested the vox principalis of its superior melodic position in favor of some other means of organization with the same inherited melos. What was lost in the process and what was gained? When the chant shifted positions within the texture there opened the possibilities for freely created melodic components that reflected the imagination and creativity of composers. As *tenor*, however, the chant still commanded a dominant position by "holding together" the more quickly moving counterpoint that unfolded about it. Its various notes remained tonally critical at the beginning and end of phrases that nevertheless began to assume aesthetic and formal dimensions of their own. This shift protected the melodic integrity of the chant (although its former rhythmic component was now quite obliterated), for which the medieval composer continued to show proper respect. But it also opened the possibility of harmonic consciousness being organized from below: since the tenor notes could not be willfully changed at the whim of the composer, the tenor became an active force in the tonal decisions that were made for everything written above it. This is bottom-to-top harmonic consciousness. However, this attitude changed again, or seemed to change, about 1450, when the cantus firmus as tenor took still another position in the polyphonic texture, *within* it and above a new bass line, the *contratenor bassus*. Even the name is significant, "against the tenor, but low." Despite the linear aspect of Renaissance polyphony that this respect for the tenor implies, a respect still to be advocated as late as Zarlino in the sixteenth century, we must ask why the tenor was moved into the interstices of the texture. And what did the addition of a bass line below it actually signify? Did the eventual organization of bottom-to-top harmonic consciousness, as evidenced in the late Renaissance (where it is reluctantly admitted by even the most conservative of twentieth-century scholars) and clearly exploited from the seventeenth century on, actually undergo a lengthy, harmonic and tonal detour for a century and a half when the tenor gracefully abdicated its earlier position as harmonic coordinator *from below* and receded into the middle of the polyphonic texture? Or, in fact, was this abdication merely clear evidence that bottom-to-top harmonic cognitive awareness was the very tonal problem that consciousness itself was in the process of solving? (I shall answer this question in the affirmative later on.) Was the eventual organization of bottom-to-top harmonic consciousness, which seems "only natural" to us, something that had to happen? And if so, why did it have to happen?

All of these questions are interrelated and bear upon a single feature of Western harmony, the importance of which the reader may not yet fully grasp. Let me therefore propose a curious hypothesis. Suppose we were to get up tomorrow morning and discover that during the night some remarkable gnomes of the Niebelungen type had turned musical harmony completely upside down. Suddenly all harmonic thought would be cognized and conceived from the top to the bottom instead of from the bottom to the top—as it was yesterday. Chords would be thought of as being built from the top note. (Assuming that one wished to continue with a system of tertian harmony, a V_7–I in F major would be C–A-flat–F–D to F–D-flat–B-flat; but perhaps the "falling fifth relationship" would have to fall up, in which case the old subdominant would become the dominant.) In orchestral scores the piccolo part would be printed on the bottom of the page and the string bass part would be at the very top. Piano scores would have their treble clef below the bass clef, with the higher notes in any texture always written below lower sounding notes. Pianos would of course be rebuilt and restrung to reflect this change. In theory classes we would teach students always to think and to learn to sing intervals down from the higher pitch. Analysis would be completely inverted. And so on!

All this sounds properly silly, both figuratively and literally speaking. Even if a piano were constructed so as to have its treble and bass strings reversed, we would still hear harmony from bottom to top. Or, we must ask, would we? Do we presently hear harmony from bottom to top? And if we do, why? Curiously, we have not ever critically sought out the physical reasons why harmony is actually conceived in the way in which it is presently given to consciousness. And if we consider the evidence we have just reviewed about the medieval and Renaissance harmonic consciousness it would seem that cognition indeed attempted to organize harmonic spectra in a fashion that was quite at variance with classic tonal modeling. This is, in part, what the modern scholar means when he states, "of course, the medieval musician did not hear his harmonies that way." That is to say, he did not hear a triad as a triad.

Current explanations as to why harmony appears as it does are based upon the structure of the overtone series. It is thought that the single *Klang* is a natural model for the way the ear operates when it hears two or more *Klänge* simultaneously. What do we hear in a single *Klang*? When we hear the pitch A sung by a bass or played on an instrument we actually hear it and the first five to eight upper partials, minutely present with varying degrees of intensity over the fundamental; these upper partials are responsible for the timbre of the tone. The pitch of that tone, however, is not any of these softer, higher pitches: it is the fundamental that is the pitch. There are no pitches beneath it, no "undertones," as Rameau was reluctantly forced to admit. In fact, the presence of upper partials do more than determine timbre. The ear relies on them also in the discrimination and resolution of the fundamental. That is, if we electronically generate enough upper partials in the absence of their respective fundamental, we will "hear" the fundamental even though it is not being generated. This is clearly an operation of the ear as it discriminates and resolves pitch.

Inasmuch as theorists assume a natural basis for harmonic spectra, it must be said that there is a translation from the harmonic order of the *Klang* itself into respective orders between simultaneously sounding *Klänge* which the ear relates to each other through processes that it considers ontic because of a physical predisposition for the single *Klang*. This is the physical basis for harmony that Rameau propounded after Sauveur had scientifically explained the phenomenon of overtones, the same physical basis that some theorists bring forward when they explain that the "historical evolution of harmony is simply an advance up the overtone series." It is of course a major premise of this book that the hearing subject and its processes of aural cognition are to be restored to their proper relationship with the tonal object that it creates. But if this is the case, we note a curious period in Western tonality during which harmony seemed to be in a state of sonic confusion concerning its own cognitive abilities and disabilities: witness the migration of the cantus firmus—as harmonic sovereign—through the various stages of its evolution, as it ostensibly organized harmony first from the top, then from the bottom, and next from within the texture of heard polyphonic complexes.

With reference to current contrapuntal versus harmonic debates, I do not believe that statements by the medieval and Renaissance theorists will ultimately reveal *what* they heard in their harmony, any more than statements by Schenker (such as "linear expansion of the III chord") reveal what contemporary audiences hear as immediately and tonally coherent in a work by Schubert. This is to say that a textbook definition of tonal coherence is not the same as the phenomenon of tonal cognition as experienced. But in terms of harmonic consciousness, it is not necessary to abandon our thoughts about medieval hearing, since we do know some facts about the phenomenon of harmonic cognition as experienced. To be sure, at the moment they must be treated speculatively when they are taken from the realm of the psychoacoustician's laboratory into the realm of heard music,[12] but they are by no means to be considered irrelevant because of it. I would like therefore to set up a general theory of audible cognition for both medieval and modern tonal hearers and follow it with a couple of more specific observations that psychoacousticians have established through empirical research. Happily, a few music theorists have noticed them as well, although they do not relate them to the topic under investigation.[13]

It is my opinion that the vox principalis was eventually placed below the organal voice for purely physical and physiological reasons that affected the cognitive operations of medieval musicians in a thoroughly unconscious manner (even as they do today) and that the musicians had no choice but to orient their intervals and eventually their triads from the bottom up. The *bassus* of a later century was eventually placed under the cantus firmus, or tenor, for the same reasons.

The physical reason may be disarmingly simple: it takes more acoustical energy to produce a low tone than it does a high one of equivalent loudness. Low frequencies create large wave forms and high frequencies create small ones. More molecules of air are excited in the production of a low tone than by a high one; more space is needed in which to produce it—as the interior of any stereophonic speaker will demonstrate or any physicist will tell you. The physiological reason follows from this acoustical law: the greater molecular activity of the low tone produces a greater state of excitation in the mechanism of the ear, and the brain is caused to respond accordingly—the greater the stimulus, the greater the response. Cognitively, tonal coordinates were (and are) determined by an integration process that interprets greater stimuli as predominating over lesser stimuli. In terms of tones, whether vertically or horizontally given, all operations of the cognitive process—rapid attention integrations, buffer-zone delays, and short- and long-term memories—would seem to orient themselves with regard to this fundamental physical phenomenon. In terms of the heard composite within the sound mass, bass tones would predominate over treble tones, and the mind

would integrate the greater sonic activity of the bass as acoustically fundamental to the harmonic structure.[14]

What I have presented here, of course, is a gross picture of the phenomenon at hand, generally stated, which attempts to relate all parts of harmonic activity at once. We can, however, now supply some tangible data to
our problem. Researchers in auditory psychophysics have discovered that
hearing is a complex affair and that the ear is not merely a passive recorder
of what it discriminates and resolves as pitch. This has profound implications for any theory of tonality. The ear's complex response to loudness, or
intensity (the physical pressure measured in decibels), is one that causes it
to react differently in different regions of the audible range. Scientific investigation of this phenomenon has led to the establishment of *equal-loudness
curves*. This means that different amounts of pressure (dB) are required to
produce impressions of equal loudness throughout the audible range.[15] For
instance, 45 dB are required to make a pitch of 100 cps sound as loud as a
1000 cps pitch of only 10 dB. These two pitches are quite far apart, but even
if we consider only male singers of medieval music, basses would still have
to sing louder in order to be perceived as matching in intensity the higher
pitches of those who sang the upper parts. (I am of course assuming
something, with absolutely no evidence, about medieval performance practice: that the sound ideal was one in which the bass was *expected* to match
in loudness parts that were sung above it.) This assumption has important
consequences for the cognition of harmonic spectra. We have already noted
that there is more sonic energy in a low tone than in a high one. If our
medieval basses produced louder strong, low tones in order to match in
intensity the high tones in any harmonic complex, they also physically
masked them, thereby rendering their own pitches even more acoustically
fundamental to the harmonic complex. Masking is defined by W. Lawrence
Gulick as "a temporary loss in sensitivity to one stimulus during simultaneous exposure to another."[16] Robert Cogan and Pozzi Escot have noted that
although "the musical consequences of masking are staggering, ... the
specific effects of masking on musical combinations . . . remain almost
completely unexamined."[17] In *Sonic Design*, these authors are primarily concerned with the effects of masking on the component of tone color, but
there are critical points to be made in terms of harmonic consciousness as
well.

A second factor that serves to weight the harmonic complex in favor of
low frequency strength is an activity that arises not in the physical, tonal
object but within the ear itself. That is, when the inner ear is stimulated by
the presence of a musical interval it "hears" or supplies additional *combination tones* with frequencies that differ from those in the objective sound
phenomenon itself. These combination tones are of two orders, termed

differential and *summational* tones by Helmholtz.[18] If the tone that the ear supplies is a difference tone it will sound *below* the two fundamental tones of the physically projected interval. If it is a summation tone it will sound *above* the interval, but it is weaker than the difference tone. It is the difference tone that interests us. For instance, the difference tone of the perfect fifth c′–g′ is c, which lends strength at the octave (c′) to the lower member of the perfect fifth. Therefore, if the tone is the same as the bottom tone of the fifth replicated at the octave below, the ear actually assists in the organization of the harmonic complex in terms of a tonal aggregate that is understood as being constructed from the bottom up. This physiological phenomenon acquires historical significance in a harmonic system in which the fifth was of paramount importance. Indeed, to quote Schenker, "the fifth returns, as it were, to its source," but the reason that nature supplied lay quite beyond the sphere of his investigation. Even the interval of the fourth proves interesting for the same—but inverted—reason. While the bottom pitch of the perfect fifth is intensified by its difference tone, the difference tone of the perfect fourth causes the upper pitch to be intensified; i.e., c′ in the interval g–c′. But this only supports the harmonic notion that in the progression I$_4^6$–V–I the tonic pitch of the inverted triad is the true root even though the fifth is the lowest sounding pitch. To be sure, this is an arbitrary selection of two intervals (fifth and fourth) from the varied sound mass of triads and chords in any given harmonic progression, but, curiously, the frequent thirds and sixths that are so important to tertian harmonic consciousness in such complexes are actually different pitches that are *not* replicas of one of the two fundamentals constituting them—as with the intervals of fifth and fourth. The important fact is that the ear itself tonally contributes to the acoustical organization of harmonic spectra and in such a fashion that it emphasizes bass to treble relationships.

How do these facts relate to the history of polyphonic consciousness? There had to be a reason (conscious or not) why the medieval composer moved his cantus firmus from the top to the bottom of his polyphonic complex. Let us review the important facts. The tonal integrity of the ecclesiastical chant had already been secured: there was a typical beginning and end of the monophonic phrase. In psalmody there was further structuring through the relatively stable recitation formulae. The chant melos generally subscribed to a cluster of diatonic pitches that were gradually organized into theoretical statements of melodic content, that is, the medieval modes. These tonal elements were not about to be given up, and gradually it was intuited (realized is much too precise a term) that this tonal cohesion and unity could continue to function best in that area of the pitch complex where natural subjectivity itself supported the greater physical and physiological response. This was a fact of human cognition that predominated over any previous judgment about where the vox principalis should be placed, for whatever reasons. I believe that the migration of the vox principalis from the top of early organum to the bottom, where it became firmly entrenched for several centuries as harmonic organizer from below, was a motion made by consciousness itself with regard to its own cognitive aural abilities in juxtaposition to the *Klang*. Stated in the most general terms, this migration brought the natural acoustical resonance and response of the ear into intervallic accord with the very harmonic components that it created as sonic object before it. Historically, this is supported by what happened to the tenor in the next stage of polyphonic rationalization. About the time of Dufay, the contratenor bassus was added below the cantus firmus through the same activity between acoustically endowed subject and sonically created tonal object. The tenor thus came to be viewed in a tension between what it had been originally set up to do compositionally, which was to organize tonal coherence, and the potential of tonal coherence itself as a harmonic and contrapuntal principle. This means that as the roots of harmonic complexes became more cognitively important, as they assumed a more encompassing sonic focus, it was also felt (however unconsciously) that an additional voice *below* the cantus (whose former tonal focus now began to act as a constraint rather than as a freely disposed agent of harmonic consciousness) could be made to serve chiefly and more freely than the cantus as a functional element in tonal cohesion. As Grout notes when discussing the cadences that appear with increasing frequency in this four-part writing, "after about 1460 the normal cadence formula was one that would be described in modern terminology as V–I. It must be understood, however, that the composers did not think of such progressions with the implications attached to the modern terms we are using to describe them."[19] But what implications ought we to attach to the fact that the chords are there? Here surfaces again our own historical consciousness about medieval and Renaissance hearing.

This consciousness, its attitudes and beliefs, our thinking about hearing, is the subject of the remainder of this chapter. Curiously, its most dramatic statement was given in Bukofzer's remarkable book, *Music in the Baroque Era*, which appeared in 1947. In a chapter ("Renaissance versus Baroque Music") that has been now read by thousands, Bukofzer sought to dichotomize the differences between Renaissance and baroque music. He felt that a proper comparison of the two styles revealed that "the most striking difference" between them was the treatment of dissonance. In Renaissance music, "the harmonic result of the combination of voices was conceived as a conjunction of intervals rather than as the unfolding of one chord. This intervallic harmony of the Renaissance was diametrically opposed to the chordal harmony of the baroque."[20] It seems that this observation was taken as gospel by the major portion of the musicological community that rapidly sprang up following World War II. True, there have been those, such as Crocker, who have challenged this position; but Lester's 1977 article reaffirms that Bukofzer had a genuine understanding of medieval and Renaissance tonality and that all we need to do is to continue to support his thesis. After all, who wishes to challenge the authority of Zarlino, who lived in the very era under investigation?

It comes as no surprise that our understanding of both medieval and Renaissance polyphony and harmony is achieved through an even larger phenomenon which we understand even less clearly—tonality. However, we can no longer avoid the consequences of our own historical consciousness which permeates all of our writing and thought about music. It is a false consciousness: it cannot correct itself; but it accurately explains the nature of polyphony and harmony in terms of current knowledge and human interests. Let me cite a few instances of this historical consciousness at work.

In a discussion of the double leading-tone cadence which was so popular in the music of the fourteenth century, Cannon, Johnson, and Waite write the following:

> The strong pull toward the final chord exerted by two voices moving upward by half steps against the downward stepwise motion of the lowest part produced an exceptional sense of finality as the tension is resolved in the last chord of the progression. With a cadential pattern of such power the composer had a tool with which he could emphasize points of division within a composition by *purely harmonic means.*[21]

And in the discussion of the Franco-Flemish Mass and motet in the latter fifteenth century, Crocker states the following:

> The treatment of three-note sonorities was the most obvious feature of the new style. The three-note chord that we call a *triad* was not yet an entity, but rather the result of enriching a fifth with a third. It was still used, as in the 1300s, because of its unstable and evocative sound. But instead of using it once in a while for special effect, composers now used it continually. The problem to be worked out was a technical one: composers had to find ways to make counterpoint produce this continual stream of harmony with convincing lyricism.[22]

It is commonly acknowledged that "traditional" tonality is a system of tertian harmonies related to one another in a sonic hierarchy that both implies and demands fixed orders of "progression" from one vertical sonority to the next. One can seek hopelessly the so-called natural reasons for the rules behind the progressions, as did Rameau, Schenker, and Hindemith, or he can admit with David Hume that custom itself both made and secured the reasons behind what historically came to be regarded as cause and effect. How and when did the triad become an entity? The initial step was laid for this possibility, of course, by the theorists of the mid-thirteenth century, who specified the essential concords of two-part discant to be unison, octave, fifth, major and minor thirds, and, later, the major sixth.[23] The triad did not become an entity before the third and the sixth had acquired legitimate status as harmonic materials in the writing of discant, which was treated according to rules set up by the theorists. The rules were determined on the basis of linear *and* vertical principles, and it is of the utmost importance to realize that from the beginning both of these principles were important to composers.

"Discant" here means a system of teaching two-part composition, in use from the thirteenth to the sixteenth centuries. As Crocker carefully demonstrates, it "shows how to combine one (and only one) note with each note of a given melodic progression by the application of two basic principles."[24] The first principle requires that discant consist primarily of concords and only secondarily (but importantly) of discords. This is a *harmonic* principle. The second principle requires contrary motion between the two parts. This is a *contrapuntal* principle. Crocker notes that the rules were absolutely binding, but there were many exceptions, and "a large part of the typical discant treatise is devoted to circumvention of this principle, laying down conditions under which similar or even parallel motion may be used."[25]

What were the concords? Taking up a suggestion offered by Thrasybulos Georgiades some years ago, Crocker constructed a tentative genealogy of the anonymous discant authors on the basis of their treatment of the intervals. The most important changes in the century between 1250 and 1350 are that the major sixth was added to the early catalog of unison, octave, fifth, fourth, major and minor thirds, and that the fourth was "demoted" to the status of a discord, the only concord, notes Crocker, to have its harmonic status changed.[26] Sometime after 1350 the minor sixth was permitted to the table of concords, although it was of course classified as imperfect along with the two thirds and the major sixth. Other intervals were dissonant.

The second principle of discant sought to explain the ways in which contrary motion (or at least oblique motion) was to control the use of the concords just mentioned. "These rules are discussed and illustrated by 13th-century writers in a bewildering variety of ways," says Crocker, "yet as rules they are broad and simple."[27] When contrary motion is not possible, similar motion is permitted, even parallel motion, admits Franco of Cologne, if the result is a beautiful effect. But the rules for two-part discant were not initially conceived with a view toward three-part writing, and they began to reveal an unforeseen tension with the permanent addition of a third voice. A new element (or cognitive operation) surfaced which began to alter the earlier procedures by which any two voices were related to each other. The theorists offered the best advice they could: "When adding the third voice, proceed as in discant."[28] This means that ostensibly the same two principles would hold; use the same concords and contrary motion whenever possible. It is here that the linear thesis of polyphonic composition seems to acquire real substance, as has been ably demonstrated before by numerous scholars. The thirteenth-century motet seems to be a veritable pastiche of different elements which not even its format on the page or pages of the manuscripts attempts to unify. The top voice (on one page) is governed by the tenor (the bottom voice); the middle voice (on a facing page) is governed by the same tenor (frequently written across the bottom of the two pages). Apparently the relationship between the two upper voices, while certainly not ignored, was harmonically of less consequence than the relationship which each had independently with the tenor.

The force lines that are drawn here for three-part harmony are critical and need to be visually demonstrated. What is expressed in the diagram is a force field. It is not simply a matter of relating three tones to each other:

1 to 2, 2 to 3, and 1 to 3 in a triangle, with equal stress between each tone. The lines of stress are primarily from the top down (2 to 1 and 3 to 1) and only secondarily (but importantly) between the two upper voices (3 to 2). I say from the top down on the basis of the acoustical integrity of sonic energy generated by bass tones and the manner in which the mind processes the data of pitch, as demonstrated earlier in this chapter.

But there is another element at work here, one which lies beyond the physical facts of audible cognition. It is the element of subjective choice. It is clearly evoked in the words from the two passages quoted above—from current scholarship. There is a "strong pull toward the final chord"; the third "enriches" the fifth; and the triad was used in the 1300s "because of its unstable and evocative" sound. Not only do these statements reveal contemporary attitudes about the birth of the triad (which historically seems to have sprung inverted from the womb of harmony), they are also confirmed by a certain medieval fascination about tertian elements and their aesthetic effect. We learn from the theorists, from John of Garland on, that the judgment of the ear is consistently invoked in the treatment of concord and discord. "A concord," says Johannes Tinctoris, "therefore is a mixture of two pitches rendered sweetly agreeable to the ear by a natural power (*naturali virtute*)."[29]

We have arrived at the core of our problem, suggested earlier by the phrase knowledge and human interests. The medieval theorist knew quite well what the consonances were. The formulae he used to describe them went back to Boethius's *De Institutione Musica*. But consonance was not enough to empower tonality with conviction and aesthetic truth, and this realization seems to be a historical element of harmonic consciousness as early as French medieval theory, clearly demonstrated by Anonymous II:

> Discant is composed principally of consonances and only incidentally of dissonances, in order that the discant per se may be more beautiful, and that we may be more delighted by the consonances. Consonance is made of diverse sounds mixed together. Dissonance is rough collision.[30]

Anonymous's statement seems precise enough, but it fails to reveal a hierarchy that was taking place within the relationships of concords as well, which had to do with the articulation of tonal form. In a discussion of the leading-tone cadence, David G. Hughes notes that

> While this cadence undoubtedly came into being as a consequence of the motion of the individual voices, the two sonorities involved acquired functions in their own right. . . . Note that this is not merely a matter of consonance and dissonance, for all the intervals concerned are consonant. It is, rather, *the selection of certain sonorities* as being conclusive or inconclusive, and using this property as a means of shaping the phrase. This type of musical thinking may be termed "harmonic," as opposed to contrapuntal or polyphonic. While it had to some extent appeared before the fourteenth century, the *Ars Nova* gave new emphasis to it. It was to continue, with increasing importance, until the end of the nineteenth century and even beyond.[31]

This statement is interesting in that it opens rather than limits the investigation of the tension between polyphonic and harmonic consciousness in medieval and Renaissance music. On the one hand, harmony is the result of linear causes—simultaneous melodic motion in several parts; on the other, harmony is the result of conscious selection. But the passage is nevertheless historically myopic. If the grounds for "harmonic" consciousness are historical (and who would deny it), what reason can we accept for determining an arbitrary moment in history for that consciousness to appear, a moment that is half a millennium short of the facts? Hughes does not know what to make of this problem, which he only dimly perceives. "Harmonic" thinking "had to some extent appeared before the fourteenth century," he admits. Indeed it had, as early as the ninth century and probably before. What Hughes seeks to do—which is rendered painfully apparent with the quotes around harmonic—is to secure "our harmony," the kind that progresses from chord to chord in a nexus of vertical relationships determined by "traditional" tonal progressions. But if harmony is the relationship between simultaneous tones, then the medieval composer or improvisor of organum knew that he had created it, and he was certainly not worried about how twentieth-century scholars would judge his activity. Whether or not a thirteenth-century motet exhibits "a strong pull toward the final chord" must ultimately be judged in the court of our own attitudes about tonal harmony.

My point is that there was harmonic thinking from that moment—loosely embraced by the ninth century—when two or more voices were sounded together. The intervals for early medieval French organum were the results of harmonic choice, and aesthetic judgment operated upon those choices with every alteration that was made upon the harmonic reservoir of vertical sonorities. Had this not been the case, the fourth would not have been demoted in status, despite its elemental security within the assumed mathematical purity of Pythagorean *harmonia*, handed to the Middle Ages by Boethius. Also, if this had not been the case, there would have been no convergence with non-French (specifically, English and Italian) tertian harmonic consciousness, which penetrated French music almost too quickly for the logical consequences of its own rules to unfold.[32] Harmonically speaking, whether or not the theorists articulate them, and however they articulate them when they do, medieval music itself testifies to feelings, attitudes, and beliefs we cannot assign consistently to accident and fortuitous consequence.

The falsity of our own attitudes about medieval music manifests itself critically in our treatment of the early stages of polyphonic consciousness. We want this consciousness to be other than it was, to hasten through the (to us) obvious stages of early tertian awareness, to secure the cadence with the proper chords, and to get on with the harmonic business of becoming like J. S. Bach. No musician in the thirteenth century ever said or thought "I am being less 'harmonic' in this passage than I could be," which is the kind of attitude that history thrusts upon him. Harmony and polyphony were not concepts toward which he yearned, and the notion of their perfection in terms of some ideal Platonic state against which they are to be weighed and judged is just another element in the historical illusion that is promulgated in the name of musicology. Comparatively speaking, "more sophisticated" and "less monotonous" are not terms (they are taken from the literature examined here) that we find in critical descriptions of medieval French dialects, simply because scholars of language do not have the temerity to state that the thirteenth-century language user thought his expression inadequate throughout the many years that he spoke. But for some reason musicologists feel justified not only in assuming but also stating as fact in textbooks (particularly for undergraduates) and in their research that medieval polyphony lacked essential elements that crippled its expression and caused it to fall short of authentic (read, later) music. Clearly our notions of harmony and polyphony are inadequate to the phenomena we attempt to explain, which is the reason that the linear-harmonic controversy cannot define its content.

The most popular harmonic closure in the three-part music of the thirteenth century was the progression vii_6^0–I, which should be regarded at the moment of its historical appearance as having nothing to do with the harmonic modeling that followed it. In no sense is the thirteenth-century composer's consciousness to be regarded as futuristic. We may properly call this tonal vehicle a progression simply because of the place in which we find it in actual music—at the end of the piece and frequently at the ends of its internal phrases. The harmony was thought to proceed or progress from the imperfect penultimate chord—with its intervals of third, fourth, and sixth—to the perfect consonant sonority that followed it. The table of discant concords (perfect and imperfect) cannot be interpreted otherwise. To be sure, this cadence came into being as a consequence of melodic motion in two-part writing. Since many chants cadence monophonically by descending to the finalis, the downward step of the lower voice was secured by the authority of the chant itself. Next to the unison, the octave was the most consonant of concords and was expected, indeed, demanded at the close of the piece. The smoothest melodic approach to the octave was through the sixth, which was minor in two modes (Dorian and Mixolydian) and major in two modes (Phrygian and Lydian). It is interesting to note that the two minor sixths were altered through musica ficta in order to secure the major sixth and half-step below the octave over the finalis. The Lydian mode already had this arrangement and a raised fourth as well. Lydian was the diatonic version of the double leading-tone cadence in three-part writing, and it was duplicated via chromatic alteration in the Dorian and Mixolydian.

Both Howard M. Brown and Donald Grout call this cadence "manneristic," for reasons not entirely clear to me. Brown judges the entire cadence a mannerism which disappeared in the course of the fifteenth century. Grout calls the ornamental resolution of the top voice (7–6–8) "almost a mannerism."[33] If the cadence was created so as to create a distinctive sonic effect, then perhaps it is manneristic; but this is not the point. Or, if it is the point, should we not also call later V–I and IV–I cadences mannerisms as well? More importantly, in three-part writing, the decision to alter the fourth and seventh degrees of the Dorian and Mixolydian modes to conform to the same sound available diatonically in Lydian was *not* a polyphonic decision; it was merely harmonically desirable. The changes that musica ficta effected upon transposed forms of the diatonic version of the Lydian statement of the cadence can only be attributed to harmonic choice that lay beyond polyphonic necessity. With regard to the critical awareness that is brought to bear upon the tonal substance of early Renaissance polyphony, this argument does not seem to me to be a very strong case for harmony following the dictates of an encompassing linear principle that "governed" harmonic consciousness. In addition, we must note that the potential for this cadence also appeared *outside* the strictures of contrapuntal voice leading. The improvisational practices of both English *faburden* and French *fauxbourdon* produce many $\frac{6}{3}$ chords, and the same cadential modeling is obtained in their harmonic closures. As is well known, both single and double leading-tone cadences gradually lost ground about 1450 to the V–I cadence, which was initially obtained even in three-part writing by crossing the two lower voices in order to avoid parallel fifths. This cadence is also interesting in that it simultaneously demonstrates a necessary tension between polyphonic and harmonic consciousness: the rule of discant concerning contrary motion was observed at the same time the composer achieved the sound he desired.

Current musicology has made it a careful principle to attempt to judge the substantive tonal character of the music of the past on the basis of what theorists who were actually contemporary with the music under question said about it. This is a commendable methodology—to a point, but the theorists of any era must also be historically understood in terms of their own knowledge and human interests. In closing, I would like to discuss this problem by returning to my opening remarks about Zarlino. The initial paragraphs of Joel Lester's article, "Major-Minor Concepts and Modal Theory in Germany, 1592–1680,"[34] properly reflect our present caution about evolutionary music history and the myth of tonal progress. But the terms *evolution* and *progress* merely disguise the fact that any musical age contains conservative and radical elements in the works of the composers who write music, and these are similarly reflected by the theorists who write about their compositions.

Despite the fact that his theories were attacked "with a violence uncommon even for the polemical spirit of the age,"[35] I cannot see the Franciscan Zarlino as anything but a conservative theorist. The attacks by Vincenzo Galilei upon him only indicate (to me) that there were others even more conservative regarding certain tonal issues than he. The Church's reluctance to accept the Ionian and Aeolian modes, which had been around since the secular songs of the troubadours (and perhaps therefore to be ignored because they *were* secular), does not exactly attest to progressive music theory, although in this one aspect Zarlino clearly understood what composers had long been doing and attempted to alter the force of theoretical tradition. As for the organization of the polyphonic voices around the tenor, mentioned at the beginning of this chapter, this is anything but radical. Zarlino conceived his theories in an age when cantus firmus technique was vanishing from his very ears. Even Palestrina, certainly no radical, ignored rigid tenor organization in favor of paraphrase and parody techniques in his some one hundred Masses. In short, the harmonic modeling of functional basses and treble-dominated songs characteristic of fifteenth- and sixteenth-century secular music would not go away. In fact, the sixteenth century created the first commercial venture of commodity music for the general public in order to exploit the economic potential of this popular style. The die had been cast. If the public wanted simple tunes with clearly defined cadences in a homophonic style, printers in Italy, France, England, and the Netherlands were more than willing to provide an abundance of them at reasonable cost and a calculated profit.

Thus, I can agree with Lester that "any systematic treatment of harmony according to the intervals over the bass would be alien to Zarlino's theories." But Zarlino and his fellow Franciscans were rapidly losing their position as the arbiters of musical taste. Their theoretical endeavors, while historically interesting to the modern theorist, were doomed to lag behind the interests of a citizenry whose music the Church had largely ignored. The Venetian, Parisian, and London bourgeoisie did not buy Zarlino's theory books to read aloud to each other for an evening's enjoyment, while they did buy a music created for them which quite ignored a compositional technique organized around a tenor. The Roman Church lost more than its political and spiritual hegemony in sixteenth-century Europe. It also lost its power to control the destiny of tonality, which was in the process of being forged by quite secular interests in the crucible of mercantile Europe. The message to the modern music theorist and musicologist is clear: we cannot do music theory—past or present—in a positivistic vacuum. Until the political, philosophical, social, economic, physical, and cognitive forces of any age are brought properly to bear upon the nature of polyphony, harmony, and tonal consciousness, there can be no adequate description of that music's true historical dimension.

7 The Dialectic of Tonic and Dominant

As the disciplines of music theory and musicology have failed to understand the relationship between polyphonic and homophonic creativity in medieval and Renaissance tonal consciousness, so also have they failed to understand the nature of tonic and dominant harmonic phenomena within these same and other musics. (The problems are interrelated.) In this chapter I wish to examine this Western harmonic concept from the standpoint of its historical evolution; to present the results of this evolution neither as the tonal jewel of common-practice tonality, that is, harmonic motion-in-itself, as did Schenker; nor as some paradigm within the *Klang* of nature that inevitably achieved, at the hands of "hecatombs of artists," an ideal of sonic utterance, definition, and perfection in classical form. Rather, I shall present it as a historical motion *within* tonal subjectivity that created, developed, and sustained its substantive content as temporal articulation through musical objects that were both formal and expressive.

The dialectic of tonic and dominant is characterized by a binary tonal relationship that entails the generalization of its motion through time as well as the particularization of its essence as concretized in half- and whole-cadence (I–V and V–I). This sentence states a good deal, but it does not provide an adequate historical notion of the tonal dialectic which I shall attempt to trace through a complex of stages that permit its ontology to appear in greater perspective. Before this, however, the subjective ego must be restored to its rightful place with relation to its sonic object, for only then is it possible to escape the limitations and contradictions which positivist theory has placed around it.

This is to say that within any musical experience the subjective ego is thrown immediately into a relationship with time and tones. What it regards as tonal within this experience has been given to it in a very secure historical sense. In one historical era the specific tonality with which it both understands and expresses itself may be its collective melos. In another era, it may acquire attendant but important instrumental accompaniment in conjunction with essentially monophonic expression. In another, it may give up its monophonic characteristics and submerge itself in polyphonic activity. And in still another, this ego may disavow any apparent connection with its once-sturdy vocal origins and achieve such singular instrumental expressions as symphony, quartet, overture, and the like. Thus we are forced to admit that what is known among musicians as tonic-dominant modeling is actually the tacit assumption of a musical heritage which we have come largely to take for granted and do not question—any more than we question that sentences should have nouns and verbs even as we supply them automatically.

The notion that tonic and dominant exhibit a fundamental relationship of interconnected tonal activity must not be too rigidly formulated at the outset, but neither should we refuse to draw any limits around such a notion at all merely because none has been attempted except for those concepts which evolved in the bourgeois age. Above all, we must suspend the theoretical speculation upon the internal nature of the *Klang* and turn to the actual formulation of heard music. But because tonic and dominant modeling is an activity of cognition and memory, I shall use the terms *expectation* and *fulfillment* when necessary, since the successful musical experience implies these cognitive acts. I shall use these terms not with any reference to the "demands of nature," which are violated by the tonal creator whenever he wishes, but rather with regard to a series of tonal configurations drawn from the activities of musicians within the course of Western music.

Implied in the present terminology of tonic and dominant is the notion that one tone (the tonic) of the scale has a relatively fixed and known relation to another tone, specifically the dominant. This also implies a sort of "loyalty to the tonic" which is secured by history itself. We must ask the crucial question: How did this relationship come into being? If it is not a given of nature, then we must have created it as a relationship ourselves. If we cannot admit with Rameau and Schenker that the dominant as second overtone within the *Klang* "seeks its natural home" by returning to it, can we isolate other features within our own historical consciousness to point to its definition and illumination? I believe that a proper introduction to this important phenomenon lies in the the ancient practice of cantillation of Jewish psalmody and its attendant tonal activity in terms of sonic motion, as discussed in chapter 3, where we attempted to establish a ground for its most rudimentary aspects. Here, we shall orient ourselves arbitrarily, but very importantly, within the habitual practice of singing of psalms in the Roman Church, where we can already outline monophonically the sources of the daily practice of tonic-dominant modeling.

An additional word about terminology is in order. The terms *tonic* and *dominant* have for modern scholars and musicians very specific meanings, the first and fifth tones of the diatonic scale (major or minor), respectively, and their attendant harmonic complexes. The term *tonus*, from which the tonic is derived, reveals a historically complex affair whose illumination is to be sought properly in the writings of the Latin theorists. At its very first appearance there we already find a music that is tonally perceived in terms of it, that is, practice preceded theory. The activity for which *tonus* came to stand as an assigned configuration of consciousness was thus already present at hand; it had only to be recognized as such. If we are to believe the theorists, we may assume that the tonus of a mode, its tonic, was thought to be most critical at the beginnings and endings of a plainchant, for such is the nature of the early tonaries, which we shall discuss shortly. *Dominant* is a much later term, one which we have superimposed upon Latin theory through historical hindsight. While the *tenor* or *tuba* reflects the dominant, it is necessary to keep in mind the fact that this dominant was apparently the third degree above the finales of the (later) church modes as often as it was the fifth degree. It is instructive to realize that *nontonic* is perhaps the better term for these relationships, although I shall frequently use dominant to express them and trust that the reader will remain open to their earlier and wider possibilities.

There are two critical aspects within Latin psalmody that focus early monophonic consciousness upon the tonal activity of tonic-dominant modeling: the recitation tones and the tonaries. When speaking of the recitation tones of the Latin Church, Willi Apel is correct when he states that "the most elementary stage of the liturgical recitative is represented by the melodic formulae used for the musical delivery of the readings and prayers that form a part of the Office of the Mass,"[1] if by this he does not mean to place this "most elementary stage" in a fixed category that historically precedes other more elaborate forms of liturgical singing such as are witnessed in the ancient Jewish Hallelujah. Nevertheless, we admit that "the style of a given chant is determined by the liturgical category to which it belongs," and that the singing of scriptures for instruction, exhortation, and prayer is a venerable tradition that lies within the very core of the Jewish and Christian religions. It is difficult to agree with Apel, however, when he states that within the general context of liturgical recitation and the various tonal formulae which are used to execute it, "the music has no independent significance and value, but only serves as a means of obtaining a distinct and clearly audible pronunciation of the words, so that they will resound into the farthest corners of the church."[2] Let the reason be made clear: the key term here is *independent*, by which Apel means that psalm tones had no musical function beyond that of liturgical recitation; but their significance and value for the structuring of tonal consciousness is of the utmost importance because these psalm tones and their tonal activity infiltrated and penetrated tonal subjectivity at the very core of collective communication. Since within the practice of liturgical recitative we are situated in the very cradle of tonic and nontonic consciousness, upon which Western music has built its tonal edifices, we disavow any a priori judgment about the value of this consciousness by stating that these formulae "are not musical items in the proper sense." The early melos knew no such restrictions. Therefore, our discussion of the liturgical recitative proceeds from the assumption that it contains as praxis the very ordering of tones out of chaos which is our tonal consciousness.

Notwithstanding Apel's historical bias, his formidable assembly of data is convincing, and I shall attempt through paraphrase to summarize the early components of this consciousness. The recitation tones for the prayers (collects) and the readings from prophecy, the Epistles, or the Gospels that form a part of the Mass, as well as for the short chapter (*capitulum*) of the canonical hours and the more extended lessons of Matins, are well known. All these tones are essentially monotone recitations sung on certain pitches (either a, c', or f, depending on the historical sources), with downward inflections to a third below.[3] It is impossible to determine the age of these tones, and we note in particular the fact that there is no rising intonation in them, that is, coming from a tonic to a tuba or tenor—the principal reciting tone. Our discussion here will concentrate intially on the psalm tones themselves, basic groups of melodic formulae that are used for the singing of complete psalms which form the core of the service in all canonical hours.[4]

Both the psalm tones and the ecclesiastical modes (though these latter less importantly) exhibit features of invested tonal order and motion. In Gregorian chant, there are eight psalm tones, one for each church mode. These tones also have the character of an inflected monotone. Their function as formulae was to provide a main note of recitation, called tenor or *repercussio* or tuba (meaning loud, and thus emphasizing its importance for vocal delivery) on which the main body of each individual verse was recited. A full psalm tone consists of: Intonation—Tenor—(Flex—Tenor)—Mediant—Tenor—Termination (See Apel, *Gregorian Chant*, Figures 44 and

49; pp. 210ff). It thus reflects the characteristic formulation of parallelismus membrorum that constitutes the two halves of nearly every psalm
verse. (For instance, "The Lord is my shepherd: I shall not want." But note
also, "We're American Airlines: doing what we do best.") Normally there
are three main inflections: the intonation at the beginning, the mediant at
the end of the first half of verse, and the termination at the end. The
additional flex and tenor are used when the first half of the psalm verse is
of such length so as to require a small inflection in its middle.

All the tenors of the psalm tones are on the dominant, that is, a fifth
away from the finalis of authentic modes, or a third away from the finalis
of plagal modes, inasmuch as it is historically proper to speak of a psalm
tone "having" a mode, for the psalm tones precede the conceptualization of
the church mode by centuries, dating back to the Jewish cantillation of
psalms in the temple and the synagogue. In fact, we must register an
important distinction between psalm tones and their respective modes. The
church modes are characterized by their finales, their ambituses, and their
dominants. Apel rightly acknowledges the latter as something "in the nature of a secondary tonal center." These secondary tonal centers, however,
are not really as consistent as the tenors of the psalm tones themselves,
which already represent the operation of the *ratio* upon the corporate melos
of liturgical recitative. As stated above, the tenor or dominant is a fifth
above the final in the authentic modes (1, 3, 5, and 7) and a third above it
in the plagal modes (2, 4, 6, and 8). The tone b, however, was not permitted to be a tenor and was replaced by c' in modes 3 and 8. And accordingly, the tenor g was raised to a in mode 4, apparently so as to correspond
to the raised c' in mode 3. But Apel notes, "these dominants are a characteristic less of the modes—they play only a minor, or at least, a very
questionable role in Gregorian melodies—than of a few special recitation
formulas associated with the modes, that is, the eight psalm tones . . . in
which they are used as the pitch for the monotone recitation."[5]

Two points must be stressed here. Apel is properly cautious. We cannot
date the great body of Latin melismatic chant before the entry of the
singing of psalms in the Christian church, although we properly register the
fact that melismatic singing was not a new invention of the Christians:
there is the ancient tradition of the Jewish Hallelujah.[6] But when we do
isolate the greatest activity of chant composition, the tonal functioning of
the psalm tones is already an established tonal phenomenon in certain
contexts but not in others. Secondly, there is the tone B, casually mentioned
above but which was never casually treated by the Latin theorists. This
critical operation of the *ratio* forms one of the important platforms of our
tonal consciousness in the first millennium of Western tonality, and we
have yet to resolve all the problems that it necessarily raises for the tonal

consciousness of the medieval mind. I quote a remark from chapter 3 of Apel's cogent book and offer a few additional comments.

> Considering the admirable variety of tonal realms afforded by the eight-mode system on a strictly diatonic basis (a variety much greater than the major-minor system was able to elicit from the much fuller material afforded by the chromatic scale), one cannot help pondering about the reasons that led to the addition of the b-flat, the single "black sheep," as it were, among the "pure-white" flock of the Gregorian pitches. Whatever answer may be given to this question—the most obvious one being that it was added in order to avoid the tritone above f—it is interesting to notice that the b-flat is not officially recognized in the earliest treatises containing information about the tonal material of the chant.[7]

Why? The reason the earliest treatises containing information about the tonal material of the chant do not officially recognize the B-flat is because their authors were not fully aware that they did not have a completely diatonic melos: the pre-notational singers of chant simply did not know there was any problem to be confronted. Until the characteristic and already widely scattered melos was brought under the control of a conforming notational practice, which had to proceed from letters to staffless puncta to the perfectibility and limitations of lines and spaces, there could be no serious grappling with the problems of a system so evolved. This affected chant in two ways. The pitch B-flat was accommodated in written notation when it was thought necessary to preserve the integrity of an inherited melos already venerated through centuries of habitual oral practice. And B was simply shelved by the Latin theorists when it became problematic to their own consciousness, which was so important to them that they moved *other* pitches within the psalm tones to correspond with changes they had made because of it. This is to say that we do not know exactly how the psalms were sung in the early but critical centuries of Christian psalmodic practice; nor can we trust a comparative analysis with Jewish cantillation (where illumination might conceivably be sought) because their own written sources are regrettably quite late. This means that the practice of tenor (or dominant) recitation may have been much stricter (or, on the other hand, even freer) regarding the selection of reciting tones than the Latin theorists ever admitted. Their late demands upon the psalmodic melos may have been quite rational to them, but they offer little assistance to the modern scholar who wishes to establish the ground for his own tonal consciousness. Having made this point with the utmost respect for what the medieval theorists did, although one still wonders exactly why they did it, let us return to the specific formal dimensions of the psalm tone. For the rather late activity of the medieval theorists and their various judgments regarding B and B-flat are not as crucial to tonic and dominant modeling as the structure of the psalm tone itself, in terms of expectation and fulfillment.

The binary structure of parallelismus membrorum decisively lent itself to the establishment of tonal expectation and fulfillment. Since the psalm verse falls into two parts, the psalm tone, accordingly, falls into halves, the first half consisting of the initial intonation figure, the tenor or dominant, and the mediant at the end of the first half of the verse; the second half consists of the tenor again and a termination of cadential conclusion. This is repeated for each subsequent verse except that the intonation figure is dropped. At least initially, then, there is a coming to the chief recitation tone and a going away from it, and it is here that we can properly isolate an early tonal function of sonic motion as dictated by the internal aesthetic of the phrase rather than superimposed from without by any general notion of the "naturalness" of the *Klang*. The center of each half of the psalmodic formulae became (in fact, had been since the beginnings of Jewish and Christian chant) the locus of a special tonal activity; the tenor was never thought of as a place of tonal rest in terms of conclusion and final repose. It was, instead, the arena of textual progression and was expected to serve the text regardless of its length. But the tenor surrendered its position of temporal dominance (the words have been carefully chosen) at the flex (when necessary), at the mediant (which only served to confirm its importance), and finally at the termination, where it gave up pitch place to the tonic (See Apel, *Gregorian Chant*, Figure 49; p. 215).

I believe that only one further point need be made at this stage: it is safe to say that these various tonal formulae were sung millions of times. A common feature between Judaism and Christianity is that the psalms formed the bedrock of their liturgies—for instruction, for praise, and for prayer. Generation after generation, they were sung for and by the members of thousands of religious communities; they became irrevocably fixed in memory, both their texts and their melodies, not because nature demanded their execution in such a manner but simply because that was the way that habit had dictated. There is something terribly Humean in this, which I did not intend, but here, I believe, is a firm and significant beginning of the dialectic of tonic and dominant. As stated in chapter 3, with even broader implications, it is characteristic of Western tonality that tonal melodic form followed tonal linguistic function. I do not mean to imply that the ancient Jews created a simple melos for the singing of psalms upon which they elaborated and ornamented their way through to much more melismatic melodies or that the early Christians did so either. Everything is much more complex. There are the hymns and the florid melodies of the

Hebrew Hallelujah, with corresponding forms in early Christianity. But it is to say that there is a specific musical (and linguistic) form which came to stand for tonal expectation and fulfillment. The beginning set of tones was followed by a middle tone; this middle tone was felt to be a state of activity and incompleteness merely because the hearer of the text knew that the text was not yet finished; and the text continued to its grammatical close and was musically finalized by tonal motion toward a predictable conclusion.

A second critical aspect of psalmody reveals particularly how the medieval theorists and psalm singers began to marshall the vast repository of the sacred melos into comprehensive and memorable units of tonal order. We find this activity documented in the tonaries. These books, of course, do not contain the earliest attempts to establish the tonality of the many hundreds of antiphons of the liturgy, but the titles that the later compilers gave their books are indeed instructive: the *Tonarius* of Regino, the *Intonarium* of Oddo, and *De modorum formulis* ascribed to Guido—these are clearly the operation of the *ratio* upon the great body of music that had been largely created, in tonal terms, as acts of unreflected consciousness. Thus, what the theorists found, when they turned their attention to the relationship between psalms and antiphons, was something in need of tonal codification and control. The results eventually were to become a remarkable sonic achievement.

Scholars of psalm tones realize that I have given a rather superficial presentation of the complex state of affairs in the singing of psalms. There is a problem of the several different terminations (*differentiae*) of the tones themselves, that is, particular endings that were chosen for the ends of the tones with regard to the antiphons that came before and after the psalm verse. The medieval practice was to sing the antiphon before and after the psalm, although according to the ancient practice of antiphonal psalmody the antiphon would also have been sung between all the verses of the psalm. Apel notes that "the connection between the Antiphon and the Psalm was made with a distinct view toward tonal unity. . . . It was this close connection between Antiphon and Psalm that led to the establishment of the two parallel systems, that of the eight modes and that of the eight tones."[8] Therefore, we find the tonaries to be compilations, tonal catalogs, if you will, in which antiphons were grouped according to the respective modes, thus assisting the singer in the selection of the proper psalm tone in which to sing the accompanying psalm.

How was the connection made between psalm and antiphon with regard to their respective tonal elements? According to the general scheme of antiphon—psalm plus doxology—antiphon, there were two important places of joining: the beginning, between the end of the antiphon and the intonation of the psalm tone; and the end, between the termination of the psalm tone (sung to the last words of the doxology) and the beginning of the repeated antiphon. Now the end of the antiphon was fairly predictable; it ended on the finalis of its mode. The beginning of the antiphon was another matter. Recall Gevaert's early work on the practice of centonization. He discovered that plainchant generally exhibited a large but finite number of melodic tropes which were used over and over again in the evolution of the collective melos into discrete and different types of chant activity. But even when we grant this practice its proper place within the "composing" of plainchant, there are still a great many ways in which to begin antiphons even when they belong to the same mode. For instance, first mode antiphons may begin on c, d, f, g, or a. This problem, Apel notes, "was ingeniously solved by providing, under the name of *differentiae*, a number of terminations closing on different pitches, and selecting for a given Antiphon that termination the closing notes of which harmonized with the initial notes of the Antiphon."[9] While tones 2, 5, and 6 (and the *tonus peregrinus*, with its two tenors) have only one ending, the other five tones have various endings because of the relationship that each tone exhibits with the repetition of the antiphon to follow it. For instance, tone 8 has three terminations, and tone 1 has ten. "Roughly speaking," notes Richard H. Hoppin in his study on medieval music, "the number of terminations for a given tone corresponds with both the total number of antiphons in the mode and the number of different characteristic patterns with which those antiphons begin."[10]

We note with interest that these connecting links, between the various differentiae and the beginnings of the antiphons, were cited as early as the *Alia Musica* (c. 900). Its commentary, the *Nova Expositio*, states that each tonus, besides having a number of differentiae, also has *loca* (places), which are actually the various typical incipits that antiphons exhibit as characteristic openings. To be sure, Apel notes that the author of the *Nova Expositio* "does not provide an unequivocal correlation between the *loca* and the *differentiae*."[11] We can, however, forgive his ambiguity, for an important element of tonal consciousness begins to surface with his efforts. We concur with Apel that the later medieval compilers of the tonaries were not so much interested in the coupling of single notes at critical tonal points as they were in the relationships between two groups of notes, that is, "the termination formula of the psalm tone and the initial passage of the Antiphon."[12] Such a relationship would have been extremely impractical had the antiphons been entirely arbitrary as to their openings. But they were not. As Gevaert was to demonstrate, and as the medieval singer must have realized through his familiarity with the many chants, they had typical beginnings and these could be approached in a fixed number of ways. That he should carry out this stage of his tonal consciousness in such a fashion does not really surprise us when we recognize what gains he hoped to achieve by his efforts. It did not occur to the medieval singer to worry unduly about the internal modeling of the chant, since he was working with an inherited melos which he considered sacrosanct. In fact, it was so sacred to him that he would not think of changing it. But the psalm tones themselves were recognized to be exactly what they were, which is formulae for the singing of psalms. These could be adjusted any number of ways so as to accommodate the various but critical tonal incipits of the many antiphons, which the singer already judged to be as important as their closures in the determination of their tonal order.[13] This is to say that here we witness tonality, or (more properly) tonal consciousness, working its way inward to the very core of its inherited melos. The beginnings and the endings of the antiphons were judged to be critically tonal: the psalm tones were also judged to be of critical tonal importance as vehicles of collective sonic coherence, and the connections between them were carefully determined. This kind of tonal connection was no less important to the medieval singer and theorist than it would later become for Mozart and Schubert, who decided within the context of their own respective tonal limitations and freedoms in which key the secondary theme of a sonata form ought to and would occur. A major premise of tonal consciousness in any era is the aspect of unity that it exhibits between large portions of musical thought as well as the internal cohesiveness of any minute temporal order of successive notes. The medieval singer did not have to worry much about the internal order: it had been given to him. But as he realized both its potential and its limitations, he also began to convey to the system as a whole the tonal continuity that he thought it so richly (and rightly) deserved.

We turn now to an investigation of tonic and dominant modeling in two-part polyphony. The annulment of certain aspects of monophonic tonal consciousness and the preservation of other of its aspects in the new polyphony of the Middle Ages can unfold here only as a series of Adornian tropes that I trust will encourage scholars of early polyphony (who are far better equipped than I) to examine this large body of literature from fresh points of view. I have examined the origins of polyphony in chapter 5 and shall bypass here a discussion of pre-twelfth-century polyphony in order to concentrate briefly on the two-voice music of the Abbey of St. Martial in Limoges and more extensively on the somewhat later activity of Notre Dame in Paris. Even this arbitrary narrowing of the field of investigation will raise questions that cannot presently, indeed may never, be answered. Nevertheless, they must be asked, if we are to keep before us the proper historical dimensions of our project. A short review is helpful.

As stated in chapter 5, the strict organum that is described in the *Musica Enchiriadis*, its companion *Scholia*, and *De Organo*, all dating from about

900, comprise the earliest technical descriptions of polyphonic practice in Europe and enjoyed a respectable circulation for their time. While a number of churches and monasteries apparently settled down to digest these polyphonic theory manuals, which were laboriously copied and carried from region to region, Rome remained aloof for several centuries from the new practice. The creation of polyphony remained largely the responsibility of the churches in France and England. And even then it was to be over a century before we see whole pieces begin to evolve in the new style. Strict organum was quite probably an early attempt by the theorists to articulate what primitive (that is, nonliturgical) singers did when they sang polyphony. It appears in retrospect to be a method to canonize what the theorists must have judged to be fairly improvisational in its original intent. This is perhaps why we find so little actual music that is rigidly parallel throughout the course of its melodic motion. The rules for parallel organum served, then, as handy ad hoc guides for those churches that chose to "ornament" the liturgical melos, and the pieces in the early treatises look much like textbook examples.

Free organum was another matter, and within its early practice lies the precise reason that the provisional rules for strict parallel organum were never followed by a durable praxis. The reason for the dominance of free over strict organum rests with the theorists who described it and who attempted to secure for polyphony the same tonal gains that had already been achieved for monophony. They could, of course, be only partially successful, but they began to forge tonal polyphony within the context of monophonic tonal modeling; at the same time they gradually created new tonal models with specific characteristics of their own.

I have stated that they could be only partially successful. Before we launch into a discussion of two-part polyphony, I would like to indicate what I mean. We find in the *Musica Enchiriadis* various arrangements of three- and four-voice organum, which may be attempts to establish contacts with variative polyphonic expression that characterized musical creativity beyond the confines and interests of medieval churches and monasteries. But what are the reasons for abandoning the remarkable potential of the *Musica Enchiriadis* for several centuries of only two-voice music? What failure of nerve can account for the almost immediate limitation of the potential polyphonic paradise to just two sung parts? A century later, how many members of the religious community at Winchester could sing the 150 organa dupla found in the manuscripts they left behind? How many of the faithful of England heard it? We are forced to leave these intriguing questions to speculation. We may safely assume, however, that the medieval musician frequently found polyphony difficult to learn and to sing. Initially it was practiced by only a few members (the soloists) of a given church or cathedral: the manuscripts bear this out. This is to say that if there were immediate gains to be made in the modeling of polyphonic tonality, they could not initially be solved within the majestic arena of multi-voice sound: they had first to be worked out in the simplest manner in two-part music. The reason, of course, is a tonal one, as we shall discover in the discussion to follow.

The first topic we must consider is the *occursus*, i.e., "in the ninth- and tenth-century organum of the fourth, the unison-confluence of the two parts employed at the beginning and end of phrases."[14] This converging organum represents a critical aspect of polyphonic tonality. While the occursus, the "coming together" of the voices in a cadential fashion, is a distinct feature of Guido's treatment of organum, we may also interpret other statements from the earliest treatises as attempts to establish from the beginning the same tonal structuring. The second rule from *De Organo* is quite clear on this point: "at the end of most melodic sections the two voices separated from each other must come together on the same note, namely, where the end of a section occurs on the final of a mode. . . ."[15] While the early treatises do not lead us to believe that oblique and contrary motions were to be adopted for their own sake (as the writings from around 1100 begin to imply), we note that they must occur for the sake of tonal focus at critical points. The reason that this motion was desired and that "symphonies" other than the interval of the fourth were occasionally permitted is explained by the author of the *Scholia*, who states that it was in order to prevent the vox organalis from passing below the fourth degree of the lower tetrachord of the gamut of pitches, thus preventing the tritone from occurring. But where this rule is applied is more important than the problematic tritone, which could easily be avoided—and was—through the use of accidentals. It was applied at the final notes, "the end of most melodic sections," where we have discovered similar care was also taken in monophonic chant to establish tonal focus. Remember that it is *chant* that is being subjected to polyphonic treatment, chant that was already tonal by virtue of certain features of its melos: organum was quickly made to serve similar requirements of tonal order.

We will never know if the early theorists were actually attempting to document two different kinds of primitive polyphony (strict and free), and ultimately it is not that important. But within two hundred years, contrary and oblique motions were not only well established; they were preferred. While parallel organum continued marginally to exist for centuries, we are told by the thirteenth-century French theorist, Elias Salomon, it did not develop much further as a compositional technique. It could not do so: it had little tonal potential in terms of its inherited melos. Even the distinctive chains of thirds and tenths in the music of Ockeghem and the first-inversion triads of English discant would be marshalled within the parameters of oblique and contrary motions that secured a tonal identity for the whole.

The second topic to be investigated is the harmony of this early polyphonic tonality itself. It is, of course, related to the occursus and cannot be treated entirely separate from it, but it also exhibits unique characteristics of its own. It is instructive to summarize what a few of the treatises state about it, since they are the apparent agents of control, although their admonitions occasionally bear little resemblance to the actual course of events in composed music.[16]

1) *Micrologus* of Guido d'Arezzo, ca. 1030.[17] It is difficult to judge Guido's treatise as indicative of a universal state of affairs in eleventh-century polyphony, although it was widely copied and apparently influenced subsequent theorists. Guido acknowledges the continuing existence of parallel organum, but his interests are specifically concerned with what happens at the occursus, the cadential coming together at the end of the phrase. He does not like the fifth and considers it hard and rigid. In addition, he finds strict organum at the fourth also rigid, and states that a piece must not end with it as the last or even penultimate interval. In progressing to and from a unison, major and minor thirds and the major second are to be used, but these are qualified. A minor third may not progress to a unison by contrary motion; the major second must also progress by oblique motion. Guido finds modes 3 and 4 "only usable" for the composition of organum; modes 5 and 8 are "especially adaptable." Although the chant is still in the top voice, crossed voices are permitted because of the occursus. No example shows more than three voices, and these are, of course, not independent voices, one being created by octave doubling.

2) *De Musica* of John Cotton, ca. 1100.[18] This theorist attempts no extensive discussion of organum, but what he does state indicates new potential for polyphonic writing. Cotton believes that of the many ways of making organum, that which uses contrary motion is the most easily comprehensible, but perhaps this is only because the problem of augmented intervals is in part avoided. It is important to note that organum is no longer to be written with just *one* interval: unisons, octaves, fourths, and fifths are freely mixed. All cadences should not be at the unison; the octave may also be used, depending on the position of the chant. Thus, crossed voices are not only sanctioned, but frequently preferred. Finally, although he gives no examples, two and three notes in the vox organalis seem to be permitted against one in the principalis. The passage concerning this is ambiguous.

3) *Ad Organum Faciendum*, ca. 1100.[19] This is the earliest treatise devoted entirely to organum, which is characterized by two important changes. The vox principalis is consistently placed on the bottom of the texture. And

second, the same chant is given several different counterpoints. This is implied by Cotton's treatise also, when it was stated that all the traditional consonances were to be mixed, but this anonymous author provides specific examples. The theoretical method by which this is obtained is unnecessarily complex. In short, organal "modes" offer different openings, middles, and ends for the organalis to be written over the same principalis.

4) *Tractatus de Musica*, twelfth century.[20] This is the earliest treatise to differentiate between discant and organum styles. We shall examine these differences in light of St. Martial organum with which the treatise is roughly contemporary. Only two short chapters of this treatise are devoted to organum.

5) An anonymous Montepellier organum treatise.[21] This treatise dates from the early twelfth century and describes eleventh-century organum. As with the *Ad Organum Faciendum*, a system of organal "modes" is advocated for the construction of different counterpoints. The organum phrase is divided into an *inceptio* (one note), middle (the organal section), and the cadence, or *copula* (two notes). As we might expect, the construction of cadences consumes a good portion of the author's attention, who suggests that they be used frequently ("phrases of more than eight notes will not be permitted"). And for the first time, major and minor thirds and sixths are given theoretical recognition as consonances. Not only are thirds and sixths freely used, they may open the organal phrase as well. It is not possible to determine whether the principalis is to be placed consistently on the bottom, and the discussion of voice crossing is no better described. This treatise has not received much attention from modern scholars. Its positive recommendation for the use of thirds and sixths, however, bridges the gap customarily assumed between actual polyphony in the twelfth century—when thirds and sixths frequently appear—and the other contemporary treatises which do not extol their use. There is a curious feature of this short treatise. It describes only note-against-note technique. Either the author was unaware of florid organum because it did not exist in his region, or he chose not to discuss it.

As mentioned above, the immediate activity of the churches of France and England centered around the creation of two-voice music. The largest early collections of this practical organum are the tenth- and early eleventh-century Winchester Tropers, in which the organal voice is still today largely undecipherable. The next sizable collections come from south-central France and the northwestern Spanish province of Galicia.[22] The French organa dupla form part of a large repository of over twenty musical manuscripts from the Abbey of St. Martial at Limoges. It cannot be stated factually that this corpus of literature necessarily represents the actual monophonic and polyphonic activity of the Abbey. Several scholars have remarked that it may more accurately represent the zeal of its librarians for collecting and preserving music. At any rate, we are grateful. The polyphonic pieces are largely contained in four manuscripts. A smaller but important group of organa dupla comes from Compostela, the pilgrimage site of thousands of Christians in the Middle Ages who came there to revere the alleged relics of St. James.

There are two distinct musical styles exhibited by the sixty-four pieces in the St. Martial repertory: melismatic organum, in which one note of the chant serves for several or a great many organal notes; and discant, syllabic text settings in note-against-note polyphony. Thus the terms organum and discant (*diaphonia*), which prior to the mid-twelfth century had been interchangeable, gradually came to stand for separate styles in two-voice music. The anonymous *Tractatus de Musica* is the first treatise to distinguish them. There is nothing in *Ad Organum Faciendum* and John Cotton's *De Musica* to forsee the extremes to which florid organum went before it gradually spent itself in the later twelfth century. Each note of the plainchant, or vox principalis, in this organum is more or less drawn out—certainly to the point that its traditional rhythmic execution in monophonic singing is thoroughly annulled. While it served thus as a sort of series of pedal points, another melody was written above it, although it often unfolds in virtually the same range as the chant, with occasional voice-crossing. This new melody is formally disposed to look, rather, to sound something like chant itself. As we would expect, some of the new monophonic music, chiefly paraliturgical, of the same period (and found in the same manuscripts) also exhibits this type of melodic similarity to chant.

The second musical style is "developed" discant, a modification of the strict note-against-note technique documented in the treatises of the early French theorists. St. Martial discant does employ strict note-against-note technique, but it is also extended to what Leo Treitler calls "neume-against-neume," in which "the ratio of duplum to tenor notes may be as high as 2:1, but where each syllable is set to no more than one neume."[23] This is exhibited in "Omnis curet homo," a *Benedicamus* trope (see Richard H. Hoppin, *Anthology of Medieval Music*, No. 30), although at the ends of poetic lines single neumatic treatment is abandoned for extended melismas on the penultimate syllable.

The two types of St. Martial polyphony, melismatic organum and discant, exhibit different features of harmonic consciousness in terms of expectation and fulfillment. This is to say that in melismatic organum the cadence comes more or less randomly, that is, when the chant (or that portion to be treated melismatically) is used up. In the strophic rhymed poetry of the sequence, versus, and prosa forms that characterize the developed discant style, however, which gradually tended toward symmetry, the formal properties of the text become critical features of tonal modeling. Literary form leads to the establishment of tonal expectation within the relatively discrete unit of the musical phrase. This can be demonstrated with virtually any of the discant pieces, for instance, "Omnis curet homo" (*AMM*, No. 30). Harmonic intervals occur in conjunction with poetic form, and the same interval has varying degrees of tonal weight depending on its context in the phrase. For instance, the two octaves of "mor-ta" in the last versicle do not shape the phrase, which has hardly begun, although the same interval is quite capable of that function at the end of the refrain. It is not only the quality of the interval but its position in the progression that secures the relationship that it administers.

The alternation of musical styles that characterizes the polyphonic sections of the St. Martial repertory is even more pronounced in that of Notre Dame. The melismatic organal sections exhibit tenors of great length, so that to call them pedal points (probably played on instruments) is a fairly accurate description of their structural function. We shall concentrate on the organal sections first. Our discussion will center chiefly around three extensive organa, readily available in standard anthologies: "Hec dies" (*Harvard Anthology of Music*, I, No. 29); "Alleluia: Nativitas" (*Anthology of Medieval Music*, No. 33); and "Alleluia: Non vos reliquam" (*Medieval Music*, eds. W. Thomas Marrocco and Nicholas Sandon, No. 43).

The typical phrase of a duplum melody in the organal sections frequently runs from two to six measures and is articulated by a rest. It is probably deceptive to give undue importance to the type of rest (short or long) that separates these phrases, since we do not know how carefully they were regarded in performance. The most characteristic melodic shape is one that begins well above the tenor and gradually descends, undulating through a series of stepwise motions and skips that terminate most frequently on a consonance. Excessive skips are rare, but do occur at the beginnings of phrases in order to move the duplum away from the tenor. There is a modest amount of repetition and sequence, for instance, the opening measures of "Hec dies."

There are two types of cadences in the organal sections: those which are articulated in the upper voice alone while the tenor is stationary, so that the motion is oblique; and those which occur when both voices move at once. Most frequently, the type of motion found at these latter cadences is contrary, although some parallel motion can be found as well. By far the most common interval on which the voices converge is the fifth, and then the unison.

The difference in the actual harmonic weight between these two types of cadence is not entirely perceptible to the modern ear. To be sure, the singers had to breathe, and the oblique motion cadences permit this articulation in the vocal line as smoothly as do the ones in contrary motion. But as stated above, we do not know how rests were actually regarded in performance. There does appear to be some difference between these cadences, however, even with nothing before us but a dead score. Contrary motion cadences occur on unisons, fifths, and octaves. (One cadence on a third does occur in contrary motion, but it is the result of crossed voices.) Oblique motion cadences, however, converge on these intervals but also on the second, third, fourth, and sixth. We must immediately qualify some of these peculiar harmonic pauses, and a glance at "Alleluia: Nativitas" exhibits what is frequently the case. In measure 63, there is a cadence on a minor third; in measure 75, one on a major second. However, in both of these instances there follows immediately another, more satisfactory cadence in terms of consonantal repose—a 2–1 appoggiatura. It would seem that the composer is jockeying into position for a full cadence and foreshadows this expected conclusion with one of a less conclusive sort—as if to suggest what can initially be, and what must ultimately be the case, harmonically speaking. This kind of double cadence is not uncommon. Another good example is the end of the versicle of "Hec dies," on the penultimate syllable "ni-." Beginning on the octave over c′, there is a long undulating melody, articulated into three phrases, the last of which ends on a major second. There is a rest, and the last measure contains only a 2–1 appoggiatura on the last syllable "am." This double cadence also occurs twice in the versicle of "Alleluia: Non vos reliquam" (see measures 121–22 and 145–46). Another curious feature of these organa is the way in which they frequently open with a kind of tonal incipit in which the octave is "established." (Major polyphonic subsections also open in a similar fashion.) In two of the pieces the octave is approached from the lower seventh. No immediate reason can be offered for this and we do not know why the medieval composers and singers apparently took delight in opening their organa with an interval that they understood to be dissonant.

Determining what constitutes a cadence in the clausulae in these two-part organa is difficult. If we take only those cases into account in which there is a dotted quarter rest in both voices or in which a word of the text is apparently terminated, the unison is the favorite concluding interval. Fifths are also popular but, as we might expect, do not occur at the ends of sections. In addition, there is the fact that in some cases a consonant cadence is left by dissonant stepwise motion. For instance, this occurs in the first clausula of "Alleluia: Non vos reliquam" (measures 29, 31, 39 and 45). In these instances, the duplum usually moves into a solitary pitch over a rest in the tenor.

We have cited a number of tonal facts about this two-voice music. What can be said of a general nature about its overall tonic-dominant modeling? First, is there any? And second, if there is, to what extent does it contribute to tonal order?

Generally, we may make the following statements. The tonal gains that had been achieved in monophonic tonality were brought into the new sphere of harmonic consciousness. Since to a large extent it is chant that was being reworked in polyphonic dress, we can expect to find preestablished areas of tonal expectation and fulfillment—chiefly, the beginning and ending of the monophonic phrase. We take note of the care that the theorists themselves invested in these areas of tonal modeling, particularly in the *Micrologus, De Musica, Ad Organum Faciendum,* and the anonymous Montepellier treatise from the early twelfth century. The occursus, the *copula,* represented areas of concern to these authors, who sought to secure for polyphony the same tonal identity which had been won in the monophony that they and their fellow musicians were still actively engaged in performing. Over this tonal ground we find a group of consonances (unison, fifth, and octave), a group of imperfect consonances (third and sixth), and a group of dissonant intervals (chiefly, second and seventh) that gradually are seen to be collectivized by ever more careful treatment of their appearance in the polyphonic complex. Even as early as the twelfth century, in the music of St. Martial, and especially in the later music of Notre Dame, we find that the fifth has come to stand for a cadential interval of openness and incompleteness. Initially, this might surprise us when we realize that the subsequent era of three-part polyphony will incorporate the fifth into the final interval complex at the cadence. But the creator of two-voice polyphony did not know this. Instead, he began to work with a series of dyads which he invested with tonal activity in relation to his formal structures. Within the context of formal definition of both text and preexisting monophonic chant, the perfect fifth came to stand for something in two-voice composition that was less conclusive than the octave or the unison. Thus we find it, generally speaking, at points of internal punctuation, or defining sections of music that are clearly in midcourse. This sense of "half" and "whole," if we are permitted to call it that, already witnessed in the binary structure of psalmody, became a conscious component of emergent harmonic motion. We shall see in our subsequent examination of three-part music that even there the normative dominant does not immediately manifest itself, although its gradual definition is a remarkable movement of the dialectic of tonic-dominant modeling in the form of the "first-inversion triad." What is of paramount importance in this short survey of monophonic and two-part polyphonic music is that—in the form of nontonic elements—a tonal place for the dominant has already been wrested from the chaos of possible pitch and interval orders of sound in motion. When it does appear, the dominant harmony will not have to create a place of its own within processive temporal order: it will be accommodated within existing harmonic structures. That it will come to establish their validity with reference to its own is another matter.

It would be instructive here to follow the dialectic in its proper stages through the appearance of three- and four-part polyphony and to do this within various geographical perimeters of that actual appearance. Surely, it is hazardous to assume that the modeling of tonic and dominant in the Renaissance was already tonally leveled at any given stage of its appearance in England, in the Franco-Flemish region, in Italy, or in Germany; that is, leveled into the classroom model of a V–I cadence in four parts with the root doubled and the voices moving to expected points of repose. But it is because we desire this notion magically to appear that we have exhibited some rather silly attitudes that we have about Renaissance polyphony in terms of its tonal coherence and motion. This area of our musical con- sciousness has become a place in academic circles where pitched battles are fought in favor of the assumed progressive or conservative platforms of a given theorist (Zarlino is a favorite), who is thought to vindicate what the scholar believes can be the only true state of affairs. Dufay and his contem- poraries are acknowledged for their V–I cadences in root position, but, as we have seen, their consciousness is then rationalized into mere accident by stating that "of course, these men did not think of their music in this fashion." Another scholar is "surprised" to find C major clearly exhibited (with its respective cadences) in the secular music of the early sixteenth century. Another decides that "any systematic treatment of harmony ac- cording to the intervals over the bass would be alien to Zarlino's theories." And still another decides that those compositions which do not measure up to "a certain standard of modal purity" but are "still not sufficiently tonal" must be thrust into a category of his own invention, haplessly labeled "monal," this category "being particularly apt for that period of incubation from approximately 1540 to 1620." From the standpoint of modern schol- ars, the implications are clear. The Renaissance composer did not know what he was doing: he was trying to be tonal in the "common-practice" sense, but he had just not acquired the necessary sophistication; he was naively tonal. The fact that he himself lived out his entire life within the limits of another common-practice period is worse than ignored; it is not even recognized.

The methodical examination of these stages must wait for a more exten- sive study that will enrich our attitudes about late medieval and Renais- sance polyphony rather than reduce them to concepts that inhibit the meaning of their project. It is folly to assume that the theorists were read in the fourteenth to sixteenth centuries with the zeal that the *Journal of Music*

Theory would lead us to believe. The composers had other things to do. To be sure, music theory achieved a status in Renaissance culture that can only be properly and historically compared to the Greek theory that preceded it. But for that reason, it is also frequently just as tedious and just as difficult to judge by its merits. Certainly, Zarlino is to be reckoned with, but, as stated in chapter 6, I find his position highly conservative and hardly to be taken as an accurate testimony of what composers themselves pandemically perceived tonally in the creation of their works. Therefore, in this section, I am going to ignore in general what theorists said composers ought to do and turn instead to an admittedly small group of well-known, three-voice pieces which exhibit exactly what early polyphonic composers thought they exhibited: a judgment against the chaos of pitch of their own largely diatonic melos. Put in the plainest of terms, this is not to say that when I find tonic-dominant modeling in these pieces I am standing on the sideline cheering their prophetic vision for the "outcome" of tonality. Rather, what I wish to examine—to the degree that such examination is possible—is why they thought such modeling was expressive, logical, and of cognitive value within their own tonal consciousness.

The first of these pieces is a motet *a*3 by Petrus de Cruce, "Aucun—Long tans—Annuntiantes" (*Historical Anthology of Music*, I, No. 34). What superficially appears to be a Schenkerian harmonic nightmare proves under closer scrutiny to be instead the conscious operation on the part of the composer to control to the best of his ability the vertical potential of the relatively new three-part counterpoint. This motet exhibits the typical Crucian style. There is a slow moving tenor, laid out in a short talea of three notes in long values, which is separated from its repetition by a rest. A second section begins at measure 37, in which the tenor melody is repeated once but without the intervening rests. The duplum moves more quickly, in phrases of five to nine measures in length; there is a modest amount of formal organization through the repetition of certain units of the rhythmic pattern of the opening phrase. The triplum moves even more quickly in parlando passages that alternate with relatively long notes. It cadences most frequently after it has sung two lines of its own text. Half of the time, when it does this, the duplum has not yet finished its own line of text, although it assists in the shaping of the cadences.

There are eleven cadences, but the seventh one, which occurs at the end of the first complete melodic statement on the tenor, is the double cadence type frequently found in early polyphony, and we shall treat it separately. While the piece begins and ends each of its two sections on F because the Lydian tenor begins and ends on this note, the harmonic scheme is not overly committed to the tonal center of F. This is due to the more abundant G, which appears eight times in the tenor melody. If Cruce did not wish G to dominate his cadential structures, he would have had to take greater pains to avoid it. Thus, there are five cadences on G (six, if we count the first half of the seventh cadence), three on C, two on F, and one on A.

Within these eleven cadences, we find a variety of cadential forms, all of them rationalized by the composer in terms of moving into consonant harmonies at the proper time. There are three first-inversion cadences, and we are not surprised where we find them: they are the first cadence in the motet and the final cadences of each section. Cruce is aware of the importance of this already familiar method of tonal control. (When speaking of a progression as a cadence there is an important feature of tonic-nontonic modeling here which must be stressed. Just as every V–I progression is not a cadence, depending on where it occurs in the harmonic phrase, so not every first-inversion progression to open fifth and octave is a cadence. This is clearly seen in measures 52–53, where the triplum has just begun its new phrase of text and is not about to participate in any cadence. The two "leading tones" do move properly by step, causing parallel fifths as the tenor moves down, but the harmonic conclusion of this phrase is cadence 10 in measures 56–57.) There are two cadences in which a fifth moves into a unison by contrasting motion. In each of these cadences one voice is absent on the penultimate harmony (the duplum in cadence 2, measures 6–7; the tenor in cadence 4, measures 16–17) because it is finishing its own phrase, but it begins again on the resolution of the cadential figure, thus serving to overlap the phrases. The fifth cadence (measures 21–22) is in root position, which is achieved by crossed voices between the duplum and the tenor. It looks like a V_7–I cadence in C, but the minor seventh resolves back up to g in the top voice! This is apparently done to avoid a full triad on a cadence, but Cruce does provide the missing e in the duplum as an afterthought, at the same time that he terminates the sounding fifth over the root. There are two cadences arrived at by parallel fifths (8, measures 41–42; 9, measures 47–48); this may in part be due to the fact that Cruce has decided in this section of the motet to let the tenor proceed in even note values from beginning to end without rests. The only cadence on A (measures 47–48) is achieved through these parallel fifth cadences, as is one of the cadences on C (measures 41–42). In either case a full triad is avoided (as elsewhere) on the point of harmonic resolution. The third, sixth, and tenth cadences (measures 10–11, 26–27, and 56–57) exhibit an octave (f–f′) proceeding to a fifth (g–d′) by contrary motion. In each case there are parallel fifths between the tenor and the triplum, but the duplum is above the triplum and proceeds down through a seventh to the fifth. And finally, we turn to the first of the two cadential figures that terminate the first complete statement of the tenor, beginning "En sa prison" in the triplum (measure 32; see Example 7-1).

hau - sa-ge Amours, et moi tout mon   vi-vant te-nir En   sa pri - son.

A   li   ne   do it   on   nul—le au - tre   com —

Example 7-1

Here we see challenged the frequently cited myth that as long as the upper voices are consonant with the tenor they need not be consonant with each other. There *is* no tenor, and the two upper voices seem to be jockeying into position for a unison e' on "sa," but they do so in a Bartokian fashion that eludes conventional notions of tonal coherence. Is the composer perhaps underscoring the nastiness of "prison" itself? From the unison e' on "sa" Cruce proceeds to a fourth between these two voices, but the tenor enters and forms a fifth and an octave with them on g. The last three-part harmony we hear in this section is a first-inversion triad moving from a sixth in the outer voices into an octave, but the triplum trails on while the root f in the tenor drops out and next so does the fifth on c'. This leaves the triplum to finish its phrase alone, but its last note is overlapped with the beginning of the second section of the motet.

What can be said in summary about this fascinating motet in terms of tonal modeling but a series of engaging questions? Is Cruce tonal? Should we decide for him that his frequent cadences on G are actually a Schenkerian "neighbor" harmony that only serves to secure the ultimate commitment to the tonic F? What is the *Urlinie*? What is the tonic? In what sense is Cruce "loyal" to it? Is the motet a vapid attempt to "prolong the triad," which failed because the composer was a poor harmonist with no real sense of his own tonal consciousness? And where are the triads?

The adjective "real" in the above sentence only indicates that we ourselves are in doubt about what should and should not be called tonal. Cruce is as tonal as Mozart, although he certainly is not as "key-centered." Like the Viennese classicist, he suffers no angst over his harmonic consciousness. Rather, he revels in it because it is his own. He is able within the limits of late medieval tonal orders to build a piece of sonic architecture that is significant to him and his tonal hearers. His frequent cadences on G in the first section of his motet are governed by a prior commitment to lay out his tenor in units of three notes to a phrase. In the second section of the piece there is only one such cadence; there are three other cadences in this section, however, one each on C, A, and F. To be sure, he is loyal to the tonic of his tenor, which is F. But his loyalty to the tonic, "in the most general sense of the term," whatever that means, is jettisoned in favor of the architectonic superstructure of his motet as a whole. In terms of a tonic, durational pre-eminence capitulates to a new, superimposed order of formal constraint. (The same may be said of Schoenberg, who was just as tonal as Petrus de Cruce.)

Our second selection of three-part polyphony comes from the same anthology, Guillaume de Machaut's ballade, "Je puis trop bien" (Example 7-2 pp. 162–63). This ballade nicely demonstrates a texture typical of fourteenth-century French polyphony. The tenor and the contratenor are textless and clearly function as accompaniment to the texted superius. While the piece begins with an open fifth on a, it quickly moves to its first cadence on C. This is a curious iii–I progression, with the contratenor e below the tenor; an incomplete dominant seventh is formed on the last beat of the measure. The tenor is not a cantus firmus and can thus more freely participate in the creation of the eight cadences, five of which are on C. The sixth cadence is the only other root position one, a V–I on C, in which the third is again missing on the interval of resolution, although Machaut discreetly supplies the e' and then leaps down to c' (measure 22). There are two cadences on D, and the ouvert cadence at the end of the first section clearly exhibits motion away from the tonic C. This is not a dominant harmony, but it is a distinct early manifestation of momentary repose on a nontonic area, giving the sensation of incompleteness and arrested motion. It is entirely proper to regard this as a half-cadence.[24] By far the most preferred cadence is the first-inversion type, which appears five times (cadences 2, 3, 4, 7, and 8). This includes two cadences at expected points of termination—the clos cadence which ends the repeat of the a section, and the concluding cadence of the ballade. The first cadence in the b section is an odd one, if indeed it ought to be called a cadence at all. On "la prioit" we find a minor ninth over the tenor and the contratenor c. The contratenor drops out, then leaps to the superius on g, only to move into a f-natural (f-sharp?), forming a second with the tenor. This dissonance resolves on the word "mais." Is this perhaps a bit of harmonic text painting? The text reads "toudis la prioit" or "out of his senses."

This ballade is a model of clarity in terms of establishing the interval C–G as a tonal center. Machaut follows the rules of fourteenth-century counterpoint, and his tonal architecture is comfortably housed within harmonic motion away from and back to the principal tone area of C. It is impossible, of course, to state that he was thinking within the harmonic context of the Ionian mode, and Glareanus is still some years in the future; but it must be admitted that this ballade is a good example of the manner in which practice will dictate what theory will eventually sanction.

Our third example is John Dunstable's motet "Quam pulchra es," which is analyzed by Donald Grout in his *History of Western Music*.[25] Here the three-part texture exhibits lines of nearly equal importance and the same text appears in all voices. The motet is divided into two sections of unequal length. There are a total of ten cadences, with C clearly defining the opening of the motet and its close. There are four cadences on C. D is again the next most important tonal locus, with three cadences, followed by F (two) and finally G (one), which closes the first half of the piece. All the cadences in "Quam pulchra es" exhibit leading-tone, first-inversion to root-position movement, including the eighth one (*punica*) with its leap from a sixth into a third on the second beat. Of interest here and in three other cadences (2, 5, and 6) is the "inserted third" which appears on a weak beat after the point of repose has been reached. This has been frequently mentioned in the historical literature as a preference by the English for consonant harmony. Indeed, it may be regional, and it reflects the tertian sonic ideal that characterizes Western harmony from the time of Dunstable to the present.

In summary, we can make some general observations about the dialectic of tonic and dominant. The tonic is a place from which and to which tonal motion is generated. In this sense, Apel's statement that being loyal to a tonic characterizes the general theory of tonal consciousness is valid, albeit not very critical. For the tonic did not acquire this authority merely by setting up its kingdom *ex nihilo* or by its own impetus. It was awarded its function gradually, as consciousness itself historically structured its melos through pragmatic, cognitive activity. While this activity did not lie solely within the context of psalmody (both Jewish and Christian), it is of critical importance in the early stages of Western tonal evolution. The medieval tonaries suggest that there was imposed upon the more elaborate forms of Latin chant a steady effort by theorists to reduce the already complex melos to categories of general tonal cognition and acceptance. Inasmuch as the chant melody was a "given" (and the Latin singer assumed that it was), only limited tampering with it was permitted. But the psalm tones—although also regarded as ancient—were taken to be genuine formulae: their cadential figures could be altered to suit tonal demands. The careful process of connecting tonal units—antiphon to psalm tone to antiphon—marked an important stage in the attempt to bring the vast Latin melos within the cognitive comprehension of the everyday liturgical singer who had to carry large portions of it in his head. The concomitant activity of reducing this melos to purely theoretical statements, that is, the church modes, represents a further operation by the *ratio* to reduce the thousands

Example 7-2. Machaut, "Je puis trop bien." Reprinted by permission of the publishers from *Historical Anthology of Music*, edited by Archibald T. Davison and Willi

of chants to predictable levels of tonal familiarity and cognitive comprehensibility. This is not to resolve the vast project of Latin chant to only two components (psalm tones and church modes) of cognitive activity regarding its already tonal melos, but certainly they merit careful consideration in any adequate investigation of monophony.

The gradual but deliberate control of this monophonic melos must not be regarded as completely separate from the activity of early polyphony. The classical period of the chant manuscripts is also the period of early polyphonic consciousness. To be sure, polyphony did not appear at once in all places, and we will never know the extent to which it was practiced before the theorists began to grapple with it. But in terms of its appearance in medieval France, we note that the invested authority of Latin chant quickly brought to bear upon polyphonic potential certain of chant's own tonal restrictions and freedoms. While the treatises suggested early on that multivoice polyphony was possible, we note that the early polyphonic singers rapidly settled down to the problems of two-voice music. Almost as rapidly the chant lost its hierarchical superiority in the top line of organum and was placed below the vox organalis. A set of possible harmonic intervals evolved. The fourth gave way to the fifth. Unisons, fifths, and octaves were regarded as the necessary intervals for cadential repose. This tonal decision marked an important concept for harmonic consciousness and set the stage for the later incorporation of the third into what was to become a thoroughly tertian system of harmony. But just as important for the immediate concerns of the early harmonicists was the fact that these intervals came to stand for ways in which intervallic stability could be regarded as compatible with the tonic areas of pre-existing monophonic chant. While the purely monophonic integrity of chant was of course annulled, its own a priori tonic modeling was preserved at the next level of consciousness. The typical openings and closes of the monophonic chant phrase were not adapted to polyphonic treatment. Instead, a way in which to preserve their important tonal integrity was found that created tonality in a new form— the harmonic interval.

Polyphonically speaking, what we have come to understand as "the dominant" historically appeared first in the realm of the nontonic, those intervallic orders which could not appear at the predetermined opening and closing moments in the harmonized chant phrase. But they could appear after the opening notes and just before the required tonic closures of specific phrases. Here, as harmony, they began to assume the activity of something in relation to the tonic; this activity defined not only the tonic but their own qualitative essence. Because music proceeds from one note to another, from one interval to another, and ultimately from one chord to another, this procession gradually acquired the character of harmonic motion. The available catalog of intervals in terms of consonance and dissonance gradually became fixed, but with adjustments, particularly with regard to the fourth.

The most frequent cadence in early three-part music was the first-inversion, leading-tone one, although this was certainly not conceived by either musicians or theorists as an inverted triad. It was merely a harmonic complex that was entirely compatible with the newly emerging rules of part writing. The motion of the cantus (once monophonic chant) was typically down by step at cadential points. It therefore continued to resolve downward to its tonic within the polyphonic complex. In the Lydian mode there were two "leading tones," which were due to the diatonic order of the mode itself. It is impossible to determine exactly how the medieval musician "felt" about or "heard" these resolutions, but we do know that he wanted them to resolve upward, even when he purposely pretended through various ornamental figures (the "Landini" cadence, for one) that the resolution in the top voice could move down instead of up. Characteristically, when the two leading tones did move upward by step, they resolved to the two most consonant intervals, the perfect fifth and the perfect octave. So attractive was the sound of this three-part resolution that we find it widely used in other modes which in their original diatonic status did not afford the same harmonic cluster of intervals. Through the use of musica ficta Dorian and Mixolydian were altered so as to shape the desired harmonic cadence. While the Ionian mode was not found in the set of eight church modes, it was soon adopted for harmonic reasons because the cadence structure that it afforded did so with only one adjustment, that is, changing F to F-sharp when a cadence was desired on G. The Aeolian mode was also altered. Because of the great flexibility of musica ficta and the freedom with which composers could utilize it, no statistics are forthcoming as to whether the double leading-tone was preferred over a first-inversion, single leading-tone cadence. Either provided the characteristic ti–do figure as the penultimate interval expanded to the octave, which was eventually governed by a rule which stated that the sixth before an octave must be major, thus securing for the other modes what was already given diatonically by the Lydian and Ionian modes. Quite importantly, this leading tone became the third of the dominant triad.

It is necessary here to bring forth again the thorny issue of the historical "contest" between contrapuntal and harmonic principles. The best evidence that the medieval musician and composer did evolve a feeling for consonant sound and a more carefully controlled use of dissonance is simply that the music itself loses a good portion of the strange (to us) and somewhat angular harshness that earlier medieval music exhibits. But a note of caution must be registered. We cannot state that the medieval musician "did not hear his harmonies the way we do" simply because we find dissonance in his music that is not characteristic of the type of control to which it was eventually subjected in the Renaissance. No such tonal evaluation can be made for medieval consciousness. More importantly, we do not hear his harmonies the way he did. But a few suggestions can be offered about his harmonic cognitive perception. If dissonance (the harsh parallel-second kind, etc.) did trouble him, it did not trouble him very much at those places in the converging of melodic lines where he let it occur. The reason for this may be fairly simple. He may indeed have had no comprehensive picture of total harmonic control through the course of a given passage of music. This kind of control had to evolve along with his tonal consciousness. It would appear that he was quite aware of the relationship of dissonance to consonance at specific places in his harmonic complex, that is, at the opening and closing of phrases. But during the course of the phrase this control was not well-established and could therefore engage in the type of dissonance that we find in the music of the thirteenth century. Having created polyphony, rather, in the very process of creating polyphony, the composer must once again wrest his tonal creation from the chaos of pitch that lay potentially within his consciousness. As stated in the discussions above, it is quite proper that he should attend first and more carefully to those characteristic places where tonal configuration was already important to his ear. Indeed, he did not hear his harmonies the way we do: but he did hear them within the context of his own tonal orders, which he gradually brought under ever more careful control. In this light, his achievement is all the more remarkable. No Schenkerian maxim can be leveled upon his mind. Certain intervals and chords did not long for "a return to the tonic," where the "revengefulness of nature," was fulfilled. Like language, harmonic motion was a creation of consciousness itself, and the dialectic of tonic and dominant had to be both created and verified by the expressive activity of the *ratio* itself. As I have suggested, I feel that harmonic motion is the cognitive product of phrase motion as typified in the shaping (particularly but certainly not exclusively) of the psalm verse in Jewish and Christian cantillation. Once agreement had been reached in early polyphony, in which it was deemed proper and necessary to maintain the tonal ground that had been won in the battle of a lengthy, previous monophonic consciousness, there remained only the active project of expanding these tonal achievements within the newly acquired potential of polyphonic endeavors. The historical facts of "voice-leading" have never been in jeopardy, although, historically, the execution of a given vocal line has frequently proved more difficult than singers care to attempt. That is not the issue. The issue is to determine as carefully as we are able the position from which counterpoint—at any given moment in its historical development—was regarded as critical to the simple and complex solutions that harmonic consciousness brought to bear upon the established order of a priori and aesthetic judgments made about acceptable orders of tones. From this standpoint, the following can be stated by way of conclusion.

Within a largely conjunct melos it is not surprising to find the counter-point of polyphony deliberately conjunct. This means that the approach to the most consonant tonic interval—the octave—encouraged the interval of the sixth as nontonic immediately before it in cadential situations. Herein lies the beginning of what was to become "the dominant," but it had already been secured in a system of music that featured nontonic areas of sonic activity with relation to tonic ones. When the dominant appeared historically, and we already see this happening in the motets of Petrus de Cruce, it was incorporated into a harmonic place that had been previously established as nontonic by thoroughly contrapuntal means. There is no evidence that composers immediately jettisoned the leading-tone, first-inversion cadence for the dominant in root position, as the works of Machaut, Dunstable, and their contemporaries clearly indicate. It is not within our province to know how these composers felt about the V–I cadence, other than to suggest that they viewed it as another potential for cadential movement. We know that they did not immediately prefer it. Perhaps the most curious feature of its activity was the fact that, if used, there was a distinctive leap in a voice at a place (closure upon a tonic) that previously had been approached by step if possible. In this light, Grout's statement about the "continual contest" between the contrapuntal and the harmonic principles of musical composition has some validity—at least in retrospect. But the degree to which composers in the late Middle Ages felt that the dominant itself was contesting for superiority over other nontonic harmonic complexes must not be qualitatively judged by the modern scholar. To be sure, there appeared during the course of the fifteenth century a quantitative difference in the preferential treatment by composers of four-voice music for the V–I in root position. But at that point the dialectic of tonic and dominant had completed the first great stage of its polyphonic development; and the other chords of the diatonic scale were being leveled into a hierarchical structure of chord vocabulary that gradually aligned itself into additional classes of tonic and nontonic tonal motion.

As stated before in less precise terms, the Middle Ages and the Renaissance offer us two rich historical areas of harmonic tonality in the course of Western musical evolution. The immediate gains that can be realized by forcing their vast legacy of harmonic consciousness into molds of tertian harmony, à la Schenker, are of extremely limited value. If what we wish to achieve is a genuine picture of their own daily praxis, we must treat their harmony as fully tonal within its own historical context. If we carry out this activity properly, we shall also be able to understand what connections *do* exist between their tonal consciousness and ours. Within their music and their theory lie the (already durable) roots of our own tonal consciousness. It is all of a piece. There is no "incubation" period for tonality: there is only music. Upon acceptance of this fact, the dialectic of tonic and dominant is properly understood as a species of moments in the rich tonal fabric of perpetual musical endeavors.

8 Tonality as Expression

Musicologists and music theorists collectively tend to disassociate themselves from the philosophical problem of musical meaning. What music does mean to them, however, frequently falls within the realm of a dualistic aesthetics of music that readily serves the most diverse kinds of interests. This dichotomy of meaning is more or less neatly housed within the contexts of *formalism* and *expression*. There are various ways of stating this polarity of musical meaning—congeneric and extrageneric, non-referential and referential, and abstract (or pure) and program. The chief error committed by those who rigorously defend separate spheres of meaning for music is, of course, the result of a number of causes—personal bias, cultural influence, academic and professional training, and naive facticity. For the most part, however, musicologists tend to shy away from the actual historicality of the meaning of music in favor of a line of defense that posits subjectivity as beyond the pale of scholarly assessment and thereby ultimately irrelevant. Those who through choice or desperation do attempt to come to grips with the meaning of music are quickly classified as aestheticians or philosophers of music and relieved of any responsibility for speaking for the combined interests of the discipline as a whole. The reason for this is simple. Since World War II musicology has legitimized itself by adopting the methodology of positivism, which it believes to be the *sine qua non* of objectivity. While music is experienced by millions of people as an emotional activity of intensity and profound social merit, even by musicologists, academically speaking, the subjective aspect of music is thought properly to slough off in the rigors of analysis, or is offered only peripherally as a reward for having acquired a "genuine" understanding of the work, or—because subjectivity itself is misunderstood—is thought to be too private a matter to be communicated in words. No more active campaign was ever waged against subjectivity in music than by Manfred Bukofzer, who, by his own admission, managed to write the history of baroque music without once using the word "beautiful."[1]

The debate over the problem of musical meaning is a thorny one with a long history that I shall not attempt even to review here—with one exception. In the nineteenth century, during which music reached a pinnacle of characteristic expressivity, Eduard Hanslick, as he said, "took up the cudgels" to prove that music meant nothing other than itself, that the beauty and meaning of a composition was specifically musical.[2] Hanslick of course was not tilting at windmills. He lived in a century when the major portion of composers assumed that the world was both to be addressed by and housed in their works. The cultural vitality of nascent nationalism, a turning toward the world of nature as a means of self-expression, and a renewed association with literature as a source of meditative, lyric, and dramatic inspiration—all of these notions figured in romanticism as important components of nonmusical reality to be brought within the sphere of the composer's imagination. Among romantic composers who remained largely aloof from the naturalist, symbolist, and metaphysical aesthetics of music there was perhaps only Brahms.

It is my opinion that the formalist and the expressive dichotomies of aesthetic meaning in music are not as separate as aestheticians have forced them to be or, once separated, that they have ever really remained divorced from one another in the manner that many contemporary aestheticians assume. While there is a certain cerebral satisfaction in viewing and experiencing a piece of music as a kind of tonal temporal geometry (this essay makes no refutation that so-called abstract music can be understood in this fashion), my task in this and the following chapter is not to be construed as taking sides in the formalist vs. expressionist debate. It is rather to restore both aspects of the problem to their relationship within the creative sonic act. What I wish to accomplish here has a two-fold purpose: to examine the historical framework in which the formal-expressive dichotomy of musical meaning arose; and to demonstrate how the apparently opposite aspects of this polarity are historically all of a piece within consciousness. That is, it is tonality itself which provides the opportunity for either manifestation: or, in Hegelian terms, this means that consciousness objectifies its essential subjectivity through characteristic and clearly definable forms of knowledge and human interests.

Historically, and largely until the end of the Middle Ages, the expressive content of music plays a minor role in tonal consciousness. This is not to say that music until that time was devoid of human expressivity, but rather that the operation of musical consciousness was one of collective activity upon a melos that did not readily encourage or afford the expression of emotion (nor would such a notion even have occurred to the medieval mind). While the oldest piece of music in existence is a song, there is no apparent evidence that the unknown Babylonian composer is using any of its pitches to express characteristically his or anybody's feelings about the goddess who is the subject of his hymn.[3] In the Middle Ages itself, the argument for the expressive content of Gregorian chant does possess some validity, although not many facts can be laid down that are not vitiated by contradictions.[4] Willi Apel points out that in the historical literature on Latin chant outstanding Gregorianists "have attributed to certain chants specific expressive values derived from the text or related to the occasion."[5] In books of a popularizing nature, where such descriptive explanations are found in abundance, they have a certain aesthetic legitimacy. But Apel feels that in scholarly writings these statements tend rather to reveal the attitudes of the (particularly, nineteenth-century) authors, whose aesthetic notions were "obviously derived from an acquaintance with the art of Wagner and Brahms."[6]

Two reasons may be offered as to why there is no marked evidence of nonmusical expressivity in monophonic Latin chant. First, the collective and anonymous nature of its composition precludes to a certain degree such consciousness. We may accurately state that the medieval conceptualization of tonal essence comprehended it only as a "species" of creative activity, as an internal generality which naturally united the many individuals who "composed" chant.[7] This is proved by the very centonate character of chant itself as established by Gevaert. To the extent that the individual composer (or perhaps more accurately, the shaper of the melos) worked within the creation and re-creation of centonic chant, he did so with a group of tonal data that he felt to be given, something simply met with, since he had no consciousness of its origin. The point at which consciousness *did* become aware of itself—that is, a self-reflective moment during which it sought its tonal origins—is historically an interesting one when applied to this particular musical activity: it was decided that Gregory I had composed the chant under the inspiration of the Holy Spirit. A more critical activity of the passage from tonal consciousness to tonal self-consciousness is seen dialectically in the specific activities of the theorists beginning as early as the ninth century.

And second, while a modest portion of text painting in medieval chant did afford nineteenth-century Gregorian scholars substantiation for their interpretations of expressive content in it, and while we ourselves are still intrigued by the possibility of such interpretations, there is an important feature of music as externalized human expression which must be admitted here: its qualitative essence had simply not yet historically and substantively appeared. This quality of tonal expressivity, at least in Western music, would be (not exclusively, but importantly) a harmonic one. It was in the sphere of consonance and dissonance that the foundation for externalized human emotion would be grounded. Guido d'Arezzo's stated dislike for the interval of the fifth in organum, in addition to his cautionary remarks about the fourth, reveal an early reflective moment in the history of the harmonic tonal dialectic. Whether Guido merely found the fifth to be "hard and rigid" on principle or whether he only judged it to be particularly inflexible at the occursus is not important now. What must be admitted, however, is that through the externalization of their own consciousness (here as before) the harmonic thought of Guido and the other theorists of the early medieval period all exhibit the gradual annulment of unreflected subjective activity in its immediacy: their harmonic "externalizations" were theoretically accomplished by their devotion to their own tonal concerns but were also done so implicitly for others. This point must be ac-knowledged for social tonal expressivity to be universally valid. The theo-rists were not only objectifying harmonic tonality for themselves: their ac-tions brought gradually into being the dynamic unity of a social, harmonic whole.[8]

With the confluence of an active polyphonic tradition in the thirteenth century in France and Italy, later in England, we note a gradual awakening to the potential of tonal expressivity in multi-voiced music that had not been apparent in earlier polyphony or in the great age of monophony that preceded it. What tendencies are found in the general sphere of polyphonic tonality that characterize the appearance of objectified human emotion? There are three that clearly differentiate polyphonic music from the monophony that preceded it: secularism, which had both a humanistic quality and, in the Renaissance, a marked economic component; the essen-tial nature of semantic domination over musical creativity; and the inter-play between the activity of the theorists and the daily praxis of composers. Although each of these has specific characteristics of its own, all three can be topically housed under the externalization by consciousness of its own subjective expressivity.

First, there is the gradual secularization of human interests on the part of composers and those for whom they wrote. Through their collective activity there flowed a humanization of spirit, a definite secularization of man in a world: temporally suspended in a triple-decker universe, and ultimately destined for heaven or hell, their immediate concerns, nevertheless, were their intellects and their pleasures, to which they devoted as much time and effort as their positions would allow. To be sure, the major portion of medieval and Renaissance music is easily characterized by its liturgical and paraliturgical intent. No proof need be offered here for the cultural dominance of the Catholic Church over the production of medieval and Renaissance art. There would be a great deal less music had composers not been financially supported largely by the Church—both the great urban churches that gradually began to tower over the European continent and England and the important princely chapels where the nobility often actively competed with one another for the best singers, musicians, and composers. But alongside this we note also the secularizing influence of literary humanism on music, both early and late, in the setting of songs in the vernacular. Early in Italy there were the madrigal, caccia, and ballata, later the frottola, strambotto, and related types, which inspired the Italian humanists (Cardinal Bembo and others) to attempt a more refined poetry than had been previously witnessed. Early chanson writing in France first utilized the old courtly *formes fixes*, ballade, virelai, and rondeau, to be followed by freely invented compositions in a mixture of polyphonic and homophonic textures. In Spain there was the amorous or idyllic villancico, the Spanish equivalent of the French virelai. And although polyphony generally developed later in Germany than in the countries just mentioned, the rise of a mercantile citizenry encouraged the development of a distinctive musical form there also, the lied.

There were more French chansons and Italian madrigals composed and printed than any of the other vernacular forms. In general, however, we may uniformly characterize all these secular forms as less contrapuntal than liturgical music, markedly rhythmic at times, and textually addressed to the activities of daily secular life—particularly wooing and loving. More importantly, music that was easily available to a consumer of cultural goods brings to the fore the the emergence of a growing bourgeois consciousness. In the long history of song, this was not characterized by the collective lyric of the lives of heroes and their brave deeds or the (also) collective melos of the faithful hoping for salvation: it was activated and characterized by a desire for music for one's self, for one's own pleasure and that of one's friends. János Maróthy has carefully traced this development and sees "ego-centeredness" (in the nonpejorative sense of that term) as the main determinant for the formulization of "song-like thinking." Song form, he notes,

> emerged in the course of a long historical process from former collective and variative musical forms. . . . The social need that gave rise to the song is linked, as to content, with the personal lyrical requirements of the isolated individual and, as to form, with the demand for a genre that could be

reproduced by him alone without the necessity of collective participation or even collective circumstance.[9]

This is to say that psychologically and aesthetically music made a turn inward, toward self-consciousness, its personal concerns, and its relationships to the social reality that impinged upon it. The potency of this internalization of consciousness could not have expressed itself as it did, of course, without the domination of words over music, which I shall discuss shortly.

Economically, this musical secularization went hand in glove with the gradual decline of feudalism and the rise of early capitalism. Perhaps the most important economic factor ever to transform the social dimension of Western civilization's musical life (other than electricity) arose peripherally from the desire to produce books more efficiently and inexpensively. The solution to speeding book production through mechanization, chiefly by means of movable type although other technological factors were also involved, was found about the middle of the fifteenth century and was not immediately applied to the printing of music. But in 1498 the Italian publisher Ottaviano dei Petrucci received from the Council of the Republic of Venice the privilege of printing music by the new method. His first musical attempt with this process, the *Harmonice Musices Odhecaton A*, appeared in 1501, a collection of ninety-six secular pieces by late Burgundian composers as well as representatives from among his own contemporaries. This occasion, like no other, marked the entry of music into the world of commodity exchange. Within twenty-two years Petrucci alone had printed or reprinted fifty-nine volumes of vocal and instrumental music, all of them through a lengthy and tedious process of triple impression printing. His success was emulated thirty years later in Paris by Pierre Attaignant, from whose presses there poured lute and organ music of diverse types, an abundance of motets and Masses, and thirty-five books of chansons. Rome, Lyons, Louvain, Antwerp, London, and Nuremberg soon established publishing firms of their own. While the Church of course benefitted from the new industry, so also did the bourgeoisie, through ready accessibility to a music especially created for their own private singing and playing activities. The lute became the first popular instrument for the home, and this in turn generated musical commodities of its own—instruction manuals on how to play it, intabulated chansons, but also original compositions and dance pieces.

Second, there is the factor of a general semantic domination over the totality of Renaissance music. Again, while there was a growing interest in musical instruments particularly for secular use and music that was written exclusively for them, the major portion of the music up to the baroque era is vocal and word-dominated. This is an important point for the topic under investigation, for it is through text (or word titles) that externalized human emotion makes its appearance in music, even—as suggested above—to some degree in Latin chant. To use a thoroughly capitalistic metaphor, words are the currency with which consciousness purchases meaning from the subjective sphere of public tonality and turns it into an object for itself—my emotion, my feeling, my activity. Take, for instance, the Italian caccia. Without words, we are of course impressed with the vigorous melodic and rhythmic activity of the two upper "hunting" voices, as they proceed apace in canon over a steadily moving bass line: some physical thing or event is being set forth in musical gesture. Without words, however, it is difficult to identify this activity with any precision. Is it a quail hunt, a sailing party, or a house on fire? All of these events are busy affairs, with a lot of running or moving about. But with the addition of the text which we have momentarily ignored, we discover that a particular human behavior is being imitated in music. This works not only in overt behavioral action but with intra-organic states as well, for instance, the sorrowful *Lachrymae* of the English composer John Dowland, who "set forth" seven "passionate pavanes for lute, viols, or violins, in five parts." Here, the falling of tears is referred to, is tonally concretized in music of continually drooping melodic lines and moderate rhythms. The music is for instruments, but the title secures an affective state for the listener which he assumes more or less represents the same affection the composer had in mind when he wrote the music. Even attitudes are indicated by the use of words, which are then subjected to musical objectification. Among the abundant lute compositions of German composers in the sixteenth century, there is the tonally abberant "Juden Tanz" by Hans Neusiedler. Compilers Archibald T. Davison and Willi Apel have declared this piece, with its "shrill dissonances, otherwise unheard of before the adventurous experiments of twentieth-century music," to be "one of the most remarkable specimens of sixteenth-century music."[10] The reason why is not readily apparent without a title for the dance. "Juden Tanz" identifies the general contempt with which Jews were regarded in the sixteenth century, which musically corresponds to a satirical use of two conflicting tonal realms that were quite at variance with the prevailing sonic consciousness of the time and therefore outcast, alien, and not "ours."

Historically, semantic prominence crystallized into an aesthetic doctrine when Adrien Petit Coclius, a pupil of Josquin, brought out a collection of compositions under the title of *Musica Reservata*.[11] Coclius claimed that Josquin had instructed him in the new style. There was a two-fold aspect of *Musica Reservata:* a new style of composition and a new style of performance. Although the latter is unrecoverable now, it was inseparable from the former. The prevailing textures of Renaissance sacred music are characterized by the systematic use of imitation through a series of progressive contrapuntal phrases that alternated with more or less chordal sections for contrast. These textures were now particularized into aesthetic content itself at the hands of each individual composer, who used them for decidedly semantic and expressive aims. A close alliance was sought with the ideas, emotions, and even objects of a given text, particularly a secular one. In performance, the musicians interpreted the musical "affects" of the score, although we cannot recapture exactly what it is that they did. Paul Henry Lang points out that "imitation and counterpoint lost some of their weight and value while the words rose to eminence."[12] The humanizing tendency and the prominence of semantic attention converged in expressive detail that turned toward immediate human concerns.

The third factor which determines the qualitative content of human expressivity in Renaissance music is a complex one—the gradual concretization of contrapuntal and harmonic rules through the activity of the theorists and the praxis of composers. I shall mention only the most crucial component of its development here. The use of dissonance and consonance as characteristic devices of expressive states of mind, attitudes, thoughts, physical events and things, or the values and properties of such events and things, was not first secured within the realm of their own immediacy as suggested and referred to within the semantic contexts I have just discussed. Curiously, this was established a priori within the realm of a consciously formal tonal activity. Initially, it was the cadence that provided this harmonic definition and function.[13] If the ultimate point of cadential repose was one of rest and the cessation from sonic activity, then the harmony immediately before it—whether contrapuntally or harmonically conceived—tonally represented a moment of tension and activity. It both implied and concretized temporal progression. As this qualitative essence of tonal motion was established (and this had been a lengthy and ongoing process, as I have suggested in the previous chapter), it could also be annexed to those affective states which the composer wished to externalize *within* the objective appearance of the work itself. Typically, reaching out from the necessity of cadential clarification, this process worked its way inward to the temporal interstices of the composition itself, thereby establishing and clarifying what had previously been only tonal structural necessity as a form of sonic truth for the composition as a whole. This is not to say that this happened all at once or particularly within the activity of any single composer. It was tacitly subscribed to by those composers who sought to work within the limitations of the theoretical system, and all did. This means that the contrapuntal processes of retardation, anticipation, suspension, and ornamental resolution were aesthetically respected because they were not only formally interesting but also psychologically effective. Initially, this process may have been more an accident than an intentional vehicle of expressive content. Until dissonance was fully realized for its potential within the context of expression and until regulatory procedures of contrapuntal control were also brought to bear upon its aesthetic function with regard to texts, there could reside in such music a halfway house of more or less randomly chosen solutions to ad hoc harmonic and contrapuntal problems. This situation gradually changed in the Renaissance. As dissonance was increasingly subjected to more and more control within the regulatory procedures of linear counterpoint, it was also realized (to the extent that such processes were articulated by creative consciousness at all) that dissonance, when presented in the general forms of anticipation and retardation, could provide the composer with powerful and expressive agents of emotive articulation should he care to use them. Historically, he did. Harmonically, this is to say that what ought to be the case was momentarily not so but would resolve itself at the necessary time as demanded by the formal exigencies of the musical phrase. Aesthetically, it is to say that the truly expressive composition was not a numbing statement of consonantal activity but rather a series of sonic relationships in which intensities and resolutions were immediately or ultimately fulfilled. And psychologically, it is to say that the reality which the composer wished to portray (chiefly through his choice of texts, which he deemed indicative of his own interests at the moment) was, indeed, a unity and concretely bound to his world of will, desire, and reason.

There was both a leveling and a particularizing tendency in this process, which objectified itself in the appearance of the tonal composition. On the one hand, there was a tacit public agreement that music should behave in a certain way, obey more or less specific rules of counterpoint as promulgated by the theorists, and tonally subscribe to accepted ways of harmonic consciousness. This is the "common practice" aspect of tonal systems. Among those who heard it there was common understanding of a known process of tonally permissive figurations for consciousness. It was precisely this compositional agreement that produced the styles of regions, nations, and, in the case of Renaissance tonality, of a given continent. What was composed in Italy could be imported to England and understood there as aesthetically true. In fact, this was a particular phenomenon of the late sixteenth century, when Italian madrigals were "Englished" for eager northern audiences. It was not the counterpoint, harmony, or tonal consciousness of the Italians which the British music lover found incomprehensible, only the texts, and these were quickly translated. In this respect, European tonality became (as it already had been to a marked degree) a "universal" language for nations whose ambassadors and emissaries had to learn

French in order to understand one another but who could enjoy music together because its remarkable leveling tendencies achieved a kind of communication that soothed the minds of men who were frequently at decisive political, economic, religious, and social variance with one another. (That music would continue to be a universal language was the result of imperialism—both English in the nineteenth century and American in the twentieth—on a world-wide scale.) On the other hand, because of this commonality of tonal consciousness there was also the potential (which became increasingly more manifest as the composer historically addressed himself to the interests of bourgeois consciousness) for externalizing within this "international" sonic communication his own emotion, psyche, and personality. We could select any of a dozen composers from the Renaissance to prove this statement. Gustave Reese notes that this particularizing tendency, which was typical of the late Renaissance, "could include the subtlety and elegance of Marenzio, the forthrightness of Sweelinck, and the declamatory writing of Wert, had room also for the striking dramatic directness and extreme chromaticism of Carlo Gesualdo, Prince of Venosa. . . ."[14] It is instructive here to make a few comments about this unique but not always princely individual.

After the death of his brother and in order to produce heirs, Gesualdo married his first cousin, Maria d'Avalos. After several years of marriage, he discovered that she had been unfaithful to him. He then murdered, or ordered the murders of, her, her lover, and a child whose paternity he had reason to doubt. He later married Leonora d'Este and resided for a time at the brilliant court of Ferrara. Upon the death of the Duke of Ferrara he returned to Naples, where he died in 1613. His biographer notes that Gesualdo, a brooding, neurotic prince, could not urinate unless he was lashed with whips. We are not surprised, therefore, to find in both his secular and sacred music a clear manifestation of psychological and aesthetic alienation that is characterized as tonal deformation. Working with both good and bad texts, Gesualdo selected literature that seemed to thrive on death, weariness, decay, pain, horror, and loneliness in order to portray a tortured spirit crying alone and in vain among the cruelness and deceit of the external world. "Expression was his primary interest—emotional expression," notes Reese. To that end, Gesualdo gradually perfected a harmonic and melodic chromaticism that tonally underscored his subjective alienation from the world. His "musical audacities—rhythmic, melodic, harmonic—spring from an approach to the text too individual to give rise to an enduring school," Reese concludes, but he apparently did attract a few contemporary musicians who wished to emulate him—to a point. In 1613, the year of his death, his six books of madrigals were published in score format, indicating some interest on the part of students of composition.

Gesualdo did not dramatically affect the tonality of his era in the same fashion as did Wagner and Schoenberg who followed him, but he stands as a unique creator of works that clearly exhibit the tension between common-practice acceptibility and an explosion of neurotic subjectivity. He annulled the diatonic order of the already weakened modal system of the late Renaissance, and through harmonic exploitation he preserved the qualitative chromaticism which that same system had permitted marginally to reside within it in the form of musica ficta.

Despite the explosion of musical forms in the seventeenth century, which were related to their social, functional activities in sacred and secular circles, there is no significant breach in the tonal consciousness from the late Renaissance to the baroque era. What we witness instead is a gradual clarification of the generalizing tendency of tonality in order to universalize its content and a concomitant suppression of troublesome modal particularities that militated against it. Within the network of social, economic, political, religious, scientific, and philosophical components, all of great importance, we find the same three tendencies previously encountered in Renaissance music—secularism, semantic domination, and the interplay between composer and theorist. In terms of the great outpouring of instrumental music in the baroque era it would seem that vocal music had reached its ascendancy, and in a certain sense this is true. But in no way did instrumental music develop in a creative vacuum unaffected by the entrenched aesthetic superiority of old and new vocal forms and styles, particularly aria and recitative. The thrust of this section, therefore, will be to state as clearly as possible the manner in which literary consciousness continued to influence the creation of instrumental music, early on through its close alliance with semantic signification, and later (albeit gradually) through a separation from semantic domination that caused it to seem quite unique in its own right, alienated from its progenitor, and potentially capable of a pure objectivity in sonic form. Thus while the causes for the advancement of instrumental music are social, political, and technological (particularly as witnessed in the perfection of the members of the string family), the success of this activity was deeply embedded in the ability of vocal music to transform its content into so-called abstract forms which were not so different in aesthetic intent from the models that had inspired their creation. From whatever point of view we choose to explain the components of baroque tonal expressivity, either vocal or instrumental, we arrive at the same conclusion—the externalization by consciousness of its immediate subjective interests.

I have just stated that there was no significant break in the tonal consciousness from the late Renaissance to the baroque era. But there is a seemingly apparent exception to this statement, and this is the gradual shift from the "modality" of the sixteenth century to the "tonality" of the seventeenth, to use these terms of differentiation in the fashion that contemporary musicologists and theorists do when they wish to point up the most remarkable tonal feature of the great flowering of music from Lassus and Palestrina to Bach and Handel. To be sure, a remarkable tonal transition took place from 1500 to 1700, one that composers and theorists themselves sensed, articulated, and objectified in their respective creative activities. We have examined it elsewhere in this book. It is instructive to approach this phenomenon again from a different point of view, but here, as before, the questions are the same. What did baroque composers annul when they abandoned the modal system? And what did they preserve from that system within the gradual development of scales and keys? And finally, what was the significance of this transition in consciousness for tonality as expression?

When the Swiss theorist Henricus Glareanus (1488–1563) published his *Dodecachordon* in 1547 he unwittingly sounded the death knell for an entrenched ecclesiastical authority over modal tonality. What Glareanus signified with the title of his book was literally the Greek word for twelve strings, and he made a plea therein for the inclusion of four more modes among the original canon of eight: Aeolian and Hypoaeolian, each with a finalis on A, and Ionian and Hypoionian, on C. Glareanus did recognize the possibility of twenty-four octave-species, since the placement of the semitones within the octave-species was the factor that differentiated one mode from another. But he was reluctant to accept twelve of these species because some of them gave rise to successions of steps that were not found in a diatonic scale. Not too surprisingly, Glareanus had powerful practical authority on his side for the adoption of these "new" modes within the modal canon. He illustrated the Aeolian and Ionian modes with compositions by Adam da Fulda, Jacob Obrecht, and the highly gifted and esteemed Josquin des Prés. He also realized that modulation between modes was a characteristic of the music of his day, but admitted that not all modes could change from one into another with equal success. However, when determining which of the group of twelve modes bore similar tonal characteristics, he did not, Joel Lester rightly notes, see the similarity of all major and minor modes. This seems curious to us, but to Glareanus, "the major or minor third is not the factor in determining closely related modes. Thus, Ionian and Dorian are listed together because in both there is no tritone within the species of fifth."[15]

Eleven years after the publication of *Dodecachordon*, Gioseffo Zarlino published his *Istitutioni Harmoniche*. Zarlino "accepts the twelve modes with neither question nor acknowledgement,"[16] remarks Lester, and his general approach to modal theory is nearly the same as that of Glareanus. Apparently the recognition of twelve modes was a matter that no longer

needed extensive deliberation. But there are two important differences between the two theorists: the ordering of the modes and their differentiation
on the basis of the imperfect consonances. Only the latter will concern us
here. Zarlino is particularly intrigued by the effect (in the sense of musica
reservata) which the imperfect consonances have upon the listener. The
passage in which he discusses this is worth quoting at length.

> The property or nature of the imperfect consonances is that some of them are
> lively and cheerful, accompanied by much sonority, and some, although they
> are sweet and smooth, tend somewhat towards sadness or languor. The first
> are the major thirds and sixths and their compounds: and the others are the
> minor. . . . There are some songs which are lively and full of cheer; and some
> others on the contrary which are rather sad or languid. The reason is that in
> the first the major imperfect consonances are often heard above the final or
> mediant notes of the modes or tones, which are the first, second, seventh,
> eighth, ninth, and tenth, as we shall see elsewhere. These modes are very
> cheerful and lively because in them we often hear the consonances placed
> according to the nature of the sonorous number: that is, the fifth divided
> harmonically into a major third and a minor third; which gives much plea-
> sure to the ear.[17]

What Zarlino regarded as distinguishing major from minor is the placement of thirds "above the final or mediant notes," that is, of modes. A
correct interpretation of the text reveals that this is clearly a *melodic* theory
of major and minor. But his treatise also contains one of "the first statements concerning the fundamental harmony, with a fifth and third over the
bass and its differentiation into major and minor according to the quality of
the third."[18] And this was a harmonic rather than a melodic consideration.
Although "the tenor is still the central voice of a composition for him—the
voice that determines the modes and the first to be composed,"[19] we note
also a significant component of so-called common-practice tonality, which
is the admission of the possibility of building harmony from bottom to top.

What did baroque composers annul when they abandoned the modal
system? One of the chief characteristics of mode construction, one on
which its very identity depended, had been the specific order of tones and
semitones that differentiated it from all other modes. These specific orders
(e.g., a half step between the first two tones in the Phrygian mode; a
whole step between the last two in the Mixolydian) were leveled by the
gradual imposition of what was felt to be their most important generalizing tendency—third relationships, to which Zarlino attests above. Thus,
specific modal expressivity was annulled in order to preserve and exploit a
more general but critical expressivity, one which all the authentic modes
(including the Aeolian and Ionian modes that were theoretically legitim-

ized in the sixteenth century) possessed at exactly the same place, a third above the final.

In answering the first of the questions posed above we have also answered the second. When we say that the modes were "given up" in favor of major-minor tonality, we are making a statement with only a partial truth. Modality did not cease to exist with the adoption of major-minor scales and harmonies: it was preserved and reified within a higher order of sonic consciousness. The most general, characteristic feature of the modes, relationships of the third in terms of major or minor, was thus preserved within the context of the (we shall see) more flexible "modern" scales. The more or less facile cognitive operation necessary to secure the distinction for consciousness between major and minor fit the baroque composer's philosophy of musical polarity quite well. Slow and fast tempos, contrapuntal and chordal textures, smooth and dotted rhythms, loud and soft volumes, and treble and bass linear emphases—all these dichotomies were further supported tonally by the critical juxtaposition of major and minor keys and harmonies.

Moreover, the leveling tendency of an earlier and specific modal consciousness by the gradual imposition of the generalizing tendency of third relationships granted tonal expression a freedom from the very limitations that had troubled Glareanus: it had not been aesthetically pleasing to move freely between all the various types of modal expression. But to move from one major key to another meant no conflict between mode species at all. And to move from a minor mode to a major one (and vice versa), habitually done in baroque music with the use of the i–III change of key center, caused no apparent formal or aesthetic problems for composers. Far from being an aesthetic problem, it was exploited as a virtue.

And finally, to answer our third question, we note that the passage quoted above testifies to an early recognition of the distinction between major and minor in terms of their qualitative expressiveness. Here is a similar statement from Sethus Calvisius's *Melopoeia sive melodiae condendae ratio* of 1592, which appeared three decades after Zarlino's *Istitutioni Harmoniche*. Calvisius notes that

> the most joyful modes are Ionian, Lydian, and Mixolydian, because the fifth is divided harmonically. The sadder and more languid [modes], on the other hand, [are] Dorian, Phrygian, and Aeolian because of the arithmetic division of the same interval. For everywhere the harmonic division expresses a smoother sound than the arithmetic.[20]

This notion of modal affection was readily received by seventeenth-century theorists. The Alsatian theologian Johannes Lippius, a student of

Calvisius, coined the phrase *trias harmonica*, or harmonic triad, for the "tonic" triad in each of the twelve modes in terms of its final, mediating third, and fifth degrees, but the leveling tendency is decisive: major triads are "lively," and minor triads are "sad."[21] Lippius's theories were transmitted to later generations by Johannes Crüger, whose *Synopsis Musicae* of 1630 attempted affectively to distinguish the modes from one another but with the same general opposites of cheerful and sad. To be sure, the die had been historically cast through the catalyzing agents of theology and numerology, but seventeenth-century composers had more direct and dramatic reasons for their actions.

The documentation by the theorists of the affective qualities of major and minor modes did not establish the emotional content of baroque music alone. As stated above, the close alliance with language and literature provided composers both early and late with the means by which to render music with the same moods and emotional expressivity that had been established throughout the Renaissance.

The attempt in the late sixteenth century by the Florentine Camerata to revive what was thought to be the actual performance practice of Greek tragedy appears in retrospect to be the happiest mistake ever made in music history. Whatever the rationale for their immediate efforts, the Camerata's members decisively altered the course of music within their own generation when they successfully objectified expressive subjectivity through the achievement of *stile rappresentativo*. From the very beginning, semantic dominance was not only apparent, it was actively sought. If early monodic recitative exhibited a musical line that was distinctly nonmelodic in character, this "certain noble neglect of song," explained Giulio Caccini in the Foreword to his *Nuove Musiche* of 1602, was intended to capture those inflections of grief, joy, and similar affective states. Camerata members may have been poor musicologists regarding Greek performance practice in classical drama, but they were quite unwittingly excellent psychologists. The purpose of stile rappresentativo, Caccini further explained, was that it "may fitly serve to the better obtaining of the musician's end, that is, to delight and move the affections of the mind."[22]

We need not raise aesthetic theories here as to how this was done in practice.[23] More important is the decisive connection between the disciplines of rhetoric and music that dominated the whole of the baroque era. The doctrine of affections and its sister doctrine of musical rhetoric is historically based in the venerable tradition of rhetoric, whose purpose was to move, to persuade, and to teach. Rhetoric had originated in ancient Greece; during the Middle Ages it was part of the formal study of the trivium—along with grammar and logic; it was still part of the curriculum of secondary schools of Germany in the eighteenth century. During the seventeenth century there was an aesthetic movement away from the Renaissance notion of music as theoretically elevated by number and reason to music that could be used in specifically purposeful ways to please and to instruct. As H. James Jensen points out in *The Muses' Concord,*

> a successful rhetorically oriented artist has to be conscious of the way audiences or spectators think and feel, of their sociological, intellectual, and emotional predilections. Rhetorical art is thus fundamentally popular, that is, created with the audience in mind: not as the audience ought to be but as it probably is, with its limitations, prejudices, wrongheadedness, and orientation to cultural and social norms.[24]

Thus, what had been initially offered as a justification through the discipline of rhetoric by the Florentine Camerata for the reason behind the stile rappresentativo resulted in throughly pragmatic approaches to the problem of depicting human emotion in the extensive development of baroque music.

In this regard, there is no more provocative a thinker in baroque music aesthetics than Johann Mattheson (1681–1765), a German composer, lexicographer, translator, cappellmeister, and the first biographer of Handel. Throughout a long and active life Mattheson gradually perfected his ideas about music and emotion, the most extensive statement of which is found in *Der vollkommene Capellmeister*, published in Hamburg in 1739. Its subtitle is instructive: *Basic proof of everything one needs to know, to be aware of, and to understand thoroughly in order to direct a chapel creditably and profitably.* Mattheson did not state what every "complete" cappellmeister already knew: that is, when new music was necessary one had to write it, as part of the regular duties of his profession. His book is, therefore, an instruction manual for the proper compositional procedures by which to write effective music for a well-run church music program (and more), and to that end he devoted extensive portions of his treatise to the then current ideas about emotion and music by explaining in concrete terms (with musical examples) "the doctrine of affections and temperaments."

According to Mattheson, music was a form of "sound speech," and it could be affectively and effectively used if it employed a collectively understood body of "figures," or *loci topici*, which "represented or depicted" the affections in music. (This same process governed the formal technique of drawing or painting. An aspiring artist might work from a sample sheet of noses—the proud nose, the evil nose, the gluttonous nose, etc.—in order to build up a profile of anatomical figures all of which contributed to a whole affection.) Mattheson stated that there were two broad categories of loci topici, the *locus notationis* and the *locus descriptionis*. The first locus dealt with actual abstract music figures such as imitation, inversion, repetition, and other common means of melodic organization. "They are particularly arresting," notes Bukofzer, "because they demonstrate how intimately the doctrine of affections and figures was bound up with the technical aspects of the musical craft."[25] The locus descriptionis depicted extramusical ideas through the use of sonic metaphor, both rhythmic and melodic.

Before we launch into an investigation of Mattheson's thought, let me briefly reflect on Bukofzer's statement. Merely to understand Mattheson's division of the loci topici into formal and affective dimensions of baroque (or any) music may be a facile means by which to establish an apparent historical dichotomy of aesthetic interests in music, but it is both myopic and wrong when pushed to extremes. To speak respectively of the locus notationis and the locus descriptionis does not mean that they thereby become mutually exclusive in any given tonal object. Herein lies the trap that ensnares virtually all who attempt to erect platforms for their arguments regarding the nature of formalism vs. expression in music. A Bach fugue may be a perfect example of Mattheson's locus notationis regarding the technique of imitation, but the opening Kyrie from the B Minor Mass, which is consistently imitative, may also objectify the religious brotherhood of collective Christian prayer. Gesualdo did not ignore the principles of imitative counterpoint in his madrigals simply because he was determined to objectify human emotion in tones. In fact, his imitative techniques and his acute chromaticism are *simultaneous* events. "Either/or" may have served the purposes of the Danish philosopher very well, but to wrench this dichotomy from the music object is an act of aesthetic violence upon the totality of its tonal utterance. What Mattheson sought to establish in his discussion of the locus descriptionis was not the excision of human subjectivity *from* the sphere of compositional techniques but, rather, concretization *within* it. With this caution in mind, the remainder of this chapter and the one to follow offer complementary views of the same tonal potential, that is, knowledge and human interests.

Early in part I, chapter 3 Mattheson takes up the gentler emotions of joy, sadness, hope, and love. When composing pieces which deal with the latter, he states that

> a composer of amorous pieces must utilize his experiences, whether past or present. Thus he will find the best example of this affect in himself and be, therefore, best able to express it musically. If he has no experiences of strong feelings of his own in this noble passion, he had best leave the subject alone. He may succeed in everything except in this all too tender sentiment.[26]

Mattheson cites here as "a charming example of love and invention thought suitable to its expression" an earlier publication by Johann David Heinichen

(1683–1729), whose *Neu erfundene und gründliche Anweisung... zu voll-kommener Erlernung des Generalbasses* was published in 1711. Heinichen had provided five different settings of the words "Bella donna che non fa?" ("What will a lovely lady not do?"), which Mattheson criticizes for their apparent lack of depth in tonally underscoring the power of beauty in favor of the "secondary matters" of "charming glances."

If love is a troublesome emotion to concretize in music, Mattheson thinks that the violent emotions are even more so, but "they are far more suitable to all sorts of musical inventions than the gentle and agreeable passions, which must be treated with more refinement." Pride, haughtiness, and arrogance "demand special seriousness and bombastic movements," writes Mattheson, but "they must never be too quick or falling, but always ascending." He is excited about these violent emotions and plunges into a lively passage of descriptions of stubbornness, anger, hate, revenge, rage, fury, fear, and jealousy; he declares this latter to be a combination of seven passions—mistrust, desire, revenge, sadness, fear, shame, and burning love. But he is suddenly overwhelmed with the project at hand and exclaims that the doctrine of affects is "like a bottomless sea; it cannot possibly be emptied, no matter how hard one may try. A book can present only the smallest part [of the subject] and much has to be left unsaid, left to everyone's own sensibility in this area."[27] He thoughtfully refers the reader to another of his own works, *Der musicalische Patriot* (1728) and a work by George Abraham Thilo, a candidate for the ministry, whose *Specimen pathologiae musicae* had been submitted to him to read.

In part II, chapter 13 Mattheson takes up the various species of melodies and their special characteristics. He launches first into a discussion of dances and their relative affects and he does so by a method quite familiar to the modern music student and scholar, i.e., the analytical dissection and examination of the various musical parts. He begins "with the minuet, so that everyone may see of what it should consist if it is not to be a freak" (*Misgeburt*). The minuet, he says, "whether it be made especially for playing, singing, dancing has no other affect than *moderate gaiety*. Even when a minuet is only sixteen measures long (it cannot be shorter than that), it will have at least some commas, one semicolon, a couple of colons and a couple of periods."[28] Note the ready references to the principles of grammar. And thus the manual proceeds: the true character of the gavotte is a "hopping quality"; the bourrée is "something filled, stuffed; settled"; the rigaudon's character "is one of flirtatious pleasantry," which in Mattheson's opinion is "one of the most pleasing" dances in its melodic elements. The rigaudon, he mentions in a modest aside, "is a real hermaphrodite, part gavotte, part bourrée."

As we might expect, Mattheson feels much more secure in delineating the expressive qualities of dances than he does of purely abstract music, and the sections on sonata, concerto grosso, and sinfonia are less conclusive. But he does try. His statements on the chamber sonata are instructive, and I shall quote them here as well as refer to them later. The purpose of the sonata

> is mainly to oblige and to give pleasure. What must rule in the sonata is a certain complaisance, ready to do anything, and of service to every listener. A person who is sad will find in it something plaintive and sympathetic; a sensualist will find something pretty; an angry person can find violence, etc., in the various movements of the sonata. The composer who keeps this in mind in his *adagio, andante, presto,* etc., will succeed.[29]

"Sensuality" reigns in the concerto grosso of the Vivaldi type. Everyone can easily guess, notes Mattheson, that the chief affective character of concertos is "contests," from which, "in fact, they derive their name." The concerto is thus a place for jealousy, revenge, envy, hatred, and other such passions. The sinfonia's more moderate affection depends on its occasion, whether for church, chamber, or theater. Church sinfonias demand the most modest treatment; in general, the character of sinfonias "must be according to the passions that predominate in the rest of the work." He finishes "this pile of species with the overture," which is apparently his favorite form of music. Its character must be noble, "but it deserves more praise than we have room for," and he simply refers the reader to a description of it in his *Neu-eröffnete Orchester* of 1713.[30]

It must be clarified that Mattheson in this lengthy description is chiefly concerned with melody and this is largely the case also with the discussion of locus notationis. In part II, chapter 4 he states that musical themes and subjects are the musical equivalent of the orator's text or thesis and "one must have a store of particular formulas that can be used in oratorical generalization." A good composer, through experiences and attentive listening to good music, will have collected a store house of these melodic figures. As proof that this is actually what is done, Mattheson demonstrates how "little turns, clever passages, and pleasant runs and jumps," that is, stock musical figures, are imaginatively turned into affective and meaningful musical wholes. Here are his own musical examples:[31]

If I had in mind, for example, three different and independent passages:

and wanted to make a connected phrase out of them, it might look like this:

The generalizing tendency of baroque melody that devolves from this type of compositional procedure is so well understood by Mattheson that he thinks the student might be afraid that he is plagiarizing another man's work when he creates music from such common tonal figures. He therefore devotes two paragraphs to this problem immediately after the examples he has just given. I quote them here in their entirety.

> Although one or two of these passages or turns may have been used by several masters before, they come to me without thinking of any particular composer; in fact, I may not even know him. Putting them together gives the whole phrase a new appearance or form, which may be considered an original invention. It is not essential that one try to do this intentionally, it can happen quite spontaneously.
>
> One must not use these devices in such a way that one has an index of them and that one treats them, in an academic manner, like a box of inventions. Rather, they should be considered in the same way as the vocabulary and the expressions used in speaking. We do not put these on paper or in a book, but keep them in mind and by means of them we are able to express ourselves in the most comfortable way without constantly consulting a dictionary.[32]

Regarding the doctrine of the affections, Mattheson's writings are a rich lode of information yet to be thoroughly mined. Only *Der vollkommene Capellmeister* has been translated in its entirety.[33] Scholars of baroque music have left him, Heinichen, and other writers on the affections largely unattended, and our notions of the importance of emotion in eighteenth-century music suffer thereby. We might smile at the finite distinctions that Mattheson makes between the various emotions; the remarkable thing historically is that he actually sought to make them. As Hans Lenneberg states in his introduction to the translation of portions of *Der vollkommene Capellmeister:*

> One can see that a composer may make subtle distinctions between the "settings" of various different emotions, but only a listener carefully schooled in a standardized musical symbolism—which would, after all, be an intellectual rather than an emotional process—could perceive definite differences between them.[34]

But this does not vitiate the Matthesonian project: it only strengthens it. The eighteenth-century mind was in the process of educating itself to its own music. Under the inspiration of the Enlightenment, there appeared more writings about music than ever before. Books, treatises, pamphlets, periodicals, dictionaries, histories, criticism—all these in addition to *collegia*, academies, and concerts, with mountains of printed music to sustain their activities point to the general universalization of a tonal consciousness for all of urban Western Europe, and an aesthetics of human expressivity developed to accompany and enrich it.

Before we leave this fascinating thinker there is one other aspect of affective tonality which must be briefly mentioned. This is the notion that specific keys convey specific emotional states. Mattheson does not treat it in *Der vollkommene Capellmeister* because he had investigated it earlier in *Das neu-eröffnete Orchester*. Lenneberg points out that in this earlier treatise Mattheson is quite willing to admit there could never be any unanimity of opinion on the subject and advises his readers to form opinions of their own. Also there he summarizes earlier opinions, although he is unaware that the Greek modes differed from the ecclesiastical modes with which he was familiar.[35] But he is aware that tuning itself would critically influence any conceptualization of this kind of affective tonal consciousness and states that he will base his descriptions upon baroque *Cammer-Ton* tuning, not *Chor-Ton*. His chief criticism, as we might expect from his thoroughness, is that general opinions are oversimplified. It is too simplistic to regard all major keys as gay and all minor keys as sad, as the theorists of the previous century had done.[36]

What Mattheson did not suspect or question was *how* the emotional modality of his loci descriptionis (or the activity of the loci descriptionis themselves, for that matter) operated in the mind as being true representations of the very affective states they attempted to objectify. We know now that no eighteenth-century theory of aesthetics was forthcoming that could have adequately explained it, with one quite simple but highly important exception, David Hume's notion of customary association that is reinforced by repetition.[37] It is habit itself rather than any intrinsic qualities of the keys themselves that procure the truth of human expressivity through their use. If enough composers use F major for pastoral attitudes and activities, then F major can come to stand tonally as a symbolic expression of those emotions and ideas. D minor comes to stand for states of psychological and physical danger in the music of Mozart simply because this is the key he uses enough times to depict such situations, from which scholars then make their observations. Historically, we have ground this notion into such generalized commercial flatness that the sung or musically accompanied commercial is unremittingly composed in major keys with few accidentals. In a brief survey in late 1977, I discovered only *one* musical commercial in a minor key out of eighty that had been randomly selected. It sought to depict the personal fulfillment one could achieve by drinking a certain California wine which apparently embodied a (stated) "mysterious" flavor that quite escaped any other combination of the same regional grapes. Needless to say, the majority of the commercials tested were written in C.

As Mattheson understood quite well, it is a fairly easy matter to set up a system of rhetorical figures of tonal expression in baroque vocal or dance music, with their clear commitment to affective definition through semantic or, in the case of dance, behavioral gesture. But it is quite another to understand how this can be done in those forms of music for which expressivity seems at first blush to be conspicuous by its absence—such as fugue, concerto, sinfonia, sonata, and overture—and Mattheson did not dwell on them long, although what he did say is interesting. Nevertheless, the baroque era offered up the first great flowering of what has come to be known as "abstract" music, and we must attempt to clarify the consciousness which imposed its interests simultaneously upon two apparently different kinds of musical thought. We want to know how it was that instrumental music achieved and has maintained the great attraction that it has for composers and audiences around the world; if its expressive content is so very much different than that of vocal and balletic forms of music; or whether instrumental music is a special form of music quite devoid of human expressivity, whose meaning is entirely congeneric, that is, as Hanslick stubbornly maintained, completely signified from within—by structural integrity and purely musical content alone. A careful look at the evidence just presented and the discussion to follow reveal that, while such meaning can be claimed for instrumental music and is appreciated as such by literally millions of listeners, the notion of music as tonal geometry is (again) a cultural value with historical precedents that rest firmly on certain unconscious processes of cognition that were developed during the course of the baroque era and have been subsequently reified in the periods that followed. A few words about the historical framework are necessary as a backdrop to this cultural phenomenon.

While France, Germany, and England were to develop independent, national characteristics within their music during the course of a century and a half, the hegemony of Italy over baroque music in general is witnessed in both the broad dissemination of Italian musical forms—concerto, opera, oratorio, chamber cantata, violin music, sonata, etc.—and the thorough penetration by Italian musicians and composers into the countries of the north and west. This explosion of musical forms was related to the fact that the Italians were about two decades ahead of other countries in the definition of the principles of the new art (particularly Venice, Florence, and Rome). Early on, Monteverdi divided the function of music into two relatively discrete stylistic categories, the *prima* and *seconda pratiche*. About the middle of the seventeenth century, the Italians also realized that their musical activities were polarizing into three definite sociological categories: *musica ecclesiastica, cubicularis,* and *theatralis* (music for church, chamber, and stage) although, as Friedrich Blume notes, "without binding definite forms or styles fast to one or another of these species."[38] With the exception of dance music, the church and the theater to a large extent shared the forms of chorus, ensemble, aria, and recitative. As time progressed, aria and recitative became common staples of opera, cantata, and oratorio, and, as witnessed above, were thoroughly governed by the doctrine of the affections and temperaments. In addition, from about 1630 on, the *bel canto* style developed into a total and remarkable exploitation of the human voice in the form of virtuoso coloratura singing.

Instrumental music was another matter. During the Renaissance it had been chiefly confined to dance music and the pleasures of the nobility and rich bourgeoisie who cultivated a taste for keyboard, lute, and viol music. The early development of these genres was not structurally independent and quite frequently reflected the compositional procedures of vocal models, for instance, the chanson and related forms. When Giovanni Gabrieli published his *Symphoniae Sacrae* in 1597, however, he made an unwittingly prophetic statement for the future of abstract music. The "melodies" of his *Sonata Pian' e Forte* are still fairly characteristic of vocal writing of the period; but the first indication of volume and the fact that the instrumental pieces in the collection request particular groups of instruments are indicative of a new attitude about instrumental music. So was the composition's title: it was a piece "for sounding," rather than for touching (*toccare*) or singing (*cantare*).

Baroque instrumental music developed with distinct social, formal/ aesthetic, and psychological tendencies. I shall treat them separately. Sociologically, instrumental music hoped to realize the potential of a commercial market at the same time that it sought to insure itself against financial disaster by appealing to the nobility to bail it out of poverty should the former prove entirely too speculative. That is, instrumental music was composed *for* someone. Recall in the particular case of the chamber sonata that Mattheson was reluctant to state a definite aim for the sonata other than to please the listener. Its purpose was "mainly to oblige and give pleasure." It had to demonstrate a certain complaisance, "ready to do anything," since private interests might not fall within the boundaries of a common civic aesthetic. Not only did the chamber sonata have to address its content to the private and ambiguous interests of a hoped-for patron, its technical requirements were frequently conceived in terms of performing abilities about which the composer had no accurate assessment. One thing was certain: the nobility could not be insulted by offering it music that it could not play.[39]

The composer's commodity was his *opus*, literally the Latin term for *work*. Commodity production involved a publisher, who frequently had to speculate on a relatively unknown talent and hope that he would be able to sell enough copies of a printing to make a profit on his investment. Such is the case of young Giuseppe Torelli's chief publisher in Bologna, Gioseffo Micheletti. Over a period of years Micheletti patiently brought out four of the seven extant opera of Torelli, who never acquired the reputation of his more aggressive and clearly more talented contemporary, Archangelo Corelli. In the meantime Torelli exercised one of the few professional alternatives available to a composer-musician and sought royal patronage. The prefaces to his first six opera, which, like other composers of his time, he produced in batches of ten or a dozen each—like cookies—reveal a willing composer, eager to solicit *benefici* which only the church and the aristocracy were fully capable of offering. Poor Torelli never did receive any of the court appointments he sought—at least as composer, although he was able to support himself as a performing musician, and, for a short time, apparently as *maestro di concerto* to Princess Sofia Charlotte in Berlin. It is safe to say that this was the fate of hundreds of composers in the seventeenth and eighteenth centuries. Some years later J.S. Bach achieved no more success, when in a similar preface, he humbly offered his services to Christian Ludwig, "Margrave of Brandenburg, et cetera, et cetera, et cetera,"[40] an insatiable collector of concertos, even though the musical merits of this "batch" of concertos have yet to be surpassed. This is to say that the bourgeoisie, who were in full accord with and supported the aims of the aristocracy in the production of opera—because it publicly represented the heroic virtues of morality to which they themselves aspired or thought they ought to aspire—were not yet entirely ready for the abstract aesthetics of purely instrumental music in the form of the commodity production of the composer. Without words, what was it all about anyway?

This brings us to our second tendency in baroque instrumental music: its seemingly apparent abstract approach to aesthetic meaning. As Friedrich Blume cogently states in a single half-sentence in his study on Renaissance and baroque music, "in the days of the Enlightenment people found themselves confronted by a certain disconcerting instrumental music that wished only to 'be,' but not to 'mean' anything."[41] Devoid of semantic meaning other than its word titles, instrumental music had to fend for itself. True, it could elicit meaning from the general office of program music, but by and large this activity was the product of the nineteenth, not the seventeenth or eighteenth, century. True, there are the *Capriccio on the Departure of a Beloved Brother* (which exemplifies an aesthetic that the young Bach did not permanently adopt), the Biblical Sonatas of Kuhnau, and the evocative "Seasons" concertos of Vivaldi, but these do not indicate a marked development of program music. Instead, we find instrumental music aesthetically and formally striking out on its own with the obvious assistance of balletic and vocal forms of music. To a large extent the meaning of abstract instrumental music was already embedded within the vocal forms that developed along with it and were simply annexed from there to the sphere of apparent abstraction. We note both from Mattheson's writings and from baroque music itself that typical rhetorical conventions which were being established in the aria also took up residence in the abstract atmosphere of congeneric music forms. There could be no other solution, since the philosophy of baroque affections was pervasive and governed both vocal and instrumental music. As with the aria, which usually displayed one prevailing emotion throughout its temporal course, expressive continuity was also both maintained and exploited in concerto, sonata, overture, sinfonia, and fugue. A given movement or section was largely monothematic, remained in the same meter and tempo from beginning to end, and introduced no new instruments after the work's orchestration had been presented at the beginning of the piece. Within the continuity of aesthetic intent for a given movement or section, was there any kind of variety at all? Not surprisingly, this was achieved in part within the realm of tonality itself. Other components of a given movement or composition remaining the same, the phenomenon of key area assumed formal importance *within* the context of aesthetic unity. This was an important concept for baroque music. What is important in a Bach fugue, concerto, or dance movement was not primarily its thematic content—for which Bach could provide hundreds of different "inventions" from a storehouse of apparently inexhaustible creativity—but the manner in which he tonally expressed its sonic differences in opposing key areas at the same time that he maintained the sonic object's formal integrity. This was the great office of baroque tonality, which it was able to achieve in part by giving up—as stated above—the particularity of pluralistic modal inflection. In their instrumental works, baroque composers did not exclude themselves from the general area of direct human expressiveness through the depiction of semantically defined affective states, although the French did not fully understand this, were not sympathetic to it, and consequently produced few instrumental works of superior quality—neither in the baroque era nor in the period which followed. But the Germans and the Italians simply internalized the rhetorical locus descriptionis within the formal dimensions of the locus notationis, and they were thereby able to capitalize on the immediacy of tonal differentiation itself if they so chose. Historically, they did.

This abstraction of consciousness into the sphere of pure sonic activity (what Blume and others have called signification through the "how" of music rather than its "what") was a major tonal contribution by baroque composers to instrumental music. That it was further exploited by classic composers and then reified by romantic composers back into the sphere of direct human expression itself (through nationalism, nature, and literature) testifies to one of the great motions of Western tonal dialectic. To be sure, the baroque era was the first great age of abstract instrumental music. But it did not spring up as an aesthetic phenomenon out of nothing. No musical appearance ever does. In this historical instance, it was very much governed by the aesthetic application of the principles of rhetoric, whose aims were to move, to persuade, and to instruct. What baroque composers discovered was that they could carry out these aims within the context of tonal differentiation itself. In the shapes of sonic, moving forms tonality was temporally externalized for its own sake. While instrumental tonality obviously annulled its commitment to *particularized* semantic definition, at the same time it concretized the affective expressivity it had inherited from the concomitant melos and preserved through a generalized musical rhetoric the form of that consciousness at a higher level. Tonality became a conscious aesthetic value unto itself.

The third tendency is the most elusive because baroque composers themselves did not leave behind any records of its ongoing activity upon their own cognitive processes, although, of course, the tonal results of those processes, music itself, reveal the objectified forms of their creative efforts. This is the psychological tendency for reification through repetition, and I shall retrace here some of the stages of the aesthetic/formal tendency but from a different point of view. To be sure, the Renaissance had exploited one of the types of musical repetition to the full. The motet, madrigal, chanson, and Mass movement are characterized in the late fifteenth and the sixteenth centuries by their careful and deliberate working out of points of imitation whereby similar melodic phrases were systematically stated in all the voices. What is largely absent in Renaissance music is the notion of organizing whole musical structures through the principle of structural repetition, that is, consistent repetition and sequence on the microlevel and sectional return of extensive portions of the work on the macrolevel. The manner in which Renaissance texts were treated had tended to preclude it. A motet did not have a single unifying theme that reappeared in the course of the composition at critical formal points. Instead, a series of points of imitation (often alternating with chordal passages) unfolded over successive phrases of text. Unity and variety were achieved through the alternation of textures instead of themes. The emergence of the *seconda prattica* and the development of many new forms of baroque music, however, brought about a change in the thinking of composers regarding musical structure, and the seventeenth century exhibits a gradually defined component of order and symmetry which as structure came to stand as an aesthetic value in and of itself. The decline of interest in consistent imitation in the early seventeenth century in favor of the polarity between treble and bass lines did not mean the abandonment of the principle of repetition entirely. But as time passed, repetition and sequence assumed roles as compositional, developmental procedures that eclipsed the activity once enjoyed by imitative counterpoint. Thousands of themes were spun out in the treble register—both vocal and instrumental—as repetition and sequence assumed formal importance in the expansion of sonic temporal length. The length of Renaissance vocal pieces is largely determined by the amount of text to be set to music. This was not the case in baroque instrumental music (or even its vocal music, as I shall demonstrate shortly). As the instrumental movement progressed, it was compelled to demonstrate some principle of unity: it easily filled this need by the exact repetition (or some varied form of it) of a principal musical idea stated at the beginning of the movement. This historically took the form of the *ritornello*, a phrase or group of phrases the last of which contains a cadence in the principal key and which quickly identified the "theme" of the work. This ritornello was normally stated in full in the tonic at the beginning and end of the movement. It was also periodically stated in full or in part during the course of the movement (medial ritornellos), either in the tonic or in nearly related keys. Between the statements of the ritornello there were episodes that were either derived from the ritornello itself or were newly composed. In the case of the solo concerto, episodic material was readily handed over to the featured instrument, whose idiomatic potential was frequently exploited through brief flashes of virtuosity.

Two aesthetic principles were thus developed in this form which met fundamental psychological criteria for enjoyable experiences with music. It provided unity: through memory the listener was rewarded by hearing in the same or different tonal areas a melody that appealed to the mind as being the most important musical idea because it was the first, last, and most frequently repeated sonic event. And it provided variety: through the presentation of new events in the form of episodes, the listener was tempted into the cognition of different melodic configurations, idiomatic excursions of technical display, and the juxtaposition of thin versus full instrumental textures—particularly in the case of solo and grosso concertos. Each time the listener was rewarded for his attention by a return to all or part of the ritornello subject, that part of the sonic phenomenon with which he was already familiar. If this formal plan appears psychologically to bear the marks of the familiar carrot-and-stick syndrome, or aesthetically to engage in a relatively simplistic approach to tonal experience, it did not seem so to the baroque listener. It must be realized that he heard many a concerto only once. He had therefore to be supplied with a ground plan for the experience which would keep him from getting lost among the ever-flowing progression of notes, and the ritornello provided a perfect scaffolding for the presentation of abstract sounds. Certainly, repetition was not a new compositional technique, but during the last half of the seventeenth century it was formalized as an abstract musical principle in a fashion that had not been previously attempted or achieved. In terms of instrumental music, the ritornello principle was developed in the works of the Bolognese concerto composers. The greatest Italian master of this form was Antonio Vivaldi, who clearly understood the mechanics of its structure and exploited it as an architectural formula. The late baroque composers freely applied the ritornello principle to the aria and the chorus. In the music of Bach we find it in arias, choruses, chorale preludes, even the preludes of some of the keyboard suites, in addition to its expected presence in all allegro concerto movements.

It would be quite wrong to give the notion that these latter two tendencies (formal/aesthetic and psychological) developed in isolation from vocal music. As Apel notes, "the term 'concerto' was first used for vocal compositions supported by an instrumental (or organ) accompaniment, in order to distinguish such pieces from the then current style of unaccompanied a capella music."[42] Even up to the early eighteenth century the term *concerto* frequently seems to mean *concertate*, music in which singers and orchestra were involved in a contrast between different groups of voices and instruments. And it would be foolish to assume that the psychological tendency for reification through repetition (both within the microform of the phrase or phrases and the macroform of whole movements) was only exhibited within instrumental music. What is here being stressed, however, is the fact that the aesthetic/formal tendency and the psychological tendency toward reification through repetition assumed the position of an interrelated value in vocal music—music which formerly had not much needed it, and, in fact, whose own principle of semantic integrity was overridden in favor of it. One of the favorite baroque aria forms was the *aria da capo* in which a complete return to the opening section of the form is carried out after a contrasting middle section (which is sometimes not very different from the corner sections). We note also in this vocal music an abundance of repetition of text; the literary idea is suspended or thwarted from rhetorical progression in favor of melodic repetition, harmonic sequence, and structural expansion through musical means. Aesthetically, it supports the general notion that "information" (in the sense of discrete bits of data) was not assumed to be of the highest significance in baroque vocal music, but rather a continuous tonal analogizing of its affective content as suggested by the words. Functionally, in the dramatic and quasi-dramatic, large-scale vocal forms, information was relegated to the activity of the recitative, where action, plot, and idea are advanced and there is little repetition of text or—for that matter—melody itself. Teleologically speaking, the dichotomy between recitative and aria, with a clear capitulation to musical ends in the case of the latter, handily demonstrates the tendencies we have just isolated within the realm of instrumental music. The interaction and interrelation between it and vocal forms is only to be expected.

From the beginning to the end of the baroque era we witness the marked influence of language and literature upon the creation, development, and maturation of both instrumental and vocal forms of music. It is an easy matter to understand the tonal means that composers utilized to objectify expressive subjectivity in the dramatic forms of recitative and aria. But similar techniques were applied to the creation of the numerous instrumental forms by the same composers. The doctrine of affections, with its manifest connections with the art of rhetoric, secured for composers the same means by which to objectify expressiveness in the so-called abstract forms of concerto, sinfonia, overture, and sonata. To be sure, this internalization of its content towards apparent abstraction and the rhetorical conventions by which it was achieved were not everywhere understood and consciously developed, particularly by the French; but the principle remained the same: the purpose of music was to move, to persuade, to instruct, and to please. In the following chapter we shall discover that the progression of this tendency toward abstraction was not the ultimate goal of tonality as form: it was merely the byproduct of a tonal dialectic at work within the sonic sphere of knowledge and human interests.

9 Tonality and Sonata Form

T he analysis of the previous chapter sought to demonstrate a commonality between baroque vocal and instrumental music in terms of a similar rhetorical, expressive, formal, and tonal dialectic. However, I initially submit here (and therefore not yet critically) that classic instrumental music by virtue of its existence did objectify an abstraction of tonal utterance that lay historically within the sphere of its interests but potentially beyond those for whom it was ostensibly created. As eighteenth-century Enlightenment French critics and their German disciples sought to encompass all art theory within a single comprehensive principle and to develop rules by which to ensure its praxis, they gradually realized that the growing popularity of instrumental music raised strong doubts as to its intrinsic ability to objectify any such aims. Instrumental music did differ from vocal music: in previous eras its function had largely determined its form. It had been the ready companion to all sorts of functions in seventeenth-century social life—eating, drinking, dancing, marching, worshipping, teaching, and diverse celebrations. But the dominant principle of baroque aesthetics was, as Mattheson and others well understood, "to please, to move, and to instruct." In the service of texts, music achieved this goal in its various vocal forms—cantata, oratorio, and opera, particularly *tragédie lyrique*. However, the same era that inspired the explosion of concerted vocal and instrumental music was also responsible for the creation and development of purely instrumental forms of music— prelude, fugue, toccata, sonata da chiesa, sonata da camera, concerto, and sinfonia. Could these "pure" forms of abstract music mean or signify anything socially?

During the eighteenth century a pitched battle was fought in Germany between a small group of composers and neoclassic critics who argued *against* meaning in abstract instrumental music and another group who argued *for* it. In the preface to his *Auserlesene mit Ernst und Lust gemengte Instrumentalmusik* (1701), Georg Muffat complained of the "ear-tickling jingle-jangle" (*"ohrkitzelndes Klingklang"*) of the new Italian instrumental style that was beguiling the minds of German music lovers. On the other hand, Mattheson devoted much of his *Der vollkommene Cappellmeister* to explaining how instrumental music could acquire aesthetic autonomy as a genre characterized by intrinsic meaning and import.

For Mattheson the rationale was simple: instrumental music acquired meaning in the same fashion as did vocal music, through the application of the principles of rhetoric developed in the classical art of oratory. Mattheson felt that the agents by which to carry out this procedure lay within the sixfold division of the *dispositio*, that is, in the application to musical composition of the parts and order of a model speech. A complete *dispositio* consisted of *exordium* (opening), *narratio* (statement of facts), *divisio* (forecast of main points in the speaker's favor), *confirmatio* (affirmative proof), *confutatio* (refutation or rebuttal), and *peroratio* or *conclusio* (conclusion). These rhetorical activities were to be musically applied to melodies, more accurately "themes," as substantive content in such a fashion that the appearing temporal form exhibited by musical analogy the same argumentative aspect as did a good speech.[1]

Mattheson's conviction was correct, although in retrospect it seems almost visionary in terms of the remarkable achievements of Haydn, Mozart, and the young Beethoven, whose concerns were decisively compositional and not specifically directed toward the confirmation of one or the other of the neoclassic critics' aesthetic platforms. In fact, when Mattheson brought the principles of rhetoric *to* the act of composing instrumental music as justification for its meaning and value, it is unlikely that he ever understood that instrumental music already contained *within* itself a far more profound and important means through which to legitimize its activity. But we can understand it now: it was the nature of the classical tonal system itself as characterized by the historical development of the phenomena of key centers and modulation. That is, devoid of textual meaning and the need to underscore and support its "conceit," instrumental music internalized the principles and forms of classical rhetoric within the role of key centers (and modes within them) as the tonal representative of sonic persuasion.[2] That classic composers chose most often to carry forth this activity in terms of the sonata-form principle needs no documentation.

It was not, of course, sonata as form alone that triumphed over all competitors as an isolated structural phenomenon, or the ambiguity about the meaning of the term *sonata* itself would not have vacillated among all conceivable instrumental forms, genres, styles, and textures. It was rather that a distinctive manner of utterance evolved in eighteenth-century instrumental music which as compositional process offered a thoroughgoing transformation of the manner in which tonality functioned within form itself. This process had not been alien to the key-centered principles of baroque tonality; but when unencumbered by the semantic requirements of the text it gradually internalized ideational substance in a dialogue with the materials of tonal utterance which was its very dialectic. As we shall see, if instrumental form was to become an autonomous art, it was required to do so.

A word of caution is in order. Although I shall attempt to assess here the notion of the sonata-form principle from the standpoint of its rhetorical and dialectical function, any hypostatization of classical form as an ideal compositional model is discouraged. Assuming that the development of musical forms and styles is not utterly unpredictable and irrational, contemporary analysts of musical form, through a "cunning of reason," have achieved results that correspond very generally to a sonic *telos* that has been constructed after the facts. That is, from the totalization of the unintended consequences of individual sonata appearances, we have decided what sonata form is. The weight of statistical evidence alone justifies the familiar, textbook model or recipe of sonata form against which the sonatas, quartets, symphonies, and concertos of composers from C. P. E. Bach to Samuel Barber have been fractured until their appearing objectivity reveals their conformity (or lack of it) to a single model of distinctly Platonic inspiration. Unfortunately, the precision of the model so evolved has tended to trivialize a lengthy period of compositional development (in which preclassic composers played a critical role) in favor of a formal analysis that notes the conformity and rationalizes the deviation of sonatas of the most gifted composers without realizing what these appearances meant historically to those who composed, performed, and heard them. The only contemporary scholar to question this pedagogic flatness with its one-dimensional approach to tonality and sonata form has been pianist and musicologist Charles Rosen whose insightful book, *Sonata Forms*, by its very title (in the plural) sought to challenge analytical thought into a new dialogue with a now frozen concept.[3] Rosen skillfully argues that classic composers did not set out to perfect a musical form which they then compositionally violated in the name of subjective expressivity. Instead, they created and developed a musical form whose potential for discursive logic dramatized tonal activity as formal truth. Thus, the motives, phrases, periods, sections, and parts within each sonata form became the very processes of sonic persuasion that claimed absolute validity and completeness as single appearances of tonal architecture.

There have been occasional attempts to explain the sonata-form principle in terms of the Hegelian dialectic with which it is contemporary. (Both Beethoven and Hegel were born in 1770, an auspicious year.) It is interesting to note, however, that Philip T. Barford, in an article that appeared in *The Music Review* in 1952, while summarily suggesting the operation of the dialectic in terms of "the movement of thesis and antithesis to a higher synthesis, the reconciliation of opposites in a transcendent whole which is more than a merely subjective affection of mind,"[4] devoted so little attention to the sonic ground in which these relations came to have expressive meaning, that is tonality itself. I shall not belabor the point here, but I believe that the movement which consciousness made in the works of pre-classic and classic composers was objectified within the realm of tonality. This is to say that the subjective activity of creative consciousness realized its potential within the contrasting components of sonic form through the processive activity of key centers. Structurally, this tonal objectification was proof of the subjective-objective reconciliation which Barford rightly identifies as the "intellectual coherence" that animates the rationality of synthetic wholes. As sonata form, each sonic edifice effectively objectified the will of the composer on virtually any level of expression he sought to activate.

I would like, however, to deepen Barford's critique. The fundamental notions beneath the evolution of sonata form (and classic form in general) were the principle of sonic identity and difference, the concept of cohesive micro- and macroform in tonal terms, and the emergence of a particular type of melodic utterance that came to be characterized as "thematic." To be sure, these notions are interrelated and exhibit historical connections with baroque music, but their marked internalization within classic instrumental music characterizes sonata form as a distinct realization of the nature of classic tonality that was uniquely flexible, logical, and dramatic. I do not mean to hypostatize sonata form into a structural object that had a life of its own, a kind of Platonic tonal ideal that hovered over the minds of composers who sought to give it definition through their own creative subjective acts. There is, however, a decisive abstract quality to sonata form, clearly evidenced by the diverse genres in which it was expressed, which readily submits to formal analysis in general terms and which I wish to discuss here. I shall do this with two sets of largely parallel terminologies—the conventional, contemporary textbook terminology because it is convenient and familiar, and the terminology of classical rhetoric because Mattheson encouraged its application to the activity of instrumental composition.

The macroform of the sonata movement exhibits five sections or parts that are temporally grounded; that is, they are noninterchangeable and progressive: introduction, exposition, development, recapitulation, and coda. In this sense, within the whole of the hierarchical order, they are "closed out" and acquire tonal logic because of this limitation.[5]

Least important is the introduction, and in fact it is often absent. In terms of the orator's *dispositio*, it corresponds with the *exordium*. Two characteristics distinguish the introduction when it is present: it is in a slower tempo than the main body of the movement, and it normally does not state principal melodic materials from it. The absence of critical melodic utterance initiates a state of expectation for the subsequent, first presentation of the movement's themes. Something is about to happen, but it is not happening now. The prefatory nature of the introduction is often tonally secured by the manner in which it articulates the two most important harmonies (tonic and dominant), as tonal disclosure of the drama about to begin.

The first major section of the sonata form is the exposition, which roughly corresponds with the *narratio* and the *divisio* of classical rhetoric. The exposition begins in the tonic key, and the clearest formative element of classic structure appears immediately. This is the short, periodic, melodic phrase. It is not only rendered melodically cohesive but also harmonically convincing through cadential activity that tends to set it off as a closed unit of low-level formation that can be treated symmetrically through repetition in the tonic key. In terms of tonal stability, the melody as theme (for it is one) both asserts itself as the vehicle for affirming the principal key of the movement and as its annulment through a detachment of its separable parts into motives that seem to suggest the very vulnerability of its melodic utterance. The principle of identity and difference is immediately activated in melodic and harmonic terms. That is, the very nature of its periodic articulation when detached from its initial tonic assertiveness begins to drift toward the dominant harmony in a passage of transition. Unfortunately, the term *transition* belittles the harmonic activity that is accomplished, for it implies that nothing of great importance ever happens here. Quite the contrary, for the hierarchic structure of the form cannot be revealed in the tonic alone. This passage to the dominant (I am considering only major key form unless otherwise noted), as Rosen notes, significantly differs from baroque harmonic movements of the same order: "the classic style dramatizes this movement—in other words, it becomes an event as well as a directional force."[6]

(The careful reader has no doubt noticed that my terminology—"asserts itself," "begins to drift toward," and the like—awards to harmonic activity the very tonal vitalism I have attempted earlier to excise from discussions of tonal consciousness. It is here that the subjective-objective relationship between the creator and his creation is the most subtle and important. The terminology is both useful and necessary because music indeed moves, but at no point do I mean to imply that musical form acquires a life of its own. The agent behind the appearing illusion of audible organic activity in musical form is the composer, not the "unfolding" of the overtone series and his assumed obedience to it. In this light, the terminology is justified because it accurately defines the historical nature of the composer's interests. If the distinction is a borderline one, it is nevertheless crucial to understanding tonal form.)

We can see the dialectic of tonic and dominant (as historically demonstrated in chapter 7) at work here on every level of the form. The polarity between the two harmonies is intensified through modulation which raises dissonance to the level of structure itself. To quote Rosen again: "A passage in a tonal work that is outside the tonic is dissonant in relation to the whole piece, and demands resolution if the form is to be completely closed and the integrity of the cadence respected."[7] This elevation of the dominant as dissonant to the level of structure is of the utmost importance to the meaning of the form. Whereas it was the dominant *chord* that was dissonant in the opening pages of the sonata, now the dominant *key* is both consonant and dissonant at the same time with respect to its new status within hierarchic structure. It is consonant because it becomes its own tonic through a resolution granted by cadential activity with *its* dominant; and it is dissonant because it is viewed as a process that has annulled the original key which must eventually be sought again and reaffirmed later in the piece.

It is not enough, however, just to modulate. This harmonic dramatization is melodically secured in one of two ways: by the presentation of a new theme (or themes), or by the repetition of the opening theme within the harmonic context of the dominant key. Rosen has attempted and rightly so to correct the mandatory recipe notion that a sonata form must present a second (and also third) theme at this moment within the structure. There are sonatas that do not present new themes, but there are many more that do. When this happens, the concept of monothematicism as witnessed in the baroque dance, fugue, even to some extent the basically monothematic character of the ritornello principle, is annulled. This principle of thematic contrast which is supported through key differentiation is critical to the understanding of sonata form. Rosen is reluctant to turn Haydn, Mozart, and Beethoven into Hegelians, but I am not.[8] Whatever else happened in the shift from baroque compositional procedures to classical ones, a plurality of thematic invention in the latter is a significant difference that must be recognized. To be sure, the terms *thetic, antithetic,* and *synthetic* are not really Hegel's terms, but they are his concepts, and the application to sonata form reveals more than it conceals.

I therefore interpret the second section of the sonata, the development, to be an antithetic motion within the tonal dialectic of the form. Here, structural opportunity is given to "unfold" the potential of themes themselves and in a more extensive fashion than was offered in the exposition. If the theme is to earn its title as theme, rather than remain a melody, it must do so by its participation in all the important phases of integration and disintegration that harmonic substantiality implies. To be sure, all the traditional compositional devices that themes can undergo are not equally employed. For instance, the augmentative and diminutive procedures of developing baroque fugue subjects diminish in importance, but other techniques acquire remarkable developmental status, particularly repetition, sequence, and imitation. The utilization of these devices unfolds the integrity and energy of the melody as it becomes a legitimate theme. It is not an accident that this section of the form was called the *fantasia* section by composers themselves, and many a composer misunderstood the function of "development" as fantasia whether he was aware of the terms or not. In this regard, Barford has pointed out Coleridge's celebrated distinction between fancy and imagination, and it is worth repeating here.

> Fancy does no more than juxtapose different images, and fanciful association does not appeal in virtue of any singleness of aesthetic purpose. Fanciful association may amuse and entertain; but there will be no certain principle of construction, no dominating inspiration.[9]

As Barford notes, for the development section to vitalize its potential content something more than "arid stretches of Alberti-bass" and "conventional scraps of Italianate melody and passage-work" had to be offered in the name of "fantasialike looseness" projected through self-conscious subjectivity. Not surprisingly, gifted composers such as the sons of Bach, along with Dussek, Clementi, Haydn, and Mozart assumed different attitudes toward this subjectivity at different times in their careers. The *Empfindsamkeit* style and the brief *Sturm und Drang* period of the seventies and eighties are accessible parts of this forced expressiveness which we cannot take up here. But if the form was to become synthetic, an integrated whole, it had to refrain from merely becoming subjective because there was nothing else expected of it at the moment. Coleridge "conceived the imagination as a faculty which struggles to idealize and to unify images with a concern for some central conception which it is desired to convey."[10] This characteristic energy thus sought to fuse the different melodic elements within sonata form that lay potentially before subjective consciousness as tonal material. Thematically, it did this by exploiting the integrative and disintegrative features of the "melodies" at work, most often through "the interpreter of the motive." Harmonically, the compositional goal of development was not explicit clarity of key—as found in the exposition—but the suggestion that such clarity lay within the wholeness of melody that was now being subjected antithetically to the wide potential of tonal consciousness itself. And aesthetically, with this assertive motion toward utter tonal freedom through the suspension of its "laws," composers decisively raised the question of tonal validity itself to the level of form.

Because these concepts are so important, I would like to state them differently, with an aim toward clarity about the creative act of sonata-form composition. I do not wish to superimpose the *dispositio* of classical rhetoric upon sonata form in any more rigid fashion than did classic composers themselves, but an important point must be made with reference to the argumentative aspect of classical rhetoric. The development section is that place in the whole of the sonata where the *confirmatio*, as affirmative proof, and the *confutatio*, as refutation or rebuttal, received their most explicit and most elaborate treatment. The purpose of rhetoric was to argue for the validity of a statement or a series of statements. The speaker was required to acknowledge, even to develop to a certain degree refutations of his own thesis. If counterargument could destroy a thesis then the thesis was not worth proposing in the first place. The speaker knew this in advance and he planned a place in his *dispositio* in which to treat it. In the sonata form, the statement or series of statements was the unfolding of melodies in the exposition. Their tonal truth was not challenged there: it was simply given as assertion. In the development section, however, the refutation of that particular tonal assertion—tonic and dominant keys as the best polarities within the abundant reservoir of key-centered potentiality—was purposely challenged and argued against. This discursive argument not only raised the harmonic possibility of other coherent key centers but also suggested through melodic fragmentation and motivic reconstruction that the melodies possessed within themselves more than had been initially asserted. These melodies were no longer simply treated as melodies per se, but as themes that actually transcend themselves into other statements with new coherences and orders. (It is this feature of the development section which romantic composers, particularly Schubert, were to understand so poorly.) But the purpose of counterargument was to secure the validity of the initial assertion in both rhetoric and the sonata-form principle. And the *peroratio* and the recapitulation followed, respectively.

The function of the recapitulation section was so well understood that there was often a short passage at the end of the development that clearly anticipated it. Haydn, in fact, was fond of beginning the recapitulation in the form of a "false reprise" only to return briefly to the developmental procedures of the middle of the movement.

In the recapitulation the synthetic unity of the classical tonal dialectic was wholly manifested. All themes had to be in the same tonic key, not because the movement would end in the wrong key if the second theme was not in the tonic—for the coda would have neatly accomplished a return to the tonic had the composer wished to use it merely for that purpose—but because what had been annulled (monothematicism) was now to be preserved on a higher tonal order (several themes, but now one pervasive key center).

There are two features of this tonal leveling in the recapitulation that merit attention, as they demonstrate how synthesis is actually accomplished within the form as a sonic whole. One is the transition passage between first and second themes. In the exposition this passage is modulatory in nature and leads to a different key area. Here, in the recapitulation, this feeling of "leading to" is again carried out by the composer, who often uses the same (exposition) transition passage but must now create the feeling that "going away from" but "right back to" the tonic is just as logical as going away from it to the dominant key had been previously in the exposition. The second feature is the change in modal quality in sonatas in minor keys. While the secondary theme had been in major in the exposition, it must be stated in minor in the recapitulation, frequently revealing characteristic turns of modal inflection (because of the various forms of the minor scale) that were unavailable in the major statement at the beginning of the movement.

Taken as a whole, the sonata's three chief sections exhibit the potential of tonality within the dialectic of an astonishing functional hierarchy. The exposition secured the tonal stability of the two most important key areas, tonic and dominant. There, the tonic assumed priority only by virtue of its being first in the processive order. (Because we are already tonal hearers we expect with a very high degree of probability that the movement will also end in the tonic, but we cannot prove it by any means offered in the exposition.) In fact, the dominant seems critically to win the first round in the tonal dialogue. In the second section, the development, tonal potential is awarded its greatest freedom. If there can be two key centers, then there can be a number of them, and it is here that the form reached its highest pinnacle of aesthetic freedom: tonal ambiguity generated a harmonic excitement that quite belied the tonal cohesion of the whole form. But the very presence of the development as central to the achievement of a formal dialectic is testimony to a concept that overruled it, formally by the passage to the third section, the recapitulation, and aesthetically by a creative rationality that demanded tonal symmetry within a temporal order. Rosen's statement regarding this cannot be improved, so let me quote it here:

> It is the classical sense for large areas of stability, impossible before and lost since, that establishes what might seem to be the one fixed rule of sonata

recapitulation: material originally exposed in the dominant must be represented in the tonic fairly completely, even if rewritten and reordered, and only material exposed in the tonic may be omitted. That is, of course, not a rule at all but a sensitivity to tonal relationships. . . . The material that already had been represented in the exposition in the tonic could be, and often was, drastically cut, but the rest of the exposition cried out for resolution in the tonic.[11]

Having stated the expository material in the recapitulation in the tonic, the movement is ostensibly over, but there is the coda. The exposition usually contains no coda, although it frequently contains codetta-like passage work and figuration (sometimes based upon themes in the exposition) which brings that section to a close in the dominant key. At that point a formal leave-taking would be inappropriate as the development must seem to follow logically from the exposition. In the recapitulation, however, this termination apparently seemed too abrupt to composers, and the coda (literally, tail) was added to bring the tonal activity to a formal and convincing close. This was carried out with short reminiscences of parts of previous themes as the harmonies passed through the most direct statements of key center, V–I in the tonic.

The harmonic possibilities of the whole sonata form depended upon individual imagination and creativity. Throughout the classic era, we witness experimentation with and refinement and reassessment of tonal potential, particularly by Austrian and German composers. One of the characteristics of their consciousness was the gradual realization that, harmonically speaking, less was more. Richard Crocker cogently underscores this point. After 1750 a subtle sense of harmonic motion became

the most important means to musical expression; not that other musical elements were neglected, but their effectiveness often depended upon the effectiveness of the harmony. Increased harmonic effectiveness was not, however, reached directly through richer chords and more intricate progressions but—paradoxically—through simpler chords and more efficient progressions. . . . Composers around 1750 capitalized on this infused sense of relationship, avoiding the now redundant effect of rapid transit through the essential chords of a key, by presenting chords one at a time—as it were—making each last somewhat longer than before. Each chord made a more individual contribution to the establishment of the key.[12]

This seeming paradox goes hand in hand with two different leveling tendencies of a thoroughly public harmonic consciousness. First, in a sociological sense, it allowed composers to communicate with each other and with a rapidly expanding international, concert-going audience on generally known and accessible levels of harmonic comprehensibility. (The classic era is not the age of the unique harmonic progression, but the generalizing one.) And second, in a psychological sense, if the cognitive and recognitive activities of thematic identity were to be secured through progressive temporal shapes and figures, harmony needed ultimately to support such thematic activity and not become an end to itself. This does not vitiate the statements made above about the question of tonal validity within the development section: it only confirms that, dialectically, questions about tonal validity are proper and necessary methods for the ultimate establishment of its concrete, historical truth. To be sure, classic harmony was an expressive device, as we have seen in chapter 8, but it was not independently so—as it would most certainly become in the personal, alienated, and irresolvable harmonic consciousness of *Tristan und Isolde*. Classic harmony's primary function was tonal confirmation, not tonal alienation, and the exceptions to this are few. A good example is the overture to Haydn's *Creation*, in which cosmic chaos is clearly and deliberately revealed through remarkable tonal ambiguity.

The sonata-form principle was a superior compositional achievement. To the men who created it, it stood not so much as an ideal of the type that modern textbooks academically claim for it but rather as a hierarchic process that provided dynamic and temporal continuity between both tonal functions and structural parts. Subjectively animated from within by tonal cohesiveness and harmonic intensity, it virtually leveled the world of instrumental music which had given it birth. Scholars of baroque music know that the ritornello was used with equal success in both concerted vocal and purely instrumental music. But because of the extensive development aspect that characterizes its middle section the sonata-form principle did not readily lend itself to vocal music. However, it *was* applied to vocal music, particularly arias and ensembles, with genuine success in the case of Mozart. The development sections there are of course insignificant or nonexistent, but both the modulation schemes and thematic content are made to function quite nicely within the limits of texted music.

Two of the numerous instances of this compositional activity are Idamante's aria in act I, scene 2 of Mozart's *Idomeneo* ("Non ho colpa") and the soprano aria, "Laudamus te," in the Mass in C Minor (K. 427). Because of a desire to see Mozart as the epitome of classicism, musicologists tend not to see how easily he assimilated the ritornello principle at the same time that he transformed its structural possibilities into sonata form. The Mass in C Minor is a telling example of this formal consciousness. The principal "theme" of the "Laudamus te" aria is really a ritornello subject with four clear motives (measures 1–3; 4–6; a transition phrase, 7–10; and a cadential motive, 11–14) in F major. The second theme has two distinct parts, both in C major. The soprano never sings the first part of this second theme, which is presented by the first violins in both exposition and recapitulation. The voice does present the second part of the theme in the exposition, in a brief imitative exchange with the oboes. Note that the cadential motive of the "ritornello" principal theme (over a dominant harmony in C) brings about the return to the recapitulation but in the manner of a facile and expected baroque convention. The second part of the second theme does not appear in the recapitulation. The closing ritornello of the movement is the transition phrase (!) of the principal theme, with a new 2-measure (and very affirmative) closing cadence. This "sonatina"-ritornello aria is an almost uncanny synthesis of the two most important vehicles of baroque and classic form. (There is a doctoral dissertation for somebody in a study of this procedure.)

In chapter 1 I viewed rather contemptuously the present day notion of judging the tonality of the classicists (sometime around the activities of the mature Haydn and Mozart and the young Beethoven) as a kind of Kantian *Ding-an-sich*, as if tonality could reach through a series of ever more precise and sophisticated stages "tonality-in-itself." I shall not retract this criticism here, for unfortunately the notion is with us still, particularly as it is hypostatized by Schenker and his followers. But by way of summary it is instructive to examine this cherished Kantian perspective in light of the classicists who actually brought it into existence. For the tonality that they "perfected" for their own ends indeed came to stand for at least a century as a paradigm of sonic consciousness in which all composers participated. But they were able to do so (and with great success) only because "tonality-in-itself" was actually in a constant Hegelian movement of the dialectic. Let us briefly review the evidence.

The most significant change in eighteenth-century tonality was "a new emphatic polarity between tonic and dominant," Rosen notes.[13] This can be seen in the total subjugation of any other cadences but I–V and V–I, as witnessed in its historical stages and demonstrated earlier in this book. As demonstrated there, these cadences function on two levels: in the particularization of their substantive essence as immediately concretized in half- and whole-cadences, and in a binary tonal relationship that entails the generalization of their motion extended through time. This is to say that subjective tonality "alienated" itself in the objective nature of the very forms that it created. One of Hegel's terms for this process is *Entäusserung*: "externalization" is a possible translation and implies a broader application than the customary meaning of alienation. In music, this externalization encountered an ontological problem of purely sonic dimensions that is not witnessed in the other arts—time that is virtually heard.[14] If tonal consciousness was to impregnate its own temporality with meaning, if it was to do so without balletic or semantic assistance (which it was perfectly willing to rely upon until the seventeenth century), it would have to develop formal and aesthetic dimensions of its own. It could not wander willy-nilly through its harmonies, punctuating them occasionally with the cudgel of a cadence and hope for the best. Nor could it continually serve up cadences as progression because they afforded the strongest statement of open and closed states of harmonic activity, for this would only weaken and annul the formal strength that cadences offered when needed. But what did devolve from the motion of cadences was externalized within the concept of harmony itself; harmonic motion came to stand for the objectified sonic rationality of the tonal work. There is a process of transcendence in this externalization of what formerly had been given to consciousness chiefly by semantic clarification and definition. This transcendence produced the notion of harmony as a concept, with concrete tonal aspects. Historically, of course, this was a gradual process and took centuries to accomplish; all periods of music from the beginning of medieval organum on participated in it. But certainly in the baroque period, when the notion was actually much freer than in its classic phase, and in the classic period, when a kind of leveling of its former diversity took place, we witness the gradual and apparently irrevocable establishment of the dominant as the prime mover within sonic temporality. In a sense, the activity of harmonic temporality in any key other than the tonic could be and was viewed as a form of dissonance—just as the dominant triad was viewed as dissonant and active before the tonic triad in a whole-cadence. Quite naturally (here meaning only through habit), the dominant itself became the principal key area for extended harmonic motion that was not tonic motion. The connective tissue between key areas, of course, was the modulation, which gradually annulled the strength of one key but preserved the validity of key area as concept at a higher level of consciousness—within the unfolding of the new key area or areas (now thought of as having a relationship with the first key), which could only be fully secured by the particularizing form of all harmonic motion, a cadence. The generalizing tendency of harmonic motion historically leveled all cadences but I–V and V–I, which became preeminent. At the same time, the externalization of these cadences in all moments of the temporal object tended also to level other possible harmonic motions in favor of the "best" harmonic motion. This process brought about the notion of "functional harmony," as defined by theorist Hugo Riemann; that is, there was a hierarchy within the catalog of triads, and secondary triads in particular were related functionally to the tonic, subdominant, or the dominant.[15] And it is on this point that Schenkerian analysis is entirely valid; but it is only valid to the extent that we may actually identify the generalizing tendency of such functional harmonic movement as germane to the composer's own cognitive interests and clearly in evidence. If tonality became a "thing-in-itself," and quite clearly Schenker thought that it did, it did so historically through this process and not through any slavish obedience to the overtone series and other "natural" causes.

Historically, the die had been cast. In a very specific sense, the classicists did perfect the conceptual aspects of harmonic motion that had begun as early as organum and had continued unabated (but with many chromatic twists and turns) right through the Renaissance and the baroque. But they were not eternal concepts and they did not remain crystallized except in the minds of theorists. While all composers up to the early Schoenberg respected the particularizing tendency of the cadence, they both explored and exploited the generalizing tendency of harmonic motion, "dissonance on the level of structure," until classic structure itself and its tonal hierarchic functionality was jeopardized, weakened, and collapsed. In the middle of the nineteenth century, Richard Wagner discovered that musical form could be organized in terms of drama itself—for those who chose to do so. And as Erik Satie irreverently proved sometime later, if one did not care to follow classic models of discursive form or Wagnerian ones he might as well write his pieces "in the shape of a pear," and ostensibly proceeded to do just that.

10 Tonality and the Nineteenth Century

T he nineteenth century exhibits an abundance of ideas and talents of such diverging character that to use the term "romantic" for the whole era is to force a unity that, historically considered, exists in name only. Never before, notes Friedrich Blume, "had music history known conditions of such confusing abundance and capricious variety,"[1] when throughout Europe composers everywhere found that the liberation they willfully granted themselves collided head on with the limitations of an extended sphere of bourgeois consciousness that both revered and abused them. And yet, for all the antinomies of romantic music—aesthetic, social, political, and philosophical—nowhere is a pervading unity more concretely both established and transformed than within the very materials of its objective appearance, that is, within tonality itself. Tonally speaking, from Beethoven through Wagner to Mahler, the frequently radical quality of music, that is to say, its indictment of an established harmonic reality, is thus grounded precisely in the dimensions where music transcended its social determination. Music emancipated itself from the given universe of tonal discourse and sonic behavior while it simultaneously preserved its overwhelming presence as artistic truth.[2]

The reasons for this remarkable activity of tonal dialectic are diverse: the conscious historicism which composers sought as inspiration for their creations; the development of harmonic alienation as a positive means to compositional individuality; the simplification of key-centered tonality through the growth of popular music; the universal establishment of equal temperament; the ratiocination of empirical science upon classical acoustics as it related to theories of harmony that evolved late in the century; the tenuous relationship between the composer as alienated individual and his audience as recipient of his creations; the infusion and inspiration of nationalism that brought music from the universal sphere of Enlightenment man down to the interests of man and his specific tonal homeland; and the belief by virtually all romantic artists that, if the concept of the infinite was ever to be objectified music above all else would open that "immense and awesome" realm of spirit. We cannot pursue these many-faceted components of romantic tonality in depth in a single chapter: they plead for a book by themselves. But I would like to discuss the first three as distinct components that shaped nineteenth-century tonal consciousness.

HISTORICISM

In the year that Mozart died, Carl Friedrich Zelter joined a new Singakademie in Berlin directed by harpsichordist, conductor, and composer Carl Friedrich Christian Fasch. Zelter became the director of the Singakademie in 1800 and during the space of thirty years turned it into one of the most important organizations of its kind, devoted to the performances of older sacred music. He had inherited a considerable collection of the music of J. S. Bach from two of the latter's pupils, Johann Philipp Kirnberger and Johann Friedrich Agricola, which he gradually drew upon for the repertory of the Singakademie. In 1811 he rehearsed the *Mass in B Minor* and four years later the *St. Matthew Passion*, but he thought it impractical to present these extensive, complex works to the Berlin public. It was through Zelter and the Singakademie that his pupil, the very young and gifted Felix Mendelssohn, began a lifelong association with the music of Bach. If Zelter's promotion of Bach's music was cautious, young Mendelssohn's had the romantic flair of unbridled enthusiasm. If the *St. Matthew Passion* were to be offered again to the German public, it should be done, Mendelssohn thought, in Leipzig on the one-hundredth anniversary of its first performance there. This did not happen, but, after some two years of rehearsals, Mendelssohn conducted the *St. Matthew Passion* in Berlin on March 11, 1829. Hegel was present in the audience.

This event, notes Nicholas Temperley, "was the decisive turning-point in Bach's reputation, for it swiftly transformed the [Bach] revival from a cult of intellectuals into a popular movement."[3] The activities of Zelter's Singakademie and the Bach performances in Germany and England (where historicism was more advanced than in Germany) are exemplary of the conscious inspiration that composers sought from the music of the past for their own creativity. To be sure, the Italians had never lost their love of

Palestrina and Carissimi; nor the French, theirs of Couperin and Rameau; nor the Germans, theirs of Graun and Handel; but the restoration of older church music that was carried forth by German romantic composers penetrated more deeply into European music than could have been accomplished by national pride alone. Moreover, we may smile or wince at some of their efforts: for instance, Mendelssohn cut from Bach's *St. Matthew* score what he thought was excessive and added what he felt was lacking; in 1807 K. F. Horn arranged and published in London twelve Bach organ fugues for string quartet—but with a figured bass! Transgressions of our own contemporary ideals regarding performance practice are not the issue here, however, but rather the transforming tendency of nineteenth-century historicism itself in tonal terms. Historically, this took the form of a new challenge from a respected tradition of polyphony upon the unleashed potential of romantic harmonic consciousness.

The dispute that the Cecilian movement generated among nineteenth-century musicians and theorists makes it difficult to establish how it affected actual musical practice beyond its own theoretical clarification.[4] If the revival of Palestrina's contrapuntal style tended to remain fixed within the realm of sacred music, the influence of Bach was more extensive. Carl Dahlhaus notes, and I think rightly so, that Bach's counterpoint became "a matter of professional equipment" for romantic composers:

> What they saw realized in exemplary fashion in the music of Bach was the idea of music at once contrapuntal and full of character, at once strict and eloquent: music in which the characteristic and the eloquent features of a contrapuntally differentiated texture were not forced on it from the outside but were actually generated by it.[5]

It is this latter cognitive and creative phenomenon that concerns us here in tonal terms.

Perhaps because of a profound lyric component that characterizes nineteenth-century music, we have tended to trivialize romantic counterpoint by opposing it to harmonic thinking. Dahlhaus has observed that modern

> textbooks, which for didactic reasons are inclined to simplify matters by setting up clear antitheses, suggest that counterpoint functions as an "opposite" to harmony, thus promoting the view that an evolution of harmony embracing varied chordal structures and methods of linking chords must necessarily entail a suppression of polyphony.[6]

I concur with Dahlhaus that our suppression of the contrapuntal aspect of romantic music in the interests of its distinctive harmonic development has misled us into believing that key-centered tonality by its very nature was to blame. This was simply not the case and I offer a couple of examples by way of correction.

The first is clearly a loaded one, the opening fugue of the Opus 131 String Quartet by Beethoven, but it handily demonstrates the concept. Sweeping through a range of key centers that prove to be prophetic for tonalities that are used in the remaining six movements, this short fugue unfolds the customary techniques of fugal writing—exposition, episode, stretto, augmentation—in such a fashion that polyphonic statement and harmonic utterance become the inevitable consequence of one another. This is remarkably demonstrated by the activity of the cadences. They are necessary in order to define the tonal areas (one hesitates to call some of them key centers here) through which the fugue moves, but Beethoven seldom prepares the listener for their appearance by leading into them in a manner that would accentuate harmonic utterance over contrapuntal activity. Instead, they devolve as the logical consequence of an unremitting control of polyphonic coherence. Let us examine this process in action. The first cadence appears almost unnoticed in the brief codetta that follows the opening exposition (measure 20). Curiously, it is a half-cadence in C-sharp minor, on the first three beats of the measure, perhaps emphasizing the fact that the opening subject is on the dominant. In the upbeat to the first episode, in the same measure, the cello suggests a V_2–i progression that harmonically evaporates because the two inner voices rest. The second cadence is just as subtle. It occurs between measures 30–31, in the prevailing quarter-note rhythm of the fugue's opening section. It too is in C-sharp minor, a V_5^6–i. It is clearly the result of the counterpoint and serves to articulate the exchange of the outer parts in *stimmtausch* fashion. The most extensively prepared cadence in the fugue, a double one, occurs in measures 41–45. While the bass does carry the roots of the triads here, first in G-sharp minor, then in E-flat minor, the pronounced linear activity in the upper parts continues uninterrupted. This facile relationship with the key of E-flat minor is dissolved by the next cadence (measures 54–55) in a return to the tonic key. The three upper strings unfold a figure from the second half of the fugue subject but in diminution, and the cello rises through interlocking thirds that lead to a *piano* statement of the subject in A (measures 62–63). The intensity generated by the active eighth-note rhythm in this passage is relieved by a quiet canon in paired voices that leads to a return to C-sharp minor. A cadence in measures 83–84, with the dominant seventh inverted, is the result of the part writing. The cello firmly supplies the root movement in the next cadence (measures 87–88), but, as with the previous E-flat minor and A major cadences, the upper parts continue unabated. The cadence in measures 90–91 is elided, as the eighth-note figure returns as counterpoint to a statement of the subject by the viola and one by the cello in augmentation. The fugue is cadentially closed by the forcible reiteration of a Neopolitan to tonic harmony that foreshadows the key of the movement in D major to follow and has a logical place within the harmonic hierarchy of the movement as a whole tonal structure. This relationship is established by the fourth note of the fugue subject itself, which in its tonic statement is the lowered supertonic, or Neapolitan root tone. Beethoven intended the listener to intuit this tonal relationship. This tone is the longest one in the subject, thus emphasizing its importance through duration, and it is approached throughout the movement with a crescendo.

It is unfair, however, to summon forth the genius of Beethoven alone in order to demonstrate a battle fought and won in the arena of contrapuntal/harmonic interests, for the problem to be solved by all composers was not the alleged dichotomy between counterpoint and harmony but between melody and harmony in which counterpoint (outside the realm of specific imitative techniques) became the developmental transformation of their respective activities. Early nineteenth-century melody and harmony so interpenetrate one another, notes Blume, "that melodic invention forfeits its character, even essential elements of its conformation, when separated from its harmonic accompaniment."[7] Thus melody's innate relation with its harmonic substance became an inhibiting factor to early romantics when applied to thematic development in the form of polyphonic gesture. Developmental techniques by their very nature were mutable ones, and composers who did not understand or who could not exploit this component of mutability tended to write music in which counterpoint was shunted into the background in favor of lyric gesture.[8] This situation changed. In the second half of the century, Wagner, Bruckner, Mahler, Brahms, and Verdi brought melodic and harmonic components into a new polyphonic fusion that had not been seen in the early stages of romanticism. This is a characteristic difference, for instance, between the early and late operas of Verdi and Wagner. One need only consider the melodic-harmonic aspect of *La Traviata* and that found in virtually every page of *Falstaff*. What characterizes the late Verdi is his ability to create a consistent ground plan in the orchestra of ongoing contrapuntal activity in which and through which the vocal utterances as melody can move uninhibited as part of the whole dramatic structure. A skillful ground plan is also found in the works of Wagner, whose mastery of the motive as a dramatic and psychological device unifies harmony and contrapuntal components so skillfully that an attempt to separate them becomes an act of excision with negligible results.

Consider, for instance, the opening of act III of *Parsifal*, where we find the concept taken down to its most *elementarisch* appearance, as Wagner once commented, where the vast potential of the orchestra is forcibly reduced to the simplest of statements. Wagner's maturity as a dramatist enables him to begin this act in a mood of utter resignation devoid of desperation despite the events that preceded it. With astonishing economy the music unfolds from a single note into four-part writing in which melodic lines, without a shred of ornamentation and without instrumental doubling by the winds or brass, combine to form a totality of polyphonic utterance. Of all the choices available to him that would cause this mood to change, Wagner chooses the simplest, a slight quickening in eighth-notes in the cello. The eighth-note figure is expanded as the upper voices rise with emerging urgency against its downward thrust. The rhythmic values of this bass figure are again halved, but the mood and polyphonic austerity of the opening passage return for a single measure (18) at *noch langsamer werdend*. The Grail motive attempts to assert itself within the figure begun in measure 12, against the descending figure in the basses that is reinforced by the bassoons. As Michael Tanner remarks, this turns hideously into Kundry's motive (measure 23), and the motive of the Pure Fool, "jerkily but insistently," emerges and continues until the end of the prelude when the polyphonic opening returns and sets the mood for the hollow groaning of Kundry's voice.[9]

No composer seems to be more subject to the false dichotomy that separates his creative process into antithetical harmonic and contrapuntal components than does Gustav Mahler. Here is a sample:

> To discuss Mahler as a harmonist seems in a sense contradictory, for he was a composer who throughout his life clung stoutly to the principle of two-part counterpoint and deliberately avoided the concept of primary harmony, so prevalent in the opulent days of his youth. It is characteristic of him to think of music, generally speaking, in terms of thematic antithesis rather than as melody supported by an undercurrent of ever-changing harmony.[10]

One wonders what Mahler's music would have sounded like if he had deliberately avoided the concept of primary harmony. To the contrary, his harmony is the warp through which is woven the substance of his highly articulate polyphony. This is true even when triads are not always present due to an inclination toward the intervals of the fourth and fifth as agents of harmonic control. This is not to say, however, that Mahler composed as Schenker would suggest—by draping his melodies over the harmonic *Ur-stoff* of the chord progression—and that melody evolved as the interpreter of the motive. To be sure, Mahler does frequently juxtapose these two components, but they never stand in opposition to one another in terms of their tonal origin. The opening pages of the finale of the Ninth Symphony are a superior example of this technique. The harmonic motion there is almost chorale-like in its steady, metric deliberation. Chord changes are even, and, if not entirely predictable, at least not surprising. Through this seemingly chordal texture the polyphony weaves a now dense, now thin complement of linear statement that attests to the complete confidence (by the composer) that one element does not tonally annul the other. This is clearly demonstrated by the facility with which the bass instruments participate in both harmonic definition and polyphonic narration. More to the point, they accomplish both simultaneously. The austerity of Mahler's deliberate use of two- and three-part counterpoint such as we find in measures 28–48 of the same movement does exhibit a distinction between polyphonic and harmonic components, but the undergirding support for this skeletal polyphony is its compatibility with harmony. This is demonstrated by the extreme range of orchestral pitch and color in which it takes place, introduced by the contrabassoon and first violin at opposite ends of the spectrum. The age of figured bass is over; now in a contrapuntal passage one does not need the harmonies "filled in" to glue tonal components together. The baroque composer may have feared that his music might harmonically fall apart if it was not continually supported by the progressive gesture of chords in motion that secured harmonic coherence: for Mahler, however, who once remarked that when he created a symphony he created a universe, there was no need to fill in the details of its harmonic validity and evolution.

Romantic counterpoint has suffered at the hands of its critics. It is to be granted that the age was one of the utmost lyricism. The melodies, expressive and beautiful, that many composers created were not commensurate with the developmental techniques of the classic sonata principle. In fact, the dialectic of sonata form precluded romantic melody's being detached from its harmonic substratum without giving the impression of fragmentation of the most disjointed sort. As Lang notes, the expansive force and possibilities of the romantic theme were often virtually exhausted with its announcement, and the thematic logic that passed for development was frequently so in name only.[11] But the fault lay not in melody as such or the tonal system that sponsored it, but rather in the aesthetic interests of the composers themselves, and as such it was not a fault at all. Certainly, counterpoint was not always readily understood by all romantic composers; nor for that matter did all express equal concern over its compositional merit. But the same has been true of every age since 1600. The consummate craft that we find in the music of Beethoven, Wagner, Brahms, and Mahler decisively demonstrates that the harmonic system of nineteenth-century tonality was not at odds with its contrapuntal thought. It could not be. Counterpoint as tonal utterance had been the very praxis from which key-centered tonality had been forged.

HARMONIC ALIENATION AS TONAL IDENTITY

A second element of nineteenth-century tonality, frequently misunderstood, is the manner in which composers alienated themselves through the conscious exploitation of chromatic harmony. This is customarily viewed from the negative standpoint of tonal disintegration. I have outlined the traditional view of this process in chapter 1. But the thesis of this book is that key-centered tonality is but a moment in the history of tonal consciousness. Whatever romantic composers did in the process of utilizing the system of key-centered tonality, they did not seek to destroy it any more than Stendhal, Balzac, and Flaubert sought to destroy French in the process of writing novels. Nor did romantic composers "use up" key centered tonality, leaving a wasted residue of broken cadences and bare ruined choirs of keys to be swept into the dustbin of atonality as sonic trash. But exploit they did, in the best sense of that term, as they put to practical use the expressive potential of a harmonic system that housed with the utmost generosity even the most radical tonal statements. I shall view this phenomenon, then, not only from the standpoint of the disintegrative elements within key-centered potentiality, for this is but one aspect of the tonal dialectic in motion. In addition, we wish to establish the astonishing flexibility of this tonality as an act of preservation that composers consciously secured for themselves in order to legitimize their very tonal liberation.

I have discussed in other chapters the role of chromaticism within tonal consciousness, but I take up now its activity as a critical component of romantic music. A few summary statements of review are in order. The relation of diatonic to chromatic pitches in major and minor scales of baroque and classic tonality had been chiefly just that, a relation of seven to five tones within the octave. The seven diatonic pitches carried the burden of melodic and harmonic statement, and the chromatic pitches fed upon the relationships within that activity. As we have established, there were two quite different functions (although they were by no means exclusive of each other) available as chromatic activity. One was modulation, and the other expressive coloring. It is important to understand on what level chromaticism was permitted in the process of modulation, because the harmony was moving to a predictable sonic place within the horizontal hierarchy. Within the context of modulation the sense of key center tended towards vagueness because of what was being given up (the original tonic) and what was being sought (the tonic of some other key). But the security of the new key was confirmed by the *same* dominant-tonic cadential processes and structures that had been utilized in the previous key. The chromaticism necessary for modulation was harmonically functional. That is, one did not modulate (and thus activate this type of chromatic function) without cause or at the wrong time and place. We do not find modulation in the beginning measures of a musical form or at its very end. Thus, the relationship between key ambiguity (with its chromatic component) and key definition (with its diatonic component) was one that devolved from harmonic macrostructure that served tonal principles of tension and repose. With the establishment of equal temperament, the composer discovered that he could move to any key center he chose, and did just that. In a sense, this modulatory, chromatic function was objective: it served to build sonic structure.

The second function of chromaticism was subjective expressivity. It is seen in the fourth note of the Beethoven Opus 131 fugue which we examined above. The scale that we construct from this subject is a curious and beautiful affair. Looking at the tonic statement (measures 4–8), it appears to be in F-sharp minor rather than C-sharp minor. What Beethoven seems to have done is to translate the top tetrachord of a harmonic minor scale (with its augmented second between pitches 6 and 7) to the bottom tetrachord, while the top tetrachord (although the fifth note is missing) remains a natural minor one. This is achieved by chromatic means for a decisive expressive effect. This chromatic tone is not an agent of motion to another key but one of immediate utterance within an ostensibly diatonic context and for expressive reasons.

Both of these chromatic functions, of course, were established prior to the nineteenth century. Let us now see how romantic composers utilized them and to what lengths they extended their potential within dominant-tonic modeling. For purposes of demonstration I shall treat these two functions as though they were completely discrete and separate, which of course they were not required to be.

Chromatic modulation in the nineteenth century made a translation from quantitative temporal gesture into a qualitative one. That is, there were no fixed rules concerning the number or length of modulatory processes (although there were certainly customary expectations that were fulfilled); and, in fact, harmonic efficiency during modulation was not necessarily to be regarded as a virtue. If the key to be reached was a distant one from the tonic, the passage to it might allude to several key areas before it arrived at its goal. But this very process gradually became an end rather than a means, and quantitative turned into qualitative utterance. The freedom not to be firmly established in a key was taken as license for not even attempting to reach one. To be sure, keys were always eventually reached in romantic music, but the potential for modulatory freedom with regard to key centers became an articulate symbol of the romantic composer's own will. Wagner is the most important composer who seized this freedom, but certainly not the only one.

It is easy to state in retrospect that Wagner's chromatic harmonies were conceived as "a musical manifestation of the romantic urge to dissolution in the infinite,"[12] and let it go at that. But Wagner consciously or unconsciously needed a poetic or dramatic reason by which to navigate through the hazards of a horizontal reality that he once characterized as a "sea of harmony." To select the best example of this harmonic activity at work from his mature operas, we know that he found this reason in the medieval legend of Tristan and Isolde, a story of two lovers who are prevented from consummating their love for one another, love so intense and irrational that it could be explained to bourgeois society only on grounds of having been drug-induced. Rivers of ink have been spilled over this work. I will not attempt to present a history of the opera's creation and public reception, but will underscore two important points regarding its (then) chromatic excesses. As Donald Grout carefully notes, public understanding of the harmonic aspect of *Tristan* depended solely on existing attitudes about tonality itself:

> The power of the *Tristan* chromaticism comes from its being founded *in* tonality. A feature of it is the ambiguity of the chords, the constant, immanent, felt possibility that almost any chord may resolve in almost any one of a dozen different directions. Yet this very ambiguity could not exist *except for* underlying tonal relations, the general tendencies of certain chord progressions within the tonal system. The continuous conflict between what *might be*, harmonically, and what *actually is*, makes the music apt at suggesting the inner state of mingled insecurity and passionate longing that pervades the drama. This emotional suggestiveness is accompanied throughout by a luxuriance of purely sensuous effect, a reveling in tone qualities and tone combinations as if for their own sake, evident in both the subdued richness of the orchestration and the whole harmonic fabric.[13]

By tonality, of course, Grout means key-centered music, from which point of departure *Tristan* took an important clue. Historically speaking, what "might be" in terms of harmony was a sense of vertical progression through chords to points of resolution in recognizable tonics and their attendant key centers. As mentioned, chromaticism was the agent by which this process had been achieved, but now in particular through an intensified use of diminished seventh chords, by which four entirely different key centers could be approached with equal ease. There was nothing uncommon about this as long as the listener's expectations were eventually fulfilled in terms of some key center. But *eventually* is a rather indecisive temporal word. What we find in Wagner (as well as Liszt) is a studied expansion of such harmonic eventuality in order to articulate frequently nonmusical effects— moods, attitudes, situations, and emotions. While chromaticism had fostered the temporal concepts of anticipation and delay, Wagner greatly assisted in the formulation of the notion that they had more than a mere formal dimension and could be extended (or collapsed) at will and quite freely. The story of *Tristan* fit this concept precisely and inspired a harmonic way of thinking that has since been tagged as "Tristan harmony." The passionate longing of the lovers, their insecurity, and their alienation were the very feelings that demanded tonal underpinning from fresh points of view: Wagner did not wish them sung about in the square form of the standard aria with its neat phrases and periodic cadences. Traditional aria structure, for instance, dictated patterns in which emotion was forcibly regulated by preconceived harmonic expectations; but emotion by its very nature was wont to determine its own form, something not given and assimilated by convention but generative and consuming by individual necessity. To be sure, there were melody and rhythm, which Wagner once conceived as the shores "at which the tonal art meets with and makes fruitful the two continents of art primevally related to it (poetry and the dance)," but tone itself was "the primeval fluid element between them, an immeasurable expanse in which the components of melody and rhythm were realized and shaped."[14] Once this great flexibility of harmonic content was understood, it could operate on all levels of the musical micro- and macrostructure and for the same emotional and psychological reasons. Thus, the whole of *Tristan* is as harmonically ambiguous as many of its individual parts. For instance, Alfred Lorenz takes the prevailing key of *Tristan* to be E major, with a tonic that is actually indistinct for most of the opera. Act I begins in the subdominant (A minor) and act III closes in the dominant (B major). The reason is clear: in a story in which love itself cannot be fulfilled neither can the ultimate repose of the tonic structurally manifest itself, and the only extended portion of the score in E major is, symbolically, a *vision* of Isolde, when Tristan lies wounded in act III.

The second function, that of immediate chromatic utterance for expressive reasons within an ostensibly diatonic context, was of course centuries old. From a Gesualdo madrigal, in which pain and suffering are persistently objectified through chromatic alteration, to the opening pages of Haydn's *Creation*, in which extensive chromaticism is used to suggest a chaotic universe yet unformed, nondiatonic tones have been the tonal reservoir from which subjectivity created expressive utterance and did so with highly individualistic approaches that characteristically separated one composer from another within the same tonal tradition.

It is generally true that chromaticism before the classic period did not uniquely characterize a given composer's harmonic vocabulary and style. Certainly, independent studies have been carried out on the chromatic activity in a single Renaissance or baroque composer's music, and these studies prove to be statistically interesting. But only the most carefully trained and astute listener can discern the harmonies of Corelli, Torelli, Manfredini, Albinoni, Martini, Vitali, and others as distinctly different vertical styles. Such characteristic harmonic distinctions were neither desired nor possible in the seventeenth century, for the limitations of competitive tuning systems before equal temperament did not permit a wide spectrum of chromatic potential from which to create a highly personal, harmonic utterance.

The general adoption of equal temperament and the genius of Beethoven were not meant historically to happen more or less simultaneously, but the outcome was prophetic. The notion of the artist as hero had begun to fill German romantic literature before 1800. It was writer and composer E. T. A. Hoffmann who believed that music was the only truly romantic art and popularized in his stories the idea of the daemonic musician. Beethoven's personality, his unbending integrity to his art, and his inner pathos appeared to be tailor-made for the romantic mind. These factors in conjunction with a unique approach to his own tonal consciousness irrevocably altered the course of nineteenth-century harmony.

We could select from any of several genres from his middle period works, but the Opus 59 Quartets are quite exemplary. The convention of writing chamber music in groups of a dozen or so, like cookies, all made from the same batch of sonic materials, had been narrowed to six in Beethoven's Opus 18, following the practices of Haydn and Mozart. With Opus 59 we cannot ignore the highly charged individualism of three quartets that so unnerved the members of the Schuppanzigh Quartet who first attempted to perform them. Joseph Kerman notes that the first quartet in C major "seems ready to go off the cliff at any minute, in this it only exaggerates a quality discernible in the others. None of them is a work at rest; all of them are explorers, and Beethoven may have been as amazed as anyone else to see where they were going."[15]

With their sonata forms expanded by an abundance of themes, their long and complex developments, and their significant codas, these quartets critically document a direct outpouring of genius and personality in the most remarkable tonal terms. This is to say that there is a type of chromaticism in these works that is not intrinsically related to form as such. Beethoven could just as easily have built them in some other harmonic fashion, and they would have remained sonatas or rondos or scherzos. That he did not do so, but instead conceived of each movement as a totality of expression regarding its utterance within its chief tonal center, reveals the composer as creator making the object his own, penetrating it, and bringing it into its own particular form by which it becomes harmonically external and strange. Every movement thus bears the personal stamp of Beethoven's imagination upon the potential of the tonal system in the form of chromatic gesture, which is one of the reasons that these works alarmed their initial audiences. Let us look at a couple of examples.

At the close of the first movement exposition of the F Major Quartet the customary repeat signs are missing. At measure 103 the main theme begins to return verbatim in the tonic key; it seems as though the exposition section is being repeated. But in measure 108 the theme lands squarely not on F but quite unexpectedly on G-flat, "a degree higher and infinitely more intense," notes Kerman. "We have been thrust into the development section, and the intensity of the shock, as much as the intensity of the chromatic note G flat itself, suffices to stir a long series of developmental modulations pointing, as will appear, to D flat."[16] Or consider the opening pages of the E Minor Quartet. Here, the rests cause one to anticipate from the very beginning what will happen next, after the opening half-cadence. A two-measure motive in the tonic is followed in sequence by the same thing on the Neapolitan harmony. This chromatic turn is not yet related to the structure of the movement: one is merely surprised that it occurs so early and so urgently. It will, as Kerman notes, color the rest of the movement; it will be used to cement it together. And importantly, "it forecasts other extremities of harmonic procedure, such as that in the highly explosive passage at the beginning of the development section. . . . When the passage explodes symmetrically a second time to begin the coda, the very structure of the piece is felt to hinge upon the harmonic audacity."[17]

Again, it is unfair to regard Beethoven as the sole agent in the progressive activity of singular harmonic expression through chromatic potential. Harmony became for each romantic composer a personal approach to the tonal system he had inherited. Certainly, it may have been thrust upon him, as Dahlhaus explains. Not only was nineteenth-century music to be original, its originality had to be authenticated through the composer's self expression, an unfolding of the emotions of his inner self, which was required to assume more or less the appearance of novelty.

> Alongside melodic ideas, what the nineteenth century valued most as "inspirations" were chords that were surprising and yet at the same time intelligible. Such chords were felt to be expressive—the word "expression" being used in a strong sense to refer to the representation of out-of-the-ordinary inner experience by use of unusual means—and were expected to take their place in the historical evolution of music, an evolution that was seen as a chain of inventions and discoveries.[18]

This aesthetic identification by the romantic composer for a personal expression within a collective harmonic consciousness went hand in glove with the expansion of musical form, particularly in dramatic and program-matic works. The composers who most strongly intuited this notion were Wagner, Liszt, and Mahler. The reason that Mahler did not name the tonic key of his Seventh Symphony is because he could not. The overall tonal motion of this work is from the B minor/E minor key *foci* of the first movement to the C major statement of the Finale, and the tonic is all of these; that is, the historically understood notion of the tonic as fundamental to the totality of form itself changes in the course of the work. Beautifully foreshadowed in the opening D minor/D major presentation of themes in the first movement of Beethoven's Ninth Symphony, this discursive quality of key and mode became for Mahler the macrostructure of the Seventh Symphony itself. Mahler's "heavenly" or "interminable" length, depending on one's point of view, becomes the temporal discourse of a symphonic continuity that requires generosity and forbearance on the part of the list-ener who expects tidy, Schenkerian formations of tonal utterance. It is not simply the "chords" in the Seventh Symphony that take on the expressive nature of the composer's subjective creativity; the whole notion of key and mode orbits through a constellation of tonal space not meant to be col-lapsed and judged as though its sonic events were heard in close juxtaposi-tion. Like all constellations, distance from them creates the necessary per-spective by which to know and to appreciate them.

It is customarily assumed that the gradual acquisition of this personal harmonic space brought about the destruction and dissolution of tonality, and there is a partial truth in this judgment when we construe tonality to be only key-centered music. That is, it is true if tonality by the end of the century, burdened with the sheer weight of its chromatic excesses, fell headlong into the dizzying abyss of atonal consciousness where it remained paralyzed, impotent, and incapable of further human expression. Histori-cally, it did not do this. Instead, what some writers have called "residual tonal elements,"[19] in the form of dominant-tonic hierarchies, remained stubbornly in view, from which appearance they are taken to be the last battered vestiges of an exhausted harmonic system. But the abdication of key-centered tonality by composers became its absolute contradiction in the form of continued and extended resourcefulness as universal sonic commu-nication. That is, the major portion of nineteenth-century music and by far the greater public understanding of that music demonstrated a remarkable simplification of the very tonal hierarchy that composers of art music were exploiting for reasons of alienated subjectivity. If all of musical Europe had followed the tonal path from Liszt and Wagner to Busoni and Reger, of "music in transition," Schoenberg would have been immediately compre-hensible and acceptable. Instead, a simplified, public key-centered tonality, running parallel to "music in transition" gradually manifested itself as an overpowering object of historical truth. The triumph of common-practice tonality is no more evident than in the virtually complete rejection of alienated, compositional subjectivity in favor of collective solidarity in tonal terms. In short, tonality could be bought and sold.

TONALITY SIMPLIFIED

In the last year of the nineteenth century, Arnold Schoenberg composed his string sextet *Verklärte Nacht,* which because it contained an inverted ninth chord with the ninth in the bass had to wait until 1902 for a public performance (see p. 233); the same year a black American musician named Scott Joplin composed and published the *Maple Leaf Rag* in Sedalia, Missouri. Joplin's most famous of all piano rags soon sold a million copies in sheet music format. Schoenberg's *Verklärte Nacht* did not. In 1918 Schoenberg founded the Society for the Private Performance of Music. In May 1921, in order to raise money to keep the Society alive, Schoenberg organized an evening of Strauss waltzes, arranged by himself, Berg, and Webern. In America, the public had purchased and was playing on its parlor pianos some three hundred thousand copies of Ethelbert Nevin's sentimental and highly popular song "The Rosary."

One would like to blame Beethoven for this situation, the gradual and unrepairable fissure between high and low cultures, and in a certain sense he is representative of the beginnings of the great schism in European culture that had profound tonal reverberations throughout the Western world. On the one hand, there was Beethoven the composer of sets of minuets, German dances, and a great quantity of piano trio arrangements of Scottish, Welsh, and Irish folksong melodies, which were published by George Thomson of Edinburgh over a period of several decades. This was music for use, for entertainment, accessible to amateur musicians whose parlor music-making began to characterize social life in thousands of bourgeois homes. On the other, there was Beethoven the composer of the middle and late string quartets, that once accessible and companionable genre, "played by amateurs in their homes, probably without rehearsal and intended simply for their pleasure"; but Beethoven's mature quartets became the vehicle for his "most exalted thought and complex structures, not uningratiating to the ear but baffling to the traditional understanding of musical grammar, syntax, and logic."[20] And, we might add, tonality. Even Schubert, twenty-six years Beethoven's junior, confessed himself puzzled and disturbed by such music. On the one hand, the progressive activity of singular harmonic expression through chromatic potential came to characterize the romantic composer of "serious" music, a tonal objectification of his inner subjectivity. This alienation was judged to be a kind of virtue.

Beethoven was fond of regarding himself as a *Tondichter*, a poet in sound, whose unique creations made unprecedented demands upon both musicians and audiences and for which Beethoven made no apologies. On the other, the remarkable and rapid growth of "light" music in numerous genres brought key-centered tonality within the realm of mass appreciation and consumption with the utmost confidence that man as a tonal creature, immediately and ultimately, could transcend all class distinctions, national rivalries, and social differences in the name of a "universal" key-centered music. Harmonically speaking, it was as if Mendelssohn, cosmopolitan, educated, and well-fed, had decided to capture all of Europe tonally for himself and won.

I shall take up the tonal implications of this phenomenon shortly. First, a brief survey of the chief genres and forms of popular musical culture is instructive.

By the beginning of the nineteenth century, the waltz was about to become the first dance fad in history. The opening of large dance halls in Vienna, the Sperl in 1807 and the Apollo in 1808 (with accommodations for six thousand dancers), provided the impetus for a generation of young bandleaders turned composers both to develop and exploit a form of music that was literally accessible to tens of thousands of people. The elder Johann Strauss's Opus 1, the *Täuberln-Walzer*, consisted of a set of seven separate waltzes, each in turn consisting of two eight-bar sections, with a final lengthened closing of sixteen bars. The refinement of waltz themes themselves either caused or at least encouraged a quickening of the tempo, and gradually social Europe plunged "into the whirlpool" of ballroom dancing at seventy bars per minute.[21] Strauss's extended tours of Germany, Holland, and Belgium in 1834–36 were so successful that they were followed by lengthy visits to France and Britain in 1837–38. Strauss had intended his three sons, Johann the younger, Josef, and Eduard, to enter the world of business, and in their own way they did; they took up pen and baton and marketed dancing. Followed by an army of imitators, they invaded Western Europe, Russia, and America and in a period of seventy-five years established their father's original orchestra as a historical institution.

Thirty years before the younger Strauss expanded his interests into the world of operetta, Jacques Offenbach had been supplying the Paris stage with complete operettas, one-act plays with music, and cabaret sketches. Along with the younger Johann Strauss, Offenbach became one of the outstanding composers of popular music in the century. Exhilarating and tuneful, his music promoted the establishment of operetta as an international genre that assisted the evolution of popular music in the twentieth century.

In addition to importing the waltz and operetta to its own shores, Britain provided its own market for the development of unique musical forms. The industrial working class bred in towns to satisfy the demands of industry produced a whole population which grew up divorced from traditional European standards of taste and culture. As Henry Raynor notes, the song and supper clubs, the choral societies, and the brass-band movement represented a kind of "nineteenth-century appetite for self-help, for moral and material improvement" that musically paralleled the nineteenth-century movement toward adult education in England and the development of the Mechanic's Institutes and Lyceums.[22] Long before the modern boys from Liverpool became famous, the notion of workers producing music for workers had become a reality. By the middle 1830s a factory or mill band was a source of pride and prestige to its owners, so much so that practicing music became a part of paid working hours, and the poaching of talented players to build rival bands a common occurrence—not unlike the "kidnapping" of talented youth by Renaissance nobility in order to enhance their private chapel choirs. Supplying music for the estimated twenty thousand bands that had evolved by the end of the century in Great Britain became a significant activity for arrangers and composers. And finally, there was the Victorian hymn, which more than any other musical form, notes Raynor, may have created a musical taste perhaps more universal than what was heard in the popular British music hall: "Hymns were the only contact which the huge and largely illiterate population of Britain outside the choral societies had with any type of musical experience."[23] Within a generation of its publication in 1861, Hymns Ancient and Modern had overcome its rivals in the hymn-book publishing industry, and its melodies (particularly those of J. B. Dykes) popularized a new and characteristic Victorian type of hymn tune. By 1912 Hymns Ancient and Modern had sold some sixty million copies. Its melodies were sung far beyond the confines of the Church of England, and were adopted by the Welsh Methodists, Scottish Presbyterians, and American Lutherans.

Similarly in America, beginning about 1820, there arose a simple and comprehensible tonal expression (with interesting undercurrents) in the forms of religious music, blackface minstrelsy, and band music, some of which led directly to city blues, jazz, and modern popular music. In 1835, "Singin' Billy" Walker of Spartanburg, South Carolina published The Southern Harmony; thirty-one years later he claimed to have sold six hundred thousand copies. It was apparent to the compilers and composers of hymn collections that any musical source could be sanctified by turning it into a hymn. Thus we find in the American anthologies folk melodies, secular song melodies, patriotic airs, and popular dance tunes alongside borrowings from the eighteenth-century Yankee composers and newly composed pieces.

In the tentative and exotic form of "Ethiopian music" the middle of the century witnessed the birth of the first real minstrel show, a full evening's entertainment by the "Virginia Minstrels" of songs, dances, and a parody "lecture on locomotives," which opened at the Masonic Temple in Boston on March 7, 1843. Musically, the ministrel shows consisted of a mixture of popular songs, adaptations from British melodies, parodied Italian opera arias (*Lucia di Lammermoor* was burlesqued as "Lucy Did Lam a Moor"), dance tunes, and dialect songs. In addition to these were the banjo jigs, the primary source of the subsequent genres of ragtime and early jazz.[24]

And finally, there was the American bandstand, architecturally remembered by a curious stone structure in the village and town parks in a thousand places throughout America still, mute and weathered testimony to the village band, the equivalent *from below* of the urban symphony orchestra. Its musical staples were quicksteps and other marches, dances (particularly the European waltz), but also the polka, occasional overtures, and "almost always a solo for keyed bugle or the novel valve cornet to amaze the audience with the newly-won agility of the brass instruments."[25]

I have given this rapid citation of a rich, complex, and varied history of nineteenth-century popular music in order to make a specific statement about its most critical tonal component, that is, its conscious and unconscious adoption of the simplest harmonic structures within the framework of key-centered tonality and its general rejection of the subjective harmonic expressivity that characterized the musical tastes of high culture and its consumers. By the very nature of its sonic collectivity, popular music rescinds unique tonal utterance. For example, because the basic harmonic progression of the twelve-bar blues is I–IV–I–V–(IV)–I, and because collective integrity to that harmonic progression "is" the blues, individual harmonic expressivity is annulled. One does not listen to "*Wein, Weib und Gesang*," "Jeannie with the Light Brown Hair," or "They Still Write Waltzes, Don't They?" for the uniqueness of its harmonic statement. Harmonic utterance is collectively understood in such music as a formal structure in which components other than harmonic ones are utilized as a means for individual expression. Largely predictable in horizontal progression through time and symmetrical in phrase structure, this harmony annuls subjectivity at the same time that it creates and preserves a universally understood harmonic object that amateurs everywhere can rapidly acquire for themselves. The same may be generally asserted for all the forms and genres cited above. Harmonically speaking, it is as if the Schenkerian *Ursatz* stepped forward and became itself the objective totality of each form's vertical appearance. To be sure, the simplicity of harmonic utterance in this music is directly proportional to the cognitive abilities and disabilities of the amateur musician of the nineteenth century, but its limitations became also its ubiquity in the form of universal tonal comprehension. As such, it stood in direct antithesis to the complex, personal, alienated, and expected harmonic development of the high-priest/hero composer of the same era who if he could not chisel his own unique harmonic expression from the bedrock of key-centered tonality was judged a harmonic copier.

Considered from its tonal standpoint, this is the difference between so-called serious music and popular music in the nineteenth century and of the twentieth as well. "Serious" tonality in the modern world is personal, subjective, alienated, and gives the illusion of tonal "progress." "Popular" tonality is impersonal, objective, numbingly collective, and makes no pretense of going anywhere at all. It cannot change as long as it gives a good return for its investors in the market. When black musician Jimi Hendrix appeared in 1967,

> using the most explosive, ear-splitting amplification yet heard, creating a volume and complexity of sound that almost literally deafened his audiences, while engaging in outrageous stage deportment that included simulated sexual acts with his guitar and concluded with a frenzied scene in which he doused the guitar with lighter fluid and burnt it, with amplification turned increasingly higher,[26]

the harmony, to the extent that it could be heard at all, paid homage to the Florentine Camerata in the early seventeenth century. The rock music phenomenon was the first movement in the history of world culture that fostered music created by and for children. Tonal limitations became quickly fixed at the level of, perhaps, the ten-year-old Chopin, and there they remain. World tonality is economic tonality. There is no spoken language on the planet which even begins to compete with the accessibility provided by common-practice tonality as a means of human communication. The reason does not stem from any largesse of human spirit for global understanding of man's aesthetic consciousness. The reason is imperialistic. The roots of the dichotomy between "serious" tonality and "popular" tonalty lay in the creation of genres and forms that appealed to the tastes of the bourgeoisie and catered to the abilities of the amateur, nineteenth-century musician. Perhaps not so curiously, it was in part initiated by Beethoven, who dedicated his Opus 59 Quartets to the Russian ambassador to Vienna and sold his arrangements of Scottish airs to a publisher in Edinburgh.

11 Atonality as Negation

I t is unfortunate but necessary to begin this essay with a brief confrontation with the vexing word *atonality*. In a fixed historical sense, it is easily understood as the antithesis of key-centered music. While Arnold Schoenberg himself always meant the words *tonal* and *tonality* to stand for the "common-practice" tonality of western Europe from 1600 to 1900, he could not at all tolerate the term *atonal* for his "method of composing with twelve tones which are related only to one another." In a footnote to the first (1911) edition of his *Harmonielehre*, Schoenberg disassociated himself from "atonality" and the "atonalists" with the remark, "Everything implied by a series of tones (*Tonreihe*) constitutes tonality," and it was this belief that led him to understand his music as the rightful, creative objectification of the given of nature—the overtone series. His argument against the use of the term *atonality* is explicit:

> That from [the above] single correct definition no reasonable opposite corresponding to the word "atonality" can be formed, must be evident. Where could the negation be introduced? Is it that *not all* implications of a series of tones, or *not any*, should characterize atonality? . . . A piece of music will always have to be tonal, at least in so far as a relation has to exist from tone to tone by virtue of which the tones, placed next to or above one another, yield a perceptible continuity. . . . If one insists on looking for names, "polytonal" or "pantonal" could be considered. Yet, before anything else, we should determine whether it is not again simply "tonal."[1]

Thus, while Schoenberg, throughout his extensive *Harmonielehre*, never took issue with the notion that key-centered tonality was a historical phenomenon of some three centuries of European sonic consciousness, he did realize in a very real sense that twelve-tone music was also tonal–even when some of his definitions of tonality marginally appeared to exclude it. For instance:

> The harmonic sense of the key (*Tonart*) in all its ramifications is comprehensible only in relation to the idea of tonality, which should therefore be explained before anything else. Tonality is a formal possibility that emerges from the nature of the tonal material, a possibility of attaining a certain completeness or closure (*Geschlossenheit*) by means of a certain uniformity.[2]

The only troublesome part of this definition is the phrase "of attaining a certain completeness or closure," by which Schoenberg may be interpreted to mean cadential closures and tonics that secure them. But Schoenberg also knew that his own music was a formal possibility of attaining completeness by means of a certain uniformity, and in that sense it was tonal.

Therefore, I think it a disservice to Schoenberg's genius and vision to continue using atonal to describe his music and herewith banish it (except for quotations) from the remainder of the chapter. Unfortunately, substitutes are also problematic. I shall use the words *twelve-tone*, or *dodecaphonic*, and *serial*, although strictly speaking much of what we shall discuss does not fit comfortably into these categories. More important is the matter at hand: How did Schoenberg come to devise his *system* (another word for which he had no great fondness), and in what sense is that negation to be understood now, eighty years into the twentieth century? Let us begin by studying his background.

Schoenberg was born in 1874 in Vienna. As a youth, he learned to play the violin and the cello. His father's death forced him to work in a bank as a clerk. He admitted once that most of the pieces he composed until he was eighteen were "imitations" of the music around him. But the music around him was that of Brahms and Wagner, which represented both the conservative and radical tendencies of then contemporary music. Schoenberg had very little musical training. Conductor and musician Alexander von Zemlinsky was his only teacher, and because Schoenberg was never overly awed by the rigor of academic tradition he was able to incorporate the opposite styles of Brahms and Wagner in a manner that other composers could not have achieved. The perpetual variation inherent in Brahms's music was not really alien to Wagner's principle of leitmotifs; both styles exhibited unifying aspects.

In 1897 Schoenberg spent a summer holiday writing the piano score of Zemlinsky's opera, *Sarema*, and composing a string quartet. This latter was well received at its first performance in Vienna and was perhaps the only work by Schoenberg that was ever to enjoy a completely favorable, initial reception. Brahms died the same year, and Joan Peyser points out that Schoenberg's composition "immediately took on a different cast."[3] He composed Opera 1, 2, and 3, a group of lieder, which were performed in a recital with Zemlinsky at the piano. The reception was hostile, but Schoenberg remembered the event with a remark that proved characteristic of the usually negative reaction to his music: "ever since this performance the riots have never stopped."

Two years later he composed *Verklärte Nacht*, which inaugurated expressionistic music. Scored for string sextet, it was the first chamber piece with a clear programmatic content. One concert society refused to play the work on the grounds that the score contained an inverted ninth chord, with the ninth in the bass. Schoenberg responded with his usual acerbic wit: "It is self-evident; there is no such thing as an inversion of a ninth chord; therefore there is no such thing as a performance of it; for one cannot perform something that does not exist. So I had to wait for several years."[4] The hostile reception to *Verklärte Nacht* at its 1902 première and similar reactions to his other music would eventually bring about an unprecedented event: in 1918 a group of composers and musicians—Mahler, Zemlinsky, and Bruno Walter among them—organized the Society for Private Musical Performances in order to educate select audiences to new music.

Anton Webern, Alban Berg, Erwin Stein, and Heinrich Jalowitz began to study composition with Schoenberg in 1904. In 1906 Schoenberg wrote his Chamber Symphony, Opus 9. Scored for fifteen solo instruments, this work is the antithesis of his mammoth *Gurrelieder*, which merits comparison with Mahler's Eighth Symphony. Begun in 1901, with a large orchestra of 140 players, five vocal soloists, one speaker, three male choirs, and one mixed chorus, *Gurrelieder* took Schoenberg a decade to orchestrate. One might dismiss this work as the last gasp of nineteenth-century romanticism were it not so beautiful. Without being in any way derivative, it easily synthesizes the style of every major composer in *fin de siècle* Western Europe. Bruckner, Wagner, Mahler, Richard Strauss, Puccini, Debussy, and Brahms—the styles of all these composers reverberate through this music in a remarkable summation of Schoenberg's understanding of the harmonic techniques of key-centered music that had become saturated with chromaticism. The Chamber Symphony, in the meantime, made a profound impression on pupil Webern, and in 1906 he showed Schoenberg a movement of a work in which the tones were not related to any particular key center. Curiously, Schoenberg rejected this visionary twelve-tone music by Webern, who thereupon wrote his next piece in C major: "but it is probable that this experiment affected Schoenberg's own next work, the String Quartet No. 2, Opus 10, in F-Sharp Minor,"[5] his last composition to contain a key signature.

The Quartet is in four movements, but traditional forms are abandoned, particularly in the last two movements in which a soprano joins the strings to sing a text of Stefan George: "I feel the air of other spheres . . . /I dissolve into tones, circling, wreathing. . . . " Biographer H. H. Stuckenschmidt notes that:

> harmony glides in long stretches beyond the frontiers of traditional tonality into a new foreign world of sound relations for which no law had hitherto been found. Schoenberg was still basing himself on chord forms which belong to the world of major and minor keys; the quartet opens and ends tonally, and frequently shows forms of harmony similar to cadences. But, in between, sounds and groups of sounds exist which in fact appear to stem "from other planets" like the air of which the text by Stefan George (*Entrük-kung*) for the finale of the quartet tells us.[6]

We must note here several paradoxes in Schoenberg's concept of tonality. In 1911 his *Harmonielehre* was published in its first edition, an exhaustive text about the principles of traditional tonality. Within a few years he was to compose the Three Piano Pieces, Op. 11; "The Book of the Hanging Gardens," Op. 15; the Five Pieces for Orchestra, Op. 16; and *Erwartung*, Op. 17—his first dodecaphonic works. In 1922 he revised and enlarged the *Harmonielehre* in a third edition, which roughly coincided with the composition of the Five Piano Pieces, Op. 23; the Serenade, Op. 24; and the Suite for Piano, Op. 25. The *Harmonielehre* is a remarkable book in light of the meager academic training that Schoenberg had in music theory. While he wrote the book "for students," it is evident that he also wished to work through the theoretical literature of the day (including Heinrich Schenker and Hugo Riemann) in order to assess not only the music he had inherited but also its traditional points of contact with the new music that he was composing.

I say paradox because Schoenberg did seek to organize the system of Western tonality in a fashion that he felt to be less deterministic, particularly in its development of the aesthetic principles of music from natural phenomena; but those few natural principles that he uncritically retained to explain his "system of presentation" of tonality prevented him from a clear assessment of the nature of all tonal phenomena—both the inherited Western system and the conceptualization of a new system that would establish the composition of music with twelve tones. To be sure, he was not writing a book about twelve-tone music, but about traditional tonality. We know, however, that Schoenberg was in the process of formulating the twelve-tone system during these years, and his private intuitions about the potential and methodology of that not-yet-articulated system hovered over his sustained efforts to explain in *Harmonielehre* the basis of tonality as key-centered music; for instance, chapter XIX, section 8, "The Chromatic Scale as a Basis for Tonality." In the first edition, Schoenberg stated that he wrote this section after completing the original manuscript because of objections and criticisms raised against it by Robert Neumann (identified only as "a young philosopher"), who had suggested a new division of the octave into a 53-note scale. In response to Neumann's criticism that Schoenberg had "established no relationship between the key and certain minor chords, but just introduced them generally in a schematic presentation," Schoenberg said he had "an idea." After two attempts to satisfy Neumann, Schoenberg suggested that "a third and more significant way, however, would be to work out an idea already mentioned in this book: to base our thought, not on the seven tones of the major scale, rather, on the twelve of the chromatic scale." In the 1911 edition this section ended abruptly with this sentence. In the third edition, however, Schoenberg offered an outline, one part of which listed in historical and (perhaps) pedagogical order the different scales that may be formed from twelve tones:

1. twelve times seven church modes;
2. twelve major and twelve minor modes;
3. a number of exotic modes . . . that are not used in European art music . . . ;
4. twelve chromatic modes;
5. one chromatic mode.[7]

Items 4 and 5 are indicative of music by Schoenberg written about the same time as the *Harmonielehre* and its revisions. I interpret "twelve chromatic modes" to mean twelve different tone centers around which are clustered the remaining eleven tones of the octave. "One chromatic mode" implies no tone center of any sort, that is, the method of composing with twelve tones that are related only to each other.

It must, however, be noted that the retention of specific and deeply embedded notions concerning *nature* and traditional tonality not only cripples Schoenberg's system of presentation for key-centered music, it also prevents illumination from being shed on a system that was in the process of emerging from his speculative activity of the very same years. Schoenberg is hardly to be criticized for the state of affairs in which he found himself, but a few points about *Harmonielehre* will demonstrate where the problems lie.

In the first chapter of *Harmonielehre*, Schoenberg confronts the nature of tonality from a refreshing point of view. It is useless to seek after a *theory* of tonality, he feels; the best that can be achieved is a *system* of careful thought that does not leave gaping holes. A theory, he states, "observes a number of phenomena, classifies them according to some common characteristics, and then derives laws from them. That is of course correct procedure, because unfortunately there is hardly any other way"[8] But at this point he also notes that the historical rationalization of consciousness fell into grave error. It falsely concluded "that these laws, since apparently correct with regard to the phenomena previously observed, must then surely hold for all future phenomena as well."[9] The laws become eternal, and aesthetic judgments based on them dominate musical creativity. Schoenberg was certain that "tonality is no natural law of music." "To hell with all these theories," he concluded, "if they always serve only to block the evolution of art and if their positive achievement consists in nothing more than helping those who will compose badly anyway to learn it quickly."[10] What Schoenberg proposed instead was a system of music theory, although he was even wary of the authoritative nature of this term as well. A system, he notes, ought to embrace a body of material that "is coherently organized and lucidly classified." Its principles ought to embrace all the facts. "Ideally, just as many facts as there actually are, no more, no less. And only such principles, which are not qualified by exceptions would have the right to be regarded as generally valid. Such principles would share with natural laws this characteristic of unconditional validity."[11]

Schoenberg was unable to establish such principles and believed that they would not be discovered very soon. "Attempts to explain artistic matters exclusively on natural grounds will continue to founder for a long time to come"[12] The best that a system could do—including his, he stated—was to "produce results something like those of a good comparison: that is, they can influence the way in which the sense organ of the *subject*, the *observer*, orients itself to the attributes of the object observed."[13]

It is unfortunate that Schoenberg, who understood so much and came so close to understanding the nature of tonality, could not have made an even greater leap of faith into the unknown. Two facts severely inhibited him from achieving a clear picture of human tonal consciousness. First, he clearly ignored the subject—despite his awareness of its relation to the tonal object. He was aware that Schopenhauer had demonstrated in his theory of colors that "a real theory should start with the subject." Just as colors are physiological phenomena, "conditions, modifications of the eye," if one were to establish a theory of tones, he "would have to go back to the subject, to the sense of hearing."[14] Schoenberg stated, however, that he did not intend "to give a theory of tones or of harmony," but merely a presentation of certain artistic means and that "this presentation does not claim any right to be taken for a theory."[15]

Having negated or, rather, ignored the subject, Schoenberg had then to determine the nature of tonality and explain the tonal system on purely objective grounds. Unfortunately, but not surprisingly, his first act of tonal legerdemain is exactly like that of Rameau and Schenker. For Schoenberg, tones are "forces" and have to be treated as such. In chapter IV, he states that the most characteristic feature of the tone is the overtone series present within it. A musical sound (*Klang*) is a composite of overtones. This is true. But Schoenberg, like others before him, was aware that the fourth degree of the scale could not be found within the spectrum of overtones, and we again witness tonal vitalism surreptitiously becoming a factor in his system. The pitch G is an overtone over C and presupposes the C as fundamental. Schoenberg drew from this presupposition the following:

> This tone, C, is likewise dependent upon the tone a fifth below it, F. Now *if* the C is taken as the midpoint, then its situation can be described by reference to two forces, one of which pulls downward, toward F, the other upward, toward G.[16]

Schoenberg immediately hypostatized these "forces" into a principle, called the tension between them a "characteristic," and promised that he would "draw a number of conclusions from it."[17] Indeed, he did. The "forces" create the Western major scale. Why they did not create the major scale for the Arabs, the Chinese, the Japanese, or the gypsies ("whose music has not evolved to such heights as ours") might, he suggested, "have to do with their imperfect instruments or with some other circumstance which cannot be investigated here." The hypostatization of the "forces" within the *Klang* into a principle is the theoretical basis for the whole of the *Harmonielehre*; by the end of the book the tone had acquired a "will" of its own.[18] The hearing subject is brought into play only to observe the tone, not to assist in its creation, and Schoenberg, like Schenker, not infrequently summoned up a disembodied "ear" to receive his tonal truth.

Schoenberg's conceptualization of Western tonal consciousness as a system is not to be dismissed with faint praise. While he clung to a cluster of concepts concerning the tonal object, concepts that were handed down to him by preceding centuries and which he could not totally escape, his speculative inquiry into the nature of tonality is much more freely conceived than the systems of Schenker or Riemann, his contemporaries. To be sure, he also could not fully understand the need to bring the hearing subject into any conceptualization of tonal phenomena, but through his own determination to break free from entrenched constraints he frequently did conceive of tonality in the most comprehensive terms of his generation. Perhaps he is to be commended for his very lack of respect for academic theory.

A second paradox is the kind of music he composed. If tones were to be thought of as exhibiting forces, and if these forces somehow registered their effect through consciousness in such a fashion that it "obeyed" their harmonic implications, the mature music of Schoenberg could only be viewed as working against nature itself. But Schoenberg did not really believe this, which seems to indicate that the "forces" theory was to be ignored at will. In fact, Schoenberg superimposed another, more general theory over the whole of the system that quietly immobilized its internal contradictions.

This general theory was that "art in its most primitive state is a simple imitation of nature."[19] Harmonically speaking, Schoenberg understood that human consciousness created music by unfolding the riches of the *Klang*. While he thought of this as a "psychological assumption," what he outlined in brief was the unfolding of Western harmonic history: "The development of the harmonic resources is explained primarily through the conscious or unconscious imitation of a prototype; every imitation so produced can then itself become a prototype that can in turn be imitated."[20] Thus he gradually came to see his music as the further extension of the given of nature, the *Klang*, a "natural" development which we have already noted was espoused by his pupil Webern.[21] It is instructive here to note how far Schoenberg was willing to take this development. What did he annul? What did he preserve?

Clearly, Schoenberg annulled the notion of key center, a historical appearance that he and everybody else of his time called tonality. Expressive music could and would proceed without it. But Schoenberg quite carefully preserved a crucial aspect of Western tonal consciousness—twelve pitches within the octave, and this preservation critically determined the development of twentieth-century music. A genuine tonal revolution would have happened if quarter-tone or any other fractional-tone pitch classes had actually overthrown the half-step pitch class system. The most isolated figure in the history of modern music is not the chromatically neurotic Gesualdo; it is Alois Hába, Schoenberg's contemporary. Ignoring the thoroughgoing and massive transformation of pedagogy that would be necessary to educate musicians to play quarter-tone or other fractional-tone music (and audiences to understand and accept it), there is a deeply embedded economic component that prohibits this phenomenon from developing under current conditions: two major families of musical instruments would have to be recreated and rebuilt—the wind and brass sections (excluding the trombone) of the modern symphony orchestra. Schoenberg *was* aware of other ways in which to divide the octave: he did not flinch before this possibility and suggested that quarter-tone music might be the next most feasible stage in any effort to expand the potential of musical material. However, he felt that "twelve tones squared by the second dimension, polyphony," offered "enough possibilities, at least to postpone for some time any necessity for further subdivision of the octave."[22]

Thus he set out to prove his point. We must turn here to the reception by the public of his works. Why was it so negative? In later years, Schoenberg spoke of his great feat in "emancipating the dissonance." By this, of course, he meant that dissonance, which had both *formal* and *psychological* functions, had been negated.

> The ear had gradually become acquainted with a great number of dissonances, and so had lost the fear of their "sense-interrupting" effect. . . . What distinguishes dissonances from consonances is not a greater or lesser degree of beauty, but greater or lesser degree of comprehensibility.[23]

Here, Schoenberg properly noted that there had been a historical development of ever freer treatment of dissonant entities in music. There was the classic composer's treatment of diminished seventh chords which "gradually eliminated the difficulty of comprehension and finally admitted not only the dominant and other seventh chords, diminished sevenths and augmented triads,"[24] but brought about the unique harmonies in the music of Wagner, Strauss, Musorgsky, Debussy, Mahler, and Reger.

This is all very nice, but the "ear" of which Schoenberg spoke was his own and that of a small group of composers and friends who followed him. In theory, the dissonance had been set free, and we ought not to think any longer of a harmony in which a series of tensions and reposes were set up both to build musical form and to underscore emotional expression. In practice, however, no such transformation of consciousness occurred, if we are considering those music lovers of the large cosmopolitan cities of Europe and America where some of Schoenberg's music was beginning to find an audience. The aesthetic gap between composer and audience, which had become appreciable by the end of the nineteenth century in bourgeois circles, became a chasm in the twentieth.

In general, composers watched with mixed emotions the gradual alienation of their works from bourgeois consciousness. Debussy, who clearly understood that he was composing for an elite audience, wrote to Ernest Chausson in 1893 and facetiously proposed: "Instead of spreading art amongst the public, I would suggest founding a Society of Musical Esotericism." In 1909 Louis Laloy, writing about Debussy, announced that appreciation of the new music was "a privilege" that was "becoming more exclusive" and glibly equated aesthetic alienation with universal purity![25] Without the slightest tinge of concern Laloy suggested that even the poor "by virtue of their intelligence" could aspire to this appreciation. Nine years later, the pupils of Schoenberg formed the *Verein für musikalische Privataufführungen* (Society for Private Musical Performances) "for the purpose of enabling Arnold Schoenberg to carry out his plan to give artists

and music-lovers a real and exact knowledge of modern music." William
Austin notes:

> A statement of aims, regulations, and achievements, by Berg, makes clear the
> complete discretionary authority of the perpetual president, Schoenberg. The
> Society's rules forbade applause, admission of nonmembers, advance an-
> nouncement of programs, and public reporting of the meetings. All sorts of
> serious new music from all parts of Europe were played, with as many
> rehearsals as necessary to achieve good performance. . . . The Society flour-
> ished until it was disrupted by the inflation of 1921. It set an example to be
> followed by looser organizations of friends of music all over the world.[26]

Tonality, which in the nineteenth century had been accessible to audiences
from Lisbon to Copenhagen, from Los Angeles to Moscow, began to speak
in tongues.

Part of the reason for the alienated position in which Schoenberg found
himself was the unique psychological character of his music. The expressionist movement in painting and literature had a similar development in
music, with Schoenberg and Berg as its chief early representatives. Visually,
expressionist artists willingly distorted real objects in order to reflect their
own inner feelings about their subjects and themselves. This was of course
an outgrowth of romanticism, but differed from it in the radical means
that were adopted to objectify human emotion. Musically, the expressionist
composer purposely jettisoned the nineteenth-century characteristics of illusion and play in favor of depicting the ego in a troubled, modern world
fraught with irrationality. To demonstrate this one has only to consider, for
instance, Donizetti's *Lucia di Lammermoor* and "the woman" (significantly,
she has no name) in Schoenberg's *Erwartung*. The threatening aspect of
Lucia's madness is permitted only on grounds that it is tonally filtered and
harmoniously falsified through the controlled agents of conventional aria
form and coloratura pyrotechnics. In fact, the real silliness of the vocal
gestures can be legitimized only because Lucia *is* mad. She is entitled to her
coloratura excesses because she has taken leave of her senses, and the
audience is encouraged to take pleasure in its illusion that she is operati-
cally insane. Donizetti's audience fully understood that *real* mad women
did not sing of their madness in major keys, with an abundance of carefully
executed trills, scales, and vocal pyrotechnics—all to the accompaniment of
a large, operatic orchestra. Opera from its beginning had demanded the
willing suspension of disbelief, and via this suspension the composer was
able to play out emotions that only operatic creatures had. Schoenberg's
Erwartung, on the other hand, is not an illusion; it is a tonal case study of a
mad woman. Its music, "which develops the eternity of the second in four

hundred bars," as Adorno notes, "is valid as an eruptive revelation of negative experience. It is closely related to actual suffering."[27] The audience
hears this tonal nightmare with the same emotion as the woman who
experiences it—as opposed to Lucia who suffers madness but is required to
render this experience (tonally) beautiful, pleasant, and entertaining for the
audience. The unleashing of the unconscious in *Erwartung* is no more
pleasant than it is in psychotherapy, and the painful moment is not the
cherished one. The willing distortion of reality is not the woman's state of
mind; it is the fractured tonal matrix of the score. I say "fractured" not to
indicate that Schoenberg did not understand what he was doing; he knew
quite well. But there had never been such sounds created before, and this
Angsttraum could (and did) only shock listeners who had no point of
reference with which to compare it except key-centered music. *Erwartung*
makes the prelude to *Tristan* seem like a gospel hymn. Here, in this Freud-
ian music drama, the emancipation of the dissonance worked at direct
cross purposes with the tonal object, and the major problem of understanding Schoenberg ran aground on a false assumption about public acceptance. Although chromaticism had evolved in part through consciously expressive means, the public's conservative attitude toward chromaticism,
dissonance, and ambiguity of key could not be utterly suspended and certainly was not emancipated. To the general listener, the dissonance was
there in the score because the text was ugly, painful, and horrible. Through
Wagner, this listener had been forced to understand that harmonic dissolution meant—among other things—expressive instability and emotional
frustration. How could even *more* harmonic dissolution now mean nothing
at all? *Erwartung* could only be publicly viewed as an exaggeration of a
decaying mode of expression, the logical extension of that freedom which
the subjective ego had gained through romanticism. Adorno notes that in
Schoenberg's expressionistic works, human passions

> are no longer simulated, but rather genuine emotions of the unconscious—of
> shock, of trauma—are registered without disguise through the medium of
> music. These emotions attack the taboos of form because these taboos subject
> such emotions to their own censure, rationalizing them and transforming
> them into images. Schoenberg's formal innovations were closely related to the
> change in the content of expression. These innovations serve the break-
> through of the reality of this content. The first atonal works are case studies
> in the sense of psychoanalytical dream case studies.[28]

But as Adorno carefully points out, Schoenberg's denial of dramatic illusion had a positive as well as a negative aspect, for this negation tended
"towards the direction of knowledge."[29] Rather than the comforting conso-

lation of a major triad after Lucia's death, expressionist music presented the untransfigured suffering of men and women as impotent figures in a fractured society. "Expressionism remains—against its will—that which art had openly professed around 1900: loneliness as style."[30] In this sense, expressionism merely fulfilled its historical necessity, and the knowledge to be gained from Schoenberg's expressionist works directly parallels Freud's discovery of the unconscious.

The next stage in Schoenberg's tonal dialectic did not follow immediately upon the heels of his expressionist phase, but "just as free atonality developed out of the fabric of large tonal chamber music, the twelve-tone procedure in turn stemmed from free atonal composition."[31] Schoenberg composed only one work between 1913 and 1923, but announced to his pupil Josef Rufer in 1921 that he had "discovered something that will assure supremacy for German music for the next hundred years." He never retracted this vision. Thus, the Five Piano Pieces of 1923, the first works in which Schoenberg deliberately used tone rows, crystallized his long years of thought, and twelve-tone music enchained music by liberating it. The best critique of this process is a long and clearly stated passage from Adorno's *Philosophy of Modern Music*, which I would like to quote in shortened form:

> The subject dominates music through the rationality of the system, only in order to succumb to the rational system itself. In twelve-tone technique the actual process of composition—the productivity of variation—is returned to the basic realm of musical material. On the whole, the freedom of the composer undergoes the same experience. This technique is realized in its ability to manipulate the material, establishing itself as alien to the subject and finally subduing the subject by its own force. . . . From the procedures which broke the blind domination of tonal material there evolves a second blind nature by means of this regulatory system. The subject subordinates itself to this blind nature, seeking protection and security, which it indicates in its despair over the impossibility of fulfilling music out of itself. The Wagnerian hypothesis upon the rule which one establishes for oneself and then follows reveals its fateful aspect. No rule proves itself more repressive than the self-determined one. It is precisely its subjective origin which, as soon as it establishes itself in a positive way with regard to the subject, exercising a regulatory function, results in the coincidental nature of any arbitrary assumption. . . . To be sure, among the rules of twelve-tone technique there is not one which does not proceed necessarily out of compositional experience—out of the progressive illumination of the natural material of music. But this experience had assumed a defensive character by virtue of its subjective sensibility that no note appear which does not fulfill its motive function within the structure of the entire work; that no harmony be employed which is not conclusively identified at a specific spot. The truth of all these desiderata rests in their incessant confrontation with the concrete form

of music to which they are applied. These desiderata indicate a factor to be approached with caution, but do not indicate how this factor is to be approached. Disaster ensues as soon as the desiderata are elevated to the level of norms and are dispensed from that confrontation. The content of the norm is identical with that of spontaneous experience. However, once this content becomes concrete, it is transformed into a self-contradiction. What once found a highly perceptive ear has been distorted to a concocted system wherein musical correctness supposedly can be guaged in the abstract.[32]

If the reader feels that Adorno is being harsh with twelve-tone music, he should read the remainder of *Philosophy of Modern Music*. Twenty-six years later Adorno changed his mind about the dialectic of twelve-tone music and reassessed his opinion of Schoenberg. But the essay in *Prisms* did stress the motion of spirit that had taken place, reminding the reader anew that nothing spiritual since Hegel had managed to escape the compelling aim of objective authority.

> The objectivity that inheres in the subject is barred from reconciliation with a state of things which negates that subjective substance precisely by aiming at full reconciliation with it, and yet which that objectivity must nevertheless become if it is to be saved from the impotence of mere "being-for-itself".[33]

Thus by the early twenties Schoenberg, through his own authoritarian nature, was in the process of enthroning above himself the very principle he had created. The idea of tonal liberation that had been offered at least since Wagner and had been subjectively carried forth in Schoenberg's expressionist works now made a desperate thrust toward heteronomous authority. Schoenberg gradually came to the understanding that such authority could be validated and sponsored by "the immanent movement of the subject-matter in the form of logically coherent composition."[34] The experiences of his expressionist phase were transformed into rules, comprehended, codified, and systematized—at which point they were "no longer open and accessible to dialectical correction."[35] It was not the creation of the system that was at fault, but its hypostatization. Historically and once again, the tonal *ratio* was seduced by its own logic, which galvanized its assumed purity—on purely objective grounds—into a principle beyond redress. Or, stated differently, music, which was never obligated to reveal its methods, a freedom which is a part of subjective reason, suddenly identified these methods with its subject-matter, which only objectively appears. Compositions became models, by which token they denied themselves self-reflection and made themselves static.

The specific coalescence of this particular moment of the tonal dialectic is no more apparent than in the music of Anton Webern, which was manifested in the guise of a new objectivity and then carried to total disaster by the composers who later serialized all components of the musical work. But first let us look at Webern himself, born in 1883 and only nine years Schoenberg's junior. The two men were remarkably similar in their spiritual attitude toward life and remarkably different in the independence and single-mindedness by which each expressed it in his music. O. W. Neighbour notes that Schoenberg greatly benefited from his association with his "disciples," and "the origin of his lifelong interest in teaching lay in the need constantly to re-enact his own exploration of the resources of music." Schoenberg the teacher, however, "refused to teach the codified knowledge that he had never learnt, mistrusting mere knowledge as the enemy of understanding."[36] Webern the musicologist simply and willingly absorbed formalized musical science in his studies at the University of Vienna where he earned a doctorate in 1906 for his work on Heinrich Isaac. The outcome in either case was the same, an act of tonal preservation.

The entire corpus of Webern's music, which he wrote in the space of thirty-seven years, can be heard in about four hours. Paul Griffiths notes that any generalizing tendency to be sought within Webern's compositional style is thwarted by several abrupt changes of emphasis in his own development as a composer in addition to an overemphasis by theorists on the music composed during his serial instrumental phase from 1927 to 1940. "Brevity, the importance of silence, the usually restrained dynamic range, clarity of texture and simplicity of harmony"[37]—these characteristics too easily turn against any clarification of style in the form of negative assessment at the same time they are open to exception in particular works. What can be positively said about Webern's music when the very words we select to describe it have such a cutting edge? The following verbs are taken from current writing about Webern's music: delimit, abbreviate, unify, emphasize, isolate, reorder, contract, interrelate, condense, separate, derive, compensate, partition, reduce, and simplify. Not so curiously, these words accurately reflect Webern's own belief that the highest principle in composing music was the element of *comprehensibility* and that the two tasks that had to be undertaken in twelve-tone composition in order to secure it were "the conquest of the tonal field and the presentation of ideas."[38] For Webern, the path to the new music was not easy. He once remarked about his Op. 9 Bagatelles for string quartet that he had the feeling in the seemingly unbounded universe of "atonality" that "once the twelve notes had run out, the piece was finished." For him, composition was "immensely difficult."[39]

Webern's approach to the conquest of the tonal field and the presentation of ideas was a heroic act of internalization and historical reflection determined to demonstrate both the coherence and the logic of twelve-tone composition. Although he distorted certain musicological facts (particularly the principle of unity in Netherlands polyphony) in order to prove his theses, his sense of Schoenberg's relation (and his own) to the historical forces within consciousness and its tonal objectification in "new music" was profound. Thus he understood the deterioration of tonality, greatly aided by Wagner, "who blew the whole thing apart," as the penultimate stage in key-centered music and Schoenberg's vision as "the final stage of the development."

During the late winter of 1932 and the spring of 1933 Webern presented a series of sixteen lectures in a private house in Vienna to audiences who sought to understand the activities of the "Second Viennese School." Again and again in these lectures he attempted to establish the historical connections between it and the previous music of Western culture. The catchword was *Zusammenhang*, used frequently by Schoenberg and constantly by Webern. The German word implies "unity" in two connections; as the relationships between entities or parts of the same entity; and also as "relatedness," or cohesion, brought about by these connections.[40] It is instructive to see this historical rationalization within the context of Webern's music, which I shall treat here as a collective legacy and with the conventional terminology of serial analysis.

Because it seemed that a set or "series" of twelve notes was too ambiguous for Webern to control and direct (see his statement above), he internalized its content. Much of his music is characterized by the structuring of smaller pitch-class sets, frequently three or four notes, within the larger and complete set drawn from the chromatic scale. These motifs became the fundamental structural elements used to provide a surface coherence that depended not so much on thematic development as on the consistency of rhythmic shape, tonal interval, and unique utterance via minute attention to the properties of musical timbre. Here, Webern's traditional musical training served him well. The statable versions of any set—prime, inversion, retrograde, retrograde-inversion—had been (literally) the canons of counterpoint since the Renaissance. They were not inimical to twelve-tone composition: in fact, through the diverse potential of instrumental timbres they disclosed a glittering surface in Webern's music that remarkably underscored his Goethean sensibilities to the form of natural phenomena—"at once analytical and contemplative, attentive to the tiniest detail and yet searching for the coincidence, the general principle." In this respect, to interpret Webern's tonal achievement negatively, as a *disintegrative* force upon key-centered tonality (the customary assessment about twelve-tone composers with regard to the tonality that preceded them) is wrongheaded. The Webernian legacy lay positively within the *integrative* capacities of polyphonic activity itself, a characteristic feature of the Netherlands polyphony of the Renaissance, which Webern greatly esteemed but felt he had surpassed in his own music. This is nicely demonstrated in his Op. 24

Concerto for nine instruments in which one three-note motif is perpetually varied through the compositional techniques of canon, palindrome, and linear variation. Indeed, notes Griffiths, it seemed that Webern had composed canons "and then willfully atomized them out of perceptivity."[41]

But this very procedure of atomic tonal activity as contrapuntal variation legislated against the logic of large-scale forms of music, the aesthetic and formal logic that Webern certainly appreciated in the music of Schoenberg and Berg, but which he never completely assimilated into his own.

Looking back to the past, he championed the technique of the Netherlands school, "where the theme was introduced by each individual part, varied in every possible way, with different entries and in different registers." There, unity was created by "repeating the theme in various combinations, by introducing something that is the theme unfolding not only horizontally but also vertically."[42] Note the *singular* "theme." Webern ignored the fact that the Renaissance motet or Mass movement was most often formally built up as a series of points of imitations on successive and different melodic utterances. That is, it had a half dozen or more "themes" each of which was developed imitatively. And he failed to recognize the procedure by which Dutch composers relieved the monotony of this constant texture, by alternating it with homophonic passages containing disguised or clearly delineated cadences.

Webern championed the "staggering polyphonic thought" of Bach's *Art of the Fugue* because "all these fugues are based on *one* single theme, which is constantly transformed." What did it mean? "The desire for maximum unity. Everything is derived from one basic idea, from the one fugue-theme! Everything is 'thematic.' "[43] But he ignored the fact that the comprehensibility demonstrated by the Bach "fugue-theme" was in part secured by presenting with it essential but nonthematic counterpoint to place it in sonic relief.

He correctly saw this desire for thematic variation "creeping into later forms, in the development section" of the classical sonata form. "This—our—type of thinking has been the ideal for composers of all periods," he concluded, "to develop everything from *one* principal idea!" "But in what form?" he immediately asked. The answer was not helpful ("That's where art comes in!") and capitulated to undisclosed mysteries of the compositional act.[44]

To be sure, Webern was attempting to demonstrate to his audiences the unity between twelve-tone compositional technique and its roots in the historical past, which it certainly had; but his uncritical approach smeared the evidence. The Renaissance motet contained in fact an abundance of "principal ideas" which unfolded in successive counterpoint; and, despite remarkable exceptions, the classic sonata form is largely characterized by its bi-thematic utterance. It was not the conquest of the tonal field that plagued him but "the presentation of ideas." He understood the relationship between key-centered tonality and the structure in which it gave "an essential foundation. It helped to build their form; in a certain sense it ensured unity. This relationship to a keynote was the essence of tonality."[45] But he failed to realize that the drama of extended forms, particularly as offered in the dialectic of different key centers within sonata form, could not be realized in twelve-tone music through any specific tonal means. The tonal drama of sonata form was substantive only to the degree that tonal differentiation was clearly sought and provided: tonally, it depended upon essential and coincidental components within sonic events. Webern hovered over this dilemma, explaining his terms to himself and his audience, but to no avail:

> What, then is differentiation? Broadly speaking, the introduction of divisions! What are divisions for? To keep things apart, to distinguish between what is principle and what is subsidiary. This is necessary, to make yourself intelligible, so it must also happen in music.[46]

It did not happen in Webern's music critically enough to secure the integrity of large-scale composition. While we find him utilizing the forms of rondo, minuet, fugue, sonata, and theme and variations, his application of them was at variance with the very integrative nature of his motivic energies. In the continual disclosure of contrapuntal variation, beautifully enhanced by his notion of *Klangfarbenmelodie*, there is no transition between essential tonal moments: all is equally important or none of it is. About 1924, after a ten-year period when he wrote only vocal music, Webern again took up purely instrumental forms. While he relied on his knowledge of historical forms of music for inspiration and assistance, the latter was never forthcoming in the development of extended formal structures. "The sorts of series he employed can be said to relate to the sorts of form he used," notes Griffiths, but "it would be an exaggeration to describe Webern's forms as 'self-generating' from their series, or to suggest that he initiated 'serial form.' "[47]

Whether or not the extreme brevity of Webern's pieces can be ultimately regarded as a virtue is moot; it consistently appeared to be a necessity for stylistic reasons. "Their brevity is a direct result of the demand for the greatest consistency," notes Adorno. "This demand precludes the superfluous. In so doing this consistency opposes expansion in time, which has been the basis for the conception of the musical work since the eighteenth century, certainly since Beethoven. The work, the age, and illusion are all struck by a single blow."[48] To be sure, this is a touchy subject, and I leave it to the reader to form his own judgment. What is more important is the fact that Webern's amazing consistency with twelve-tone technique soon brought about its next stage and its own negation.

Schoenberg died in 1951, and a year later *The Score* devoted a portion of its spring issue to an evaluation of his achievements. The most critical statement came from the young Pierre Boulez, whose "Schoenberg is Dead" essay clearly registered that the next stage in the dodecaphonic dialectic had indeed begun. Boulez felt that Schoenberg's greatest contributions had been in his music, not his system, which was full of "misunderstandings and contradictions," although one could certainly learn from Schoenberg's "errors." With some inconsistency himself, Boulez suggested that "we might convince ourselves that the tone-row is an historical necessity," but because of his misguided application of it, "perhaps it would be better to dissociate Schoenberg's work altogether from the phenomenon of the tone-row." The importance of Schoenberg, exterior to *Pierrot Lunaire* "and a few other outstanding works," was not his system but the principle of the tone row, which "could be applied to the five elements of sound, *viz.*, pitch, duration, tone-production, intensity, timbre."[49]

The development of this principle had already begun, almost simultaneously in America and Europe. In 1948 Milton Babbitt composed his *Three Compositions for Piano*, *Composition for Four Instruments*, and *Composition for Twelve Instruments*. And a year later, Olivier Messiaen composed *Mode de valeurs et d'intensités*, an etude in a set of piano pieces. Here in these works, the all-inclusive premise of "total organization" structured the music in a fashion that was indebted more to Webern than to Schoenberg. Tone color, dynamics, register, durations, rests, tempos, meters, attacks, and decays were brought under the leveling principle of serialism, and the ultimate objectivity was achieved. Thus the strict serialists of the 1950s organized all parameters of the musical image according to a rule that Schoenberg had formulated for tones only. In this light, Webern became "a real hero," as Stravinsky hailed him—at least for a while. In a world that viewed one piece of music as being more or less tonal than another, this was the ultimate tonality. No more careful decisions were ever made against the chaos of pitch.

It is important at this juncture to realize that the events described here initially affected only a small portion of the Western world's composers, although it affected those few critically. Schoenberg's music had been banned by Adolf Hitler, and from 1933 to 1945 German composers were excluded from any vital contact with continuing or emerging trends in twentieth-century music. Thus in postwar German culture, Schoenberg and the method of composing with twelve tones was essentially a revelation to young composers. The Polish-French composer and theorist René Leibowitz studied with Schoenberg in Berlin from 1930 to 1933 and in Vienna with Webern. In 1947 he published *Schoenberg et son école*, which argued for serialism as "the contemporary stage of the language of music," the book's subtitle. Not only did Leibowitz adopt serial composition, he became the foremost exponent of the method in France. In 1948 he lectured at Darmstadt on the possibility of an uncompromising dodecaphonic composition, i.e., total serialization.

We now know that Leibowitz's "contemporary stage of the language of music" was short-lived, at least as he envisioned it. To be sure, while a number of composers in both Europe and America began to adopt twelve-tone technique, wholly or in part, audiences had been turning from the music since early Schoenberg and continued to do so. As Henry Pleasants noted in 1955, modern music had become agony rather than pleasure, but had to be endured because it was "serious." There were two general reactions to this mid-century crisis: retreat under the guise of academic respectibility or a self-correcting humanization of serial techniques. The first can be dismissed in a paragraph, and the second, we shall discover, is the negation of "atonality" as negation.

Total serialism (and other forms of maximum rationalization and control in music) would continue to be cultivated if the composer could find a patron. He did. "The fact that the universities tend to be the centers for its cultivation," notes Daniel Kingman, "often pursued with the aid of foundation grants, has helped to foster the analogy of this type of composition to pure scientific research."[50] The fact that nobody was listening seemed to be of no genuine concern. For composer Charles Wuorinen, music had "grown too rich and complex to be handled by the illiterate."[51] In fact, it was even assumed that such music might somehow be "better" if no public application was sought for it at all. In a now-famous article, Milton Babbitt suggested that

> the composer would do himself and his music an immediate and eventual service by total, resolute, and voluntary withdrawal from this public world to one of the private performance and electronic media, with its very real possibility of *complete elimination of the public and social aspects of musical composition.*[52]

Thus, total serialism as *die neue Sachlichkeit* (the new objectivity) ensconced itself within the academic citadel and in a few cities here and abroad—New York, Darmstadt, and Paris. This music became

> concerned with embodying the extensions, generalisations, and fusions of certain techniques contained in the music of Schoenberg, Webern, and Berg,

and above all with applying the pitch operations of the twelve-tone system to non-pitch elements: durational rhythm, dynamics, phrase rhythm, timbre, and register, in such a manner as to preserve the most significant properties associated with these operations in the pitch domain where they are applied in these other domains.[53]

Music became concerned with its own internal compositional procedures, as the titles of the works themselves aptly demonstrate: *Three Compositions for Piano, Formel, Punkte, Kontra-Punkte, Structures Ia, Structures Ib, Structures II, Polyphonie X*. Streamlined and sleek, music raced toward a multiple, integrated set of determinate, particular relations among all discernible components—to use the jargon of its sonic authenticity. Trendy and "pre-compositional," composition by virtue of its extreme rationality (and perhaps boredom and exhaustion) unwittingly headed for its own critique in the form of irrationality and chance. I will not continue the chronology here.

But other composers were neither as disenchanted with the public's ability to absorb twelve-tone tonality nor as uncommitted to encouraging them to do so. I wish to devote the remainder of this chapter to the tonal odyssey of one of these composers, Hans Werner Henze, who was judged by composer and music critic Hans H. Stuckenschmidt in 1957 to be "the richest artistic personality" of a trio of young musicians (Geselher Klebe and Karlheinz Stockhausen are the other two) whose imaginations were kindled by the possibilities of "serial thinking."[54]

For Henze, music is a tonal gesture, a sonic sign full of information, emotion, and beauty.[55] It is almost amusing in the late twentieth century to hear a composer consistently describe his music as beautiful, and perhaps it is because Henze does this, and also because he rejected *die neue Sachlichkeit*, that he has been frequently and uncritically labeled a romantic. It is unnecessary to dwell upon the negative or positive contexts of this label. More important to the thesis of this chapter is the historical and social self-correction that Henze's music exhibits with regard to the progressive dialectic of tonal consciousness. We have already covered the first two stages of this process, but it is necessary to examine again a particular facet of the early stage of twelve-tone music—expressionism.

Expressionism, as Donald Grout notes, was born out of a need to express "all the elemental irrational drives of the subconscious," and was characterized "both by desperate intensity of feeling and revolutionary modes of utterance."[56] Musically speaking, a quick glance at the early works of Schoenberg and those of Berg bears this out. But the list of emotions and psychological states of mind that are accredited to early expressionist art is usually negative and short, mentioning only anxiety, fear, and guilt. Certainly,

Schoenberg's *Verklärte Nacht* is a concrete example of these states of the psyche. But half of that score is also devoted to the transfiguration of the guilty night into one of splendor and joy when the man offers forgiveness to the woman he loves. The positive aspects of expressionism, while meager, are usually forgotten or intentionally omitted. Expressionist art did more than annul the taboo against objectifying the inner human consciousness, however irrational its anxiety, fear, and guilt; it also affirmed the positive aspect of the whole human condition through the same intense and new musical means. Alban Berg's Violin Concerto, after forty years, remains one of the most beautiful testimonies of human care and courage in modern music. While the Concerto audibly portrays the death of a young girl, while it takes the listener up to and through the actual catastrophe of Manon Gropius's death (the technique is similarly used for Marie's murder in *Wozzeck*), and while there is a profound sense of grief in this music, this grief is both transcended and rationalized by the historical tonal properties of the score—a tone row constructed in minor and major triads; the interval of the tritone rationalized through Bach's harmonization of Ahle's chorale melody, "Es ist genug"; and the conscious quotations of Viennese folk tunes. Berg's Violin Concerto is an early foreshadowing of the negation of "atonality as negation."

Critics are wont to declare these "common-practice" features of Berg's score to be "touches of tonality," perhaps analogous to the faint and barely discernible shape of a human face in an otherwise abstract painting. Sometimes there is even the suggestion that such encounters with key-centered music are indiscreet and indicate a serialist failure of nerve. Unfortunately, these remarks indicate how little is understood about the progressive character of twelve-tone music. When Henze states that he writes "freely invented compositions without serial parameters," he places himself firmly on the other side of strict serialism, *die neue Sachlichkeit*, and the sterility of an elite, hermetic, and academic music. The political crises he has undergone with regard to his commitment to music for people have generated a consciousness in the late twentieth century that is both passionate and critical, personally involved and socially committed. As he has stated on numerous occasions, "my music is *for* people—the taxi cab driver, the nurse, and the fisherman."[57]

It would be easy to dismiss this statement with a hasty judgment of populism if populism itself were not in acute need of critical analysis. Only the human cognitive aspect of it will be treated here. I shall attempt to do this with Henze's instrumental music, not because his vocal music fails to exhibit the same characteristics, but because it is particularly in his instrumental music that Henze has faced the contemporary problems of aesthetic comprehension and appreciation: "namely whether it could be possible to produce, in purely instrumental music, a language which, without the assistance of text, or other nonmusical means of communication, can be received by the listener to a performance without misunderstanding."[58]

In response to the sterility of *die neue Sachlichkeit*, Henze made a strong affirmation for "music with melody." This lyric quality in his music has been observed by many critics who are wont to credit it to the effect of Mediterranean lyricism upon a German consciousness, but the reason lies more critically in the nature of music as tonal gesture. Along with its rhythm, melody is that succession of tone events that the listener immediately and tacitly assumes has been created *for him* to comprehend as *linear* thinking. Since the melody is for him, it must be comprehensible to him. As a tonal act, it is successful because it is melodically conceived as a statement from the societal repository of pitches—those the listener has already acquired for himself through the habitual process of melodic identification. But it is also historically progressive in the sense of expanding the listener's consciousness in terms of the potentiality for melodic configurations. The initial inaccessibility of Beethoven's Opus 59 Quartets and Wagner's "unending melody" is a case in point. Henze's melody is largely disjunct, asymmetric in phrase length, and consistently chromatic—although in a harmonic context as thoroughly twelve-tone as his, the opposition of "chromatic" and "diatonic" is no longer a useful distinction. These characteristics mean little: they could also apply to the strictest of serial composition. However, if the listener is to be encouraged, if he wishes to follow the melodic content available within the vast potential of twelve-tone configurations, if he wishes to remember what he hears, and if remembering is important, what kinds of assistance might the composer offer him instead of a randomly or purposely chosen series of nearly a half billion twelve-tone successions? It is doubtful that Henze has consciously sought the answer to this question, but his avowed melodic consciousness exhibits an intuitive awareness of the abilities and disabilities of those for whom he writes.

The general cognitive component of Henze's music that makes it tonally accessible is a simple one—repetition, but it is repetition that is neither mindless nor so hermetic so as to be discovered only in the presence of the score. Lest this seem at first blush to be a carrot-and-stick technique, let us consider what repetition offers in the musical image. Subjectively, it generates familiarity—so much so in some music that Schoenberg expressed contempt for it. Objectively, it generates form, both on the micro- and the macrolevel. Because Henze's structures are so very much transformational ones, both of these levels are important, although he is not concerned that the listener "know" the form of his music, but, rather, its meaning. It is this quest for meaning that dissolves the subjective/objective dichotomy by means of lyric composition that affixes to the multiplicity of potential tone

combinations an indispensable seal of cognitive understanding and approval through repetitive tonal gestures. This paraphrase of Sartre (who was
speaking of abstract art) decisively extends into the world of music. Since
the ear has as its immediate stimulus communication, representing the
incessantly recreated completion and perpetual animation of the twelve-
tone work, the composer must give it his immediate and constant attention:
"Meaning, since it is revealed through unification and since its revelation
promotes unity, must be by nature communicable. To establish the condition without providing the means for fulfilling it is to risk exposing the
work to the perils of indetermination."[59] Like language, which does not
attempt to establish meaning with a *different* word or semiotic gesture with
every single utterance, Henze's music establishes the means of cognitive
comprehension through micro- and macro-repetitive lyric gestures that insure both unity and expressive content. These general remarks can now be
substantiated.

Henze's melody is not serial, but it is freely twelve-tone. Instead of an
unremitting cycle of twelve pitches in strict order until the whole image
becomes static, he conceives of a melody in which conscious repetition of
tones and groups of tones offers a focal point—however conjunct or disjunct—with which to weight the tension, strength, energy, and significance
of melodic utterance as a whole. Example 11-1 gives the theme of the
Second Piano Concerto.

Example 11-1

This technique is consistent with the cognitive abilities of the listener and—
not surprisingly—with Schoenberg's vision of a tonality in which the pitches
are related only to each other. The immediate repetition of tones 3 through
6 in this twelve-tone theme does not create a tonic around which the
remaining notes must be structured, but it does negate the steady advance
of all twelve tones in predetermined succession. Whether or not the listener
is conscious of this technique is irrelevant. A painter does not ask his
viewers to know how much of a certain pigment was used in a given color,
and Henze does not ask the listener to count notes, only to feel their
progression as logical. A transformation of this theme occurs shortly thereafter, as shown in Example 11-2. Here, the repetition scheme is more

extensive, and the theme doubles back upon itself three times before ending—as it did in its initial statement—with the first pitch of the series. The left hand accompaniment is contrapuntal with a free use of all pitches.

Example 11-2

This melodic technique runs the gamut from the subtlety of the above examples to melodies in which a group of tones revolves and turns upon itself, contracting and expanding, in a fashion that is clearly projected and heard as melodically meaningful. This can be seen in Example 11-3, a passage for unison violas near the end of the same concerto.

Example 11-3

Intervallically speaking, no single melodic configuration is more important than another. Major and minor thirds are not avoided nor are perfect fifths, but thirds in chains are largely absent because of the fixed association with tertian harmony. As mentioned above, disjunct melodic motion characterizes much of the linear shape (especially in the above), but conjunct motion—both whole- and half-step—is abundant.

A given melodic line is quite frequently enforced with octave doubling in order to bring it into clear audible relief. Schoenberg, of course, felt that the reinforcement of the octave was one of the strongest elements of key-centered tonality, and ruled that it should be rigorously avoided in his system. Curiously, with Henze, its conscious adoption forms a strong cognitive component within thoroughly twelve-tone music but one that never summons forth the specter of the roots of triads or chords. In a texture rich in polyphonic activity, this important technique serves as guaranteed *Hauptstimme* projection for melodic cognition.

Henze makes no effort at periodic phrase structure, nor—in orchestral music—does he favor a given group of instruments to articulate either short or lengthy melodic statements. In fact, it is in the large expanse of symphonic expression that his dialectic of melodic consciousness has a most characteristic utterance. A melody may run many measures, moving from one instrument to another, from one group of instruments to another group, or from a solo instrument to a group of instruments, through a wide ambitus that reflects their respective range capabilities, with "couplings" to insure continuity when this is desired rather than phrase articulation through rests. Because of the pronounced dialogic quality of his melodic thinking, the positive appearance of the melody is its immediate ability to nurture the exchange of ideas between respective instruments and families of instruments, and to transform itself in the process.

While imitation is infrequent, the contrapuntal interplay of several melodies (often more than two) characterizes Henze's music to a marked degree, although these melodies may be of quite different weight and character. Thus we may find two melodies of relatively matched contours moving together, or a longer and slower lyric melody juxtaposed with a faster moving one, either or both of which may be collectively articulated in the method described above. It becomes apparent in Henze's music that the project of melody, whether minimally or densely polyphonic, is but one integral part— although a highly important one—of a dramatic structure that unfolds as all musical elements contribute to it.

Consistent with his melodic consciousness, Henze's harmony is twelve-tone but not serial. With regard to triadic tonality, it is thoroughly "non-functional," but Henze's harmony does function in a dramatic and organic sense that corrects the static harmonic consciousness of serialism. Again, it is the principle of repetition that corrects it. Henze does not have a chord vocabulary that he divides into dissonant and consonant categories to be determined by "natural" principles of vertical organization. Using one of his favorite English terms, he explains that "what happens harmonically is dependent on the musical expression I want to bring across: the chords give the proper light to the melodies. So the harmonies are always *invented* for dramatic purposes."[60]

Given the polyphonic nature of Henze's melodic dialogues it follows that a good portion of the vertical combinations are the result of intersecting melodic lines. This is not a fault, since any combination of notes is possible for Henze *if* their spacing is convincing, of which more shortly. The resultant harmonic component provided by melodic consciousness is rationalized by the potential of twelve-tone thinking.

Of paramount importance to the way Henze creates harmony is what he wishes to accomplish at any given time. With a harmonic palette consisting of sounds ranging from an interval to (frequently) eight-note chord complexes, there appear three typical functions that vertically assist in the creation of sonic architecture.

The first function is one of harmonic *disclosure* in which Henze brings into open sonic space a vertical complex sustained through duration at the same time that part of it may be changed through alteration. Cognitively speaking, there is an introductory character to this technique, and we find it at the beginnings of movements or sections within them. While examples are abundant, note the opening of the Second Piano Concerto and also the beginning of its third section (measures 900ff.). In the first instance, Henze reaches for the upper part of the orchestral canvas, gradually filling in with pitches until a six-note chord is formed at the fortissimo, a cluster of whole- and half-steps. At the beginning of the third section, a similar disclosure of harmonic space evolves from the middle of the orchestra, and the first oboe solo enters above it. Note also the beginning of the *Marcia funebre* (measures 1055ff.), where the harmonic space opens from the bottom, in the contrabasses, is sustained up through the texture and with the pitches of the original twelve-tone theme. Perhaps one of the most beautiful of these harmonic disclosures in all of Henze's music is the opening of the andante (measures 252ff.) of the *Doppio Concerto per Oboe, Arpa et Archi*. In each of these instances, the *spacing* and *doubling* of the tones is critical: other tones might have been chosen, but the specific arrangement of these particular ones, their instrumental timbres, and their careful doublings disclose unique harmonic atmospheres from which melodies take their point of entry. Functionally, consciousness understands that a world of twelve-tone sound is being opened for it to comprehend and that which follows will be internally consistent.

A second function of *crystallization* accounts for a great deal more harmonic activity in Henze's compositional technique than disclosure. A problematic feature of serialism is that the persistent cycling of the tones through a given row does not permit the listener to establish for himself harmonic intensity, stability, and the vertical rationale that any one harmonic complex should follow another: the omnipresence of all tones denies the necessity for any in particular, and the music becomes static. Henze's harmonic structures do not become static. While the traditional function of harmonic motion in key-centered tonality is absent, substantive shape is given to vertical space so that the listener knows that what he is presently hearing has a relation both to that which preceded and that which will follow it. There are several means by which this is accomplished, but each one is secured through either duration or repetition.

The simplest of these is an alternation of two intervals (or chord complexes) through brief or moderately extensive repetition. In the Second Piano Concerto, we hear this immediately after the opening harmony and the first statement of the theme in the piano. The strings sustain a chord while *divisi* flutes alternate a two-interval complex in thirty-second notes (measures 11–12). After a second statement of the piano theme, the first bassoon joins the flutes for a similar harmonic ostinato (measures 18–19), and a longer one in the flutes accompanies the entire transformation of the theme given above (Example 11-2, measures 27–34). Note also that the first interval (a minor seventh on E-flat) is solidified by five beats of quadruple meter. What this technique does is give definite shape to a harmonic sonority that stabilizes the vertical space through which the piano moves as it transforms the initial theme. The listener is given a sense of vertical stability even though other harmonic components are in motion.

A second technique that crystallizes harmonic consciousness entails a rapid statement of the pitch data that tends to assume melodic substance because of its length but cannot do so because of its rapidity. An important structural one in this Concerto is found in measures 554–61, a rising motive that states (*acquires* is perhaps a better term) all twelve pitches, shown in Example 11-4. While this is achieved by the violins and the flute, the remaining instruments sustain an eight-note chord.

Example 11-4

A cadence follows immediately both here and at the end of the section (measures 886–90). In these two instances, this rapid motivic pattern gives definite sonic substance to harmonic consciousness. It is a repetitive tonal device like that found in key-centered music. But, as with the harmony of key-centered tonality, it also serves melodic consciousness as well. Note again the viola melody quoted above in Example 11-3. That passage begins with a viola solo, but when the remaining violas join it (*con sordino*, measure 1112), what had formerly been too rapid to be melodically appreciated earlier in the piece (see Example 11-4) is transformed here at the end of the Concerto into a graceful melody with a rhythm of its own.

Repeated or sustained chords account for extended stretches of harmony. Woodwinds, brass, and strings are equally utilized in creating these vertical shapes, in which doubling, spacing, timbre, and dynamics are carefully controlled components of harmonic articulation. For instance, the *Ancora meno mosso* section (measures 168ff.) in the Second Piano Concerto is a thickly orchestrated passage in which complex chords, frequently with common tones between them, absorb the sonic space. The point of entry into one of these massive vertical complexes is usually one of two types. It may be instantaneously stated in all parts, as in this passage, or it may gradually fill up orchestral space, as it does at measures 206ff., again with spacings and doublings that clearly project a harmonic sphere of moving shapes.

The *termination* of such vertical complexes is the third function in Henze's harmonic technique. Structurally, he builds sonic architecture that is temporally shaped to conclude harmonically as convincingly as it began. This cadential aspect assumes the same function as in key-centered music but without any assistance from dominant to tonic modeling. The means are to sustain the harmony, suspended in time, until cognition perceives that no other complex need follow it, or to resolve from this complex a less dense harmonic entity, or simply to end quickly and efficiently—frequently after ostinato figures.

Henze's music is tonal in that he decides for each work how to control the vast potential for melodic and harmonic thought within twelve-tone consciousness. The features mentioned above are of a general sort and are not meant to box him into an inflexible compositional corner. In addition to these, there are ad hoc solutions to the problem of building tonal architecture. For example, the *Doppio Concerto per Oboe, Arpa et Archi* of 1966 is cohesively structured upon a single opening "head motive" stated by the oboe in the first measures, which permeates the entire work. Variation technique is utilized in the *Sonata per Archi* (1957/1958). The recent *Il Vitalino raddoppiato* (Chaconne for Solo Violin and Chamber Orchestra, 1978) is purposely tonally restricted to the repeated chaconne harmony that undergoes progressive vertical transformation.

The point is not that Henze is "more" or "less" tonal, as the popular parlance of modern criticism is wont to describe any composer who moves toward or away from key-centered music. It is, rather, that as a sonic gesture, a composer's music is a single consciousness that is shaped from the historical dimensions of his culture. As individuals, composers have always altered historical tonality at the same time that they have worked within certain common conceptions of what constitutes expressive sonic communication. Henze believes that the progressive tendency of aesthetic creation should neither lag behind nor rush ahead of human aesthetic enjoyment and understanding. The appropriation of musical works is a tonal appropriation of a sonic object of and for man. It cannot appear as a mere sonic thing for itself, however rational, "total," or objective the methodology is that produces it. Henze establishes a specific relation in his music that he feels satisfies a specific human need, and he encourages the listener to appropriate his sonic objects for their human significance. The determinate form, the tonal work itself, is neither hermetic nor banal. To be sure, there are millions of people for whom this dialogue with the creative artist is not yet possible. No dialogue can be established as long as alienated, aesthetic consciousness is manipulated solely in terms of consumption for profit. (The reasons for this tonal alienation will have to be examined at another time.) But to acknowledge that man is tonally alienated is also to recall that at one time this was not the case. To paraphrase Adolfo Sánchez Vásquez: Henze composes for those who feel a need for a totality of vital human manifestations through music, although present-day capitalist society engenders for the most part a type of man who at present does not feel that need. As the self-correcting negation of "atonality as negation," Henze believes that his music not only transcends the socio-historical conditions that created his dilemma but will also "continue to live when current conditions become only a dim memory or a forgotten matter."[61]

In summary, critics have been quick to point out the "neo-romantic" tendencies in Henze's music, without realizing that the wider applicability of the term is itself a genuine critique of a predominant tendency throughout the century: expressionism. While several other "isms" have gained momentary or lasting credence in modern music (impressionism has been thoroughly absorbed into the contemporary film score), the essential subjectivism of expressionist music—in which the composer tonally objectifies his consciousness as intensely and as directly as possible and does so through the once radical techniques of twelve-tone composition—remains a philosophy that infuses contemporary music with continuing validity. In fact, such music is regarded as radical still because its point of reference is precisely drawn *not* against electronic music, aleatoric music, minimal music, or some other manifestation of avant-gardism but against the ubiquitous presence of key-centered tonality which was once its point of departure.

A century of psychology and psychoanalysis has given empirical substance to the chaotic state of man's daily consciousness. If early expressionism attempted sonically to objectify the tension between man and his society, in the psychic expressions of fear, dread, guilt, and angst, it did so because there were the dominant ills that artists in all media felt were in most need of examination, analysis, and understanding. But a century of psychology and psychoanalysis has also deepened the whole of man's daily consciousness. If the education of feeling is a critical component in music, then man's joy, love, awe, and surprise at modern life are just as important to establish and to sustain as enduring components of his desire to live both well and in full possession of his emotional faculties.

In this light, expressionist music is very much alive. In 1911 Kandinsky wrote that "the refusal to employ the habitual forms of the beautiful leads one to admit as sacred all the procedures which permit the artist to manifest his own personality." His judgment that "the Viennese composer, Arnold Schoenberg, alone follows this direction" has undergone historical correction. That is, during the last seven decades we have seen that the dialectic of atonality as the negation of key-centered music was but a moment within a larger and more encompassing sonic consciousness. While the sterility of its serialist phase in mid century was the consequence of the tonal *ratio* at work on its own objectivity, there appears now a self-correcting humanism of twelve-tone composition in the music of Henze and other composers. When Schoenberg once stated that he had discovered a method of composing that would ensure the hegemony of German music for another hundred years, he perhaps did so with more pride than vision. His retreat in some of his later works from the very principles he had established in the early stages of serialism offered its own critique for the integrity of a method of composing with twelve tones that are related only to one another. "Twelve tones squared by the second dimension, polyphony," continue to offer the "atonal" composer a substantive content for his thought. In no other century has the relationship between tonal theory and its praxis been so drastically challenged. Perhaps this is the reason both for the confusion and the optimism.

Conclusion

I believe there is an activity of consciousness that is tonal. Theories of hearing map this activity between the ear and the brain and involve such processes as reception, transmission, and interpretation. In this area I have no expertise. However, these processes when directed toward cognizable pitches and their orders produce a physical, temporal form, the musical object, which in its appearance (whether heard or only "read" as a musical score) manifests specific learned orders of perception, identity, and interpretation that are tonal on a profound and general level.

The customary method by which to investigate the tonal consciousness of Western music has been to isolate it historically as to stylistic period, thus losing the connections between what that tonality *preserved* from previously established sonic materials and their orders that made its appearance possible, and what it *annulled* in them in order to make its own appearance new and different. This division of tonal analysis has both discouraged and denied an understanding of the general nature of tonal phenomena at the same time that, historically speaking, it has elevated the music of the "common-practice" period to a paradigm of remarkable tenacity. For literally thousands of musicologists, theorists, and pedagogues it has encouraged a belief in tonal perfection that historically was never achieved in praxis. This assumption, which equates key-centeredness with true tonality, is the basis upon which modern musicology and music theory founders: to the extent that these disciplines accept this false assumption, they can neither define their content nor assess its meaning.

Generally speaking, the connections betweeen successive tonal appearances in history are those components discussed in chapter 3. Whether these components can serve as a theory of general tonality is beyond the scope of this book. However, I wish to suggest that the profound *generality* of Western tonal consciousness, far from being vacuous and hopelessly encompassing as some have suggested, is its most critical and revealing attribute. This generalizing tendency of tonal consciousness lies at the very core of all investigations about music whether it is assumed to be present or not. Tonality emerged and developed through a human desire for expressive modes of utterance that were not available in spoken discourse. This emergence was largely pre-reflective and relatively unconcerned with its origins other than to place them within the assumed precision of mathematics (as did the Pythagoreans) or in the hands of the gods (as did the Greek poets). Tonality was frequently observed as an activity of consciousness whose explanatory procedures of creativity were already encrusted by authoritative, theoretical, or theological interests. No more decisive example of this can be observed than in the transmission of Greek music theory to the Middle Ages through Boethius, which was largely misinterpreted by the medieval theorists as constituting the bedrock from which the emergent ecclesiastical modes had been mined. Throughout modern scholarship it has been the unfortunate fate of tonal analysis to be based on chronological texts whose relationship to the historical praxis of music composition is narrowly confined to the immediate interests of a given theorist. Consciousness must break free from these restraints if it wishes to disclose the nature of its object. In short, tonality is other than we thought.

With Schoenberg I propose that the word *tonal* is entirely sufficient to describe the vast corpus of Western music—notwithstanding various attempts of avant-garde music-making to create entirely new sonic materials and new orders for their presentation. Nevertheless, the historical development and manipulation of the societal repository of pitch data consistently projects a direct relationship between the creative subject (who more or less consciously preserves this repository as useful to his interests) and the autonomous object that subjectivity creates from it—for whatever reasons.

Within this context, certain "tonal" words are simply unsuitable and inaccurate because they project upon tonal consciousness a commitment that it never possessed. "Pre-" and "post-" tonal are two of the most misleading. What they respectively indicate is a historical projection toward the harmonic efficiency and expressivity of key-centered music of the baroque, classic, and romantic eras, and a subsequent decline of interest in this harmonic efficiency (although not in popular music) due to subjective alienation of the romantic composer. In addition, and perhaps more perniciously, these terms assume for tonality, in the form of key-centered harmony, a paradigm for tonal expression that historically never occurred. There has never appeared a perfect tonal moment in the history of music, any more than there has appeared a perfect legal, social, economic, or linguistic moment in the history of human consciousness. This is not to confuse tonal utterance with the autonomous nature of its appearing forms in individual works of music.

"Modal" is a useful term only to the degree that it reflects the historical moments of preservation and annulment of its own tonal dialectic. To set up modal against tonal—each with its own neat and tidy descriptive categories—is to miss entirely both the nature of modal creativity within its own historical ascendency and the preservation of characteristically modal features that were chronologically carried forward and developed, refined, or leveled in the activities of the so-called common-practice period.

And finally, "atonal" ought simply to be scrapped as a piece of historical juvenilia coined by early twentieth-century composers and critics who were reluctantly forced to admit that tonality was not immune from its own dialectic. "Twelve-tone" adequately describes music in which the older order of 7 + 5 diatonic and chromatic pitches is no longer of hierarchic validity within the act of composition. And "serial" handily serves to describe twelve-tone music that has become specifically and systematically ordered within preselected statements, that is, tone rows, drawn from the potential of its own historical materials.

Far more useful as well as being historically accurate are the terms *monophonic, polyphonic,* and *homophonic* tonality. But even these latter two must be permitted to demonstrate the connections between their distinguishing components in the music that they characterize. I shall use this division here. They are separable on principle, but they are also historically connected and determined.

Beginning quite generally with Greek antiquity, we assume that music was largely monophonic, sung in unison (or octaves) by men and women. Singers of the melos were not, nor had reason to be, interested in whatever variative-polyphonic elements coexisted with a leveling monophonic tendency. Plato was aware of heterophonic components within Greek music; he both mistrusted and proscribed them. The degree to which instrumental music polyphonically or harmonically embellished this melos is not recoverable.

To be sure, part of the Greek legacy to the Middle Ages was a scientifically founded acoustical theory of music, a system of scale-formation based on tetrachords, and a musical terminology, but the extent to which these components influenced the actual praxis of the early Christian church or a concomitant secular melos outside it must be historically understood within the context of an abundant musical creativity already in place. If the shap-

ing of modern tonality was the praxis of the Christian church, and I believe
that it was, then tonal modeling received both its historical impetus and its
formal justification from the prevailing musical practices of mixed Orien-
tal-Hellenistic societies around the Eastern Mediterranean crescent which
were taken up and absorbed by Christians during the early centuries of
their activity.

In short, the practice of parallelismus membrorum—both in Jewish cantillation and Christian psalmody—became the crucible of a specific kind of
musical phrase, articulated by consciousness in the form of cognitive expectations, through the delivery of sacred texts; and preserved by memory as
both musically and formally coherent. Antithetic to it (and as pronounced
as the later seventeenth-century dichotomy between recitative and aria)
were the florid, melismatic features found in the Hebrew *Hallelujah* and
the Christian *Alleluia*, although by no means restricted to them. At least in
one critical dimension, here can be observed the separable intentions of
didactic and expressive musics.

Toward the end of the first Christian millennium, the anonymous, orally
created and transmitted melos met with the leveling tendency of modal
theory at roughly the same time that an enormous body of ecclesiastical
music was being subjected (and critically so in tonal terms) to the legiti-
mizing features of written notation. Characteristic regional expressions of
the melos (now irretrievably lost) were gradually brought under the leveling
force of Greek music theory, transmitted to the Middle Ages by Boethius but
misunderstood by the medieval theorists. The collective melos, which had
never been completely diatonic, was forced to become so if possible. For
instance, the durable presence of the pitch B-flat jeopardized the tidiness of
the modal system, particularly in modes 3 and 4, at the same time that its
preservation contained the very seeds of diatonic disintegration. The notion
of tonic and nontonic pitches was clearly in place in this music: the medieval tonaries testify to the gradual penetration of tonic validity from the
beginnings and endings of chant into the more freely disposed middle
portions of a given melody. Tonal validity becomes evident through the
examination of relationships between antiphons and psalm tones.

Furthermore, it is important to underscore that an early, decisive manifestation of tonal "vitalism" in the form of active and passive sonic stages
within temporal succession grew out of the medieval identification of these
tonic and nontonic components. This identification was secured by a human desire for tonal expectation and fulfillment, largely but not exclusively,
through the binary structure of parallelismus membrorum. That is, tonal
function in the form of sonic motion was dictated by the internal logic of
the texted phrase rather than superimposed from without by any general
notion as to the "naturalness" of the *Klang*. It is characteristic of early

Western tonality that tonal melodic form follows sonic linguistic function. The generality of this statement is not vitiated by the exceptions in early music that tend to oppose it: it is instead confirmed by them.

The emergence of polyphonic tonality sometime around the ninth century testifies to a residual polyphony in secular music that had been ignored by or excised from the Christian melos in its formative centuries. Thus the medieval theorists chose to treat it as a form of "ornament" to the chant for those musicians who wished to use it. Many did, but early acceptance of its existence even then did not inspire an immediate flowering of its potential. In retrospect, the music of St. Martial, Notre Dame, Compostela, and Winchester vibrates still with a rare and angular beauty, but their independent activities did not quickly secure any prevailing polyphonic practice for all of medieval Europe. Germany, for instance, was quite slow to adopt the polyphonic consciousness of France, Italy, and England.

Polyphonic tonality both absorbed and transformed the great monophonic legacy of the Church at the same time that it was itself determined by it. In a sense it represents a unique manifestation of "historicism" in the minds of independent composers who worked within the fixedness of a religious, musical praxis. While they revered the vast body of monophonic chant, and while it served as inspiration for polyphonic composition, at the same time it operated as a form of tonal control that directed polyphonic activity from within. For instance, there was the question about what to do with the previously composed chant in the first place. Over the course of several centuries it was placed in all possible positions within the vertical complex—top, bottom, and middle. As stated in chapter 5, I feel that the ecclesiastical chant was originally placed in the top voice of organum for purely theological reasons, that this particular form of treble domination by the cantus firmus was later abandoned for purely tonal reasons, and that the cantus firmus was even later moved from the bass to the tenor line for similar tonal reasons. Second, there were the orders of possible vertical combinations. Notions of harmonic motion were clarified by two activities: 1) the previously established formal validity of tonic repose at the monophonic cadence was preserved within the context of the new polyphonic phrase; and 2) the choices that were actually made for the intervallic orders within the polyphonic phrase juxtapose the creativity of harmonic composition against the tenuous classifications of consonant and dissonant sonorities. Thus, we find that the fourth was demoted from its position as a perfect consonance (the only interval ever to be harmonically devalued) and that thirds and sixths were given imperfect status as consonances perhaps because their very sonority (often called "sweet") was more important to composers than their theoretical position within the hierarchy of intervals.

The periodic debate in academic circles over the contrapuntal versus harmonic, or polyphonic versus homophonic, components of medieval and Renaissance tonality is, I think, a pseudoproblem. Polyphonic and homophonic writing exist side by side in literally thousands of pieces of music from 1350 to 1600, freely alternate with one another during the course of those pieces, and never indicate any angst on the part of composers that one style was about to overcome and gobble up the other in a war of vested tonal interests.

By the end of the sixteenth century, however, the polyphonic style, while perhaps not ever in conflict with the homophonic style, was gradually but decisively abandoned in favor of the latter. The reasons lay not in the dual principles of the polyphonic and homophonic styles at war with each other, but in the cognitive, social, and economic interests of composers and music makers themselves. Cognitively, it is still easier today to learn and to sing a homophonic chanson than a highly contrapuntal motet, and so must it have been in the Renaissance. With the invention of music printing from movable type around 1500, everyday consumption of music changed dramatically. The performance of vocal and instrumental music became accessible to thousands of musicians throughout Western Europe. What these frequently amateur musicians demanded, what they could perform without extensive training and constant practice were the light airy *frottole* and *balletti*, chansons and madrigals by the same composers who excelled also in the complexities of Renaissance contrapuntal art. Its accessibility ensured by treble dominated textures, with an easy rhythmic flow, and largely in major modes, this music was in these respects identical to the popular music currently aired on the modern, soft-rock radio station.

To characterize the seventeenth century as the happy emergence of key-centered music is to fail to understand its tonal roots in the music, both monophonic and polyphonic, that preceded it, a myopic exercise in naive facticity and poor musicology, a play with no prologue and a *dramatis personae* known only to its playwright. No such tonal phenomenon ever happened in Western music, and the dichotomy that current scholarship both describes and evaluates between Renaissance and baroque harmonic consciousness is at best unfortunate. The facts of the case are more accurately stated as follows.

It is a commonplace to characterize the key-centered homophonic practice of "common-practice" tonality as a distinguishing feature of the music composed from about 1600 to 1900. This is not the problem, but the origins of this key-centered tonal consciousness certainly are. Whether through cognitive necessity or aesthetic demands for recapitulation and symmetry, or both, these origins begin when consciousness chose to repeat any given pitch within its collective body of pitch data. It matters little now whether or not this "choice" was raised to the level of reflection and judgment or, ultimately, whether or not once brought to the level of reflection the motives given for such choice were actually the real ones at stake. I sincerely feel that my argument about Zarlino's conservatism regarding organizational of a polyphonic complex around the tenor ("this part being the principal guide for each mode, over which the song is composed") is a particular case in point. This is to say that all the music before the baroque era that demonstrates tones, intervals, chords, or chord complexes in succession in any fashion "centering"—through constant repetition—around certain pitch phenomena to the exclusion of the remaining pitches of the syntactic vocabulary was tonal music. It was key-centered in the most general sense. And this includes virtually all the music composed before the baroque era.

Let these remarks not be misunderstood. Part of what makes a piece of music by Bach key-centered is the notion of a tonic triad that functions *structurally* in the form of half- and whole-cadences at the same time as it functions *temporally* within harmonic successions in the form of prolongations of its sonority. This loyalty to and prolongation of a tonic occurs also in the thirteenth-century Montpellier motet *Quant voi—Virgo—Hec dies*, which is well-known to most readers of this book. There is of course no triad at strategic cadential points in this three-voice motet, only the interval A–E; but we do find this interval (which is determined by the tonal coherence of the previously existing chant *Hec dies*) and not a random series of fifths (over C–sharp, E–flat, and what have you) pulled out of a hat. Thus, tonal specificity was determined to a degree thought necessarily coherent by the composer. I am merely equating tonic loyalty of some sort— in terms of the operative agents of control directed toward pitch, interval, triad, or chord—as essential to *any* notion of key-centeredness, and this medieval motet possesses critical instances of such tonal specificity. What is *not* found in any given music makes it tonal just as importantly as what *is* found there.

The problem in current musicology and music theory is to establish and to understand the logic of this development without also subordinating it to the interests of the remarkable efficiency of key-centered music in its classic phase. One can only be surprised by "crystal clear expressions of C major" in early sixteenth-century music when he does not expect to find them there. When he expects them he rightly begins to understand the historical truth of the nature of tonal coherence as temporally generated through the practice of psalmody, cadential formulae in organa dupla, the use of the first-inversion "triad" in Machaut's music, and a great deal more. I will not therefore summarily restate the content of chapters 4 through 7 other than to underscore the notion that key-centeredness has both a general and a specific dimensionality and that the latter is absorbed within the former.

This *general* notion of key-centeredness is both the legacy of Landini and the exploitation (in the best sense of the term) of Mahler; it is a fundamental principle of tonal coherence enduring from the time of Gregory I to that of Barry Gibb. Key-centeredness predicates tonality with all the richness that it so rightly deserves in the form of unity, historical truth, and expressiveness. The differences are those of degree, not of kind.

Nonetheless, the seventeenth and eighteenth centuries brought into critical focus the unique features of a restrictive but thoroughly expressive mode of tonal coherence accurately characterized as being key-centered in the specific sense. Here the system of tonal functions gradually leveled chord vocabulary in the interests of establishing three main chords—the tonic, the dominant, and the subdominant triads—as the chief foci of both harmonic and melodic substance. Other triads assumed roles of substitution and extension for these three primary triads. As the system of equal temperament gained hegemony over all competing tuning systems, the potential of harmonic, key-centered tonality emerged as a strong, characteristic feature. Composers could move freely from one key to any other key no matter how distant it lay from it in the circle of fifths. The process of modulation by which transition was made from one key to another became the very critique of the inherent freedom that its momentary tonal ambiguity afforded.

In the nineteenth century the inherent freedom of modulatory procedures began to efface the clarity of the key centers it had formerly advanced. The freedom not to be established firmly in a key was taken as license for not attempting to reach one. This type of modulatory chromaticism, which had fostered the temporal concepts of anticipation and delay of key centers, was expanded beyond its mere formal dimension into the ongoing harmonic substructure of the work itself. In addition, immediate chromatic utterance for expressive reasons within an ostensibly diatonic context, a context that had been present in music for centuries, became in the hands of romantic composers an agent for personal harmonic expression. Expressive, chromatic harmony became alienated harmony in a good sense. It meant the tonal representation of the out-of-the-ordinary, the objectification of inner states, moods, and perceptions of composers who as tonal artist-heros were expected to authenticate their visions as both melodically and harmonically unique. In the rarefied world of German cultural idealism this exaltation of individualism led to the destruction of a common tonal language and prepared the world for tonal modernism.

Thus, it was during the romantic period that tonality gradually began to part company with itself. The customary judgment of this ever-encompassing harmonic freedom through chromatic excess is that it led directly and irrevocably into the dizzying abyss of twelve-tone consciousness. This judgment *is* true for the works of the composer-hero who had unwittingly also assumed the role of tonal prophet for the system so exploited—Wagner not so unwittingly. But it is *not* true for the greatest portion of the music composed during the nineteenth century (beginning with the waltz craze of the Strauss dynasty) nor for that music most popular with audiences. The abdication of key-centered tonality by the alienated, elitist composer became its absolute contradiction in the form of continued and extended resourcefulness as simplified, universal sonic communication. Thus, a simplified, public key-centered tonality, running parallel to a "music in transition," gradually manifested itself as an overpowering object of historical truth. Tonality became a commodity to be bought and sold.

Before I remark on this simplified, mainstream tonality, let me take up the thorny issue of "atonal tonality." First, twelve-tone tonality was but a species of moment in a general negation, felt at the turn of the twentieth century, that manifested itself among a plurality of less radical tonal appearances: bitonality, polytonality, pantonality, neomodality, neoprimitivism, neoclassicism, futurism, and neoromanticism. None of these appearances possessed characteristic tonal features of such profound dissimilarity to key-centered music as did twelve-tone music. Second, twelve-tone music in its mature stage did annul the notion of key-centeredness in its specific dimensionality, although not always in its general dimensionality of loyalty to pitches and intervals and chords (for instance, the music of Berg). But if twelve-tone music can—and does at times—completely efface key-centered music (and all characteristic loyalties), how does it remain tonal? The answer is a simple one: by the continuing operation of the cognitive *ratio* as composer upon the inherited reservoir of pitch data, that is, twelve pitches within the chromatic scale. Taking the half-step as the smallest melodic and harmonic point of reference, twelve-tone composers both speculated upon and composed a music in which loyalties were ignored in favor of other forms of tonal coherence. Not so curiously, this music still tended toward the customary notions of anticipation, delay, and fulfillment but did so with other than the harmonic means available to key-centered music. Thus, tonal disclosure, stasis, unfolding, succession, progression, and conclusion were still objectified by such means as timbre, rhythm, texture, melodic gesture, intervallic coherence and order, volume, tempo, and so forth. To be sure, the most aggressive attempt to obliterate these temporal components entirely from twelve-tone music appears most critically in total serialism. But even there, while the techniques used were largely successful in bringing about the deterioration and destruction of what we might call "temporally understood" tonality, they were not wholly successful (a fact that serialists did not fully comprehend but John Cage did). Whether or not twelve-tone composition as generally conceived will surface as a dominant form of tonal utterance in the remaining years of this century and into the next is a matter of speculation. Since the principle by which its most successful works have been conceived and composed is human expression (instead of artifice for its own sake), I feel that it can. The dialectic by which this method of composition works has been suggested in chapter 11.

It is not twelve-tone tonality that will determine the tonality of the future, however, although it will certainly figure in it. The future of tonal consciousness will be determined by the interests of the ruling forces in society. In the case of capitalistic societies they are economic; in those that are aesthetically characterized by socialist realism they are comprehensibility and collectivity. (At least this is what the defenders of socialist music claim.) In either case the outcome is the same—tonality simplified.

It is folly to assume that there will be a tonal revolution in the near future. Such an assumption can only be held by those who also assume that there have been tonal revolutions in the past. That is, if revolution means the overthrow of one class, government, or social system, with another taking its place, then by analogy this never happened in the history of Western music. Key-centered, homophonic tonality did not overthrow modal, polyphonic tonality (such knee-jerk analysis is much too simplistic): it only transformed it. The reason we cannot claim a tonal revolution is that since the appearance of the monophonic melos in Western culture the same chromatic scale, as a potential historically suggested by the earliest recognition of the half-step in the Greek tetrachord, has been theoretically ready to serve the interests of musical creation—from early Christian chant to the present. I do not wish to raise the notion of scale to an ontological status within musical consciousness, only to suggest the importance of the *ratio* to its interests.

But there has been a revolution *with* music, and it was made possible through the implicit nature of its utterance in mass tonality, in the sonic form of what I have identified in chapter 10 as tonality simplified. The birth and development of rock and roll music heralded the first significant body of music in the world ever to be created, produced, and consumed by children, which the baby booms in America, Europe, and Japan provided in great abundance following World War II. By the late 1950s, youngsters between the ages of nine or ten and seventeen or eighteen, predominantly the children of working-class parents, constituted a new class of customers and consumers that was a relatively larger portion of the population than ever before in the twentieth century. While the musical segment of the culture industry—Capitol Records, MGM, RCA Victor, Columbia Records, and ABC Records—catered to and exploited the tastes of its young audience, the audience decisively determined the nature of the tonal image by its willingness to accept the most mundane key-centered music in the form of thousands of dance-songs that fed their insatiable appetite for novelty, frequently sustained by soft and hard drugs. Unschooled in anything but the most rudimentary principles of chordal harmony, they consciously sought to revolutionize music: they did so successfully in the realm of lyrics, tempo, beat, and volume; but since no tonal revolution had even been dimly conceived (more accurately, did not even appear to consciousness), tonality rigidified and hardened around tonal components far less radical than those of a fifteenth-century chanson.

In none of the current literature has anybody admitted that the phenomenon of mass tonality is the single most pervading component of those forms of mass culture which in any fashion whatsoever are involved with music: specifically radio, television, film, and the making of live and recorded music. This tonality is understood on both the unconscious and the conscious level by hundreds of millions of people around the world. This tonality easily accounts for *all* the popular music of the last two centuries—from the waltz, brass-band music, operetta, and the Victorian hymn in the nineteenth, to American band music, ragtime, jazz, blues, swing, rock, country and western, reggae, easy listening, gospel (black and white), soul, and the Broadway musical in the twentieth. There is no form of popular music in the modern, industrialized world that exists outside the province of mass tonal consciousness. It is the tonality of the church, school, office, parade, convention, cafeteria, workplace, airport, airplane, automobile, truck, tractor, lounge, lobby, bar, gym, brothel, bank, and elevator. Afraid of being without it while on foot, humans are presently strapping it to their bodies in order to walk to it, run to it, work to it, and relax to it. It is everywhere. It is music and it writes the songs.

This tonality is held in contempt by the elite tonalist at the same time that he demands that its "fundamentals" be taught (and tested and graded) in music schools, conservatories, colleges, and universities here and abroad—all this study in order that the "true" young musician who seeks wisdom may learn these fundamentals and then reject them as a form of authentic music making. The establishment justifies the ideological position that it takes toward the required education of this tonality on the premise that it is the basis of the "common-practice" period, but it must not be commonly practiced by those who aspire to membership within the elect and elite sphere of the serious musician. (The study of jazz, the most recent addition to the university curriculum, is an exception.) The general assumption is that because mass tonality is a commodity, because it exists in the interests of profit making and profit sharing, it is contaminated. The fact that Monteverdi made his livelihood from it is forgotten.

Because the meaning of a given historical form of tonality is located both in its function as a social symbol and its utility as an object of human productivity, the late twentieth century is tonally characterized by the most profound contradictions in the form of musical objects. Critical tonality (an early, working title for this book) is an attempt to interpret these contradictions with the utmost clarity. Current writing about tonality discloses its own weaknesses and is largely unaware of its ideology. It does not understand that the cognitive abilities and disabilities of human music makers (which this book has been able only to suggest because they lie within the sphere of psychology and physiology) decisively determine musical objects. The undeniable fact that the music of mass culture (both serious and popular) is exploited as a commodity, rather than as a product of true human usefulness and resourcefulness, figures in none of the reasons that are offered for the conservative approach taken toward the traditional training of "common-practice" tonality in academic institutions. In addition, current tonal analysis fails to realize that, along with the phenomena of number, the physical gesture, and the visual picture, tonality as semiotic gesture offers daily confirmation that there are fundamental vehicles for human communication that quite encompass and absorb the customary social divisions of nation and language. These crucial components of musical understanding and communication are shunted aside by the modern music theorist and musicologist in favor of explanatory modes of analysis that are rigidified and imprisoned within the precision of a system. This system is hypostatized through the authoritative agents of a *ratio* that is impressed with its own fascination with mathematics, that is quite unaware of its dependency upon sonic vitalism to maintain its interests, and—most unfortunately—that guards its utility as musical thought so forcibly that criticism of its activity is regarded as treason. Critical tonality is a restoration of the creating subject to the sphere of investigation of tonal works. Its usefulness lies not in any forecast for the future of tonal consciousness; rather it lies in a necessary, at times surprising, self-correction of what has been a historically misunderstood development of man's potential and desire for making music.

=========== **Notes**

Complete publishing information can be found in the Bibliography.

INTRODUCTION

1. Apel, *Harvard Dictionary of Music*, p. 855.
2. Cazden, "Tonal Functions and Sonority in the Study of Harmony," p. 21.
3. Kim, "Carl Gustav Hempel," pp. 473–74. Hempel's "covering-law model" first appeared in "Studies in the Logic of Explanation" (1948, with Paul Oppenheim). Its application to historical explanation aroused extensive controversy. For a collection of viewpoints, see Dray, *Philosophical Analysis and History*. For the complete text of Mendel's address, see "Evidence and Explanation," pp. 3–18.
4. Williams, *Culture and Society, 1780–1950*, p. 323.
5. In the early stages of writing this book, I coined this phrase in an effort to restore tonality to its creator-subject. With or without its Hegelian perspective, it appears in Leibowitz, *Schoenberg and His School*, p. 32.

CHAPTER 1

1. Adorno, *Negative Dialectics*, p. 25. The central thesis of these essays is ably demonstrated by a modest paraphrase from Adorno. He was not, of course, speaking of tonality in this passage, although his credentials and interest in things musical would have qualified him to participate in its critique. He was speaking of the *concept* of a philosophic system, and it is the modern concept of tonality as system and its necessary negation that is of concern here.

It is impossible to express my debt to Adorno even in this longish note. *Negative*

Dialectics should be read by those who wish fully to understand my methodology. I have relied heavily on it, particularly for the critique of tonal speculation under consideration in the first two chapters. See also his *Philosophy of Modern Music*, *Introduction to the Sociology of Music*, and *Prisms*. Only gradually are the Adorno musical articles in European sources being translated into English, an activity for which the editors of *Telos* deserve just praise. Anne Mitchell Culver has completed a dissertation on Adorno; see "Adorno's *Philosophy of Modern Music*: Evaluation and Commentary." See also Blomster, "Adorno and His Critics: Adorno's Musico-Socio-logical Thought in the Decade Following His Death"; and Subotnik, "Adorno's Diagnosis of Beethoven's Late Style: Early Symptom of a Fatal Condition." Professor Subotnik writes that even though Martin Jay's book (*The Dialectical Imagination*) "has aroused considerable attention in other disciplines, American musicology has continued to show little interest in one particularly celebrated member of the Frankfurt School, Theodor W. Adorno (1903–1969), an outstanding musical scholar, philosopher, and critic who developed some provocative theories of art: that Western art has tended toward increasing autonomy from society; that the more autonomous the work of art is, the more deeply it embodies the most profound social tendencies of its time; and that proper analysis can decipher the social meaning of artistic structure so as to criticize art and society simultaneously" (p. 242). Until Adorno is digested (and this is difficult) as the most direct musical spokesman of Critical Theory, there can be no further progress in current musicology. He is the only effective antidote for Pythagoras.

In view of this high praise, which Adorno certainly deserves, I must also register here a word of caution for those who attempt to understand him. Adorno "has been criticized for being a Marxist; for being a poor Marxist; for being a bourgeois reactionary and elitist; and for being intolerably fatalistic" (ibid., p. 270). To me, obviously, being a Marxist is not a fault: Adorno would not have accomplished what he did within the context of any other philosophy. Indeed, he was a Marxist of a rather curious stripe, and I cannot develop and analyze here the contradictions that his work exhibits. Had he lived longer, we can only speculate on whether or not he would have seen his own negation of the negation at work in contemporary music, for in new music we see this active motion of spirit. Its path is clear: from classic tonality to Schoenberg to Hans Werner Henze there runs the Adornian double negation, of tonality, of consciousness which, happily, in the works of Henze, has arrived at an authentic commitment to music as a vehicle of social energy that is both critical and passionate at the same time. Henze's *Das Floss der 'Medusa'* is the perfect tonal analog of Picasso's *Guernica*. I shall develop this dialectic in chapter 11. A very fine general introduction to the genesis of Critical Theory is the book mentioned above, by Jay, *The Dialectical Imagination*.

2. By virtue of my definition I regard all musics of all societies as tonal. Music in nonliterate societies may afford absolutely no theoretical speculation as to its creation, but unconscious decisions made against the chaos of pitch are no less important than conscious ones. The tonality discussed in this book is Western tonality—from Ancient Greece to the present. I have great admiration for but no expertise in ethnomusicology. However, particularly with regard to chapter 3, comparative to-

nality is not only possible but highly germane to the assessment of human tonal consciousness.

3. Adorno, *Negative Dialectics*, p. 11.

4. Treitler, "On Historical Criticism," p. 201.

5. Ibid., p. 202.

6. Křenek, *Music Here and Now*, pp. 131–40.

7. Treitler, "On Historical Criticism," p. 200. Treitler is quoting a summary paragraph of Crocker, *A History of Musical Style*, p. 525, which I shall give here in full: "Musical materials have to be 'used up,' their potential fully exploited, before style can move ahead on the long line of history. As in a development section by Beethoven, the material already introduced has to be shredded down to its constituent fibers, all its meaning extracted, before new material will seem meaningful."

8. Webern, *The Path to the New Music*. In the winter of 1932, Webern, whose music was already proscribed by the Nazi regime, gave a series of eight lectures in a private house in Vienna, to an audience paying a small entrance fee. These were perhaps the first formal lectures on atonality. In the spring of 1933 he presented a second series of eight lectures. The two series are quite different in content. In the former, Webern was more didactic, attempting to explain the coherence of his own music, as well as Schoenberg's and Berg's, through appeals of unity and comprehensibility. The transcriptions of these lectures from shorthand notes by Dr. Rudolf Ploderer are necessarily brief because Webern spent much of the time playing music at the piano. He seemed eager in these lectures to jettison "tonality in its last throes" in favor of music that was to be conceived in light of "new laws." The following year, however, he sought a different approach in the second set of lectures. Goethe, who had earlier been cited as an authority on artistic production, became the main court of appeal to justify the new music. Webern's plan now seemed to be to prove that atonal music was the most natural thing in the world, that is, that it proceeded—as Schenker also believed that tonality did—"according to true and natural laws." The following is typical:

"Goethe sees art as a product of nature in general, taking the particular form of human nature. This is to say, there is no essential contrast between a product of nature and a product of art, but that it is all the same, that what we regard as and call a work of art is basically nothing but a product of nature in general. . . . Just as a researcher into nature strives to discover the rules of order that are the basis of nature, we must strive to discover the laws according to which nature, in its particular form 'man,' is productive" (pp. 10–11).

The thrust of this later series of lectures was to prove that musical notes evolved through "natural law as related to the sense of hearing, just as Goethe had sought to prove that 'color is natural law as related to the sense of sight.' " Thus twelve-tone music was merely following a physical determinist course, thoughtfully using the gifts of a natural world, this in a world that had become so unnatural that Schoenberg fled Europe for fear of his life. Readers of the English edition of the lectures should note that editor Willi Reich has reversed the presentation of the two lecture series in order to point up the assumed "natural" foundations that the new music sought as a way in which to rationalize its path to social legitimacy.

9. Adorno, *Negative Dialectics*, p. 333.

10. Narmour, *Beyond Schenkerism*, p. 31.

11. Berry, *Structural Functions in Music*, p. 27.

12. Ibid.

13. Ibid., p. 28; emphasis mine.

14. Reimer and Evans, *The Experience of Music*, p. 76.

CHAPTER 2

1. Lang, *Music in Western Civilization*, p. 974.

2. For an examination of the historical notion of tonality, see Simms, "Choron, Fétis, and the Theory of Tonality," pp. 112–39.

3. Bukofzer, *Music in the Baroque Era*, pp. 219–20.

4. Ibid., p. 12.

5. Ibid.

6. Simms, "Choron, Fétis, and the Theory of Tonality," p. 119.

7. Ibid., pp. 115–19.

8. Ibid., p. 120.

9. Boyden, *An Introduction to Music*, 1st ed., p. 36; unchanged in the 2nd edition, 1970.

10. Blume, *Renaissance and Baroque Music*, p. 128.

11. Ibid., p. 129.

12. Stevenson, *Western Music*, p. 100.

13. Lowinsky, *Tonality and Atonality in Sixteenth-Century Music*, p. 62.

14. Wienpahl, "Modality, Monality and Tonality in the Sixteenth and Seventeenth Centuries," 52:404–17; 53:59–73. See also his "The Evolutionary Significance of 15th Century Cadential Formulae," pp. 131–52. The first article is largely a reduction of part of Wienpahl's dissertation, "The Emergence of Tonality." The title is unfortunate.

15. Rosen, *The Classical Style: Haydn, Mozart, Beethoven*, p. 23.

16. Hoppin, *Medieval Music*, p. 72.

17. Apel, *Harvard Dictionary of Music*, p. 855.

18. Reimer and Evans, *The Experience of Music*, p. 52.

19. Christ, Delone, and Winold, *Involvement with Music*, p. 52.

20. Berry, *Structural Functions in Music*, p. 27.

21. Rameau did not consider diminished and augmented triads to be "chords," since no complete chord could exist without a perfect fifth. Cf. *Treatise on Harmony*, pp. 48–52; *Code de musique*, pp. 95ff. It is instructive here to mention the "Rameau-is-not-at-all-like-Schenker" debate but, it is to be hoped, without getting embroiled in its argument. Eugene Narmour notes that "some writers have allied Schenker to Rameau—e.g., Michael Mann, "Schenker's Contribution to Music Theory," *The Music Review* 10 (February 1949):19. But this conclusion is mistaken. . . . In Rameau, tone generation from acoustical phenomena is translated directly into chord generation (musical phenomena); a succession of chords identified by the *basse fondamentale* 'explains' the function of the voices. In Schenker, however, the

theory is somewhat the opposite: contrapuntal voice-leading principles determine the function of the chords." See *Beyond Schenkerism*, p. 4, n. 3.

We may quibble about how Rameau and Schenker evolved their methodologies, but the platform on which they erected them remains the same—the generation of musical tones, that is, human tonal production from natural sonic phenomena. This notion is bourgeois idealism and in both cases it leads to contradictions which neither theorist ever resolved. With his own "implication-realization" model Narmour has successfully freed himself from the spell of Schenker. For its application to tonality, see pp. 135–36. Note the critique that Narmour himself gives of his model in chapter 12, especially "the lack of a good psychological theory of memory, particularly as it pertains to syntactic systems" (p. 213).

22. Summarized in Shirlaw, *The Theory of Harmony*, 2nd ed., p. 134.

23. Ibid., p. 135.

24. *New Grove Dictionary*, 15:561.

25. Actually, *fundamental bass* is a theoretical statement about harmonic motion. It does not sound: it actualizes itself in the actual bass, or *basso continuo*. Compare these remarks by Joan Ferris about Rameau's *basse fondamentale* with the Schenkerian scale-step to be discussed shortly: "The bass should proceed slowly with respect to the upper parts, moving by consonant intervals so that each sound harmonizes with the preceding sound. The upper parts should move diatonically and generally more quickly than the bass (*Traité de l'harmonie*, p.50). . . . The fundamental bass is not a sounding part, but is only given to show how the harmonies move. The fundamental bass notes bear all kinds of chords (i.e., chords in root position and in inversion)." See Ferris, "The Evolution of Rameau's Harmonic Theories," p. 240.

There is a remarkable connection to be made here. The conceptualization by Zarlino of the *harmonia perfetta* has two aspects: the harmonic generation of the triad via the *senario*; and—stated acoustically—the notion that this triad was bottom heavy in frequency value. Zarlino's *Istitutioni Harmoniche* appeared a century and a half before Rameau's *Traité* and testifies, I think, to the popular, modern tonality of its time. When sixteenth-century composers in Italy imitated the secular music of the citizenry around them, they wrote simple, chordal pieces with sturdy basses on diatonic tones. Two things were happening harmonically between 1400 and 1600: the cantus firmus itself began to disappear, first by migrating throughout the upper voices; in secular music it was missing entirely. And second, the bass began to carry the harmony. Rameau did not have to establish the fundamental bass in the bottom voice. It had already been placed there by Renaissance practice. (I shall take up this topic in detail in chapter 6.) Rameau's contribution to tonal modeling lies importantly in his statement that this fundamental bass *as such* could detach itself from its bass and bottom position and move freely *as an abstraction* throughout the texture of the music. A good basso continuo realization would testify to the inner logic of the composer's harmony. This was a significant day for classic tonality.

26. Schenker, *Harmony*, p. 29.

27. Ibid.

28. Ibid., p. 40.
29. Ferris, "Evolution of Rameau's Harmonic Theories," p. 236.
30. Ibid., p. 232.
31. Schenker, *Harmony*, p. 38.
32. Ibid.
33. Ibid., p. 52.
34. Ibid., p. 53.
35. Rameau, *Treatise on Harmony*, p. 62. Gossett's translation of this passage reads: "If each of these sounds bore a perfect chord, the mind, not desiring anything more after such a chord, would be uncertain upon which of these two sounds to rest. Dissonance seems needed here in order that its harshness should make the listener desire the rest which follows."
36. Mackey, "The Evolution of the Leading Tone in Western European Music to *circa* 1600 A. D." A bewildering study.
37. Only the tonic should be a perfect chord. Sevenths should appear on all the other root tones of the diatonic scale. If the dominant was not to be followed by the tonic, it could appear without its seventh; otherwise, in perfect cadences, it must be a seventh chord. Cf. Rameau, *Treatise on Harmony*, bk. II, chap. 13; bk. III, chap. 6.
38. Schenker, *Harmony*, pp. 21–25.
39. Schenker, "The Dissonance Always Consists of Passing Notes; It Never Constitutes Harmonies."
40. Schenker, *Harmony*, pp. 133–53.
41. Ibid., p. 152.
42. Ibid.; see the musical examples in Section 80, "How to Recognize Scale-Steps: Some Hints," pp. 141–51.
43. Ibid., p. 212. The cognitive organization of the ego's personality is reinforced, narrowed, or expanded through what Schenker calls its attentiveness to "harmonizability."
44. Ibid.; see Sections 116 and 117, pp. 212–14.
45. Ibid., p. 213.
46. Ibid., p. 256.
47. Ibid., p. 261.
48. Ibid., pp. 272–73.
49. Ibid., p. 288.
50. Ibid., pp. 321–36.
51. I have left untouched Schenker's contrapuntal studies—the second volume (in two parts) of *Neue musikalische Theorien und Phantasien*, 1910 and 1922, which, with the *Harmonielehre*, the issues of *Tonwille*, and the Yearbooks, are synthesized in *Der freie Satz*, published in the year of Schenker's death. This total system has yet to be adequately evaluated. *Der freie Satz* was first translated by Krueger as a doctoral dissertation, *"Der Freie Satz* by Heinrich Schenker: A Complete Translation and Re-editing"; there is a new "official translation" by Ernst Oster. A portion of the yearbooks has been translated; see Kalib, "Thirteen Essays from the Three Yearbooks *Das Meisterwerk in der Music* by Heinrich Schenker: An Annotated Translation." This is a welcome addition to the Schenker translations, despite its great bulk

which could have been alleviated by a smaller typescript. Kalib's Glossary (Vol. I; repeated in Vol. II) is helpful. For those who want only the translations, they are all in Vol. II.

I refuse to collaborate in any way with Schenker by actually citing any of of his highly idiosyncratic remarks about the world of music as he saw it. The reader can only be amused or angered by what he finds scattered throughout the pages of *Der freie Satz* and the essays. Sylvan Kalib is quite generous with Schenker in this regard and offers the following reason for his troubled Weltanschauung: "Still another difficulty encountered in the reading of Schenker is due to the fact that one frequently encounters derogatory statements and many attacks on theorists, composers, musical styles, and/or attitudes concerning them. . . .

"[Schenker] concludes that the definition of music as an art had to be based on the organizational possibilities of tones themselves in the absolute sense, without the assistance of any secondary source such as a text, program, colors, textures, etc. He deduced the basis of such an absolute art to be found in the natural overtone series and its unfolding by the assistance of the extended application of the centuries-long established principles of voice-leading, as expressed in strict counterpoint. As is well known, Schenker found the realization of that definition to be exemplified most ideally in the works of the great masters of the eighteenth and nineteenth centuries—more specifically, only twelve composers in all: D. Scarlatti, J. S. Bach, Handel, C. P. E. Bach, Haydn, Mozart, Beethoven, Schubert, Schumann, Mendelssohn, Chopin, and Brahms. Living in the latter part of the nineteenth and early part of the twentieth centuries, Schenker lived through the period that witnessed the trend of composers of that time to depart more and more from the composition of absolute music and to concentrate increasingly on works based on dramatic and programmatic content. These trends, in addition to the gradual departure from the principles of tonality, were viewed by him as a withdrawal farther and farther from the principles of structural organization embodied in the above definition, and consequently, as the disintegration of music as an art. In consequence of this, he viewed with contempt and personally identified deep resentment any factor contributing to or pointing in any way to that trend. It is the expression of this feeling that is at the root of all angry condemnations in his writings." See Kalib, "Thirteen Essays," Vol. I, pp. xiii–xv.

52. There are a number of *systems* of classic tonality, and I have selected two which I thought were of paramount importance here. A good general survey is Shirlaw's *Theory of Harmony*. As a system for analyzing, describing, and evaluating the structural functions of harmony, *Funktionslehre* has always been popular. It was developed by Karl Wilhelm Julius Hugo Riemann (1849–1919), a distinguished German musicologist in the late nineteenth century, whose prodigious efforts covering every branch of musical science—particularly those in harmony and the history of it—were instrumental in laying the foundations of modern musicology. Riemann's attempt to structure the essentials of harmonic progressions "is based on the idea that in a given key there are only three 'functionally' different chords, namely tonic (I), dominant (V), and subdominant (IV). All other combinations, even the most complex and chromatic, are variants of one of these three chords,

i.e., they have a tonic-function, dominant-function, or subdominant-function" (Apel, *Harvard Dictionary of Music*, p. 337). The remaining chords in the diatonic scale and chromatic alterations of it become substitutions for the tonal strength believed to reside in the primary triads. Of course there are problems. The substitution triad may come from a third above or a third below the primary triad. Thus, both vi and iii may stand for I in a given progression. Since iii can stand for both I and V, which in tonal modeling are assumed to be opposites, the ambiguity caused by the mediant triad is then determined by its function within the course of the progression. The "directive force" of the progression somehow decides whether iii is articulating the extension and/or substitution of the tonic or the dominant qualities of harmonic motion.

Developed in *Vereinfachte Harmonielehre* (1893), Riemann's system gained a following outside Germany and is taught today—with sundry modifications—as a method which, like Schenker's, allows harmonic motion to be conceived in terms of its chief focal points. See Riemann, *Harmony Simplified*; cf. Shirlaw, *Theory of Harmony*, pp. 387–410.

53. See Adorno, *Negative Dialectics*, p. 196.
54. Schenker, *Harmony*, p. 133.
55. Mann, "Schenker's Contribution to Music Theory," pp. 3–26. The reader may wish to consult the meager early biographic data before 1949 and the initial attempts to describe the system. See Mann's References, pp. 3–5.
56. Ibid., p. 21.
57. Forte, "Schenker's Conception of Musical Structure," p. 3.
58. Warfield, *Layer Analysis: A Primer of Elementary Tonal Structures*, p. 92.
59. Cogan and Escot, *Sonic Design*, pp. 71–78.
60. Berry, *Structural Functions in Music*, pp. 40–41.
61. Salzer, *Structural Hearing*, vol. I, p. 30.
62. Horkheimer, "Traditional and Critical Theory," p. 196.
63. Ibid., p. 197.
64. Ibid., p. 198.
65. Ibid., p. 200; emphasis mine.
66. Ibid., p. 231.
67. Ibid., p. 210–11.
68. Ibid., p. 201.

CHAPTER 3

1. Kilmer, Crocker, and Brown, "Sounds from Silence." See the illustrated booklet that accompanies the recording of a Hurrian Cult Song from Ancient Ugarit (ca. 1400 B.C.). This is a fascinating tonal study.
2. Burkert, *Lore and Science in Ancient Pythagoreanism*, chapters 4 and 5.
3. Weber, *Rational and Social Foundations of Music*, p. 40.
4. Ouspensky, *In Search of the Miraculous*, particularly chapter 7. This is heady stuff.
5. Marx, "Production and Consumption," pp. 34–35; emphasis mine.

6. See Meyer's "Law of Good Continuation," in *Emotion and Meaning in Music,* pp. 92–127; also "Process continuation," in the Index, p. 303.

7. Lukács, "Art as Self-Consciousness in Man's Development," pp. 233–34.

8. Adorno, "On the Fetish-Character in Music and the Regression of Listening," pp. 270–99. It is unfortunate that Adorno became so involved in a knee-jerk reaction to the fetish-character in music (which indeed exists) that he failed to understand the deeper levels of cognitive appropriation of tonality through melodic activity. In 1938 he writes: "Melody comes to mean eight-beat [-bar?] symmetrical treble melody. This is catalogued as the composer's 'idea' which one thinks he can put in his pocket and take home, just as it is ascribed to the composer as his basic property.... A Beethoven symphony as a whole, spontaneously experienced, can never be appropriated. The man who in the subway triumphantly whistles loudly the theme of the finale of Brahms' First is already primarily involved with its debris. But since the disintegration of the fetishes puts these themselves in danger and virtually assimilates them to hit songs, it produces a counter-tendency in order to preserve their fetish character" (pp. 277, 281).

To be sure, Adorno is to be credited for underscoring the fact that melodic success is achieved by "the memorability of disconnected parts, thanks to climaxes and repetitions, [and] has a precursor in great music itself, in the technique of late romantic compositions, especially those of Wagner" (p. 281). And certainly, melody was doomed to become the debris of fetishization of late industrial capitalism. But a societal and thereby cognitive component exists historically before Adorno's problem, where its moral imperative is ontologically grounded in the very nature of sonic phenomena. Adorno did not see this fact, although Marx did—as witnessed in the quotation above. I have stated it several times in this section: a melody is *for* someone, and its success as communication depends primarily upon the social character of human personality. A melody must have a content, either linguistic, symbolic, behavioral, or purely figural, and this content must be comprehensible to the listener.

There is a critical moment in the life of Charles Ives that renders this fact clearly evident. As is well known, Ives declined to market his music because he knew that through commodity exchange the integrity of his own self-production would evaporate in the vicissitudes of an illusory public freedom and economic necessity. But early in May of 1923, "a thin, balding New York business man in his late forties left at the New York Public Library a book that he had just had privately printed." The book was a copy of Ives' now famous "114 Songs," which he brought to the Library as a curious public act of commitment to tonal communication. "Some of the songs," wrote Ives in a typical 'Postface,' that tried to explain his highly subjective creations, "cannot be sung." But a song, he continued, "has a *few* rights, the same as other ordinary citizens." The metaphor of the song as citizen is one that the Greek philosopher of music Damon would have readily understood. For a song has duties too, to be a song for someone, which duty the librarians dimly understood, the Library being the acknowledged repository for the collective melos. It kept the book of this unknown composer and someone penciled in a note on the back of the title page: "Composer, May 18, 1923." Thus the unique tonal vision of Charles Ives began its own long, often unnoticed, sonic odyssey through the uncharted seas of the

American melos. Paradoxically, the first serious attention paid to Ives' melodies was by a recording company whose reputation had been founded on the preservation of *folk* music. Quotations from Charters, brochure for "Charles Ives Songs."

9. Nettl, *Music in Primitive Culture*, pp. 136–37.
10. Weber, *Rational and Social Foundations of Music*, p. 40.
11. Gerson-Kiwi, "Religious Chant: A Pan-Asiatic Conception of Music," p. 64.
12. Ibid., p. 67.
13. Ibid., p. 65.
14. Werner, *The Sacred Bridge*, p. 129.
15. *Liber Usualis*, p. 117.
16. Werner, *The Sacred Bridge*, p. 347.
17. Ibid.
18. All percentages are approximate.
19. See n. 6.
20. *New Grove Dictionary*, 15:483.
21. Ibid., 13:799.
22. Ibid., 8:186.

CHAPTER 4

1. Burkert, *Lore and Science in Ancient Pythagoreanism*, p. 224.
2. The sifting out of early Pythagoreanism from the Platonized Pythagoreanism reflected in the Academy would founder but for Aristotle, who sought to distinguish between Platonism and Pythagoreanism. A thorough Aristotelian critique is difficult to achieve, and perhaps it is impossible without the few authentic fragments of Philolaus; but it is apparent to Burkert and Kahn that it yields positive results. Cf. Kahn, "Pythagorean Philosophy Before Plato," pp. 161–85; Burkert, *Lore and Science*, pp. 15–52. Scholars of pre-Socratic philosophy have no doubt discovered Burkert's book, but permit me to recommend it to all musicians who are interested in early Greek music theory. It is a superb piece of research and thought. See in particular, part V, "Pythagorean Musical Theory," to which I am indebted far beyond mere footnote citations. Cf. Crocker, "Pythagorean Mathematics and Music," pp. 189–98; 325–35. Crocker's reconstruction of Pythagorean music theory does not seek to penetrate beyond 400 B.C.
3. Burkert, *Lore and Science*, p. 378.
4. Homer, *Odyssey*, 5.246–48.
5. "B" numbers refer to the *Fragmente* sections of Diels, *Die Fragmente der Vorsokratiker*, 6th ed., I, pp. 406–19; trans. Freeman, *Ancilla to the Presocratic Philosophers*, pp. 73–77. For B1, B2, and the first half of B6, I have given Burkert's translations—with a few modifications to point up their specific use of the term *harmonia* and its derivatives. See Burkert, *Lore and Science*, pp. 250–53 for the Greek and his translations. Note that he does not give all of B2 and that he connects the first half of B6 to it, for reasons that are explained in part III, chapter 2. The remainder of B2 is my translation.

6. Guthrie, *The Earlier Presocratics and the Pythagoreans*, p. 280.

7. Burkert's translation; see *Lore and Science*, pp. 251–52.

8. My translation; cf. Freeman, *Ancilla*, p. 74.

9. Burkert, *Lore and Science*, p. 40.

10. Plato, *Republic* 617b; cf. 530d and *Cratylus* 405c.

11. Burkert, *Lore and Science*, p. 355.

12. Plutarch, *De Defectu Oraculorum* 422b.

13. Cicero, *Academica Posteriora*, II, 39.

14. Cf. Schrade, "Music in the Philosophy of Boethius," pp. 188–200; Ellinwood, "Ars Musica," pp. 290–99; Chamberlain, "Philosophy of Music in the *Consolatio* of Boethius," pp. 80–97. A comprehensive study of Boethius and his historical influence on music has yet to be written.

15. Bower, "Boethius' *The Principles of Music*, An Introduction, Translation, and Commentary."

16. Knowles, "Boethius," 1:330.

17. Ibid.

18. Ibid., p. 329.

19. Ibid.

20. Boethius' friend Cassiodorus, who also worked in the court of Theodoric, tells us that Boethius translated "Ptolemy the astronomer." This treatise was mentioned by Gerbert, but it has not survived.

21. See Weisheipl, "Classifications of the Sciences in Medieval Thought," pp. 54–90; cf. Stahl, *Martianus Capella and the Seven Liberal Arts*.

22. Varro's influence is recoverable through Aulus Gellius, Censorinus, Augustine, Cassiodorus, and Isidore of Seville, an interesting set of connections.

23. Bower, "Boethius' *Principles*," p. 17.

24. Plato, *Republic* 532b.

25. Boethius, *De Institutione Arithematica*, I, i. Quoted in Bower, "Boethius' *Principles*," p. 27. Bower's dissertation also includes an English translation of the first book of *De Institutione Arithematica*.

26. Wiora, *The Four Ages of Music*, p. 127.

27. For a detailed examination of the sources for *De Institutione Musica*, see Bower's Commentary, "Boethius' *Principles*," pp. 333–69.

28. It would be amazing (not to say exciting) if we could establish a link between Greek music theory and early Christian musical practice, but even Nicomachus' Syrian connections afford us no platform from which to launch any such investigation. Victor Tcherikover notes that "of the cultural activity of the Greek cities of Palestine in the Hellenistic period we hear absolutely nothing. Nor can they be compared with the Hellenistic cultural centers of Egypt or Asia Minor, such as Alexandria or Pergamum. Palestine was a remote corner from the Greek cultural point of view, and when we have said this we have exhausted the issue" (Tcherikover, *Hellenistic Civilization and the Jews*, p. 115).

29. Cazden, "Pythagoras and Aristoxenus Reconciled," p. 101. Unfortunately, Hellenistic-minded medieval theorists did not subscribe to *JAMS* and there was no reconciliation. Pythagorean concepts dominated theoretical activity for some two millennia.

30. Ibid., p. 98.

31. Cf. Reese, *Music in the Middle Ages*, pp. 38–40; Winnington-Ingram, *Mode in Ancient Greek Music*, pp. 62–71.

32. Bower, "Boethius' *Principles*," pp. 275–78.

33. Ibid., p. 276n.

34. Ibid., p. 289.

35. Ibid., p. 289n.

36. Reese, *Music in the Middle Ages*, p. 155.

37. Bower, "Boethius' *Principles*," pp. 467–69.

CHAPTER 5

1. Apel, *Harvard Dictionary of Music*, p. 687.

2. Bower et al., "A Bibliography of Early Organum," p. 45.

3. Spiess, "An Introduction to the Pre-History of Polyphony," p. 14. Spiess's concluding paragraph reads: "On the basis of available evidence it is not possible to show satisfactorily the existence of a continuous practice of polyphony before the ninth century works which have sometimes been attributed to Hucbald. If we except theoretical references (which do not necessarily point to a contemporary polyphonic practice) and the heterophony of Greek antiquity, there is no scientific evidence extant to prove beyond question that there was a rudimentary polyphonic practice before the organum of the ninth century."

4. Apel, *Harvard Dictionary of Music*, p. 383.

5. Worner, *History of Music*, p. 20.

6. The first problem this will solve will be to permit a better understanding for polyphony in thirds in medieval Britain in favor of an initial preference for polyphony in fifths and fourths on the Continent.

7. Unfortunately, Maróthy's early development of this concept is found in *Az europai nepdal születese* (The Birth of European Folk Song, 1960), which has not been translated; but its thesis is liberally scattered throughout his *Music and the Bourgeois; Music and the Proletarian*. For a review of this book, see Norton and Bokina, *Telos*, 28:227–234.

8. Spiess, "Introduction to the Pre-History of Polyphony," p. 11.

9. Worner, *History of Music*, p. 19. The categories themselves are respectable enough; it is the manner in which they were determined that weakens their effectiveness. Very briefly, and to quote Adorno, we are "no longer entitled to transpose, as a residual definition, a kind of minimum object into the direct data by means of subjective reduction." The more "purified" polyphony becomes via its early categories, the scantier and the more abstract are the data to secure them. All tension between the cognitive abilities and disabilities in which the phenomenon of monophonic/ur-polyphonic/polyphonic expression arose is lost as the subject defines a sphere of absolute origins. See Adorno, *Negative Dialectics*, especially part II.

10. Worner, *History of Music*, p. 21; emphasis mine.

11. Reese, *Music in the Middle Ages*, p. 256.

12. Spiess, "Introduction to the Pre-History of Polyphony," p. 11.

13. Reese, *Music in the Middle Ages*, p. 255.

CHAPTER 6

1. Crocker, "Discant, Counterpoint, and Harmony," p. 1.

2. Lester, "Major-Minor Concepts and Modal Theory," p. 218, n. 26.

3. Ibid.

4. Grout, *History of Western Music*, p. 109.

5. Among the current music history texts one finds remarks to the effect that if the medieval composer had "paid attention" to his harmony, he would have produced vertical sonorities more acceptable to modern harmonic analysis. He is thereby subjected to both cognitive deficiency and an irresponsible attitude toward the perfection of Western tonality. It is difficult to see why he should be judged in these terms.

6. Ultan, *Music Theory*, p. 163; emphasis mine.

7. Ibid., p. 206.

8. Crocker, "Discant, Counterpoint, and Harmony," p. 1.

9. The following passage from Franco of Cologne's *Ars cantus mensurabilis* is frequently cited with reference to this procedure: "He who shall wish to construct a triplum ought to have the tenor and discant in mind, so that if the triplum be discordant with the tenor, it will not be discordant with the discant, and vice versa. And let him proceed further by concords, ascending or descending now with the tenor, now with the discant, so that his triplum is not always with either one alone." See Strunk, *Source Readings in Music History*, p. 155.

10. Gustave Reese, for example; see p. 115 above.

11. The fifteenth century exhibits diverse activity in the treatment of the tenor, whose migration I have generalized in its most important aspects here—top, bottom, and middle of the polyphonic texture. For an extensive study of its activity in the Middle Renaissance, see Sparks, *Cantus Firmus in Mass and Motet*.

12. Readings in the *Journal of the American Society of Acoustics* over the last half-century reveal that most often psychoacoustical observations are made with only the sine wave (because there are fewer variables), less often with composite tones (single *Klänge*) such as are heard in (monophonic) music, and very infrequently with composite dyads (two *Klänge* heard simultaneously). The literature on triadic cognition and how the ear processes this tonal data is virtually nonexistent; and it is with the psychoacoustical observation of the triad, of course, that (classic) tonality must establish its sonic ontology.

13. In this regard, one of the most open approaches to the problem of tonality and psychoacoustics is made by Westergaard in his unassuming but provocative chapter "What are We Talking About?" in *An Introduction to Tonal Theory*. See also the Appendix.

14. For those who are unfamiliar with the process of auditory cognition (and that includes many of us), I recommend a short and readable book, Blumenthal, *The Process of Cognition*.

15. Cogan and Escot, *Sonic Design*, p. 447.

16. Gulick, *Hearing: Physiology and Psychophysics*, p. 174.

17. Cogan and Escot, *Sonic Design*, p. 379.

18. Combination tones were observed by the German organist Georg Andreas Sorge in his most important work, *Vorgemach der musicalischen Composition* (3 vols.; 1745–47), but with the credit of discovery laid to the famous Italian violinist Giuseppe Tartini, who claimed to have observed first order difference tones (albeit incorrectly) in 1714. Helmholtz writes: "The pitch of a combination tone is generally different from that of either of the generating tones, or of their harmonic upper partials. In experiments, the combinational are readily distinguished from the upper partial tones, by not being heard simultaneously with the second tone. Combinational tones are of two kinds. The first class, discovered by Sorge and Tartini, I have termed *differential* tones, because their pitch number is the difference of the pitch numbers of the generating tones. The second class of *summational tones* having their pitch equal to the *sum* of the pitch numbers of the generating tones, were discovered by myself" (Helmholtz, *On the Sensations of Tone*, p. 153).

19. Grout, *History of Western Music*, p. 164.

20. Bukofzer, *Music in the Baroque Era*, p. 10.

21. Cannon, Johnson, and Waite, *The Art of Music*, p. 128; emphasis mine.

22. Crocker, *A History of Musical Style*, p. 154; cf. p. 142.

23. Crocker, "Discant, Counterpoint, and Harmony," pp. 6–7.

24. Ibid., pp. 2–3.

25. Ibid., p. 3.

26. Ibid., pp. 6–7.

27. Ibid., p. 9.

28. Ibid., p. 12; cf. n. 9 supra.

29. Quoted in Crocker, "Discant, Counterpoint, and Harmony," p. 4.

30. Ibid.

31. Hughes, *History of European Music*, p. 86; emphasis mine.

32. Reese, *Music in the Middle Ages*, p. 295; cf. pp. 388ff.

33. Grout, *History of Western Music*, p. 125; cf. Brown, *Music in the Renaissance*, p. 35.

34. Lester, "Major-Minor Concepts and Modal Theory," pp. 208–09 and the notes.

35. Slonimsky, *Baker's Biographical Dictionary of Musicians*, p. 1937.

CHAPTER 7

1. Apel, *Gregorian Chant*, p. 203.

2. Ibid.

3. Ibid., p. 205; see Figure 37.

4. For reasons of economy only, I restrict myself to a general discussion of the psalm tones. There are, of course, in addition to the tones for prayers and collects, the tones for the Canticles (similar to but more elaborate than the psalm tones), the melodies for the verses of the Introits (also a system of eight tones), the responsorial tones, and the tones of the Invitatory Psalm (whose many tones were never organ-

ized into a system that corresponded with the eight church modes). See ibid., pp. 226ff.

5. Apel, *Harvard Dictionary of Music*, p. 166. Apel does not feel that g was raised in mode 4 in order to correspond with the raising of b to c' in mode 3. The alterations in modes 3, 4, and 8 "appear as early as the eleventh century, in the *De Musica* of Johannes Cotton, and remained unchanged thereafter." Apel bases his opinion on the fact that in the *Commemoratio brevis* (c. 900) the tenor was either g or g–a (with two tenors, as in the *tonus peregrinus*). This a could not have been explained "in consequence of the raise of the tenor in the third psalm tone, since the tenor had not yet changed" (See *Gregorian Chant*, pp. 211ff.).

6. Werner, *The Sacred Bridge*, pp. 144–59. The chief strata of liturgical music in the synagogue and the early Christian church can be grouped into three important categories: psalmody, hymn, and melismatic song. Tonally, all of these practices are highly significant, but certainly psalmody is to be reckoned as one of the greatest gifts from the vast cultural wealth of ancient Jewish religion. Up to the fourth century, all the primitive Christian liturgies—Syrian, Jewish, Byzantine—were in some part made up of quotations, paraphrases, and transformations of the Psalter, which itself was centrally located in the oldest and most venerable practice of scriptural lessons. Regarding *parallelismus membrorum*, Werner notes, "without the parallelism of diction our musical and liturgical expressions would be so much poorer, probably as monotonous as only constant hymn-singing could be. The abundance of varied forms, the scope of artistic imagery, all this is only understandable in light of the fundamental concept of scriptural dichotomy" (p. 129).

7. Apel, *Gregorian Chant*, p. 152.

8. Ibid., p. 218.

9. Ibid., p. 219.

10. Hoppin, *Medieval Music*, p. 83.

11. Apel, *Gregorian Chant*, p. 222.

12. Ibid.

13. This was a characteristic concern of the authors of the medieval *tonaria*. For a careful study of one of these tonal catalogs, see Le Roux, "The *De Harmonica Institutione* and *Tonarius* of Regino of Prüm": Latin text with English translation of *De Harmonica Institutione*, chapter 2; background and sources for the history and development of the *tonaria*, chapter 3; a comparative study of the *tonaria*, including Regino of Prüm's *Tonarius*, chapter 4.

14. Apel, *Harvard Dictionary of Music*, p. 589.

15. Quoted in Riemann, *History of Music Theory*, p. 13.

16. Similarities in terminology relate the five treatises. Cf. Riemann, ibid., pp. 253–56; Apel, "The Earliest Polyphonic Composition and its Theoretical Background," pp. 129–37; Spiess, "Diatonic 'Chromaticism' of the *Enchiriadis* Treatises," pp. 1–6. The chapters on organum in *Musica Enchiriadis* are 13–18. In some manuscripts, the Paris *De Organo* is found in this section of the *Musica Enchiriadis* instead. Excerpts of the *Scholia* are found in Strunk, *Source Readings in Music History*, pp. 126–38.

17. Cf. Riemann, *History of Music Theory*, pp. 61–70; Reese, *Music in the Middle*

Ages, pp. 259–60. Critical Latin edition in *Corpus Scriptorum de Musica*, 4. Four independent commentaries from the Middle Ages can be found in *Expositiones in Micrologum Guidonis Aretini*.

18. Cf. Riemann, ibid., pp. 76–79; Reese, ibid., pp. 261ff. Critical Latin edition in *Corpus Scriptorum de Musica*, 1.

19. Cf. Riemann, ibid., pp. 70–75; Reese, ibid., pp. 262ff. Ed., with an introduction, translation, and notes by Huff, *Music Theorists in Translation*, 8.

20. De la Fage, *Essais de dipthérographic musicale*, 1, pp. 355ff; partly reprinted in Handschin, "Zur Geschichte der Lehre vom Organum," pp. 321ff. See Waite, "Discantus, Copula, Organum," pp. 77–87.

21. Translated and discussed by Fred Blum, "Another Look at the Montpellier Organum Treatise," pp. 15–24.

22. One (Bibliotheque Nationale MS 1139) dates from the end of the eleventh century, two (BN MSS 3719 and 3549) from the twelfth century, and the fourth (British Museum Additional MS 36681) seems to be a composite of fragments from several places and times.

23. Treitler, "The Polyphony of St. Martial," p. 33.

24. Hoppin, "Tonal Organization in Music Before the Renaissance," p. 26. Concerning *ouvert* and *clos* endings and their tonal coherence, Hoppin writes: "In secular monophony, *ouvert* and *clos* endings furnish logical proof that a consciousness of the tonal center must have been established at the beginning. The *ouvert* ending, after all, comes before the *clos* and would be utterly pointless if the hearer did not already know that it was not the final. The same situation, of course, exists in the polyphonic ballade, although the vertical combinations and progressions of polyphony greatly increase the means by which incompleteness in the *ouvert* ending may be indicated." Hoppin's essay is a superior piece of scholarship and thought, with some provocative statements directed at the "common-practice" theory of tonality. Hoppin rightly "wonders whether this view of tonality is not too narrow. Music since 1900 has surely taught us that functional harmony within the major-minor system is no longer a *sine qua non* for the establishment of tonal centers. Perhaps it never was" (p. 25).

25. Grout, *History of Western Music*, pp. 154–56.

CHAPTER 8

1. Bukofzer, *Music in the Baroque Era*, p. xiv.

2. Hanslick, *The Beautiful in Music*, p. 11.

3. See chapter 3, n. 1.

4. Apel, *Gregorian Chant*, pp. 301–04, especially the last paragraph.

5. Ibid., p. 302.

6. Ibid., p. 303.

7. See Marx's critique of Feuerbach in the Sixth Thesis; cf. Lukács, *The Young Hegel*, p. 477.

8. Ibid., pp. 483ff.

9. Maróthy, *Music and the Bourgeois; Music and the Proletarian*, pp. 17–18.

10. Davison and Apel, *Historical Anthology of Music*, vol. 1, p. 227. See No. 105b for the music.

11. *New Grove Dictionary*, 4:513–14.

12. Lang, *Music in Western Civilization*, p. 223.

13. The reader may begin to think by now that my view of tonality is one which always sees tonal consciousness working its way inward from the beginning and end of the phrase, be it *parallelismus membrorum* or, as here, a Renaissance chanson. I submit that this is indeed true if other factors of tonal consciousness are also kept in focus. The several descriptions of the activities of the beginning and end melodic units (here and elsehwere) mean that they were the first places where consciousness became self-conscious to the degree that it established orders which all would cognize as formal necessities.

14. Reese, *Music in the Renaissance*, p. 430.

15. Lester, "Major-Minor Concepts and Modal Theory," p. 212.

16. Ibid., p. 213.

17. Ibid., p. 216.

18. Ibid., p. 218.

19. Ibid.

20. Ibid., p. 221.

21. *New Grove Dictionary*, 11:17.

22. Strunk, *Source Readings in Music History*, p. 382.

23. Kivy, *The Corded Shell*.

24. Jensen, *The Muses' Concord*, p. 48.

25. Bukofzer, *Music in the Baroque Era*, p. 300.

26. Lenneberg, "Johann Mattheson on Affect and Rhetoric in Music," p. 48. Cf. Harriss, *Johann Mattheson's "Der vollkommene Cappellmeister*," p. 105. This chapter was written when only Lenneberg's English translation of certain portions of *Der vollkommene Cappellmeister* was available. Either out of stubbornness or gratitude I give his translations for the discussion here. The corresponding passage in Harriss's complete translation is given for each citation.

27. Ibid., p. 56; cf. Harriss, p. 110.

28. Ibid., p. 57; cf. Harriss, pp. 451–52.

29. Ibid., p. 68; cf. Harriss, p. 466.

30. Ibid., p. 69; cf. Harriss, p. 467.

31. Ibid., pp. 69–70; cf. Harriss, pp. 283–84.

32. Ibid., p. 70; cf. Harriss, p. 284.

33. Harriss, *Johann Mattheson's "Der vollkommene Cappellmeister*," formely Harriss's dissertation.

34. Lenneberg, "Johann Mattheson," p. 48.

35. Mattheson cites Athanasius Kircher, author of *Masurgia universalis* (1650); Glareanus; and Johann Michael Crovinus, author of *Heptachordum danicum* (1646); see ibid., p. 234.

36. Ibid., pp. 234–36.

37. For a discussion of this in musical terms, see chapter 8, "Contour and Convention," in Kivy, *The Corded Shell*, pp. 71–83.

38. Blume, *Renaissance and Baroque Music*, pp. 121–22.

39. Blume notes that "the Italian Baroque brought forth the showy forms of musical vital to court and church ceremony. Court and church requirements blended so intimately that the Baroque became without more ado the age of court art and aristocratic cultivation of music and the aristocratic spirit set its stamp upon this music. . . . Almost every published work was dedicated to a patron, a Maecenas, a spiritual or worldly lord, ruler, gentleman. . . . If in the Renaissance period the cultivation of music by a high-ranking citizenry was responsible for musical creativity—even the courts of the period bore this burgher-like stamp, and the prince was the first among his subjects—in the Baroque, the emphasis shifted heavily toward the side of court and church aristocracy, and here the personality of the ruler or dignitary assumed a central position" (ibid., pp. 157–58).

40. For a translation of Bach's title page and dedication, see David and Mendel, *The Bach Reader*, pp. 82–83.

41. Blume, *Renaissance and Baroque Music*, p. 111.

42. Apel, *Harvard Dictionary of Music*, p. 194.

CHAPTER 9

1. Mattheson, *Der vollkommene Capellmeister*, part II, chapter 14. Mattheson immediately cautions against a rigid application of these parts of a good speech to musical form, but does suggest that "with diligent examination of good speeches as well as good melodies, these components, or most of them, can actually be discovered in a clever sequence. . . . "

2. I am indebted to Professor Herbert Brün of the University of Illinois at Champaign not only for the particular phraseology given here but also for sharing his insights into the nature of tonality and classic form in music.

3. Rosen, *Sonata Forms*. Rosen's notion of tonality is not mine, but this book is a superb achievement.

4. Barford, "The Sonata Principle," p. 261.

5. Because my analysis of the sonata-form principle is already an effort to bring to bear upon it the activities of classical rhetoric and Hegelian dialectic, I have omitted a still further—but closely related and very useful—concept, that of hierarchic construction, which the sonata clearly exhibits. My use of the adjective hierarchic is intended to reflect this concept, however, and a brief explanation is in order for those who wish it. I am indebted to Leonard Meyer's discussion and development of this concept in *Music, the Arts, and Ideas*.

Functionalism in music, notes Meyer, "may be defined as the implications which one musical event—be it a tone, a motive, a phrase, or a section—has for some other musical event either on its own hierarchic level of some other" (p. 296). Although they are by no means mutually exclusive, we can isolate two distinct types of tonal function in baroque and classic music—*additive* and *hierarchic* construction.

A number of baroque musical forms can be accurately characterized as consisting of additive components that were more or less interchangeable in nature. This process had its roots in the Renaissance motet, madrigal, chanson, and Mass movement in which lines of text were successively set forth in polyphonic or chordal fashion until a whole was built up of units that housed a specific portion of poetry. In the baroque period, fugue, chorale prelude, theme and variation (including passacaglia and chaconne), and ritornello technique also exhibit this additive process. On the microlevel, the ritornello subject itself is built up from a series of short phrases added one to the other, to be terminated in a cadential phrase that secures the key. (The first movement of Bach's second Brandenburg Concerto is a superior example of this.) On the macrolevel, as the form unfolds in time, these phrases are not so much developed as they are added together in different combinations, and "development" consists of different arrangements of this subject matter in various keys with episodes between them for contrast.

Hierarchic construction was of a different order, and the drama of tonality in instrumental forms came to depend on the gradual realization that its dynamic and its dialectic rested on a principle that lay parallel to the additive process but transformed it from within. By analogy, let me explain this process in the familiar terms of the modern university system. Its activities, responsibilities, and privileges are hierarchically ordered one above the other, all the way from the student who may apply for a work-study grant to the chancellor who may not. An exemplary system might feature a chancellor, vice-chancellors, deans, associate and assistant deans, department chairmen, faculty, nonacademic staff, and students. Some of the activities of these levels must be viewed as "closed out" in terms of their function; others are not. For example, a chancellor may teach a course in his discipline if his schedule permits, say chemistry, but a secretary cannot enter into contract negotiations and hire a professor for the chemistry department. To paraphrase Meyer here, the function of each component of the academic system, broadly speaking, may be defined as the *implications* that one professional activity has for some other professional activity either on its own hierarchic level or some other. Classic composers created the sonata form on the order of hierarchic structure that tonally functioned in terms of key centers that became its very dialectic.

6. Rosen, *The Classical Style*, p. 70.
7. Ibid., p. 26.
8. Ibid., p. 83.
9. Barford, "The Sonata Principle," p. 258.
10. Ibid.
11. Rosen, *The Classical Style*, pp. 72–73.
12. Crocker, *A History of Musical Style*, p. 356.
13. Rosen, *The Classical Style*, p. 26.
14. As applied to the temporal musical object, "virtual" and "virtually" in this book signify a more precise context than is customarily assumed. For a discussion of this notion, as developed by Susanne Langer, see my article "What is Virtuality?"
15. See chapter 2, n. 52.

CHAPTER 10

1. Blume, *Classic and Romantic Music*, p. 122.
2. I know no better way to establish the thesis of this chapter than through this conscious paraphrase of a statement from Marcuse, *The Aesthetic Dimension*, p. 6.

3. *New Grove Dictionary*, 1:884.

4. *New Grove Dictionary*, 4:47–48.

5. *New Grove Dictionary*, 4:849.

6. Ibid.

7. Blume, *Classic and Romantic Music*, p. 145.

8. See Lang, *Music in Western Civilization*, pp. 816–25, for an excellent discussion of this problem.

9. Tanner, "The Total Work of Art," p. 214.

10. Redlich, *Bruckner and Mahler*, p. 153.

11. Lang, *Music in Western Civilization*, p. 818.

12. Ibid., p. 885.

13. Grout, *A Short History of Opera*, p. 415; first two emphases mine.

14. Quoted in Crocker, *A History of Musical Style*, p. 458.

15. Kerman, *The Beethoven Quartets*, p. 119.

16. Ibid., p. 95.

17. Ibid., p. 123.

18. *New Grove Dictionary*, 8:181.

19. Samson, *Music in Transition*, pp. 156ff.

20. Raynor, *Music and Society*, p. 150.

21. *New Grove Dictionary*, 20:203.

22. Raynor, *Music and Society*, p. 154.

23. Ibid., p. 153.

24. Hitchcock, *Music in the United States*, p. 108.

25. Ibid., p. 114.

26. *New Grove Dictionary*, 15:117.

CHAPTER 11

1. Schoenberg, *Theory of Harmony*, p. 432.

2. Ibid., p. 27.

3. Peyser, *The New Music*, p. 15.

4. Ibid., pp. 16–17.

5. Ibid., p. 21.

6. Stuckenschmidt, *Arnold Schoenberg*, p. 42.

7. Schoenberg, *Theory of Harmony*, pp. 387–88.

8. Ibid., p. 13.

9. Ibid.

10. Ibid., p. 15.

11. Ibid., p. 10.

12. Ibid., p. 11.

13. Ibid.

14. Ibid., p. 18.

15. Ibid., p. 19.

16. Ibid., p. 23; emphasis mine.

17. Ibid., p. 24.

18. Ibid., p. 399.

19. Ibid., p. 24.

20. Ibid., p. 385.

21. See chapter 1, n. 8.

22. Schoenberg, *Theory of Harmony*, p. 425.

23. Schoenberg, *Style and Idea*, p. 104.

24. Ibid., p. 105.

25. Quoted in Austin, *Music in the Twentieth Century*, p. vi.

26. Ibid., p. 222.

27. Adorno, *Philosophy of Modern Music*, pp. 30, 37.

28. Ibid., p. 39.

29. Ibid., p. 41.

30. Ibid., p. 46.

31. Adorno, *Prisms*, p. 162.

32. Adorno, *Philosophy of Modern Music*, pp. 68–69.

33. Adorno, *Prisms*, p. 165.

34. Ibid.

35. Ibid., p. 166. I have compressed Adorno's dialectic here through paraphrase and minimal quotation. Some of the Schoenberg essay in *Prisms* is quite woolly, but I suggest that it be read before *Philosophy of Modern Music*.

36. *New Grove Dictionary*, 16:706.

37. *New Grove Dictionary*, 20:278.

38. Webern, *Path to the New Music*, p. 32.

39. *New Grove Dictionary*, 20:273.

40. See Translator's Preface (Leo Black) to the Universal Edition, Webern, *Path to the New Music*.

41. *New Grove Dictionary*, 20:276.

42. Webern, *Path to the New Music*, p. 34.

43. Ibid., pp. 34–35.

44. Ibid., p. 35.

45. Ibid., p. 37.

46. Ibid., p. 18.

47. *New Grove Dictionary*, 20:279.

48. Adorno, *Philosophy of Modern Music*, p. 37.

49. Boulez, "Schoenberg is Dead," pp. 21–22.

50. Kingman, *American Music: A Panorama*, p. 518.

51. Wuorinen, "What Concerns Me is Music," p. 18.

52. Babbitt, "Who Cares If You Listen?" p. 126; emphasis mine.

53. Sleeve note, CRI 138; quoted in Griffiths, *Modern Music*, pp. 37–38.

54. Stuckenschmidt, "German Musical Life," p. 352.

55. For a semiotic analysis of this statement, see Norton, "Musik als tonal Geste," pp. 9–31.

56. Grout, *A History of Western Music*, p. 727.

57. See, in particular, "An Interview with Hans Werner Henze," broadcast on WFMT-Radio, Chicago, 3 December 1972.

58. Liner notes for Henze, *Doppio Concerto per Oboe, Arpa et Archi*, DGG 139396.
59. Sartre, *Essays in Aesthetics*, pp. 71–72.
60. Correspondence with the composer.
61. Vásquez, *Art and Society*, p. 265.

Bibliography

In the bibliographic entries that follow, *New Grove Dictionary* refers to *The New Grove Dictionary of Music and Musicians*, edited by Stanley Sadie, 20 volumes (London: Macmillan, 1980).

BOOKS AND ARTICLES

Adorno, Theodor W. *Introduction to the Sociology of Music*. Translated by E. B. Ashton. New York: Seabury, 1976.

———. *Negative Dialectics*. Translated by E. B. Ashton. New York: Seabury, 1973.

———. "On the Fetish-Character in Music and the Regression of Listening." In *The Essential Frankfurt School Reader*. Edited by Andrew Arato and Eike Gebhardt. New York: Urizen Books, 1978.

———. *Philosophy of Modern Music*. Translated by Anne G. Mitchell and Wesley V. Blomster. New York: Seabury, 1973.

———. *Prisms*. Translated by Samuel and Shierry Weber. London: Neville Spearman, 1967.

Apel, Willi. "The Earliest Polyphonic Composition and its Theoretical Background." *Revue Belge de Musicologie* 10 (1956): 129–37.

———. *Gregorian Chant*. Bloomington: Indiana University Press, 1958.

———, ed. *Harvard Dictionary of Music*. 2nd ed. Cambridge: Harvard University Press, 1969.

Aristotle. *The Works of Aristotle*. Edited by W. David Ross. 12 vols. Oxford: Clarendon Press, 1921.

Austin, William W. *Music in the Twentieth Century*. New York: Norton, 1966.

Barford, Philip T. "The Sonata Principle." *Music Review* 13 (1952): 255–63.

Berry, Wallace. *Structural Functions in Music.* Englewood Cliffs, N.J.: Prentice-Hall, 1976.

Blomster, Wesley V. "Adorno and His Critics: Adorno's Musico-Sociological Thought in the Decade Following His Death." In *Musicology at the University of Colorado.* Boulder: University of Colorado, 1977.

Blum, Fred. "Another Look at the Montepellier Organum Treatise." *Musica Disciplina* 13 (1959): 15–24.

Blume, Friedrich. *Classic and Romantic Music.* Translated by M. D. Herter Norton. New York: Norton, 1970.

———. *Renaissance and Baroque Music.* Translated by M. D. Herter Norton. New York: Norton, 1967.

Blumenthal, Arthur L. *The Process of Cognition.* Englewood Cliffs, N.J.: Prentice-Hall, 1977.

Boulez, Pierre. "Schoenberg is Dead." *The Score* 6 (1952): 18–22.

Bower, Calvin Martin. "Boethius' *The Principles of Music:* An Introduction, Translation, and Commentary." Ph.D. dissertation, George Peabody College for Teachers, 1966.

———, James R. Briscoe, Dean Douglas File, Judith Fisher, and Ross W. Ellison. "A Bibliography of Early Organum." *Current Musicology* 21 (1976): 16–45.

Boyden, David D. *Introduction to Music.* New York: Knopf, 1964.

Brown, Howard M. *Music in the Renaissance.* Englewood Cliffs, N.J.: Prentice-Hall, 1976.

Buelow, George J. "Johannes Lippius." *New Grove Dictionary* 11:17.

Bukofzer, Manfred F. *Music in the Baroque Era.* New York: Norton, 1947.

Burkert, Walter. *Lore and Science in Ancient Pythagoreanism.* Translated by Edwin L. Minar, Jr. Cambridge: Harvard University Press, 1972.

Cannon, Beekman C., Alvin H. Johnson, and William G. Waite. *The Art of Music.* New York: Thomas Y. Crowell, 1960.

Cazden, Norman. "Pythagoras and Aristoxenus Reconciled." *Journal of the American Musicological Society* 11 (1958): 97–105.

———. "Tonal Function and Sonority in the Study of Harmony." *Journal of Research in Music Education* 2 (1954): 21–34.

Chamberlain, David S. "Philosophy of Music in the *Consolatio* of Boethius." *Speculum* 45 (1970): 80–97.

Christ, William, Richard Delone, and Allen Winold. *Involvement With Music.* New York: Harper and Row, 1975.

Cicero. *Academica Posteriora.* Translated by H. Rackham. Cambridge: Harvard University Press, 1933.

Cogan, Robert, and Pozzi Escot. *Sonic Design.* Englewood Cliffs, N.J.: Prentice-Hall, 1976.

Coker, Wilson. *Music and Meaning.* New York: Free Press, 1972.

Crocker, Richard L. "Discant, Counterpoint, and Harmony." *Journal of the American Musicological Society* 15 (1962): 1–21.

———. *A History of Musical Style.* New York: McGraw-Hill, 1966.

———. "Pythagorean Mathematics and Music." *Journal of the American Musicological Society* 22 (1963): 189–98; 325–35.

Dahlhaus, Carl. "Counterpoint." *New Grove Dictionary* 4: 843–52.

———. "Harmony." *New Grove Dictionary* 8: 175–88.

David, Hans T., and Arthur Mendel, eds. *The Bach Reader.* New York: Norton, 1966.

Davison, Archibald T., and Willi Apel, eds. *Historical Anthology of Music.* Vol. 1. Cambridge: Harvard University Press, 1946.

Diels, Hermann, ed. *Die Fragmente der Vorsokratiker.* 6th ed. Vol. 1. Dublin: Weidmann, 1964.

Dray, William H., ed. *Philosophical Analysis and History.* New York: Harper & Row, 1966.

Dunning, Albert. "Adrianus Petit Coclico." *New Grove Dictionary* 4: 513–14.

Ellinwood, Leonard. "Ars Musica." *Speculum* 20 (1945): 290–99.

Fage, Juste Adrien L. de la. *Essais de dipthérographic musicale.* Vol. 1. Paris, 1864.

Fellerer, Karl Gustav. "Cecilian Movement." *New Grove Dictionary* 4: 47–48.

Ferris, Joan. "The Evolution of Rameau's Harmonic Theories." *Journal of Music Theory* 3 (1959): 231–56.

Forte, Allen. "Schenker's Conception of Musical Structure." *Journal of Music Theory* 3 (1959): 1–30.

Freeman, Kathleen. *Ancilla to the Presocratic Philosophers.* Cambridge: Harvard University Press, 1962.

Gerson-Kiwi, Edith. "Religious Chant: A Pan-Asiatic Conception of Music." *International Folk Music Council Journal* 13 (1961): 64–67.

Girdlestone, Cuthbert. "Jean-Phillipe Rameau." *New Grove Dictionary* 15: 559–73.

Griffiths, Paul. "Anton Webern." *New Grove Dictionary* 20: 270–82.

———. *Modern Music: The Avant Garde since 1945.* New York: George Braziller, 1981.

Grout, Donald Jay. *A History of Western Music.* 2nd ed. New York: Norton, 1973.

———. *A Short History of Opera.* 2nd ed. New York: Columbia University Press, 1965.

Gulick, W. Lawrence. *Hearing: Physiology and Psychophysics.* New York: Oxford University Press, 1971.

Guthrie, W. K. C. *A History of Greek Philosophy.* Vol. 1. *The Earlier Presocratics and the Pythagoreans.* Cambridge: Cambridge University Press, 1962.

Hamm, Charles. "Popular Music." *New Grove Dictionary* 15: 97–121.

Handschin, Jacques. "Zur Geschichte der Lehre vom Organum." *Zeitschrift für Musikwissenschaft* 8 (1926): 321–41.

Hanslick, Eduard. *The Beautiful in Music.* Translated by Gustav Cohen from the 7th (1855) Leipzig edition. New York: Da Capo, 1974.

Harriss, Ernest C. *Johann Mattheson's "Der vollkommene Cappellmeister": A Revised Translation with Critical Commentary.* Ann Arbor: University Microfilms International Research Press, 1981.

Helmholtz, Hermann. *On the Sensations of Tone.* Translated by Alexander J. Ellis. New York: Dover, 1954.

Hempel, Carl Gustav, and Paul Oppenheim. "Studies in the Logic of Explanation." *Philosophy of Science* 15 (1948): 135–75.

Hitchcock, H. Wiley. *Music in the United States: A Historical Introduction.* Englewood Cliffs, N.J.: Prentice-Hall, 1969.

Homer. *Odyssey.* Translated by Richmond Lattimore. New York: Harper and Row, 1967.

Hoppin, Richard H. *Medieval Music.* New York: Norton, 1978.

———. "Tonal Organization in Music Before the Renaissance." In *Paul A. Pisk, Essays in His Honor.* Edited by John Glowacki. Austin: University of Texas, 1966.

Horkheimer, Max. "Traditional and Critical Theory." In *Critical Theory: Selected Essays.* Translated by Matthew J. O'Connell et al. New York: Seabury, 1972.

Huff, Jay A., trans. *Music Theorists in Translation.* Vol. 8. *Ad Organum Faciendum.* Brooklyn: Brooklyn Institute of Medieval Music, n.d.

Hughes, David G. *A History of European Music.* New York: McGraw, 1974.

Jay, Martin. *The Dialectical Imagination.* Boston: Little, Brown, 1973.

Jensen, H. James. *The Muses' Concord.* Bloomington: Indiana University Press, 1976.

Kahn, Charles H. "Pythagorean Philosophy Before Plato." In *The Pre-Socratics.* Edited by Alexander P. D. Mourelatos. New York: Anchor Books, 1974.

Kalib, Sylvan. "Thirteen Essays from the Three Yearbooks *Das Meisterwerk in der Musik* by Heinrich Schenker: An Annotated Translation." Ph.D. dissertation, Northwestern University, 1973.

Kerman, Joseph. *The Beethoven Quartets.* New York: Norton, 1966.

Kim, Jaegwon. "Carl Gustav Hempel." *The Encyclopedia of Philosophy.* Vol. 3. Edited by Paul Edwards. New York: Collier Macmillan, 1967.

Kingman, Daniel. *American Music: A Panorama.* New York: Schirmer, 1979.

Kivy, Peter. *The Corded Shell.* Princeton: Princeton University Press, 1980.

Knowles, David. "Boethius." *The Encyclopedia of Philosophy.* Vol. 1. Edited by Paul Edwards. New York: Collier Macmillan, 1967.

Křenek, Ernest. *Music Here and Now.* Translated by Barthold Fles. New York: Russell and Russell, 1967.

Krueger, Theodore Howard. "*Der Freie Satz* by Heinrich Schenker: A Complete Translation and Re-editing." Ph.D. dissertation, University of Iowa, 1960.

Lamb, Andrew. "Waltz." *New Grove Dictionary* 20: 200–06.

Lang, Paul Henry. *Music in Western Civilization.* New York: Norton, 1941.

Leibowitz, René. *Schoenberg and His School.* Translated by Dika Newlin. New York: Da Capo, 1975.

Lenneberg, Hans. "Johann Mattheson and Affect and Rhetoric in Music." *Journal of Music Theory* 2 (1958): 47–84; 193–236.

Le Roux, Mary Protase. "The *De Harmonica Institutione* and *Tonarius* of Regino of Prüm." Ph. D. dissertation, Catholic University of America, 1965.

Lester, Joel. "Major-Minor Concepts and Modal Theory in Germany, 1592–1680." *Journal of the American Musicological Society* 30 (1977): 208–53.

The Liber Usualis. Edited by the Benedictines of Solesmes. Tournai (Belgium): Desclee, 1965.

Lindley, Mark. "Pythagorean Intonation." *New Grove Dictionary* 15: 485–87.

Lowinsky, Edward E. *Tonality and Atonality in Sixteenth-Century Music*. Berkeley: University of California Press, 1962.

Lukács, Georg. "Art as Self-Consciousness in Man's Development." In *Marxism and Art*. Edited by Berel Lang and Forrest Williams. New York: David McKay, 1972.

———. *The Young Hegel*. Translated by Rodney Livingstone. Cambridge: Massachusetts Institute of Technology Press, 1976.

Mackey, Mary Lourdes. "The Evolution of the Leading Tone in Western European Music to *circa* 1600 A. D." Ph. D. dissertation, Catholic University of America, 1962.

Mann, Michael. "Schenker's Contributions to Music Theory." *Music Review* 10 (1949): 3–26.

Marcuse, Herbert. *The Aesthetic Dimension*. Boston: Beacon Press, 1978.

Maróthy, János. *Music and the Bourgeois; Music and the Proletarian*. Translated by Eva Róna. Budapest: Akademiai Kiado, 1974.

Marx, Karl. "Production and Consumption." In *Marxism and Art*. Edited by Berel Lang and Forrest Williams. New York: David McKay, 1972.

Mendel, Arthur. "Evidence and Explanation." In *International Musicological Society, Report of the Eighth Congress, New York, 1961*. New York: American Musicological Society, 1962.

Meyer, Leonard B. *Emotion and Meaning in Music*. Chicago: University of Chicago Press, 1956.

———. *Music, the Arts, and Ideas*. Chicago: University of Chicago Press, 1967.

Neighbor, O. W. "Arnold Schoenberg." *New Grove Dictionary* 16: 701–24.

Nettl, Bruno. *Music in Primitive Culture*. Cambridge: Harvard University Press, 1956.

Norton, Richard. "Musik als tonale Geste." In *Neue Aspekte der Musikalischen Ästhetik II. Die Zeichen*. Frankfurt: Fischer Verlag. 1981.

———. "What is Virtuality?" *Journal of Aesthetics and Art Criticism* 30 (1972): 499–505.

Norton, Richard, and John Bokina. Review of *Music and the Bourgeois; Music and the Proletarian* by János Maróthy. *Telos* 28 (1976): 227–34.

Narmour, Eugene. *Beyond Schenkerism*. Chicago: University of Chicago Press, 1977.

Ouspensky, P. D. *In Search of the Miraculous*. New York: Harcourt, Brace and World, 1949.

Peyser, Joan. *The New Music*. New York: Delacorte, 1971.

Plato. *The Collected Dialogues*. Edited by Edith Hamilton and Huntington Cairns. Princeton: Princeton University Press, 1961.

Rameau, Jean-Philippe. *Treatise on Harmony*. Translated by Philip Gossett. New York: Dover, 1971.

Raynor, Henry. *Music and Society*. New York: Taplinger, 1978.

Reckow, Fritz. "Organum." *New Grove Dictionary* 13: 796–803.

Redlich, H. F. *Bruckner and Mahler*. London: J. M. Dent, 1955.

Reese, Gustave. *Music in the Middle Ages*. New York: Norton, 1940.

———. *Music in the Renaissance*. New York: Norton, 1954.

Reimer, Bennett, and Edward G. Evans, Jr. *The Experience of Music*. Englewood Cliffs, N.J.: Prentice-Hall, 1972.

Riemann, Hugo, *Harmony Simplified, or The Theory of the Tonal Functions of Chords.* Translated by H. Bewerunge. London: Augener, 1895.
———. *History of Music Theory.* Books I and II. Translated by Raymond H. Haggh. New York: Da Capo, 1974.
Rosen, Charles. *The Classical Style: Haydn, Mozart, Beethoven.* New York: Norton, 1972.
———. *Sonata Forms.* New York: Norton, 1980.
Salzer, Felix. *Structural Hearing.* 2 vols. New York: C. Boni, 1952.
Samson, Jim. *Music in Transition.* New York: Norton, 1977.
Sartre, Jean-Paul. *Essays in Aesthetics.* Translated by Wade Baskin. New York: Citadel Press, 1966.
Schenker, Heinrich. *Harmony.* Translated by Elizabeth Mann Borgese. Edited by Oswald Jonas. Chicago: University of Chicago Press, 1954.
Schoenberg, Arnold. *Style and Idea.* New York: Philosophical Library, 1950.
———. *Theory of Harmony.* Translated by Roy E. Carter. Berkeley: University of California Press, 1978.
Schrade, Leo. "Music in the Philosophy of Boethius." *The Musical Quarterly* 33 (1947): 188–200.
Schwartz, Elliott and Barney Childs, eds. *Contemporary Composers on Contemporary Music.* New York: Holt, Rinehart and Winston, 1967.
Shirlaw, Matthew. *The Theory of Harmony.* New York: Da Capo, 1969.
Simms, Bryan. "Choron, Fétis, and the Theory of Tonality." *Journal of Music Theory* 19 (1975): 112–39.
Slonimsky, Nicolas, ed. *Baker's Biographical Dictionary of Musicians.* 6th ed. New York: G. Schirmer, 1978.
Sparks, Edgar H. *Cantus Firmus in Mass and Motet, 1420–1520.* Berkeley: University of California Press, 1963.
Spiess, Lincoln Bunce. "An Introduction to the Pre-History of Polyphony." In *Essays on Music in Honor of Archibald Thompson Davison.* Cambridge: Harvard University Press, 1957.
———. "Diatonic 'Chromaticism' of the *Enchiriadis* Treatises." *Journal of the American Musicological Society* 12 (1959): 1–6.
Stahl, W. H. *Martianus Capella and the Seven Liberal Arts.* New York: Columbia University Press, 1971.
Stevenson, Ronald. *Western Music.* New York: St. Martin's Press, 1971.
Strunk, Oliver. *Source Readings in Music History.* New York: Norton, 1950.
Stuckenschmidt, Hans H. *Arnold Schoenberg.* Translated by Edith Temple Roberts and Humphrey Searle. London: J. Calder, 1959.
———. "German Musical Life: Patterns of Conservatism and Experiment." In *Postwar German Culture.* Edited by Charles E. McClelland and Steven P. Scher. New York: E. P. Dutton, 1974.
Subotnik, Rose Rosengard. "Adorno's Diagnosis of Beethoven's Late Style: Early Symptom of a Fatal Condition." *Journal of the American Musicological Society* 29 (1976): 242–75.
Tanner, Michael. "The Total Work of Art." In *The Wagner Companion.* Edited by

Peter Burbidge and Richard Sutton. New York: Cambridge University Press, 1979.

Tcherikover, Victor. *Hellenistic Civilization and the Jews.* Translated by S. Applebaum. Philadelphia: Jewish Publication Society of America, 1959.

Temperley, Nicholas. "Bach Revival." *New Grove Dictionary* 1: 883–86.

Treitler, Leo. "On Historical Criticism." *The Musical Quarterly* 53 (1967): 188–205.

———. "The Polyphony of St. Martial." *Journal of the American Musicological Society* 17 (1964): 29–42.

Ultan, Lloyd. *Music Theory: Problems and Practices in the Middle Ages and Renaissance.* Minneapolis: University of Minnesota Press, 1977.

Vásquez, Adolfo Sánchez. *Art and Society.* Translated by Maro Riofrancos. New York: Monthly Review Press, 1973.

Waesberghe, Joseph Smits van, ed. *Corpus Scriptorum de Musica.* Vols. 1 and 4. Rome: American Institute of Musicology, 1950, 1955.

———. *Expositiones in Micrologum Guidonis Aretini.* Amsterdam: Musicologies Medii Aevi, 1957.

Waite, William G. "Discantus, Copula, Organum." *Journal of the American Musicological Society* 5 (1952): 77–87.

Warfield, Gerald. *Layer Analysis: A Primer of Elementary Tonal Structures.* New York: Longman, 1976.

Weber, Max. *The Rational and Social Foundations of Music.* Translated and edited by Don Martindale, Johannes Riedel, and Gertrude Neuwirth. Carbondale and Edwardsville: Southern Illinois University Press, 1958.

Webern, Anton. *The Path to the New Music.* Translated by Leo Black. Edited by Willi Reich. Bryn Mawr: Theodore Presser, 1963.

Weisheipl, James A. "Classifications of the Sciences in Medieval Thought." *Medieval Studies* 27 (1965): 54–90.

Werner, Eric. *The Sacred Bridge.* New York: Columbia University Press, 1959.

Westergaard, Peter. *An Introduction to Tonal Theory.* New York: Norton, 1975.

Wienpahl, Robert E. "The Emergence of Tonality." Ph. D. dissertation, University of California at Los Angeles, 1953.

———. "The Evolutionary Significance of 15th Century Cadential Formulae." *Journal of Music Theory* 4 (1960): 131–52.

———. "Modality, Monality and Tonality in the Sixteenth and Seventeenth Centuries." *Music and Letters* 52 (1971): 404–17; 53 (1972): 59–73.

Williams, Raymond. *Culture and Society, 1780–1950.* London: Chatto and Windus, 1958.

Winnington-Ingram, R. P. *Mode in Ancient Greek Music.* Amsterdam: A. M. Hakkert, 1968.

Wiora, Walter. *The Four Ages of Music.* Translated by M. D. Herter Norton. New York: Norton, 1965.

Worner, Karl H. *The History of Music: A Book for Study and Reference.* Translated by Willis Wager. New York: Free Press, 1973.

Wuorinen, Charles. "What Concerns Me Is Music." *Genesis West* 1 (1962): 11–18.

Revised in Barney Childs and Elliott Schwartz, *Contemporary Composers on Contemporary Music*. New York: Holt, Rinehart, and Winston, 1967.

Liner Notes and Interviews

Charters, Samuel. *Charles Ives Songs*. Folkways FM 3344, 3345.

Henze, Hans Werner. *Doppio Concerto per Oboe, Arpa et Archi*. Deutsche Grammophon 139396.

"An Interview with Hans Werner Henze." WFMT-Radio, Chicago, 3 December 1972.

Kilmer, Anne Draffkorn, Richard L. Crocker, and Robert R. Brown. *Sounds from Silence: Recent Discoveries in Ancient Near Eastern Music*. Berkeley: Bīt Enki Records, BTNK 101.

Index